Privatization

CHATHAM HOUSE SERIES ON CHANGE IN AMERICAN POLITICS

SERIES EDITOR: Aaron Wildavsky
University of California, Berkeley

PRIVATIZATION
The Key to Better Government

E.S. SAVAS

Baruch College
City University of New York

CHATHAM HOUSE PUBLISHERS, INC.
Chatham, New Jersey

PRIVATIZATION
The Key to Better Government

CHATHAM HOUSE PUBLISHERS, INC.
Post Office Box One
Chatham, New Jersey 07928

PUBLISHER: Edward Artinian
ILLUSTRATIONS: Adrienne Shubert
JACKET AND COVER DESIGN: Lawrence Ratzkin
COMPOSITION: Chatham Composer
PRINTING AND BINDING: R. R. Donnelley

LIBRARY OF CONGRESS CATALOGING-IN-PUBLICATION DATA

Savas, Emanuel S.

    Privatization : the key to better government.

    (Chatham House series on change in American politics)
Includes index.
    1. Government productivity—United States.
2. Privatization—United States. 3. Administrative
agencies—United States—Cost effectiveness. I. Title.
II. Series.
JK468.P75S28 1987   353.001'47   87-23831
ISBN 0-934540-59-4
ISBN 0-934540-58-6 (pbk.)

Manufactured in the United States of America
10   9   8   7   6   5   4   3   2   1

Contents

Part One. The Background for Privatization   1

  1. Introduction   3
    Pressures for Privatization   4
    Overview   11
  2. The Growth of Government   13
    The Size of Government   13
    Why Government Grows   17
    Conclusion   30

Part Two. The Theory of Privatization   33

  3. Basic Characteristics of Goods and Services   35
    Exclusion   35
    Consumption   36
    Classifying Goods and Services   37
    Private Goods   44
    Common-Pool Goods   45
    Toll Goods   47
    Collective Goods   47
    The Growth of Collective and Common-Pool Goods   51
    Summary   56
  4. Alternative Arrangements for Providing Goods and Services   58
    Providing, Arranging, and Producing Services   60
    Service Arrangements   62
    Multiple, Hybrid, and Partial Arrangements   82
    Privatization   88
    Summary   89
  5. An Analysis and Comparison of Alternative Arrangements   93
    The Nature of Goods and the Choice of Arrangements   93
    Factors in Evaluating Arrangements   95
    Comparison of Arrangements   107
    Characteristics of the Privatization Alternatives   109
    Summary   115

Part Three. Privatization in Practice 119

  6. Applications in Physical and Commercial Services 121

    Solid-Waste Management 124

    Street Services 131

    Transportation 137

    Water Supply and Treatment 148

    Electric Power 149

    Communications 152

    Commercial and Administrative Activities 155

    State-Owned Property 162

    State-Owned Enterprises 166

    Miscellaneous and Prospective Applications 170

    Conclusion 171

  7. Applications in Protective and Human Services 181

    Public Safety 181

    National Defense 188

    Health Care 189

    Housing and Urban Development 196

    Social Services 206

    Education 212

    Recreation and Leisure 218

    Conclusion 223

Part Four. Toward Successful Privatization 231

  8. How to Privatize 233

    Load Shedding 234

    Load Shedding by Denationalization 241

    Limited-Government Arrangements 247

    User Charges 248

    Competition 250

    Contracting for Services 255

    Summary 272

  9. Problems with Privatization 277

    Problems That Arise from the Concept 277

    Necessary Conditions for Successful Privatization 278

    Implementation Obstacles 280

    Summary 285

  10. Conclusion 288

Name and Subject Indexes 292

Figures

1.1 Conceptual Representation of Services Desired by
Society, Divided between Governmental (Public) and
Nongovernmental (Private) Sectors   6

3.1 Exclusion and Consumption Properties of Transportation
Services and Facilities   38

3.2 Exclusion and Consumption Properties of Water-supply Services   39

3.3 Exclusion and Consumption Properties of Various Goods
and Services   40

3.4 Four Kinds of Goods in Terms of Their Intrinsic Characteristics 56

4.1 Illustrative Relationship between Consumer, Producer,
and Arranger   61

4.2 Overview of the Ten Institutional Arrangements for Delivering
Services   63

4.3 Government Service, Paid by Taxes   64

4.4 Government Service, with User Fee   64

4.5 Government Vending   65

4.6 Intergovernmental Agreement   66

4.7 Contracting   68

4.8 Exclusive Franchise   75

4.9 Multiple Franchise   76

4.10 Grant Arrangement   77

4.11 Voucher Arrangement   78

4.12 Market Arrangement   80

4.13 Voluntary Arrangement   80

4.14 Voluntary Arrangement with Contracting   81

4.15 Self-service Arrangement   82

4.16 Different Service Models   91

6.1 Extent of State-owned Enterprises, by Country   168

7.1 The Improvement in Measures of Adequate Housing   198

8.1 Characteristics of Particular State-owned Enterprises in France 242

Tables

1.1	The Forces Behind Privatization	5
2.1	Number of Government Units in the United States	14
2.2	Federal, State, and Local Government Expenditures	15
2.3	Tax Revenues as a Percentage of Gross Domestic Product	16
2.4	Government Employment	17
3.1	Comparison of Private and Collective Goods	50
3.2	Government Spending for Private and Toll Goods	55
4.1	Producers of Services to Municipalities under Intergovernmental Agreements	66
4.2	Percentage of Cities and Counties that Use Intergovernmental Agreements to Supply Services	67
4.3	Percentage of Cities and Counties that Contract with Private Organizations to Supply Services	70
4.4	City and County Services Provided Contractually by Private Firms	73
4.5	Percentage of Cities and Counties that Franchise Private Firms to Supply Services	76
4.6	Examples of Institutional Arrangements Used for Common Urban Services	84
4.7	Functional Division of Service Activities	87
4.8	Ranking of Arrangements by Degree of Privatization	88
4.9	Institutional Arrangements for Providing Public Services	90
5.1	Types of Goods and Institutional Arrangements that Can Be Used for Their Delivery	94
5.2	Characteristics of Different Arrangements	108
5.3	Survey of Public Officials' Opinions about Contracting	112
6.1	Summary of Comparative Studies of Public and Private Residential Refuse Collection	126
6.2	Comparison of Municipal and Contract Residential Collection	128
6.3	Comparison of Public and Private Bus Operations in New York City	138

6.4 Examples of Commercial and Administrative Activities in
     Government   156
7.1 Monthly Cost per Child for Day-Care Centers   209
8.1 Ranking of Institutional Arrangements to Reduce Government
     Expenditures, by Type of Good   248
9.1 Necessary Conditions for Successful Privatization   279
9.2 Hypothetical Illustration: "Cream Skimming" Can Reduce
     Public Costs   285
9.3 Hypothetical Illustration: "Cream Skimming" When There Is
     a User Charge   286

Acknowledgments

I first happened upon the concept that came to be called privatization in 1969, when I served as First Deputy City Administrator of New York under Mayor John V. Lindsay. At the time I was seeking a strategy to bring about lasting improvements in the management and performance of government agencies. Since then, as professor, researcher, consultant, and observer of governments, and during a second tour of duty in government (as Assistant Seceretary of Housing and Urban Development under President Reagan, while on leave from academia), I learned much more that also has been distilled into this volume. Therefore I am grateful to all those in and out of government, known and un-known public officials and private-sector practitioners, and colleagues in aca-demia, in the think tanks, and in the consulting field, who have contributed (not always knowingly or willingly) to my education and my conclusions about this vitally important area of public policy. Obviously they cannot all be named here, but I would be remiss if I did not identify and thank John Diebold, Lin Ostrom, Barbara Stevens, and Aaron Wildavsky.

The Manhattan Institute for Policy Research, under the enlightened leader-ship of William M.H. Hammett, has supported my work, and I am grateful for that. To my good friend, Peter Tropp, for whom government is both voca-tion and avocation, I owe a large debt of gratitude for his thorough and in-sightful reading and rereading of numerous drafts, and for his persistence in getting me to revise passages and to improve the book's organization despite my initial reluctance to do so. Finally, I want to thank my graduate assistant, Srini Muktevi, for his help.

This book is lovingly dedicated to
my wonderful and supportive family:
HELEN, JONATHAN, *and* STEPHEN

PART ONE

The Background for Privatization

1. Introduction

Privatization is a new word that is rapidly coming into popular usage despite its awkward sound. The word *privatize* first appeared in a dictionary in 1983 and was defined narrowly as "to make private, especially to change (as a business or industry) from public to private control or ownership."[1] But the word has already acquired a broader meaning; it has come to symbolize a new way of looking at society's needs, and a rethinking of the role of government in fulfilling them. It means relying more on society's private institutions and less on government to satisfy the needs of the people. *Privatization is the act of reducing the role of government, or increasing the role of the private sector, in an activity or in the ownership of assets.* (A further discussion of the definition, and the precise actions encompassed by privatization, is in chapter 4.)

Some opponents of privatization regard it as a simplistic call to cut back government and regress to a harsh state where only the fittest survive and the poor and sick are left to cope as best they can. Yet privatization can be at least as compassionate as the welfare state; moreover, when applied properly, it offers even more for the less fortunate among us.

Privatization appears in several forms. Contracting with private firms to finance, construct, and operate waterworks or prisons, or to sweep the streets, prune trees, or repair ships, is a form of privatization. So is contracting with a not-for-profit agency to deliver "meals on wheels" to elderly shut-ins, or to operate a halfway house. Issuing food stamps and housing vouchers to the poor are examples of privatization that are far different from having government-run farms and grocery stores, and public housing projects. Urban dwellers practice privatization when they form neighborhood security patrols, and so do suburbanites who join volunteer fire departments. Selling off or denationalizing a state-owned airline, factory, or coal mine is privatization, and it is privatization when government retires from the business of insuring home mortgages or running commuter buses and lets the marketplace provide those services.

The distinction between *public* and *private* is elusive. We speak of a park or a government office building as being publicly owned, but we use the same term to describe IBM because it has many stockholders and any member of the public may buy part of the company; it is a private firm that is publicly owned. In the same way, a public restaurant is one that is open to the public at large, although it may be owned by a sole proprietor. Confusingly, we use the same word, *public,* to describe three very different circumstances: government ownership, widespread ownership, and widespread access. This semantic confusion is nevertheless instructive, for it implies that government ownership — and by extension, government action — is not necessary to achieve widespread (i.e., "public") benefits. Privatization capitalizes on this underappreciated truism and takes advantage of the full array of ownership and operating relations to serve the public interest by satisfying people's wants and needs.

It should be clear that, throughout this book, the term *service* or *public service* refers not only to a narrow task such as collecting trash, delivering mail, putting out fires, or running railroads but to broad functions as well, such as assuring economic security in old age, supplying food, defending the nation against external threats, clothing the populace, producing manufactured goods, and protecting endangered species of ocean life. As is implied by this brief list, the analysis in this book is applicable to all cultures and socioeconomic systems, regardless of the institutional means by which goods and services for people are currently provided.

Pressures for Privatization

Several major forces, or pressures, are behind the privatization movement: pragmatic, ideological, commercial, and populist. The goal of the pragmatists is better government, in the sense of a more cost-effective one. The goal of those who approach the matter ideologically is less government, one that plays a smaller role vis-à-vis private institutions. The goal of commercial interests is to get more business by having more of government's spending redirected toward them. And the goal of the populists is to achieve a better society by giving people greater power to satisfy their common needs, while diminishing that of large public and private bureaucracies.

The characteristics of these four forces are summarized in table 1.1, and each is discussed in turn.

PRAGMATIC PRESSURE

When governments face severe fiscal stress, that is, when the cost of government activities is rising but the public's resistance to higher taxes is also rising, public officials seek any promising solution to their quandary. Typically, the first resort is to creative bookkeeping that masks the magnitude of the disparity between revenues and expenditures. The second resort is borrowing to close

4

TABLE I.I

THE FORCES BEHIND PRIVATIZATION

Force	Goal	Reasoning
Pragmatic	Better government	Prudent privatization leads to more cost-effective public services.
Ideological	Less government	Government is too big, too powerful, too intrusive in people's lives and therefore is a danger to democracy. Government's decisions are political, thus are inherently less trustworthy than free-market decisions.
Commercial	More business	Government spending is a large part of the economy; more of it can and should be directed toward private firms. State-owned enterprises and assets can be put to better use by the private sector.
Populist	Better society	People should have more choice in public services. They should be empowered to define and address common needs, and to establish a sense of community by relying more on family, neighborhood, church, and ethnic and voluntary associations and less on distant bureaucratic structures.

the gap. But lenders are unwilling to support wasteful government enterprises, particularly in developing countries. In industrialized nations, public antipathy to more government spending leads to voter rejection of bond referenda, and the growing adoption of generally accepted accounting principles in government tends to foreclose the surreptitious option of creative bookkeeping. The remaining choices for public officials are then narrowed to two: reduced activities or greater productivity.

Naturally, eliminating or cutting back government activities is unpopular among beneficiaries of the activity, and therefore increasing productivity seems more attractive politically. But even this encounters opposition, for it often creates resentment among the affected public employees, and in any event it is difficult to do. The history of modern government is replete with efforts to improve government by centralizing, decentralizing, reorganizing, introducing performance budgeting, PPBS (planning-programming-budgeting systems), ZBB (zero-based budgeting), MBO (management by objectives), management training, sensitivity training, organization development, worker incentives, shared savings, labor-management committees, productivity councils, computerization, management science, operations research, and numerous other techniques. Their overall impact has been modest, however, for reasons that will become clearer later in this volume. A more fundamental, strategic approach is needed.

Privatization is a strategic approach to improving the productivity of government agencies and thereby to give people more for their money. Chapters 6 and 7 present strong evidence that privatization, properly carried out, generally leads to large increases in efficiency while improving or at least maintaining the level and quality of public services. For this reason, cost-conscious public officials, spurred by good-government groups and others who favor privatization, are turning to privatization as an important tool for better public management and as the key to more cost-effective government.

IDEOLOGICAL PRESSURE

The role of government differs in different societies, and even within a single society it changes over time, waxing and waning over decades and centuries. One can visualize the situation conceptually as in figure 1.1. The goods and services (in the broad sense described above) that a society enjoys are represented as points, and responsibility for providing them is divided between the governmental and nongovernmental (i.e., private) sectors. The location of the boundary line between the two is different in different countries; for example, in the Soviet Union the governmental sector occupies almost the entire area.

The boundary also changes its shape and shifts position over time. For example, in the United States more and more mail is being delivered by the private sector, and the role of the government mail service is shrinking in relative terms. In contrast, government's role in medical care has expanded enormously in recent decades. In other words, different sections of the boundary can be moving in opposite directions at the same time.

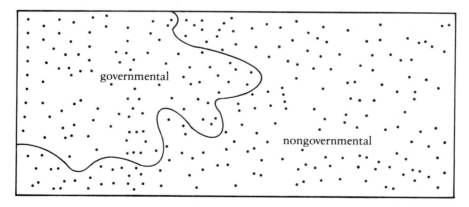

FIGURE 1.1

CONCEPTUAL REPRESENTATION OF SERVICES DESIRED BY SOCIETY, DIVIDED BE-
TWEEN GOVERNMENTAL (PUBLIC) AND NONGOVERNMENTAL (PRIVATE) SECTORS

Despite these contrary shifts, in the United States overall there has been much waxing but little waning of government. Chapter 2 summarizes the facts about the size and growth of government, and discusses why government grows. Many view this trend with alarm and see it as a danger to democracy. Their rallying cry is "Get government off our backs and out of our pockets."

The reasoning of those who subscribe to this view is based on political and economic philosophy. As more of people's earnings are taken by government, as decisions about the disposition of these moneys are made by increasingly distant and unresponsive organs of government, and as government's presence pervades more areas of human activity, there is a loss of freedom. In drawing up the Constitution and the Bill of Rights, America's Founding Fathers took great pains to protect citizens from their government. The history of civilization showed them that government could be a serious threat to the individual rights they cherished. Government institutions could become instruments of tyranny even in a democratic society; those who mobilize majority support could use government's coercive sanctions to deprive those in the minority. Therefore, the framers of the Constitution designed a system that imposed the minimal level of collective coercion necessary to secure the blessings of liberty. At each turn, the power of government was circumscribed by checks and balances.

Individual freedom is not the only value endangered by a powerful government. Justice is also highly prized, and equality is an important component of justice. Reasonable and humane people will differ on the degree of inequality or the extent of redistribution that is acceptable and can still be considered just, but it is clear that government greatly affects the level of justice, for better and for worse, by taking from some and giving to others.

In a world of finite resources, efficiency is also an important societal goal. We should extract the maximum from each ton of raw material and from each hour of work. Efficiency is good because it produces a higher standard of living. Just as freedom and justice are menaced by an overly powerful government, so is efficiency.

Freedom, justice, and efficiency are all essential, and each is alloyed with the other. They are different and sometimes conflicting goals, and a balance must be struck among them, for example, trading some individual freedom or some economic efficiency for more justice. Government is a tool that society employs to help attain these goals and to strike the balance, but in excess it threatens all three goals.

Another dimension to the ideological concern about big government is the harm that comes from distrust of government. Modern civilization requires individuals to cede substantial control over vital aspects of their lives to impersonal institutions. Personal autonomy has been reduced, and responsibility

7

for the well-being of the individual has been assumed by collective institutions — principally government. But government is not sufficiently responsive or accountable, and if it acquires a life of its own, then people feel that it is not living up to its end of an implied agreement: to do those things that only government is supposed to be able to do. They lose faith in government. This attitude was revealed clearly in a survey conducted in 1980 in the United States. Only 21 percent of the people believed government is largely run for the benefit of all; the figure improved somewhat to 29 percent in 1982.[2] In some countries, people view government as an evil to be endured, a horde of self-aggrandizing officials and civil servants.

Antigovernment sentiment grew more rapidly than antibusiness sentiment between 1958 and 1980 in the United States.[3] This feeling, too, abated somewhat after 1980, at the same time that a new administration began to change the role of the federal government; perhaps the two phenomena are related.

When it comes to ability to get things done, the public considers the private sector superior to political institutions.[4] As for quality of service, local governments and public transportation are rated at the very bottom, together with real estate firms and even lower than auto repair shops.[5]

The election of President Jimmy Carter (the non-Washington candidate) and the two elections of President Ronald Reagan (the avowed anti-Washington and anti-big-government candidate) reflect in part a popular reaction against the growing role that government has assumed. The much-needed social and business reforms adopted earlier in this century are themselves in need of reform, as mistakes, excesses, and waste proliferate, and as institutional arteriosclerosis inevitably sets in.

Up to this point we have reviewed the ideologues' arguments against big government from the perspective of political philosophy. Another line of their argument is based on economic philosophy. The long-term well-being of society will be maximized if economic decisions are left mostly to the marketplace (with government assuring that no one is left without the basic necessities of life). But government, by definition, has a strong effect on the economy, and this inevitably means that decisions affecting the economy will be made on political grounds instead of economic grounds. Therefore, big government, in contrast to small government, will gradually make a society poorer than it otherwise would be.

Based on political and economic philosophy, therefore, advocates of these viewpoints want to shift the boundary line in figure 1.1 much farther to the left, reducing the role of government and expanding the role of the private sector. This is privatization, and hence the movement has drawn its strongest support from this quarter. Paradoxically, the ideologists who do not want government made more efficient (because this will encourage a continuation of its current role) find themselves allied with the pragmatists who support privatization for that very reason. The ideological proponents of privatization want *less* government; the pragmatic proponents merely want *smaller* government, in the sense of a more efficient one.

COMMERCIAL PRESSURE

Further support for privatization comes from commercial interests. The thinking is straightforward. Government spends a lot of money, much of it on salaries for its employees. Much of the work performed by government employees consists of routine commercial activities that are in no way unique to government, such as maintenance of buildings, grounds, vehicles, ships, and airplanes; typing and data processing; handling insurance claims and sending out bills; and collecting trash and repairing streets. Business groups advocate more privatization of these in-house government activities and support legislation that would prohibit using government employees to perform work that private, tax-paying businesses can perform.

Another segment of the private sector sees substantial business opportunities in large capital projects for government. These include prisons, wastewater-treatment plants, and waste-to-energy plants. Private firms can finance, build, or operate any of these kinds of facilities. The novel element here is financing the facility; in many circumstances this can be an appealing option to a hard-pressed government that is unable to raise capital funds in a timely manner, yet must build a facility to relieve overcrowding in its prisons or a waste-treatment plant to eliminate an environmental hazard.

In countries with nationalized industries or assets (and no country is entirely without them), commercial pressures come from business leaders who see mismanagement, underutilized assets, and slothful practices in an environment sheltered from competition. They encourage denationalization, which is a particular form of privatization, because they see excellent prospects for that industry or those assets if they were sold and brought into the private sector; they see the potential for innovation, whereas they predict continuing stagnation and growing inefficiency if the enterprise is left unperturbed in the public sector. This reasoning applies to the entire array of state-owned enterprises, including manufacturing plants, mines, oil fields, transportation lines, communication systems, banks, timber forests, and open land.

For these various reasons, commercial forces are active supporters of privatization, although their interests are very different from those of the pragmatists and those who endorse privatization on the basis of political or economic philosophy.

POPULIST PRESSURE

The final source of support can be called *populist*. Populists are *against* both big government and big business and *for* other, more local institutions and the empowerment of people. This point of view has been articulated in the following terms:

> This country's "public" systems, governmental and private, have become too institutionalized, too bureaucratized, too professionalized, too protective of their own interests. . . . These major systems must be made instead to work for people. . . . It is possible to redesign the institutional arrangements . . . to make the life-support systems of a community both competitive and equitable. . . . Choices should be expanded. . . . No private or public buyer should rely on a sole source of supply.[6]

The two elements of the populist position are that people should have greater choice in public services than they now have, and they should be empowered to define their common needs and address them without undue reliance on distant bureaucracies. They can rely instead, to a much greater degree, on family, neighborhood, church, and ethnic and voluntary associations. The process of formulating common needs, and working through traditional local institutions to satisfy those needs, will reinforce a much-needed sense of community.

Such institutions are imperiled, however. A large and powerful government can displace and swamp them. The family gives way to Departments of Health, Education, Welfare, Housing, and Human Services. The minister is replaced by a community mental health agency. Voluntary groups are supplanted by issue-oriented lobbies that seek to use the force and majesty of government to impose their values on others.

These other institutions provide safety to society by their very redundance and help arrive at an adaptive equilibrium among the conflicting goals of freedom, justice, and efficiency. To the extent that one institution, such as government, gains great strength at the expense of the others, it limits their contribution to these goals, eliminates the diversity they afford, and thereby increases society's dependence on government alone to choose and impose particular allotments of freedom, justice, and efficiency.

Adherents of this world view endorse privatization because it enhances choice and affords opportunities for strengthening traditional institutions and reinforcing a local sense of community. In seeking a better society, populists also press for privatization, and join forces with those ideologically committed to less government, pragmatists who want better government, and commercial interests that seek to do more of government's work.

Overview

The book is divided into four parts: the background, theory, and practice of privatization, and steps toward successful privatization. Chapter 2 completes the background discussion by reviewing the growth of government.

Part 2 presents the theoretical basis for privatization. It is necessary to start at the beginning and examine the basic goods and services that people want and need. This is done in chapter 3, which shows that the various goods and services have intrinsic characteristics that permit them to be categorized in a particularly useful way: as private, toll, common-pool, or collective goods. Chapter 4 goes on to clarify the role of collective action in supplying each of these kinds of goods. It describes ten different institutional arrangements or structures for delivering them: direct government provision, intergovernmental agreements, franchising, contracting for service, voucher systems, grants, voluntary associations, self-help or self-service, the marketplace, and government vending. Seven of these are privatization approaches.

Chapter 5 completes the theoretical section. It shows that each category of goods can be delivered by any one of several delivery arrangements, although certain kinds of goods cannot be supplied by certain arrangements. The chapter presents an extended comparison of the different service arrangements, pointing out the advantages and disadvantages of each and shedding light on the question of which arrangement to use when there is a choice.

Part 3, which examines privatization in practice, consists of two chapters, 6 and 7. They review the major empirical studies of the relative performance of different arrangements. They also survey a wide variety of experiences with privatization and discuss how it may be applied in different areas.

In part 4, which consists of three chapters, chapter 8 describes how to implement privatization through a multipronged approach that would (1) reduce government provision or subsidization of certain services (i.e., "load shedding"); (2) make greater use of those service-delivery arrangements that require a lesser role for government; (3) employ user charges to make the true costs of government services more visible and thereby stimulate demand for alternative arrangements; and (4) utilize competition to the fullest possible extent to overcome the harmful consequences of unnecessary government monopolies. The chapter discusses in detail how to assure successful contracting for services. Chapter 9 presents the other side of the coin and discusses the problems with privatization. Finally, chapter 10 draws together the principal conclusions about privatization as the key to better government.

Notes

1. *Webster's New Collegiate Dictionary,* 9th ed. (Springfield, Mass.: Merriam, 1983), 936. The earliest use appears to have been in Peter F. Drucker, in *The Age of Discontinuity* (New York: Harper & Row, 1969); he used the term "reprivatization." Robert W. Poole, Jr., shortened it to "privatization" and used it in the Reason Foundation newsletters (Santa Monica, Calif.) beginning in 1976.

2. Adam Clymer, "Poll Finds Trust in Government Edging Back Up," *New York Times,* 15 July 1983.

3. S.M. Lipset and W. Schneider, *The Confidence Gap* (New York: Free Press, 1983), 33.

4. Ibid., 75.

5. "Groceries' Service Rated High," *New York Times,* 10 March 1986.

6. Ted Kolderie, "An Equitable and Competitive Public Sector" (Minneapolis: Hubert H. Humphrey Institute of Public Affairs, University of Minnesota, 1984).

2. The Growth of Government

Governments have grown in both democratic and totalitarian systems, in capitalist and in socialist countries. This chapter first examines the size and growth of governments in the United States by reference to the number of government units, their expenditures, the taxes they levy, and the number of people they employ. The remainder of the chapter then explores the reasons why governments grow.

The Size of Government

Some striking statistics illustrate the size of the U.S. federal government:

- ☐ It employs 2.8 million people.
- ☐ It purchases more than $130 billion annually in goods and services.
- ☐ It owns one-third of the land in the United States.
- ☐ It occupies 2.6 billion square feet of office space, an area four times as large as all the office space in the ten largest cities in the United States.
- ☐ It owns and operates 437,000 nonmilitary vehicles.
- ☐ It has more than 17,000 computers.
- ☐ It provides 95 million subsidized meals a day.
- ☐ It issues 4.8 billion publications annually.

These figures are mind-boggling and serve the purpose of capturing attention; however, a more systematic examination of the size of government is needed.

NUMBER OF GOVERNMENTS

People sometimes think of government as a single, monolithic giant, but in fact there are many governments in the United States, 82,341 of them in 1982 to be exact. Table 2.1 shows the number of different government units and how it has changed over time. The number of municipalities has been growing slowly, an indication of increasing urbanization and the accompanying incorpora-

TABLE 2.1

NUMBER OF GOVERNMENT UNITS IN THE UNITED STATES

Kind of government	1942	1952	1962	1972	1982
Federal	1	1	1	1	1
State	48	50	50	50	50
County	3,050	3,052	3,043	3,044	3,041
Town and township	18,919	17,202	17,142	16,991	16,734
Municipal	16,220	16,807	18,000	18,517	19,076
School district	108,579	67,355	34,678	15,781	14,851
Special district	8,299	12,340	18,323	23,885	28,588
TOTAL	155,116	116,807	91,237	78,269	82,341

SOURCE: Bureau of the Census, Department of Commerce, *1982 Census of Governments, Governmental Organization* (Washington, D.C.: Government Printing Office, August 1983), table A.

tion of previously unincorporated areas. The number of special districts shows rapid growth, a reflection of the continuous creation of intergovernmental arrangements to perform various functions in metropolitan areas. In fact, this has caused an upturn in the total number of government units, after a prolonged decline that resulted from the extensive consolidation of school districts.

GOVERNMENT EXPENDITURES

Total government expenditures in 1984 amounted to $1,258 billion. Table 2.2 shows the growth of these expenditures. In about fifty years, government expenditures have grown a hundredfold, from an eighth to more than a third of the gross national product (GNP). Even when adjusted by subtracting expenditures for national defense, foreign aid, and veterans' benefits, the growth pattern persists. Per capita expenditures, adjusted in this manner and expressed in constant dollars, have increased more than sevenfold during this period.

The growth has not occurred uniformly at all levels of government. Federal expenditures have grown much more rapidly than nonfederal ones, and state expenditures in turn have grown more rapidly than local ones; therefore the latter have been shrinking steadily in relative terms. This represents an increasing centralization of power at higher levels of government and, by contrast, a waning of local government.

The data in table 2.2 on government budget expenditures do not reflect "off-budget spending." This category includes outstanding federal loans, guaranteed loans, and borrowing by federally sponsored enterprises, which exceeded $400 billion by 1985 but did not appear as budgeted expenditures.[1] As loan defaults occur, honest bookkeeping would require that the losses appear somewhere as expenditures.

TABLE 2.2
FEDERAL, STATE, AND LOCAL GOVERNMENT EXPENDITURES

(1) Year	(2) Total (billions)	(3) As percentage of GNP	(4) Total, excluding national defense and veteran expenditures (billions)	(5) (4) as percentage of GNP	(6) (4) in constant 1967 dollars (billions)	(7) (4) as per capita expenditures in constant 1967 dollars
1930	$11.1	12.2	$9.6	10.6	$23.9	$194
1940	18.4	18.4	16.3	16.3	44.4	336
1950	61.0	21.3	41.4	14.5	61.1	404
1960	136.4	27.0	83.7	16.5	96.3	537
1970	313.4	31.6	223.7	22.5	193.4	951
1980	869.0	33.1	707.0	26.9	313.3	1,383
1983	1,167.5	35.3	922.8	27.9	338.8	1,445

SOURCE: Derived from *Facts and Figures on Government Finance*, 23d ed. (Washington, D.C.: Tax Foundation, 1986), tables A7, A31, B37.

TAX LEVELS

International comparisons can be made by examining tax revenues in relation to the gross domestic product (GDP) in different countries. Table 2.3 presents this comparison and shows the United States to be at the lower end of the range of industrialized nations, near Japan and Switzerland. Some Western European nations have significantly higher fractions of their economies in the hands of government.

TABLE 2.3

TAX REVENUES AS A PERCENTAGE OF GROSS DOMESTIC PRODUCT, 1982

Country	Tax revenues
Japan	27.2
United States	30.5
Switzerland	30.9
Australia	31.0
Greece	31.9
Canada	34.9
West Germany	37.3
Italy	38.3
United Kingdom	39.6
France	43.7
Denmark	44.0
Netherlands	45.5
Belgium	46.7
Sweden	50.3

SOURCE: *Facts and Figures on Government Finance,* 23d ed. (Washington, D.C.: Tax Foundation, 1986), table A33.

GOVERNMENT EMPLOYMENT

Corroborating evidence concerning the size and growth of government can be found in the employment data shown in table 2.4. In 1983, the number of full-time-equivalent government employees, not counting the military, was 13.9 million, or about 1 out of every 7 nonagricultural civilian workers. If part-time workers are included, the total is 16 million; if military personnel are added, the total is 18.3 million. In the thirty-five years between 1948 and 1983, the government workforce grew at a compounded annual rate of 2.8 percent, much more than that of private-sector employment (1.8 percent) and twice that of the population as a whole (1.4 percent).

Remarkably, 30,000 of the 82,000 governments in the United States have *no* employees! These "zero-employee governments," generally serving very small

TABLE 2.4

GOVERNMENT EMPLOYMENT

Year	Number of employees[a] (millions)	As percentage of population	As percentage of all employees[b]
1929	2.92	2.4	7.9
1939	5.79	4.4	16.0
1950	5.69	3.8	11.0
1960	7.89	4.4	13.1
1970	11.35	5.6	15.1
1980	14.12	6.2	14.7
1983	13.86	5.9	14.2

SOURCE: *Facts and Figures on Government Finance,* 23d ed. (Washington, D.C.: Tax Foundation, 1986), tables A30, B1, B5.

a. Full-time equivalents, excluding military.
b. Includes only nonagricultural civilian workers.

communities, have dedicated volunteers who negotiate and supervise contracts for services with larger communities nearby.[2]

Why Government Grows

Three major factors have contributed to the growth of government: (1) a demand for more government services, by current and would-be recipients of the services; (2) a desire to supply more government services, by the producers of the services; and (3) increased inefficiency, which results in more government spending to provide the same services.

INCREASED DEMAND FOR SERVICES

Demographic Change. Inflation, population growth, and an increase in defense-related expenditures account for much of the absolute growth of government; but, as table 2.2 showed, the real growth was large even after allowing for these effects. Part of the explanation has to do with a change in the composition of the population to one that demands more government services. For example, if the number of retirees increases relative to the number of working adults, and if pension payments of constant size in constant dollars are made to them out of general government funds rather than from an actuarially sound retirement fund, government expenditures will increase even if all else remains unchanged.

The same phenomenon can be observed at the local government level when the population of a city changes so that a larger fraction of its residents are welfare recipients, even though population size remains unchanged. Faced with this increased demand, welfare and welfare-related expenditures will rise to accommodate the increased workload. Yet this explains only part of the observed increase. Of the $3.9 billion increase in the human services budget in New York City in a ten-year period, only 40 percent was the result of inflation and a larger workload; 60 percent was caused by other factors.[3]

Urbanization also creates a demand for services. As urbanization increases, people get in one another's way. More police officers are needed. New kinds of government action are called for to regulate and ameliorate harmful and potentially harmful side effects of individual actions — for instance, to control air and water pollution, to reduce noise, to test foods and drugs, to inspect restaurants, and to segregate certain activities by zoning. All these require government expenditures.

Income Growth. The growth in real per capita income is sometimes cited to explain the growth in government spending, for it is said that people demand disproportionately more government services as their incomes rise. This may be seen in the demand, in wealthy communities, for more expensive education programs (e.g., more specialized courses, more luxurious school facilities and furnishings, more costly equipment), larger budgets for libraries and cultural events, a higher level of services such as street repair and recreation programs, and a willingness to spend more for environmental protection.

The opposite phenomenon can also be observed. With more money, people rely less on government services. Instead of patronizing public swimming pools, they build their own. They use private automobiles instead of buses, and arrange for their own recreation by joining tennis and golf clubs instead of patronizing public facilities. They buy books instead of borrowing them from libraries, and increase their personal security by installing alarms and locks and hiring guards. If they question the quality of their drinking water, they switch to bottled water.

From these contradictory factors, Borcherding estimates that only about a fourth of the real increase in public spending in this century can be attributed to the increasing affluence of the populace.[4]

Income Redistribution. The areas of income security, welfare, health, housing, and education have been the principal focal points of large and rapid government growth. But unlike public safety, for example, there is little agreement about the extent to which government should supply or pay for such services.

Scandalous abuse has gone hand in hand with new, humane programs. There is unemployment insurance not only for war veterans, but also for school employees and forest rangers on seasonal vacations. There are health clinics for infants, but also assembly-line eye tests prescribed by greedy doctors. There are classes for the handicapped, but also remedial reading courses in universities. Humane programs have been stigmatized by abuse. "There's a lot of money in poverty," but some of it went not to the deserving poor but to shady opportunists who operated will-o'-the-wisp, "nonprofit" neighborhood programs with unknown goals and dubious achievements.

The net effect of programs in these areas is to redistribute income, whether it is money per se that is being redistributed or the services that government pays for and distributes. Proponents of income redistribution view government as a convenient mechanism for this purpose. (Sometimes, however, they seem oblivious to basic arithmetic, ignoring the indisputable fact that 10 percent of the population will inevitably be in the lowest income decile, except under ruthlessly perfect egalitarianism.)

One theory attributes much of the growth of government to the fact that the median voter has a median income, which is less than the average income; in other words, a majority of voters have lower-than-average incomes. Therefore, "those with the lowest income use the political process to increase their income. Politicians . . . attract voters with incomes near the median by offering benefits . . . that impose a net cost on those with incomes above the median."[5] This is especially feasible when taxation is progressive. This analysis concludes on a somber note that government grows in every society where the majority remains free to express its will, despite the fact that large government is a threat to freedom.

This bleak forecast could be wrong, however. Perhaps the median voter does not vote. That is, while the median *eligible* voter earns less than an average income, the median *actual* voter may not. Voter turnout is embarrassingly low in the United States, and the poor are much less likely to vote than the wealthy. Furthermore, "one man, one vote" in no way means that every voter has the same degree of influence over public policy. The inexorable growth of government and the slide into totalitarianism or anarchy implied by this voting analysis are not the inevitable destiny of democracies—we hope. Moreover, although government has grown, the income redistribution predicted by this theory has not occurred: The proportions of total income going to the highest and lowest quintiles in the United States have been essentially constant for many decades.

Rectification of Societal Ills. There are strong demands for government action to cure or at least ameliorate a wide variety of perceived shortcomings in society. This approach rests on the assumption that (1) there is a broad consensus as to what constitutes a desirable improvement; (2) we know how to bring about the improvement; and (3) government can do it.

Dissatisfaction with circumstances once accepted as an inevitable part of life brings forth efforts—sometimes presumptuous efforts—to change those circumstances. Rewards accrue in the political arena for publicizing problems and initiating programs that purport to solve them, however intractable the causes.[6] Thus the vainglorious attempts to eradicate poverty, to provide high-paying jobs for the unskilled, and to find a quick cure for every disease. Unfortunately, not every deplorable condition succumbs to government programs.

Risk Aversion. Government programs have been initiated to absorb societal risks. For example, governments make large, risky investments in basic research, such as nuclear fission and space exploration. This is all well and good, but they are also drawn into financing the production of synthetic fuels, where the role of government can be questioned: Once outside the laboratory, a process should stand on its own in the marketplace.

Another kind of risk is also imposed on government by popular demand: risks that are inherently personal in nature. Examples are mortgage insurance for people who want to buy houses but cannot afford it, guarantees for bank accounts in mismanaged institutions, and guaranteed markets for producers of unwanted, surplus products.

These are manifestations of the understandable yearning to create a riskless society; alas, such a society can be found only in the cemetery. Life is risky, and any attempt to protect everyone against economic harm by collectivizing the risk is doomed to costly failure.[7]

Public Standards. In some countries more than others, government growth is spurred in part by demands for government involvement in television, theater, and the arts in order to assure high standards. Left to private patrons, the standards presumably would be too plebeian and insufficiently uplifting.

The problem with this ennobling vision, of course, is that the elevated activities can readily be transformed into propaganda vehicles for the state. Moreover, there is no evidence that the aesthetic tastes of government bureaucrats are markedly superior to those of private philanthropists.

Fiscal Illusion. Fueling the increase in government spending is the illusion that government services are a bargain. Clearly this is the case for every special-interest group, for its benefits are visible and individual, but the costs are diffuse and shared by all. Only in the aggregate are costs recognized as counterbalancing benefits, at best, but the aggregate has no identifiable constituency. Legislators who want to curry favor with interest groups point to the benefits but ignore the costs.

Contributing to this illusion is the naive notion that because government does not make a profit, its services are a bargain. Studies of municipal services, reviewed in chapters 6 and 7, disprove this common assertion by demonstrating that the prices charged by profit-making contractors are substantially lower than the cost of nonprofit municipal work.[8]

Ordinary citizens are often misled as to the cost of government. Surveys show that they consistently underestimate the amount of taxes they pay because of the ingenious "fiscal extraction devices" used by governments to raise revenues without the conscious knowledge of the taxpayer.[9] Property taxes are concealed in rents and mortgage payments. Sales taxes are collected by every retailer. It is no wonder that the value-added tax appears attractive to legislators.

The ultimate fiscal illusion may be found in the Soviet Union, where sophisticated individuals will tell a foreign friend in all sincerity that they pay little in the way of taxes and that only a very modest amount is withheld from their pay. A moment's reflection is needed to realize that when everyone is an employee of the state, all he knows is his take-home pay—he knows neither his true wages nor the amount withheld.

Indeed, the Soviet Union offers many excellent examples of this fallacy. For example, I found myself in a friendly confrontation in Moscow after listening to smug assertions about "free medical care" there, in pointed contrast to the medical care system in the United States. I noted, however, that doctors and nurses are paid in the Soviet Union, and so are the construction workers who build hospitals and the workers who produce hospital supplies (although all workers are expected to "volunteer" on several Saturdays a year). Obviously, the Soviet people pay all these costs. The service is not free; the people are merely ignorant of the cost, which is a different matter altogether.

Even government officials in the United States are generally unaware of the cost of their services. A large-scale study found that the true costs of a particular municipal service were 30 percent greater on average than the amounts reported in the cities' budgets.[10]

The end result of fiscal illusion is pressure for government services in the belief that they are free, or at least a bargain.

Program Preservation. One might imagine that as times and needs change, new programs will emerge and old ones will disappear. The former occurs readily, but the latter occurs slowly, at best. Political leaders learned long ago that depriving someone of an existing benefit is like snatching a lion cub from its mother. Pirie recounts the amusing story of public bathhouses that survive to this day in England. When their closure is periodically attempted, on grounds of economy and because they are no longer needed, the few users chain themselves to the railings and cause such a fuss that the budget-cutters' will is sapped and they retire in defeat. In contrast, the loudest advocates of lower taxes and smaller government would be deemed mad if *they* were to chain themselves to bathhouse doors and demand their closure for such piddling savings.[11]

Backlash. The foregoing factors and forces do not mean that the demand for more services is inevitable and ever increasing; government growth is not a one-way street. In cities with severe financial problems the size of municipal government has been cut in real terms. Throughout the country, Proposition 13 and its progeny have come forth as an antidote to demands for more government services. The public, apparently despairing of the ability or will of its elected representatives to reduce expenditures, has taken the matter directly into its hands and reduced government revenues, like a parent rebuking a spendthrift child by cutting his allowance. President Reagan, giving effective voice to this public mood and marshaling bipartisan support, drastically slashed personal income taxes and put an end to "bracket creep" whereby tax collections rose more rapidly than inflation.

Increased Supply of Services

Whereas increased demand provides the "pull" for more government services, the desire by producers to supply more services provides a "push."

Political Imperatives. Elected officials gain considerable "political income" when government grows. From this point of view, it is far better to levy taxes and distribute them as subsidies to all than not to collect them, even though each individual citizen may be no better off. That is, an ideal program from a political viewpoint is one that extracts taxes as invisibly and painlessly as fiscal illusion can permit, and sends a check, signed by the elected official, individually to each citizen. The raising of revenues to be distributed is often hidden and diffuse, while the spending is frequently concentrated on particular, identifiable beneficiaries.

Ogden Nash expressed the point well in a delightful bit of doggerel entitled "The Politician":

> He gains votes ever and anew
> By taking money from everybody and
>   giving it to a few,

While explaining that every penny
Was extracted from the few to be given to the many.[12]

The institution of representative government itself facilitates this outcome. Individuals elect representatives and expect them to take care of government business on their behalf. Sensible individuals will then pay no attention to the details of government except for those few actions that affect them greatly.

Consider a bill that would increase government spending for constructing dams by $100 million. This would mean substantial contracts for a handful of construction companies and suppliers of construction materials, jobs for a few thousand construction workers, and some indirect benefits to local residents. The cost of this program would be a dollar for the average taxpayer. There is no rational reason for the taxpayer to bother himself for even a moment about this program. He knows little about the subject and is oblivious to the bill's consequences because they will not affect him. Yet you can be sure that the direct beneficiaries will know a great deal about the bill and all its intricacies (they probably helped draft it) and will exert themselves to the fullest to assure its passage. Legislators know that this is how people behave and that by supporting the bill they are likely to get the votes of the beneficiaries at the next election, but their action will have no effect on the votes of citizens who have no interest in the bill.[13] In short, politicians use public money to buy votes. (More direct bribes to voters at the polls are illegal, of course.)

Congressmen earn electoral credits by establishing various federal programs; in addition,

> The legislation is drafted in very general terms, so some agency must translate a vague policy mandate into a functioning program, a process that necessitates the promulgation of rules and regulations. . . . At the next stage, aggrieved and/or hopeful constituents petition their Congressmen to intervene in the complex process of the bureaucracy. The cycle closes when the Congressman lends a sympathetic ear, piously denounces the evils of bureaucracy, intervenes in the latter's decisions, and rides a grateful electorate to ever more impressive electoral showings. Congressmen take credit coming and going.[14]

Larger government brings other political benefits. The officeholder can utilize his staff in his election campaigns. This is a time-honored tradition that is widely observed and diligently followed. The larger the agency, the larger the campaign staff.

Budgetary Imperialism. James Buchanan, the Nobel Laureate, points to other incentives for growth that act on those within the government. More government work and more government expenditures inevitably mean more opportunities for larger salaries, higher status, more perquisites, and bigger bribes.[15] The larger the organization to be managed, and the greater the total resources under one's responsibility, the greater the salary. Along with a more imperial scope come suitably larger and nicer offices, more assistants, car and chauffeur, plaques and photographs of handshakings on office walls, invitations to governors' mansions and the White House, and assorted other status symbols.

The effect of larger public agencies can be seen in education. The consolidation of small school districts into larger ones results in more administrators per pupil and higher salaries for administrators and teachers. In the absence of any proven relationship between educational inputs and outputs, the effect of court decisions equalizing per-pupil expenditures is to transfer income to teachers and administrators when education expenditures rise in total.[16]

Further support for this thesis is found in income data: The highest median income in the country is in the environs of Washington, D.C., and the inflation of job titles and federal salaries has resulted in much higher pay in government than for corresponding work in the private sector.[17]

Budget maximization is a powerful driving force in government agencies, as Niskanen notes insightfully, and much of the observed growth can be attributed to this motivating principle.[18] Bureaucrats take those actions that will maximize their budgets, and they do so not only for the pecuniary motives ascribed by Buchanan but also for nobler purposes that are directly in accord with the public interest. If a public official wants to change the thrust of his agency so that it will be more effective, it is much easier, quicker, and more painless to do so if the agency is expanding. To fire incompetents, change inherited attitudes, turn around a misguided unit, or galvanize a tired one into action is a lot harder than getting more money, creating a new unit, staffing it with fresh people, and setting it off with enthusiasm in a promising new direction. In short, even the most selfless public servant can honestly say that he is better able to serve the public interest if he has a bigger budget.

A final point in this category: It's *fun* spending other people's money! Anyone who has ever served in government and been in a position to make expenditure decisions will admit to the satisfying thrill and the regal sense of power and self-worth—to say nothing of the flattery from grateful beneficiaries —that comes with dispensing tax moneys. And all this is realized at no cost to one's own pocket!

The Problem-Finding Elite. Another factor reportedly at work is the desire of an intellectual elite to gain influence. Our society has been producing a large number of educated people, many of whom do relatively better in government than in the private sector, according to this view.[19] They are particularly adept at detecting societal ills, from rare occupational hazards to obscure but endangered fish species. They constitute a problem-finding elite[20] whose numbers multiply as they seek ever more problems and offer their services to search for solutions.

Command-and-Control Syndrome. In many developing countries, particularly those with short histories of independence from colonial rule, the problem of nation building was thought to demand strong, centralized planning and control. The few educated people were brought into government to run the economy. Western lenders provided money, but only to the government (for convenience and for what proved to be illusory security). Government growth was forced, as government tried to run practically everything: farms, factories, mines, hotels, utilities, transportation systems, and all kinds of businesses. Only in this way, it was thought, could rapid, purposeful progress be made. Market alternatives seemed too untidy, uncoordinated, slow, and, above all, insufficiently responsive to direction from the nation's commanders; certainly markets could not be entrusted with the country's meager capital resources. Command and control of an economy dominated by government agencies was to be the shortcut to development. Unfortunately, time has already judged many of these efforts harshly.

Government Monopolies. Many government agencies are monopolies, in effect.[21] They find themselves in this situation as a result of several contributing factors. In the first place, a principal function of government is to provide services that by their nature are monopolies. Second, in the name of administrative efficiency and rational management, bureaus with partially overlapping functions have generally been combined, leaving the surviving agency with monopoly status. Third, at the local government level, the process of consolidation, school board mergers, annexation, formation of a regional government or authority, and city expansion to encompass previously unincorporated areas can result in the creation of an areawide monopoly.[22]

Lacking competitors, a monopoly agency is inexorably driven to exercise its power and exploit its monolithically secure position. It does so in a variety of ways. For one thing, its budget is particularly resistant to reduction. When asked to cut back on expenditures, the agency head typically presents a budget with the cuts focused on the politically most visible and popular programs; when asked if the reductions could not be made in its other, less sensitive programs, he shrugs his shoulders helplessly.

One of the iniquitous practices of private monopolies is forcing consumers to purchase unwanted goods and services: "tie-in sales." If they do not buy these goods, they may not be permitted to buy the monopolized good they really want. Government monopolies behave no differently. Consider a city police department that says, in effect, "If you want uniformed police to do patrol work, you have to have uniformed police to answer the telephones and enforce parking regulations too." Such a department often resists creation of a separate, low-cost, specialized, civilian unit whose function is solely to enforce parking regulations. Its reasons for resistance include a desire to maximize both the number of police officers and the departmental budget, but also, it is alleged, to retain the power to extend courtesies to grateful offenders and police-fund contributors.

Should this illustration of governmental "tie-in sales" tactics strike one as far-fetched, note that the city of Plaquemine, Louisiana, tried to force some of its water customers to purchase city power as well. However, the U.S. Supreme Court ruled that the city is not automatically exempt from antitrust laws that prohibit such actions.[23]

The net effect of government's monopoly status is pressure for more government growth.

Employee Voting. For the aforementioned reasons, it is in the self-interest of public employees to have government grow. More than the average voter, therefore, they are motivated to vote, and to vote for candidates whose programs will enlarge government expenditures. After all, they are the most direct beneficiaries of government spending, except for citizens and firms who receive direct payments from government. Furthermore, they are numerically strong enough to affect the outcome of elections.

There is evidence to support the contention that government employees are more likely to vote and that their voting strength is significant. It is estimated from available data that public employees, who represent a sixth of the workforce, cast more than a quarter of the votes.[24] The conventional wisdom in New York City is that municipal employees, each of whom can influence the votes of three relatives or friends, control a million votes, a number that greatly exceeds the margin of victory in any mayoral election.

The political power of public employees and their unions is not restricted to their voting strength. Political campaign contributors and campaign workers are a potent influence on office seekers. The situation lends itself to collusion whereby officeholders can award substantial pay raises to employees with the unspoken understanding that some of the bread cast upon those particular waters will return as contributions; furthermore, a sudden increase in worker absenteeism during the campaign season might be conveniently overlooked by the city official who understands that the workers are temporarily engaged in a higher calling.

In recognition of this danger, the Hatch Act prohibited direct political activity by federal employees. There is no counterpart legislation at state or local levels, however, and the effectiveness of the Hatch Act itself has been diluted by court decisions. Similar considerations were no doubt responsible, at least in part, for the fact that until 1961, residents of the District of Columbia were denied the right to vote in federal elections; the residents all were presumed to be direct or indirect employees of the federal government.

Demand for Government Jobs. Not to be overlooked for its contribution to the growth of government is the simple demand for a government job. Perhaps the boldest expression of this occurred in New York City just before the superficial fiscal symptoms of its deep-seated managerial distress first surfaced. In response to an announcement of several hundred job openings for police officers, more than one hundred thousand people applied for the civil service examination. (This is stunning evidence of the desirability of such jobs, but that is not the point here.) Tens of thousands passed the test, but, of course, relatively few were hired because of the city's limited need; the names of the others were put on the list of eligibles from which additional appointments might someday be made. What happened next was straight from the theater of the absurd: The people on the list formed an association, conducted demonstrations, and lobbied vigorously among city and state officials, demanding the enlargement of the police department and the appointment of more police officers.

Many developing countries have succumbed to such demands and have alloted a significant portion of their foreign aid funds to create government jobs, with little or no work expected from many of the jobholders. This has not proven to be a promising route to economic development.

Overproduction. Yet another factor on the supply side favoring government growth is the overproduction of services. This refers to the supply of more or better services than the public would willingly select if it had a direct choice and knew the true cost. In one commonplace public service, residential refuse collection, a detailed study shed light on this issue by examining the frequency of collection in cities where residents had both a greater choice of service level and more information about the cost of different service levels than in other cities.[25] Where a government agency performed the work directly, or hired a private firm to do it at direct government expense, collection was more frequent than in cities where collection was mandatory but each household made its own arrangement with a private firm and paid the latter directly for the service. Evidently the close connection between costs and benefits in the latter cities led to thriftier citizen choices.

INEFFICIENCY

A third major factor that accounts for the growth of government is growing inefficiency: spending more money and employing more people to do the same work. Of course, this happens in private firms, too, but a harsh correction tends to occur quickly in this sector.

Overstaffing. Evidence can readily be found in New York City, not because it is worse than other governments but, on the contrary, because it is relatively open to scrutiny. Perhaps the most remarkable statistic is drawn from the police department: Over a twenty-five-year period, the number of police officers rose from 16,000 to 24,000, but the total annual hours worked by the entire force actually declined slightly. The entire 50 percent increase in manpower was completely devoted to shortening the workweek, lengthening the lunch hour and vacation period, and providing more holidays and paid sick leave.

Inefficient staffing was legitimized by a state law that called for an equal number of police officers on duty on each shift, despite the fact that crime statistics showed few criminals working in the small hours of the morning. Because of this legislated inefficiency, if more police were needed for assignment to evening duty, when most street crimes occur, more would also have to be hired and assigned when there was little or no work for them to do.

In the New York City school system, during a period of constant pupil enrollment, a 50 percent increase in the number of teachers and the addition of one paraprofessional for every two teachers produced only a slight decrease in class size. Instead, classroom time was reduced for teachers, and some teacher duties were delegated to the paraprofessionals. It is by no means obvious that the result was better teacher preparation and better pupil education.

Overpaying. Inefficiency in the form of overpayment to employees is evident in publicly operated mass transit. Because the great preponderance of passenger trips occurs during rush hours, few bus drivers are needed between those two periods and "split-shift" scheduling using part-time drivers makes obvious sense. Some drivers for the New York Metropolitan Transportation Authority, however, drove a total of eight hours a day but were also paid (at overtime rates) for a four-hour Mediterranean-style break at midday.

Numerous studies show that the total remuneration of public employees per hour worked is high compared to similar workers in the private sector.[26] The key here lies in the terms "total remuneration" (which often includes generous fringe benefits) and "per hour worked" (which adjusts for the relatively liberal vacation, holiday, and sick-leave policies in the public sector). A study by the Bureau of Labor Statistics confirms the fact that fringe benefits in the public sector are relatively high; the benefits of federal employees were 27 percent greater than those of private-sector, nonagricultural employees.[27] Overall, the average annual pay of government workers (excluding members of the armed forces) was 5.7 percent higher than that of private-sector workers, but this calculation does not take into consideration any differences in activities.[28] Public-employee compensation reflects not only their productive services on the job, however, but also their political activities.[29]

A careful study of the growth of New York City expenditures for health, education, and welfare concluded that enormous additional sums were spent on higher real salaries and more jobs without evidence of increased outputs or higher quality of services.[30] Labor-to-output ratios for several public services during a period in the mid-1960s revealed that average productivity was either unchanged or had declined for state and local government employees.[31] Thus, while inefficiency is surely not restricted to government activity, declining productivity and increasing inefficiency help explain the growth in the size and cost of government.

Overbuilding. Another contribution to inefficiency is the government bias toward capital spending and against routine maintenance. This bias can best be understood by considering the high visibility of the former and the near invisibility of the latter. A ground breaking or a ribbon cutting presents an excellent opportunity for crowds, speeches, photographs, television coverage, news stories, durable mementos, and wine-and-cheese receptions for potential campaign contributors. Thus, capital budgets create political capital and cement political ties. In contrast, what kind of ceremony can one organize to celebrate the prompt repair of a leaky sewer?

Simple cost-benefit analysis also reveals the virtues of capital projects: The sponsoring politician gets 100 percent of the credit but incurs only 3 percent of the cost, assuming thirty-year bonds.[32]

THE EFFECT OF SPENDING COALITIONS

It would be misleading to leave the impression that the three factors discussed here—recipient demands, producer pressures, and inefficiency—operate separately and in isolation. In fact, they are closely linked.

James Q. Wilson analyzed how the costs and benefits of public-sector programs are distributed. In most tax-paid programs, either costs and benefits are both spread over a large number of individuals or the costs are widespread but the benefits are targeted on a small group. Both kinds of programs are immensely attractive to office seekers.[33] These characteristics of federal government programs in the United States result in the formation of spending coalitions that cause these programs to grow.[34] The coalition that forms to nurture, protect, and expand a program is comprised of four groups: beneficiaries and near-beneficiaries (the latter are those who expect to become beneficiaries as the program expands); service providers (e.g., construction firms and construction workers engaged in road-building programs); government administrators; and political activists (e.g., officeholders, office seekers, and problem-finding elites). The partners in the coalition interact in almost a choreographed manner to gain gradual increases in spending for their program. Inefficiency comes into play as the number of beneficiaries, providers, and administrators is enlarged to gather more adherents into the spending coalition.

Conclusion

There are strong and undeniable pressures for government to grow in response to public demands, in response to the desires of service producers to supply more services, and as a consequence of ineffcicency. If unchecked, these factors would lead to an unstable and uncontrollable spiral of continued growth: the bigger the government, the greater the force for even bigger government. According to this view, budgets will expand, resulting in the appointment of more officials and the hiring of more workers. These will go to work at once to enlarge their budgets, do less work, hire still more workers, obtain better-than-average raises, and vote for more spending programs, while encouraging their constitutents and beneficiaries to do the same. The forecast seems ominous: Sooner or later, eveyone will be working for government.

But simple extrapolations of this sort are not correct. Countervailing, homeostatic forces come into play from time to time, as in the taxpayer revolts that are symbolized by Proposition 13, in state-mandated "caps" on local expenditures, in proposals for a constitutional amendment requiring a balanced budget, and in the Gramm-Rudman-Hollings Act. At times political leaders can gain more support by cutting back on spending programs than by initiating new ones. Revenue cuts and revenue limitations are politically popular. Voters frequently reject spending proposals, elect more frugal officials, and flee from high-tax jurisdictions. Ronald Reagan was elected governor and President because of his antigovernment stance: Get the government off the backs of the people.

Moreover, public employees are not united in a headless conspiracy; they feel just as victimized as other taxpayers when they receive poor and costly services in return for their tax dollars: Proposition 13 was supported by 44 percent of families that included public employees.[35] Under budgetary stringency, the objectives of one government bureau are at odds with those of another, and instead of making common cause to enlarge their total budget, they fight each other to obtain a larger share of the pie.

A more educated, critical, and sophisticated citizenry no longer regards government action as synonymous with the public interest. It is learning to expect unintended, adverse consequences of attempts at social engineering, and it recognizes limits in the state's ability to define—let alone attain—the public good.

Notes

1. James T. Bennett and Thomas J. DiLorenzo, *Underground Government: The Off-Budget Public Sector* (Washington, D.C.: Cato Institute, 1983).

2. Alan Schenker, "Zero Employee Governments," *Small Town* 16, no. 2 (September/October 1985).

3. Charles Brecher, *Where Have All the Dollars Gone?* (New York: Praeger, 1974), 94.

4. Thomas E. Borcherding, ed., *Budgets and Bureaucrats: The Sources of Government Growth* (Durham, N.C.: Duke University Press, 1977), 50.

5. Allan H. Meltzer and Scott F. Richard, "Why Government Grows (and Grows) in a Democracy," *Public Interest,* no. 52 (Summer 1978): 111-18.

6. Charles Wolf, Jr., "A Theory of Non-market Failure," *Public Interest,* no. 55 (Spring 1979): 114-33.

7. For an excellent discussion of risk in the context of health, see Aaron Wildavsky, "Richer Is Safer," *Public Interest,* no. 60 (Summer 1980): 23-39.

8. For example, see E.S. Savas, "Public vs. Private Refuse Collection: A Critical Review of the Evidence," *Journal of Urban Analysis* 6 (1979): 1-13. See also chapter 6.

9. Richard E. Wagner, "Revenue Structure, Fiscal Illusion, and Budgetary Choice," *Public Choice* 25 (Spring 1976): 45-61. Also, James M. Buchanan, "Why Does Government Grow?" in Borcherding, *Budgets and Bureaucrats*.

10. E.S. Savas, "How Much Do Government Services Really Cost?" *Urban Affairs Quarterly* 15 (September 1979): 23-42.

11. Madsen Pirie, *Dismantling the State* (Dallas: National Center for Policy Analysis, 1985), 20-21.

12. Odgen Nash, *I'm a Stranger Here Myself* (Boston: Little, Brown, 1938), 193.

13. Gordon Tullock, "Why Politicians Won't Cut Taxes," *Taxing and Spending,* October/November 1978, 12-14.

14. Morris P. Fiorina, *Congress: Keystone of the Washington Establishment* (New Haven: Yale University Press, 1977).

15. Buchanan, "Why Does Government Grow?" 13.

16. Robert J. Staaf, "The Public School System in Transition: Consolidation and Parental Choice," in Borcherding, *Budgets and Bureaucrats,* 143-46.

17. Tom Bethell, "The Wealth of Washington," *Harper's Magazine,* June 1978, 41-60.

18. William A. Niskanen, Jr., *Bureaucracy and Representative Government* (Chicago: Aldine-Atherton, 1971), 36-42.

19. Bethell, "The Wealth of Washington."

20. E.S. Savas, "New Directions for Urban Analysis," *Interfaces* 6 (November 1975): 1-9.

21. E.S. Savas, "Municipal Monopoly," *Harper's Magazine,* December 1971, 55-60.

22. Robert L. Bish and Robert Warren, "Scale and Monopoly Problems in Urban Government Services," *Urban Affairs Quarterly* 8 (September 1972): 97-122.

23. *City of Lafayette, Louisiana, and City of Plaquemine, Louisiana* v. *Louisiana Power & Light Company,* 435 U.S. 389 (1978).

24. Thomas E. Borcherding, Winston C. Bush, and Robert M. Spann, "The Effects on Public Spending of the Divisibility of Public Outputs in Consumption, Bureaucratic Power, and the Size of the Tax-Sharing Group," in Borcherding, *Budgets and Bureaucrats,* 219.

25. E.S. Savas, *The Organization and Efficiency of Solid Waste Collection* (Lexington, Mass: Lexington Books, 1977), 67-78.

26. For example, see Sharon Smith, "Public-Private Wage Differentials in Metropolitan Areas," in *Public Sector Labor Markets,* ed. Peter Mieszkowski and George E. Peterson (Washington, D.C.: Urban Institute, 1981), 81-102; see also Don Bellante and James Long, "The Political Economy of the Rent-seeking Society: The Case of Public Employees and Their Unions," *Journal of Labor Research* 2 (Spring 1981): 1-14.

27. Bureau of Labor Statistics, "Employee Compensation in the Professional, Administrative, Technical and Clerical Survey," *Industry Surveys,* no. 464 (Washington, D.C.: 1975).

28. Bureau of Labor Statistics, "Average Annual Pay by State and Industry, 1984," *News,* 13 August 1985, table 4.

29. Bernhard F. Lentz, "Political and Economic Determinants of County Government Pay," *Public Choice* 36 (Spring 1981): 253-71.

30. Brecher, *Where Have All the Dollars Gone?* 99.

31. Robert M. Spann, "Rates of Productivity Change and the Growth of State and Local Governmental Expenditures," in Borcherding, *Budgets and Bureaucrats,* 100-129.

32. I am grateful to Edward V. Regan, comptroller of the State of New York, for this lucid observation.

33. James Q. Wilson, *Political Organizations* (New York: Basic Books, 1973), 330-33.

34. Stuart M. Butler, *Privatizing Federal Spending: A Strategy to Eliminate the Deficit* (New York: Universe Books, 1985), 9-28.

35. Jacob Citrin, "The Alienated Voter," *Taxing and Spending* (October/November 1978): 7-11.

PART TWO

The Theory of Privatization

3. Basic Characteristics of Goods and Services

To determine the appropriate roles for government and for the private sector in modern civilization, let us begin at the beginning by looking at the kinds of goods and services that people want and then examining the proper nature of government involvement in satisfying those needs.

Human beings require many different kinds of goods and services. Air, water, food, clothing, and shelter are the basic necessities of life, but unless one is a hermit, additional goods and services are desired: fire protection and banking services, education and old-age security, transportation and communication, recreation, health care and waste removal, theaters and cemeteries, museums and beauty parlors, landscaping and tailoring, books and locks, money and satellites. Advanced societies, no less than primitive tribes, seek protection from human enemies and assistance from divine beings, and therefore they support warriors and weapon makers to provide the former and priests and shamans to provide the latter services.

An examination of the basic characteristics of these and other goods and services reveals that certain kinds of goods have special attributes that require some sort of collective action. To start this inquiry it is useful to classify this vast jumble of goods and services, not in alphabetical order, as in the Yellow Pages, but according to two important concepts: exclusion and consumption.[1]

Exclusion

Goods and *services*—henceforth these terms will be used synonymously, for the distinction between goods and services is not important in this discussion— have the characteristic of exclusion if the potential user of the goods can be denied the goods or excluded from their use unless he meets the conditions set by the potential supplier. In other words, the goods can change hands only if both the buyer and seller agree on the terms.

Now this is a perfectly ordinary sort of condition. All the commonplace goods and services that we buy in the marketplace clearly fall into this category; all have this exclusion property. I may walk off with my bag of groceries only after my grocer agrees. (We can ignore the possibility of theft—we know it occurs, but it is not germane to the discussion.) But there are vast numbers of other goods and services that do not possess this simple property. A consumer can simply help himself to such goods as long as Mother Nature or another supplier makes them available. As one example of such a good, consider a lighthouse. Built at considerable expense on a rocky coast, and consuming large amounts of costly energy, the lighthouse sends forth its beacon to help seamen navigate the treacherous waters nearby. This is a valuable service for the seafarer, but he does not pay the lighthouse keeper for it; he can avail himself of it freely and cannot be excluded from doing so. After all, what is the keeper to do? Turn off the beacon when he knows that a particular nonpaying user is in the area? (Conceivably one could transform a lighthouse into an excludable good by using a radio beacon instead of a conventional light. Only paying subscribers who are supplied with the proper receivers and provided with regular information about the frequency currently in use could avail themselves of the service. I'd like to have the lifeboat concession in the vicinity of such a beacon!)

The water of a large freshwater lake is another example of a good whose consumption cannot conveniently be prevented or excluded. Consumers can drink freely of the water, and can use it for irrigation purposes without paying anyone for its use.

It should be recognized that exclusion is a matter of cost more than logic; exclusion is feasible or infeasible to the extent that the cost of enforcing exclusion is relatively low or high. Hence, exclusion admits of degrees. Exclusion from the services of a lighthouse is rather infeasible; exclusion in the purchase of goods from a store is easily feasible. But other goods cannot be classified quite so neatly. For example, it is feasible to charge admission (and therefore to practice exclusion) for a grandstand seat to a fireworks display, but many others outside the grounds will also see the show, although perhaps not as well as those in the seats. It is simply not feasible to enclose a large enough area so that no one can witness the show free of charge—unless the show is a poor one with no high-altitude bursts.

Consumption

The other important characteristic of goods and services that is relevant here has to do with consumption. Some goods may be used or consumed jointly and simultaneously by many customers without being diminished in quality or quantity, while other goods are available only for individual (rather than joint) consumption; that is, if they are used by one consumer, they are not available for consumption by another. A fish and a haircut are examples of a good and a service subject to individual consumption; the fish is no longer available to another diner, and neither are the services of the barber while he is cutting someone's hair. (Other, comparable barbers may be available to others in need of tonsorial attention — just as similar fish are available to other diners — and the very same chair and barber will be available in a few minutes, but the fact remains that the services of that particular barber at that particular time are devoted to and consumed entirely by the one user.)

Contrast these cases with a television broadcast. My family's "consumption" of a program, by enjoying it on our television set in our living room, in no way limits its "consumption" by anyone else, or even by millions of other viewers who may turn on their sets. The program remains equally available for joint consumption by many users and is in no way diminished or made less useful by our act of consumption.

We should not be confused by the fact that the fish may be fed to several people at a dinner party; that act does not confer upon the fish the property of joint consumption, in the rigorous sense that we have used the term here. Similarly, my solitary viewing of a television show does not transform that telecast into an individually consumed good.

Another illustration of a joint-consumption good is national defense. The protection I receive from the armed forces in no way subtracts from the protection available to my neighbor; his consumption of that particular good is undiminished by my own.

Other examples of goods that are subject to joint consumption are parks and streets. One person's use of Grand Canyon National Park does not preclude another's use of it; it is a jointly consumed good, as is a city street. In both cases, however, if the total number of joint users is large relative to the capacity of the park or street, then the quantity and quality of the available goods are severely diminished. In other words, these goods — parks and streets — are not pure joint-consumption goods like the television broadcast. To a degree, they are like a haircut, an individually consumed good. In fact, few goods are pure joint-consumption goods; most fall along a continuum between pure individual and pure joint consumption.

Classifying Goods and Services

What has been said so far can be displayed in the form of a diagram, as in figure 3.1 for several transportation-related services; figure 3.2 shows water supply represented in a similar diagram. The two properties, exclusion and con-

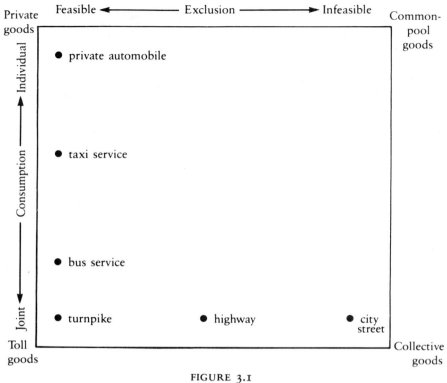

FIGURE 3.1

EXCLUSION AND CONSUMPTION PROPERTIES OF
TRANSPORTATION SERVICES AND FACILITIES

sumption, constitute the two dimensions of the diagram and are shown as continuous variables; their extreme values are at the ends of the scales.

Figure 3.3 (on page 40) further illustrates the concept by displaying additional goods and services, located in accordance with their respective degrees of exclusion and joint consumption. Obviously, subjective judgment is involved in the precise placement of services in this diagram; the reader is invited to draw his or her own version.

The four corners of the diagram correspond to pure forms: (1) pure individually consumed goods for which exclusion is completely feasible; (2) pure jointly consumed goods for which exclusion is completely feasible; (3) pure individually consumed goods for which exclusion is completely infeasible; and (4) pure jointly consumed goods for which exclusion is completely infeasible. These four idealized types of goods and services are important enough and will be referred to often enough to justify naming them; this has been done

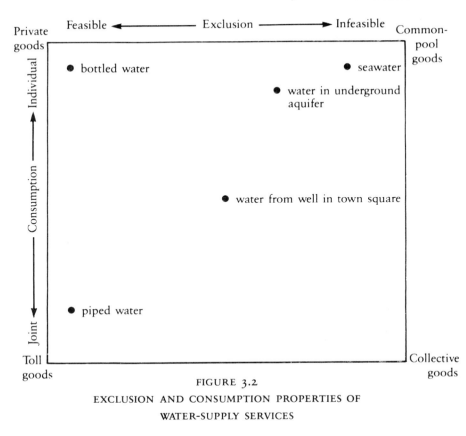

FIGURE 3.2

EXCLUSION AND CONSUMPTION PROPERTIES OF
WATER-SUPPLY SERVICES

in the diagram. In the sequence listed above, they are called (1) private goods, (2) toll goods, (3) common-pool goods, and (4) collective goods.

The reason for classifying goods in this manner is that the nature of the good determines whether or not it will be produced at all, and the conditions needed to assure that it will be supplied. Private goods are consumed individually and cannot be obtained by the user without the assent of the supplier, which is usually obtained by making payment. Common-pool goods are consumed individually, and it is virtually impossible to prevent anyone from taking them freely. Toll goods are used jointly, but the users must pay, and those who won't pay can easily be excluded from enjoying the use of the goods. The more difficult or costly it is to exclude a consumer from the use of a toll good, the more like a collective good it is. Collective goods are used jointly, and it is impossible to exclude anyone from their use, which means that people generally will not pay for them without coercion. This important discussion of the relation between the nature of the good and how to assure an adequate supply of the

39

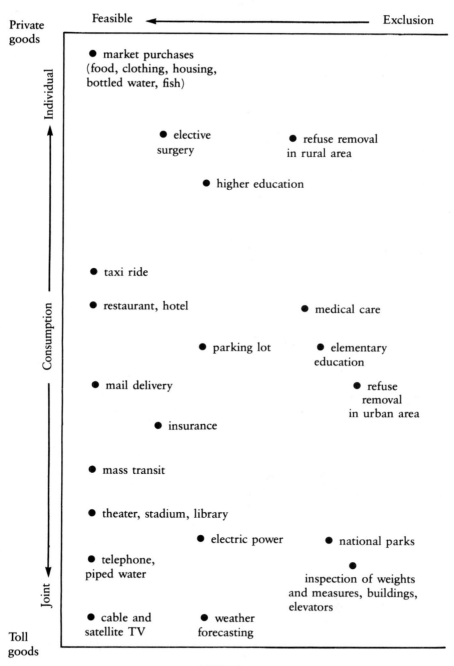

Private
goods

Feasible ⟵——————————————— Exclusion

Individual

Consumption

Joint

Toll
goods

● market purchases
(food, clothing, housing,
bottled water, fish)

● elective
surgery

● refuse removal
in rural area

● higher education

● taxi ride

● restaurant, hotel

● medical care

● parking lot

● elementary
education

● mail delivery

● refuse
removal
in urban area

● insurance

● mass transit

● theater, stadium, library

● electric power

● national parks

● telephone,
piped water

●
inspection of weights
and measures, buildings,
elevators

● cable and
satellite TV

● weather
forecasting

FIGURE 3.3

EXCLUSION AND CONSUMPTION PROPERTIES OF VARIOUS GOODS

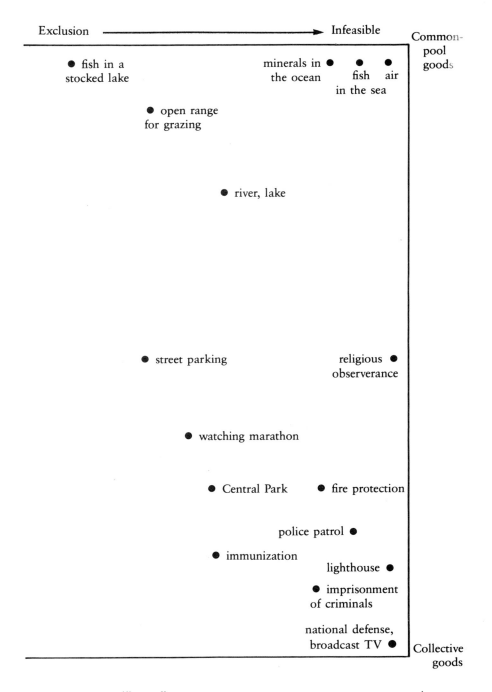

Exclusion ———————→ Infeasible | Common-
pool
goods

● fish in a
stocked lake

minerals in ● ● ●
the ocean fish air
in the sea

● open range
for grazing

● river, lake

● street parking

religious ●
observerance

● watching marathon

● Central Park

● fire protection

police patrol ●

● immunization

lighthouse ●

● imprisonment
of criminals

national defense,
broadcast TV ●

| Collective
goods

AND SERVICES ("PURE" GOODS ARE SHOWN AT THE FOUR CORNERS)

good will be resumed more fully after reviewing and classifying some of the principal goods used in a modern society.

The goods that appear in figure 3.3 near the corners can be considered private goods, toll goods, common-pool goods, or collective goods, although it should be remembered that none of them are pure or ideal types. In the upper left of the diagram appear the ordinary goods and services that one buys in the marketplace: shoes, bread, automobiles, housing, haircuts, dry cleaning, watch repair, etc. They are all pure or nearly pure private goods.

In the lower right of the diagram are collective goods. Air pollution control is as pure a collective good as one can find. National defense is a collective good, but even this is impure: An army busy defending one part of a country may be unavailable to protect another part. Police protection is almost as pure a collective good, but any finite force on patrol can be "consumed" by individual calls for service, making the good temporarily unavailable to others. For this reason, it is shown above and to the left of national defense. On the other hand, fire protection used to be a toll good or even a somewhat private good, for it was common in the nineteenth century to have private fire companies that protected only their paying subscribers, whose homes were marked with identifying placards. Today, particularly in urban areas, we recognize that when a house is on fire, many people besides the homeowner benefit by having the blaze extinguished before it spreads. Furthermore, it is no longer technically feasible to exclude service in densely packed, high-rise, multiple dwellings. Changing conditions have caused fire protection in urban areas to migrate into the class of collective goods.

Central Park in New York City was also a toll good when it was first built. It has a wall around it, interrupted by many gates that were once tended by gatekeepers who charged admission. The wall and gates are still there, but the gatekeepers have long since gone, exclusion is no longer practiced, and the park is used — and abused — as a collective good. National parks have limited access points and are therefore toll goods, but a determined backpacker can hike into one through the wilderness and, realistically, cannot be excluded. Because the quality of a park depends on the number of users and the uses they make of it, parks are shown as being more individually consumed than some other toll and collective goods.

Air is a common-pool good. It can be used and taken freely and compressed, but upon compression it is changed into a purely private good. Air can also be used and soiled, thereby rendering it unavailable to others in its original condition. Similarly, a fish in the sea is a common-pool good, and a fish in a stocked lake is somewhere between a common-pool good and private good (the lake could be patrolled and only those who purchase a license could be granted access to the fish), but once a fish is caught and in the creel, it is clearly a private good.

Water in an underground aquifer is a common-pool good, free to be tapped by any well digger who owns a tiny parcel of land above it, but once it is brought into a water distribution system, it becomes a toll good. Rivers, lakes, and other waterways are common-pool goods of sorts, whether they are used for transportation, as sources of water, or to dispose of waste material. As figure 3.3 (pages 40-41) shows, they are decidedly impure common-pool goods because exclusion is by no means impossible.

Telephone service is a toll good whose quality is actually enhanced when other users consume it jointly; can you imagine a telephone system with only one subscriber? Whom would one call? The more subscribers, the more useful and valuable the communication network—provided it is not saturated. The same is true of postal and telegraph services, and insurance.

Sewer service and electric power are toll goods, as are bridges, turnpikes, stadiums, theaters, and libraries, although none of these is as pure a toll good as cable TV. Even broadcast television becomes a toll good, like cable TV, if receivers must be licensed, as is the case in some countries.

Some readers may be confused upon seeing, in figure 3.3, weather forecasts identified as toll goods, inasmuch as people in the United States are used to getting weather forecasts free on radio, TV, and in newspapers. This occurs because the U.S. Weather Bureau gives away this toll good, which is produced at public expense. The bureau could conceivably charge for the information, and the media could buy it, just as they purchase information from international wire services. Alternatively, private firms could provide weather forecasts to the media, either by sale or free as a way to advertise their more specialized and localized forecasting services.

While mass transit is a toll good, taxi service is more of a private good, and a private automobile is a more purely private good. In general, on-street parking is a collective good, although where there are parking meters it has been made into a toll good that is impure insofar as the street has limited capacity. Streets are a collective good, for it is difficult to exclude the use of a street for passage; that is, it is costly to construct and to man barriers.

To exclude someone from a school is not difficult, but at least an elementary education can be obtained without formal schooling. Furthermore, particularly with elementary education, joint consumption occurs to some degree. The relative positions of elementary and higher education are displayed in figure 3.3. Accepting one applicant into medical school means rejecting another (as a famous reverse-discrimination case has shown); and therefore the higher the level of education under consideration, the more the service resembles a private good.

Health care presents an interesting case that cannot be analyzed without considering separate portions of the health-care system. Elective and cosmetic surgery, treatment for vitamin deficiencies and metabolic disorders, and medical care after accidental injury are private goods. On the other hand, public health services such as mosquito abatement, rat control, and immigration control to prevent the entry of contagious diseases are obviously collective goods.

Immunization and treatment for communicable diseases, whether sore throats or diphtheria, at first glance seem to satisfy all the criteria of private goods. A person with such an illness can certainly be denied treatment, and, if admitted to a hospital, the bed he occupies and the nursing and medical care he receives are no longer available to others. It is evident, however, that treating such illnesses provides important side benefits—"positive externalities"— in that others are not exposed to the illnesses. Therefore, many people receive benefits, or partake of the fruits of this particular good, at the same time as the patient and without reducing the latter's benefits. Surely this is a collective good. Going back to the elective surgery mentioned above, this service, too, can benefit others, if the patient is better able to work and support his family and provide employment to his workers. Clearly, however, except for the aforementioned public health measures, health care has the exclusion property and is a private or toll good.

This lengthy exercise in classifying goods and services makes it clear that the nature of the good—private, toll, common-pool, or collective—determines the willingness of consumers to pay for it, and therefore, inevitably, the willingness of producers to supply it. Hence the nature of the good determines whether or not collective intervention is needed to procure the good in satisfactory quantity and quality. The next four sections explore this issue for each type of good.

Private Goods

Private goods pose no conceptual problem of supply; the marketplace provides them. Consumers demand the goods; entrepreneurs recognize the demand, produce the goods, and sell them to willing buyers at a mutually satisfactory price. Collective action with respect to private goods for the most part is confined to assuring their safety (e.g., of food, drugs, elevators, and buildings), honest reporting (of weights and measures, interest rates, labels), and the like. Of course, no one will be able to secure all the private goods he may deserve, and some may to be too poor to afford even the rudimentary necessities without assistance.

One should note that private goods are sometimes supplied by governments even though the market can supply them. This is true of virtually all

44

private goods in the Soviet Union, for example, but it is also true of some private goods in the United States.

Common-Pool Goods

Common-pool goods do pose a supply problem. With no need to pay for such goods, and with no means to prevent their consumption, such goods will be consumed—even squandered—to the point of exhaustion, as long as the cost of collecting, harvesting, extracting, appropriating, or otherwise taking direct possession of the free goods does not exceed the value of the goods to the consumer. No rational supplier will produce such goods, and they would exist only through the beneficence of nature. (We will see later, however, that this is not quite the case.)

Whales, tigers, and elephants are living—or rather dying—proof of the problem of managing common-pool goods that belong to whoever takes them. They are being consumed to the point of extinction, even though they are naturally renewable.

Market mechanisms cannot supply common-pool goods. One way to conserve the natural supply, however, is through collective action. In the case of whales and animals, this takes the form of international efforts to achieve voluntary agreement among the consumers to limit their consumption. (This is also true of Antarctica, currently a common-pool good.) Alas, this has proven to be too thin a reed to support such a burden, as enforcement is next to impossible. Another approach is to ban the sale of common-pool goods after they have been appropriated from their natural state. (Not all common-pool goods lend themselves to this approach.) Following this tactic, in the United States the sale of products made of alligator hides, tiger skins, ostrich feathers, and other endangered species is prohibited; and in Kenya the government tries to prohibit the sale of elephant tusks and rhinoceros horns. This approach, too, has had limited success. Note that the commissions, agencies, regulatory bodies, and enforcement units created to deal with the problem of common-pool goods are providing a service that is, in effect, a collective good.

Just as whales and tigers have been appropriated from the common pool and used as private goods, some rivers and lakes represent common-pool goods that have been used freely as dumps for toxic and noxious wastes and therefore have been debased into lower-quality, less available, partly consumed private goods. This destruction of common-pool goods, the pollution of waterways, has also called forth collective action. Controls have been established over sources of pollution such as industrial plants and sewage treatment facilities. In effect, a new service is provided, water pollution control (a collective good), in order to assure a continued supply of the desired common-pool good —unpolluted waterways.

The moon is a far-out example of a common-pool good. It could be used as a source of raw materials or as a communication or military base, but it is at least temporarily protected from overconsumption because of the high cost of using it. Nevertheless, outer space is already being degraded as a common-pool good as more and more waste products from space explorations orbit the Earth.

These examples illustrate the problems inherent in common-pool goods: the danger of depletion, the conventional approach to the problem by creating collective goods (that is, services usually performed by government agencies) to safeguard the common-pool goods, and the limited effectiveness of such efforts because exclusion is difficult to achieve.

Because of the inadequacy of this approach, a diametrically different alternative is receiving growing attention. It is an approach based on the concept of property rights, about which Alchian[2] and DeAlessi,[3] for example, have written widely. Simply put, when a common-pool good is transformed into a private good and belongs to a single owner, conservation and successful management become possible. A private owner (of elephants, wilderness land, or water) wants to maximize the long-term value of his property and will follow prudent practices in husbanding the erstwhile common-pool goods that he owns. For the same reason, an underground oil deposit whose drilling rights belong to a single producer can be managed more effectively than one that can be tapped from dozens of overlying parcels of land. Conversely, land that is owned by "the public" tends to be treated as a common-pool good, and is overgrazed and destroyed—"the tragedy of the commons."[4]

An interesting extension of these ideas can be applied to ocean fishing. In the United States, the price of fish has risen rapidly, even along the ocean shore. Paradoxically, fish is expensive because fish are free. That is, as a quintessential common-pool good, they are free for the taking, and, as a result, the ocean is overfished, the supply is depleted (just like the overgrazed commons), each fishing boat catches few fish, and thus the process is inefficient and the cost per fish is high. It has been suggested that off-shore fish be treated the same as off-shore oil, as the property of all U.S. citizens; scientific quotas should be set on the annual catch permitted, and rights to catch fish within that quota should be sold at auction. Transforming the common-pool good into a private good in this way, by creating transferable property rights—the privatization of ocean fisheries, if you will—is likely to solve the problem of overfishing.[5]

Butler has described the analogous failures caused by government land ownership in the United States, and he advocates the privatization of wilderness lands in order to conserve them.[6] This is discussed further in chapter 6.

Toll Goods

Unlike common-pool goods, toll goods can be supplied by the marketplace. Because exclusion is readily possible, users will pay and therefore suppliers will supply the goods, theoretically in the quantity and quality demanded by the users. Nevertheless, some toll goods present problems that require collective action. These are the toll goods said to be natural monopolies, which is to say that as the number of users increases, the cost per user decreases. The result is that it is most economical to have a single supplier. This is true of cable television, communication networks, and utilities such as electric power, gas distribution, water supply, and sewer service. Collective action is often taken to create and award these monopolies in the first place, and then to regulate them so that the owners do not exploit their monopoly privileges unfairly.

A growing number of economists disagree with this rationale for regulation.[7] They cite the fact that many toll goods that were once monopolies no longer are. Railroads face competition from airplanes, trucks, buses, barges, and boats. Telephone communication is challenged by microwave and facsimile transmission, and cable TV by satellites and videotapes. Indeed, it is argued, if a monopoly is "natural," there is surely no need to protect it by legislation! Moreover, even natural monopolies may be contestable.[8] If there is no alternative, a monopoly could be established for only a fixed period of time and could be awarded by competitive bidding.[9] Collective action is required to carry out this competitive process among would-be suppliers operating in the marketplace.

In any event, toll goods, like private goods, can be supplied in the marketplace, but in many countries toll goods are supplied by government (usually with a user charge). The wisdom of government provision of such goods is explored in chapter 6.

Collective Goods

It is collective goods that pose a serious problem in the organization of a society. The marketplace is unable to supply such goods because, by their nature, they are used simultaneously by many people and no one can be excluded from enjoying them. Every individual has an economic incentive to become a "free rider," that is, to make full use of such goods without paying for them and without contributing a fair share of the effort required to supply them. Aristotle said it long ago: "That which is common to the greatest number has the least care bestowed upon it." If no one volunteers to pay for such goods, surely no one will volunteer to produce them, at least not in adequate supply. Therefore, collective contributions—usually taxes—have to be obtained in order to assure a supply of the goods. In small groups, social pressures may be sufficient

47

to assure that each person contributes his or her fair share to secure the collective goods, but in larger, more diverse groups, legally sanctioned coercion (such as tax collection and compulsory military service) is necessary.

Having said this, however, it is necessary to examine some collective goods more closely to resolve apparent inconsistencies. Take the example of the lighthouse referred to earlier in this chapter. Is it possible for a private, profit-making organization to provide that collective good? Consider a consortium of companies that sell marine insurance. Conceivably they could maintain and operate lighthouses throughout the world and they could include the cost in the premiums they charge for marine insurance. A moment's reflection reveals the weakness in this scheme, however: it requires an OPEC-like, oligopolistic cartel, and, by analogy with OPEC, there is a great incentive for every firm to sell insurance without the lighthouse premium, thereby becoming a free rider and underselling its competitors. Thus, sooner or later the scheme will falter. The inherent nature of the lighthouse as a collective good will shine forth, and the consortium will dissolve if it lacks sufficient coercive power to enforce payment.

Broadcast TV is also defined as a collective good in figure 3.3. How is this possible, inasmuch as it is free to viewers and not paid for by taxes? The answer is that it is paid for by advertisers, and the "good" they receive in exchange for their money as sponsors is access to potential customers. The latter ultimately pay collectively for their "free" TV viewing, in the price of the product. Moreover, the cost of the TV program is treated as a tax-deductible business expense, and so it might be argued that taxpayers *do* pay after all for this collective good, just as theory predicts!

MEASURING AND CHOOSING COLLECTIVE GOODS

Collective goods have other properties that exacerbate the already serious consequences of their joint-consumption and nonexclusion characteristics. They are generally hard to measure and they offer little choice to the consumer.

Unlike private goods, which are relatively easy to count, account for, and package for unit sales, collective goods generally do not allow such ease of handling. How many units of national defense should be purchased? How much police protection? One can count the number of firemen in a fire department, but that number offers no reliable measure of the amount of fire protection they provide. One can report the area of a park, but that says little about it; appearance and ambience are inherent aspects of that particular good. Street mileage can be measured and traffic and potholes can be counted, but these hard facts barely begin to capture the important features of that particular collective good. The product of an air pollution control department can be measured only indirectly, in terms of air quality, and even that is subject to extraneous factors, such as a strong breeze. For these reasons, it is difficult—but by no means impossible—to define and measure the performance of an organization charged with providing a collective good. And this difficulty means that it is difficult to specify the amount of the good to be provided and to estimate what it should cost.

The very nature of a collective good means that an individual has little choice with respect to consuming the good, and he must generally accept it in the quantity and quality available. The ordinary citizen can demand that a policeman be stationed in front of his home, that his street be swept daily, and that his neighborhood park look like a royal garden; but his voice is diluted, and although his taxes may rise, the collective goods he receives are not likely to change much. Neither the individual who feels that the country is in danger and needs more military might nor the individual who feels that the nation's security is threatened by too much military power in the hands of fallible mortals will be satisfied, for he has no individual choice in the matter. He may lobby his congressman, but must settle for what he can get.

A further consequence of these characteristics is that because it is impossible to charge directly for the use of collective goods, payment for them is unrelated to demand or consumption. Therefore, instead of relying on a market mechanism, one must rely on a political process to decide how much each user must pay, and whether or not some users are to receive a discount. Furthermore, to the extent that most collective goods are impure, and permit individual consumption to some degree, the decision as to who gets them is also relegated to the political process, as is the decision about how much of the goods to produce.

At this point it is worth reviewing and summarizing the important differences between private and collective goods in order to appreciate better the profound nature of the differences; this is done in table 3.1.

HOW LARGE SHOULD THE COLLECTIVE BE?

A further important issue arises with respect to collective goods. How big is the collective that has to provide them? There may be agreement that a collective assessment (e.g., taxes) is required to assure supply of a collective good, but what is the scale of the community that should be assessed? The entire nation? A region, state, county, or city? A neighborhood? The residents on a city block, or in a condominium on that block?

A basic principle of public finance says that the beneficiaries of a collective good should pay, but they may not be so easy to identify. While it is easy to see that national defense benefits the entire nation, and so everyone should pay for it, at the other end of the scale consider the lowly pothole. Located

TABLE 3.1

COMPARISON OF PRIVATE AND COLLECTIVE GOODS

Characteristic	Private good	Collective good
Consumption	Entirely by an individual	Joint and simultaneous by many people
Payment for goods	Related to consumption; paid by consumer	Unrelated to consumption; paid by collective contributions
Exclusion of someone who will not pay	Easy	Difficult
Measurement of quantity and quality of goods	Easy	Difficult
Measurement of performance of goods producer	Easy	Difficult
Individual choice in consuming or not	Yes	No
Individual choice as to quantity and quality of goods consumed	Yes	No
Allocation decisions	Made by market mechanism	Made by political process

just below the street surface, lying quietly in wait for the unwary motorist, the pothole jars teeth, rattles bones, destroys front-end alignments, snatches hubcaps, and, in its most virulent form, bends wheel rims and snaps axles. Surely its elimination (pothole repair) would benefit many and is a collective good. But who should pay? One line of reasoning is that potholes are found all over the country and are a nationwide problem, therefore, they are a national problem; ergo they should be repaired using funds from the national government, collected from taxpayers nationally. This beguiling syllogism is badly awry, however. By this reasoning, every widespread problem, including solid-waste disposal and poor study habits, can be propelled into the lap of the largest available collective agent, the national government.

A more careful analysis of the matter can be carried out. The basic principle to follow is that *the smallest collective unit that embraces most of the beneficiaries should provide the collective good*. In the case of potholes on city streets that are public thoroughfares, the city is the appropriate unit in size (although we will see in the next section an approach to charging individual users of streets). City taxpayers should pay. Note how this policy affects out-of-town visitors: They benefit from well-paved streets, but to the extent that they purchase gas, go shopping, stay in hotels, and eat in restaurants, they contribute both directly and indirectly to the city's coffers and thereby pay a share of the street-maintenance costs. Similarly, distant purchasers of goods manufactured in the city benefit from well-paved streets in that city, because their goods are not damaged when trucked through that city's streets. They pay for the benefit, however, because the price they pay includes the cost of local taxes paid by the manufacturer and trucker to maintain their city's streets. In other words, we see that even with a small and local collective unit, beneficiaries pay for the collective good regardless of where they are located; the basic principle articulated above remains intact and is confirmed.

The reader will note that this discussion has placed us squarely in the midst of the unending debate on federalism, which deals with the proper allocation of responsibilities among the different levels of government. We have seen that it is the nature of each collective good, and the identification of its beneficiaries, that determines the appropriate level of responsibility for supplying the good.

The Growth of Collective and Common-Pool Goods

The problem of providing collective goods is compounded further by the fact that the number of such goods has grown in recent decades. This has occurred for three reasons. First, individuals can and do create collective goods by transforming their private goods, thereby shifting the burden of payment onto collective shoulders. For example, the person who throws his garbage into the street instead of subscribing to a refuse-collection service eschews the private good called waste collection and creates a need for the collective good called street cleaning.

The reverse is also occurring. Some collective goods can be replaced, in part at least, by private goods. Locks, burglar alarms, karate lessons, smoke alarms, home fire extinguishers, and automatic fire sprinklers are examples of private goods being used increasingly as partial substitutes for the collective goods of police and fire protection. Furthermore, a very wealthy person could transform collective goods into private goods by having his own guards, a large estate with private roads, and private park and gardens, as at Versailles. Given sufficient incentive, more metering and exclusion devices could be invented that would make it possible to transform other collective goods into toll or private goods; for example, autos could be charged for the use of particular city streets during congested periods, as advocated by Vickrey.[10]

The second reason for the growth of collective goods is that the basic nature of some goods has changed, either because of changing technology that affects their exclusion and consumption characteristics or because of changed conditions. The migration of fire protection from private good to collective good, due to urbanization, exemplifies this shift. The same is true of refuse removal; this may be almost a pure private good in a rural setting, but in a city it is more of a collective good; after all, both my neighbor and I will benefit if he has his refuse collected regularly, and we will both suffer if he does not.

Consider also the following whimsical instance of a migrating good. As we've said, a fish in the sea is a prototypical example of a common-pool good. Indeed, until 1977 the fish outside the 12-mile limit in international waters off the New England coast were so regarded. Then the United States in effect appropriated these fish for its citizens, and redefined them to be collective goods by extending to 200 miles the limits of its territorial waters and sending the Coast Guard to watch over them. (In reality, of course, it was a side effect — the well-being of the local fishing industry — that was deemed a collective good. This particular collective action and its political side benefits further illustrate why and how government grows.)

The third reason for the growth of collective goods is that some have been created by the need to husband common-pool goods whose scarcity has only recently been recognized. Air and water pollution control, and the negotiation and enforcement of international agreements concerning common-pool goods such as whales, tigers, and Antarctica, are examples of such newly created collective goods.

WORTHY GOODS

The largest cause of government growth, as was pointed out earlier, was the societal decision that certain private and toll goods, such as food, education, and mass transit, are so worthy that their consumption should be encouraged regardless of the consumer's ability to pay. As a result, these worthy goods have either been subsidized by government or produced directly by government and supplied to those deemed to require consumption (by force if necessary, in the case of education) of these goods. If no use is made of the exclusion property of private and toll goods, that is, if there is little or no charge for their use, then in effect the good is being treated as a common-pool or collective good.

There are two different conceptual ways to view this transformation. One way, which is more rigorous intellectually, is to adhere scrupulously to the basic definitions. Private and toll goods, because of their innate exclusion and consumption characteristics (as long as the technological means of delivery remain unchanged), cannot be redefined and they do not migrate. What has happened with worthy goods, simply put, is that society, acting through government, decided to provide certain private and toll goods completely or partly at collective expense.

The other way to view the transformation is to consider certain designated private and toll goods as having migrated into the class of collective goods; that is, on figures 3.1 to 3.3 these goods have settled into the lower-right corner. The explanation of this migration is that (1) everyone benefits to some degree when worthy goods are consumed (i.e., there are positive externalities) and so their consumption can be considered partly joint, which causes a drop downward on the diagram; (2) exclusion has been abandoned because these are worthy, and so the goods have shifted to the right on the diagram; the result is more collective goods. These two different formulations can be considered complementary rather than competing.

The collective political decision to supply and encourage the consumption of certain worthy goods regardless of the consumer's ability or willingness to pay results in subsidies to private individuals and enterprises, or in direct production of service by a government unit. Examples abound: Recreation services that are toll goods according to our definition are given away free of charge to the user. Bridges, mass transit, and other transportation services that are toll goods are often subsidized. Similarly, theaters, concert halls, opera houses, sports arenas, stadiums, museums, and exhibition halls are often built with government funds and receive operating subsidies as well.

The straightforward toll goods of electric, gas, and telephone service may be in the early stages of being similarly treated. For example, a demand that they be provided without charge under certain circumstances, hence rendering them indistinguishable in practice from collective goods, arose following a particularly tragic incident in New England one winter when an elderly couple, incapable of caring for themselves yet living alone, froze to death when their utilities were unwittingly turned off for nonpayment of bills.

Not long ago education was regarded as a private good. Exclusion and individual consumption were clearly identifiable attributes of this good. An education bestowed great and obvious benefits on the recipient, and this much-prized good was sought and sold in the marketplace. In time, however, a new understanding gained ground: The entire society benefited significantly if everyone was educated, much like vaccination. Education was considered to have major, positive side effects associated with it, and therefore it was not only made freely available to all, but its consumption was actually made compulsory, up to a certain age or grade level.

An even better example of changing social values, and the designation of a private good as a worthy one to be supplied at no cost to the beneficiary, is the most basic good: food. How could there be a purer private good? Nevertheless, the inevitable consequence of treating food as a purely private good is that some would starve. Therefore, collective action is taken to distribute food to the poor. Another private good, housing, was similarly defined as a worthy good, and public housing was built for eligible consumers. (Unfortunately, public housing has had a mixed record. A better approach for delivering this worthy private good is described in chapter 7.)

At the extreme, one can claim that every good has some joint-consumption character by saying that a citizen who lacks a particular private good, and therefore has an unfulfilled need, will become disaffected from the larger society; this in turn will lead to social instability, which threatens everyone. By this reasoning, all private goods have side benefits that benefit everyone in the society at large and hence should be provided at collective expense.

Such actions have unfortunate consequences, however. As has been said, all goods are somewhat subject to individual consumption, for there are no pure joint-consumption goods. When subsidized, underpriced, or given away without charge, the demand for the good increases, and public expenditures must be made to supply more of it. But what often happens with such goods, regrettably, is that they become indistinguishable from common-pool goods, and are subject to all the problems inherent in such goods: rampant waste, thoughtless consumption, and possible exhaustion. To the extent that the handling of "junk mail" is underpriced, postal service is an example of an impure toll good that has tended to become a casually consumed, exhaustible, common-pool good. Unmetered municipal water is another case in point. Anyone associated with free-lunch programs in schools is keenly aware of the prodigious waste that occurs, and scandals associated with free summer lunch programs in large cities revealed the same thing: large amounts of food treated as a worthless good and discarded. Public schooling is treated in much the same way by some careless consumers.

The recent experience with medical care in the United States offers an even more dramatic illustration of this process. As was discussed above, most medical care could be characterized an an individually consumed good readily subject to exclusion, that is, a private good. However, a gradual change in societal values led to the recognition that individual medical care has joint-consumption properties: A lot of people feel better when a sick person is cured. Thus, medical care was subsidized or provided at nominal or no charge as a result of various collective decisions embodied in legislation. What happened next was an explosion of demand, a proliferation of multiple visits to greedy doctors in "Medicaid mills," and a large increase in unnecessary laboratory tests, hospital admissions, and surgical procedures. Thus, to a significant degree, medical care became like a common-pool good, there for the taking like the fish in the sea. Predictably, commissions were created to investigate and agencies were set up to control the waste and high cost (to the public) of this low-cost (to the consumer) good.

One can postulate the general rule that private goods and impure toll goods subsidized to a significant degree or provided without a user charge—that is, goods whose exclusion property is abandoned — will be treated as common-pool goods, subject to all the problems of such goods. The only restraints to infinite consumption of such goods are their exhaustion and the cost of taking the goods. In the case of medical care, it is the nurses, doctors, and hospital beds that can be exhausted, and it is the fuss and bother of making appointments, waiting in lines, and filling out reimbursement claims that constitute the cost of taking the toll-free goods.

Nevertheless, there is general agreement that a humane society should assure food, shelter, and a subsistence income for the deserving poor. The welfare debate centers on the amount of assistance, the means of providing it, who should be eligible for it, and what conditions society should impose on the recipient.

The growth of government-supplied private and toll goods is evidenced by the changing pattern of government expenditures. As illustrated in table 3.2, spending for health, education, income maintenance, housing, and transportation—all of which are predominantly private and toll goods, as we have seen—now constitutes 45 percent of all government expenditures. If defense spending and interest payments on debt are excluded, these private and toll goods ac-

TABLE 3.2

GOVERNMENT SPENDING FOR PRIVATE AND
TOLL GOODS, FISCAL YEAR 1983[a]
(IN BILLIONS OF DOLLARS)

Functions	Federal	State	Local	Total
Private and toll goods	$297	$144	$169	$608
National defense and foreign aid	229	0	0	229
Interest on general debt	109	11	13	133
Other direct expenditures	151	78	150	379
TOTAL	$786	$233	$332	$1,351

NOTE: Because of rounding, details may not add to totals.

a. Consists of government expenditures for education, public welfare, health, hospitals, social insurance administration, housing, insurance trust (except employee retirement), and transportation (air and water only). Does not include agriculture subsidies, which could be considered a form of welfare payment and hence a private good.

SOURCE: Derived from *Facts and Figures on Government Finance,* 23d ed. (Washington, D.C.: Tax Foundation, 1986), tables A6 and A7.

count for two-thirds of federal expenditures and 58 percent of state and local expenditures.

Summary

The starting point for determining the proper roles of government and the private sector is an examination of the goods and services needed in a modern society. Two important properties are useful for classifying goods and services: exclusion and consumption. A good is characterized as having the property of exclusion if its acquisition or use can readily be denied by the supplier. A suit of clothes has this property; a fish in the sea does not. A good is characterized as a joint-consumption good or an individual-consumption good depending on whether it can or cannot be consumed jointly and simultaneously by many users. TV broadcasting is a joint-consumption good; a loaf of bread is not.

Goods can be classified according to the degree to which they possess these two properties. The result is four idealized types of goods: private goods (characterized by exclusion and individual consumption), toll goods (exclusion and joint consumption), common-pool goods (nonexclusion and individual consumption), and collective goods (nonexclusion and joint consumption). Figure 3.4 summarizes these relationships.

	Easy to deny access	Difficult to deny access
Individual consumption	private goods	common-pool goods
Joint consumption	toll goods	collective goods

FIGURE 3.4

FOUR KINDS OF GOODS IN TERMS OF THEIR INTRINSIC CHARACTERISTICS

Private goods and toll goods can be supplied by the marketplace, and collective action plays a relatively minor role with respect to such goods, primarily establishing ground rules for market transactions, ensuring the safety of private goods, and regulating the means of supplying those toll goods that are natural monopolies. Collective action is indispensable for assuring a continued supply of common-pool goods and collective goods, however, and for providing those private and toll goods that society decides are to be subsidized and supplied as though they were collective goods.

More and more private and toll goods have been deemed "worthy" and are being treated as collective or common-pool goods. Indeed, the big growth in government has taken place in expenditures for private and toll goods. This has occurred both at the federal and local levels. Such goods now account for 45 percent of all government spending, up from only 31 percent in 1960. They represent 62 percent of nondefense, noninterest spending, up from 51 percent. In other words, providing goods and services that are intrinsically collective by nature, which is one of the fundamental reasons for the creation and existence of governments, is no longer the dominant activity of governments in the United States.

Notes

1. The typology employing these concepts draws heavily on Vincent and Elinor Ostrom, "Public Goods and Public Choices," in *Alternatives for Delivering Public Services,* ed. E.S. Savas (Boulder, Colo.: Westview, 1977), 7-14.

2. A.A. Alchian and R.A. Kessel, "Competition, Monopoly and the Pursuit of Money," in *Aspects of Labor Economics,* ed. National Bureau of Economic Research (Princeton: Princeton University Press, 1962).

3. L. DeAlessi, "The Economics of Property Rights: A Review of the Evidence," *Research in Law and Economics* 2 (1980): 1; idem, "Property Rights and Privatization," in *Prospects for Privatization,* Proceedings of the Academy of Political Science 36, no. 3 (1987): 24-35.

4. Garrett Hardin, "The Tragedy of the Commons," *Science* 162 (13 December 1968): 1243-48.

5. S. Fred Singer, "Free-for-All Fishing Depletes Stock," *Wall Street Journal,* 10 October 1985.

6. Stuart M. Butler, *Privatizing Federal Spending: A Strategy to Reduce the Deficit* (New York: Universe Books, 1985), 82-91.

7. For an excellent exposition of this issue, see Walter J. Primeaux, Jr., "Some Problems with Natural Monopoly," *Antitrust Bulletin* 24, no. 1 (Spring 1979): 63-85.

8. William J. Baumol, J.C. Panzar, and R.D. Willig, *Contestable Markets and the Theory of Industry Structure* (San Diego: Harcourt Brace, 1982).

9. Steve H. Hanke, "The Theory of Privatization," in *The Privatization Option,* ed. Stuart M. Butler (Washington, D.C.: Heritage Foundation, 1985).

10. William Vickrey, "Optimization of Traffic and Facilities," *Journal of Transport Economics and Policy* 1, no. 2 (May 1967): 123-36.

4. Alternative Arrangements for Providing Goods and Services

In the preceding chapter we saw the role of collective action with respect to supplying each of the four kinds of goods. For goods that are intrinsically—that is, by their nature and before any redefinition—private goods or toll goods or common-pool goods, collective action is needed primarily for regulation. In effect, such regulation is a collective good created to assure satisfactory supplies of those goods.

With respect to collective goods, collective action is necessary to pay for the goods and thereby to make sure that they are produced. With respect to worthy goods, collective action is needed (1) to decide which private and toll goods are to be defined as worthy goods, (2) to decide on the level of supply, and (3) to pay for them. The essence of collective action, therefore, consists of making decisions and raising money. This is true of all the collective actions described, for all four kinds of goods.

Stating those functions in this way makes it readily apparent that collective action is by no means synonymous with government action. Groups of people can and do agree on collective decisions and collective fund raising even without the formal methods and sanctions available to governments. For example, recreation facilities such as beaches, swimming pools, golf courses, tennis courts, flower gardens, and cultural institutions are often provided by government, but identical services and facilities are also provided by voluntary membership associations. People interested in consuming one or more of these common recreation services agree to form a club and pay for the desired facility through membership dues, entrance fees, and other collective fund-raising actions. Carpools and vanpools represent more informal collective activity.

It might be argued that these instances of voluntary collective action are possible only because the goods are intrinsically toll goods, and exclusion is therefore possible. Can voluntary associations take collective action to provide collective goods where exclusion is truly infeasible? The answer is yes. An example can be seen in cities with enclaves of private streets. The care and maintenance of these streets is provided by homeowner, civic, or neighborhood associations. Money to pay for street cleaning, snow removal, and sometimes even private police patrol is obtained from local residents through membership dues or pro rata user charges.

Collective action in such circumstances may be enforceable by a requirement or covenant written into the property deed so that anyone buying property in the area is required to belong to the association and pay a just portion of the expenses of the association in exchange for voting rights in it. Housing cooperatives and condominiums have such features.

But collective action can be entirely voluntary and still be effective in providing collective goods. When the collective organization is relatively small and the members have similar values and interests, informal social pressures can be adequate to assure that everyone contributes his or her fair share and no one is a free rider. A volunteer fire department is an excellent and commonplace example. Tenant patrols and block patrols in crime-ridden areas of large cities are other examples of successful voluntary collective action used to provide collective goods. (Payment can be in the form of contributed services, rather than money.) So are the associations in unincorporated communities that, despite their lack of government authority, nevertheless contract with private firms for refuse-collection service to their members. (However, like recreation goods and unlike fire protection, the service can be denied to a would-be free rider.)

It is when the number of affected individuals becomes large and interests are diverse and conflicting that purely voluntary action is no longer adequate to provide collective goods. In such circumstances, organizations have to be created with the authority to exercise force to take the money or property that is necessary to assure the supply of collective goods. In short, government can be viewed as an instrument for making and enforcing decisions about collective goods: which ones to provide, which ones (of those that are intrinsically private or toll goods) are to be financed at least in part by involuntary collective contributions, how to allocate the costs or contributions, and how to allocate the goods themselves if they are not pure collective goods.

The reader may have noticed the noncommittal verbs used to describe the role of government with respect to goods: provide, supply, assure the availability of, arrange payment for, and so on. Nothing that has been said so far requires that collective goods be *delivered* by government workers. They may be produced directly by public employees working for public agencies, but they need not be. Other institutional arrangements also exist for delivering collective goods; for example, governments can purchase collective goods from private firms. Hence the argument that a particular service is "inherently governmental" or that it is a "basic function of government" should be treated with caution. The service may be inherently a collective good, and may even be provided as a government responsibility, but it need not be produced by a government agency and government employees.

Providing, Arranging, and Producing Services

In order to clarify the matter, and before we can define and discuss the different institutional arrangements for providing services, it is necessary to distinguish the three basic participants in the delivery of a service: the service consumer, the service producer, and the service arranger or provider.

The consumer directly obtains or receives the service. The consumer might be an individual, a household, everyone residing in a defined geographic area, or a class of individuals with common characteristics (e.g., poor people, students, exporters, auto workers, or farmers).

The service producer is the agent that actually and directly performs the work or delivers the service to the consumer. A producer can be a unit of government (local, county, state, or federal), a multipurpose or unifunctional special district, a voluntary association of citizens, a private firm, a nonprofit agency, or, in certain instances, the consumer himself. The Department of Defense produces national defense services, as does Boeing. A county government may produce public health services. A tenant association produces a service when it patrols its building. A doctor produces services when he treats his patients. An individual who hauls his own trash to the town dump is acting as both producer and consumer of the service.

The service arranger (sometimes called the service provider) is the agent who assigns the producer to the consumer, or vice versa, or selects the producer who will serve the consumer. Frequently, but not always, the arranger is a government unit. Thus the service arranger may be the municipality in which the consumer is located, the federal government, a voluntary association, or the service consumer himself. For collective goods, the arranger can usefully be viewed as the collective-decision unit, that is, the unit that articulates the demand for such goods. As we see below, it is possible to have joint arrangers.

The relationship of the three service participants is illustrated in figure 4.1. The consumer, the producer, and the arranger are connected by certain flows—of authorization, of service delivery, and of payment.

When a city government hires a paving contractor to resurface a street with asphalt, the city is the arranger, the firm is the producer, and the people who use the street are the consumers of this particular collective good—street repaving. A state government is the service arranger when it contracts with a

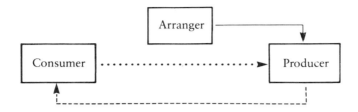

FIGURE 4.1
ILLUSTRATIVE RELATIONSHIP BETWEEN CONSUMER, PRODUCER,
AND ARRANGER WHERE THE ARRANGER SELECTS, ASSIGNS,
AND AUTHORIZES THE PRODUCER (SOLID LINE); THE PRODUCER
DELIVERS THE SERVICE TO THE CONSUMER (DASHED LINE);
AND THE CONSUMER PAYS THE PRODUCER DIRECTLY FOR
THE SERVICE (DOTTED LINE) IN THIS EXAMPLE

church group, the producer, to operate a day-care center for working mothers, the consumers. A National Merit Scholarship winner is a consumer of educational services, but he is also acting as service arranger when he selects the college of his choice to produce his educational service.

With respect to collective goods, the arranger has significant responsibilities. He must have authority to levy and collect assessments despite a lack of unanimous consent, relying instead on rules established by majority vote, for example. Similarly, on the demand side, the arranger must establish procedures to decide which services are to be provided, the level of service, and level of expenditures to be made, again in the absence of unanimous agreement among all members of the collective unit.

The distinction between providing or arranging a service and producing it is profound. It is at the heart of the entire concept of privatization and puts the role of government in perspective. With respect to many collective goods, government is essentially an arranger or provider—an instrument of society for deciding what shall be done collectively, for whom, to what degree or at what level of supply, and how to pay for it. For example, it may levy taxes to pay for cleaning the sidewalks, or it may require property owners to clean them at their own expense or effort.

Producing the service, however, is a separate matter. A government that decides that a service is to be provided at collective expense does not have to produce it using government equipment and government employees. As noted above, there are different possible producers. Opposition to privatization often comes from those who do not appreciate the difference between providing and producing, and mistakenly assume that if government divests itself of the producer function, it must automatically abandon its role of provider as well. Thus, false alarms are raised about privatizing services that are said to be "inherently governmental"; the responsibility for providing the service can be retained by government, but government does not have to continue producing it.

Service Arrangements

With the distinction between providing and producing services firmly in mind, we can proceed to discuss the different institutional arrangements for delivering services.

Different arrangements arise because government can serve as arranger or producer, and so can the private sector. This leads to four classes of arrangements, which can be further divided into ten particular arrangements according to the specific ways that the arranger, producer, and consumer interact. Figure 4.2 depicts the conceptual relationship among the ten arrangements. Special attention is drawn to the seven arrangements in which the private sector is the producer. Privatization generally involves the use of one or more of these arrangements, as discussed near the end of the chapter. The ten arrangements, to be examined in turn, are (1) government service, (2) government vending, (3) intergovernmental agreement, (4) contract, (5) franchise, (6) grant, (7) voucher, (8) free market, (9) voluntary service, and (10) self-service.

GOVERNMENT SERVICE

The term *government service* denotes the delivery of a service by a government agency using its own employees; government acts as both the service arranger and the service producer. The schematic relationship is shown in figure 4.3.[1] When there is a user charge for the government service, the situation is as depicted in figure 4.4. Examples of conventional municipal, county, state, and federal government services abound.

One should also note the case of nationalized or state-owned enterprises. For example, Renault, the French automobile manufacturer, was nationalized shortly after World War II, and so the French government, in effect, makes automobiles. In the Soviet Union, city governments operate hotels, restaurants, bakeries, breweries, retail shops, and factories that make household goods.[2] As is true of nationalized industries in noncommunist countries, these activities are carried out by state-owned and state-run enterprises rather than by government bureaus, strictly speaking, but for our purposes they all come under the heading of government service.

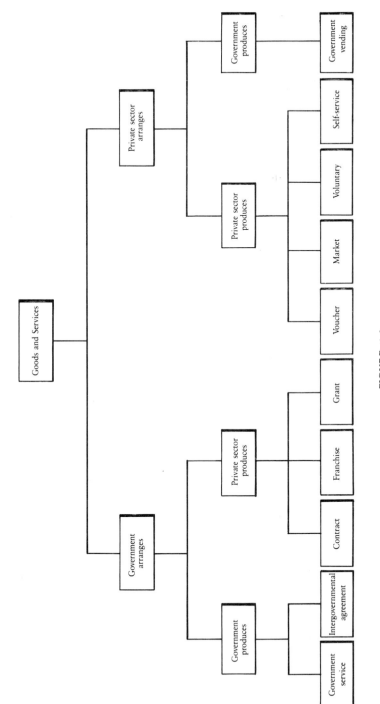

FIGURE 4.2

OVERVIEW OF THE TEN INSTITUTIONAL ARRANGEMENTS FOR DELIVERING SERVICES

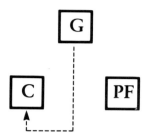

FIGURE 4.3
GOVERNMENT SERVICE, PAID BY TAXES, WHERE GOVERNMENT (G)
PRODUCES AND DELIVERS SERVICE (DASHED LINE) TO CONSUMER (C)

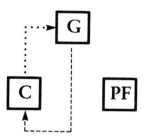

FIGURE 4.4
GOVERNMENT SERVICE, WITH USER FEE, WHERE DOTTED LINE
SHOWS DIRECT PAYMENT; PRIVATE FIRM (PF) PLAYS NO ROLE

GOVERNMENT VENDING

Someone may arrange to purchase goods and services from a government agency. For example, he can buy rights from government for water, minerals, timber, and for grazing on government-owned land. As another example, a privately owned sports arena may arrange for crowd control by the local police department instead of hiring private guards; it would pay the government for this service. Similarly, a private sponsor of a parade on public streets or a picnic in a public park may pay to have a public agency clean up afterward. In essence, government is competing with private firms to perform this work. A private individual or organization is the arranger, and government is the producer. This arrangement, called *government vending,* is depicted in figure 4.5 on page 65.

Government vending, as defined here, is not the same as imposing a user fee on government services. When government charges for supplying water,

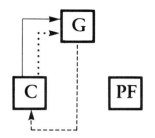

FIGURE 4.5
GOVERNMENT VENDING, WHERE CONSUMER, AS ARRANGER,
AUTHORIZES (SOLID LINE) AND PAYS (DOTTED LINE) GOVERNMENT
TO DELIVER SERVICE (DASHED LINE)

power, or bus rides, it is merely charging the consumer directly for the private and toll goods it is supplying as direct government services, for which the government is the arranger. In government vending, the consumer is the arranger. (Compare figures 4.4. and 4.5.)

INTERGOVERNMENTAL AGREEMENT

A government can hire or pay another government to supply a service. A local school district does that when, lacking a high school of its own, it arranges to send its pupils to the high school in a neighboring district and pays the latter jurisdiction for the service. It is also commonplace for small communities to purchase library, recreation, and fire-protection services from a specialized government unit that is organized by and sells its service to several general-purpose governments in the area. Counties sometimes contract with cities and pay the latter to maintain county roads within city limits. States contract with cities and counties to provide social services to families and individuals. Reassignment of service responsibilities between jurisdictions is occurring to a significant degree in an attempt to handle regional problems better and cope with rising costs. We refer to such institutional arrangements as *intergovernmental agreements*. One government is the producer, but another is the service arranger. This is shown conceptually in figure 4.6.

Intergovernmental agreements are common. A 1973 survey of 2,375 municipalities in the United States revealed that no less than 62 percent had formal or informal agreements for the provision of services to their citizens by other government units. Moreover, 43 percent of all cities produced services for other governments.[3] The relative roles of different service producers is shown in table 4.1. Counties were the most common producers of services under inter-

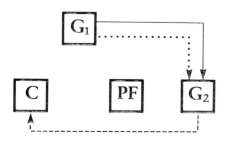

FIGURE 4.6

INTERGOVERNMENTAL AGREEMENT, WHERE ONE GOVERNMENT
AUTHORIZES AND PAYS ANOTHER TO DELIVER SERVICE

governmental agreements. Other municipalities serve as producers for 40 percent of the cities that have intergovernmental agreements.

A 1982 survey of 1,780 local governments, conducted for the U.S. Department of Housing and Urban Development, determined the extent to which
intergovernmental agreements were used for particular local services in the
United States. Table 4.2 lists the services provided through this arrangement
by more than 25 percent of the responding localities. It can be seen that health

TABLE 4.1

PRODUCERS OF SERVICES TO MUNICIPALITIES
UNDER INTERGOVERNMENTAL AGREEMENTS

Government producer	Frequency
County	62%
Municipality	40
State	29
Special district (other than school)	28
School district	25
Public authority	17

NOTE: That is, 62 percent of the municipalities that received
one or more services through intergovernmental agreements
identified the county as the producer. (Total adds to more than
100 percent because many cities arrange for services from more
than one kind of producer.)

SOURCE: Derived from *The Challenge of Local Governmental
Reorganization,* vol. 3 (Washington, D.C.: Government Printing Office, Advisory Committee on Intergovernmental Relations, February 1974), table 3.3. Data are from a 1973 survey.

TABLE 4.2

PERCENTAGE OF CITIES AND COUNTIES THAT USE
INTERGOVERNMENTAL AGREEMENTS TO SUPPLY SERVICES

Service	Number of governments reporting	Percentage using inter-governmental agreements
Public housing	602	43
Bus system	508	42
Sanitary inspection	939	36
Mental health	512	34
Solid-waste disposal	1,223	31
Animal shelter	1,225	30
Public health	721	30
Drug/alcohol treatment	626	30
Paratransit system	560	29
Insect/rodent control	1,037	29
Tax assessing	1,038	29
Child welfare	558	28
Libraries	1,153	28
Airport operation	530	26
Hospital management	361	25

NOTE: Based on responses to a survey of 1,780 local governments.

SOURCE: Derived from *Rethinking Local Services: Examining Alternative Service Delivery Approaches* (Washington, D.C.: International City Management Association, 1984), table B.

and transportation services are most commonly handled in this manner. These agreements are frequently between a locality and a county or special governmental authority.[4]

The Lakewood Plan makes extensive use of this particular institutional arrangement for service delivery. In 1981, Lakewood, a city in the county of Los Angeles, was purchasing forty-one different services from the county; seventy-six other cities also purchased one or more services from the county. All these cities purchased election services from the county, and other county services being marketed included animal regulation; emergency ambulance service; enforcement of health ordinances; engineering services; fire and police protection; library; sewer maintenance; park maintenance; recreation services; assessment and collection of taxes; hospitalization of city prisoners; personnel staff services such as recruitment, examination, and certification; prosecution; building inspection; weed abatement; school fire-safety officers; mobile-home and trailer-park inspection; milk inspection; rodent control; mental health services; tree trimming; bridge maintenance; preparation and installation of street signs; street sweeping; traffic-signal maintenance; traffic striping and marking;

traffic-law enforcement; business-license issuing and enforcement; and crossing guards.

The cities involved have even formed an organization to tend to their common concerns, the California Contract Cities Association.

CONTRACTS

Governments contract not only with other governments but also with private firms and nonprofit organizations for delivery of goods and services. In this arrangement the private organization is the producer and government is the arranger, which pays the producer, as shown in figure 4.7. Such "contracting out" is the arrangement most commonly referred to in discussions about privatizing conventional public services (as distinguished from privatizing state-owned enterprises). In a contract arrangement, government ideally is (1) an articulator of democratically expressed demands for public goods and services, (2) a skillful purchasing agent, (3) a sophisticated inspector of the goods and services that it purchases from the private sector, (4) an efficient collector of fair taxes, and (5) a parsimonious disburser of proper and timely payments to the contractor.

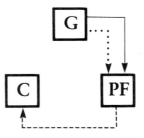

FIGURE 4.7
CONTRACTING, WHERE GOVERNMENT AUTHORIZES
AND PAYS PRIVATE FIRM TO DELIVER SERVICE

Examples of government contracting are legion. Most of the tangible goods — supplies, equipment, and facilities — used by governments in the United States are purchased from contractors, as little manufacturing, construction, or food production is actually done by government employees. This is true even of sensitive military equipment, for although some munitions are manufactured in federal arsenals, most are obtained from private producers. Military equipment is purchased from contractors, but sometimes with inadequate managerial oversight; this subject is pursued further in chapter 7. At the local level, roads, schools, and government offices are generally constructed for governments by private builders under contractual arrangements, and pencils, desks, fire hoses, uniforms, food (for pupils, patients, and prisoners), ferry boats, automobiles, guns, garbage trucks, and computers are bought from private vendors.

In addition to these material goods, governments contract out for a wide variety of services: grounds maintenance, custodial functions, cafeterias, secretarial and clerical work, libraries, laundries, computer centers, data conversion, vehicle repair, microfilming, photography, printing, claims processing, transportation, and so on.

More unusual examples also abound. The U.S. Mint contracts out part of its coin-production work. For many years, a private contractor manned and operated the Distant Early Warning line, to detect airplanes and missiles coming toward North America over the Arctic Ocean. The U.S. government purchased the services of a private firm to carry out monitoring and surveillance of the cease-fire line in Sinai between Egyptian and Israeli forces, a task that traditionally would have been performed by a military unit. Mercenary troops have been used since ancient times and are still being used in clandestine wars by various nations. Similarly, private air forces have come into being in recent years to engage in war under contract.

More benign contracts with private firms are used at the municipal level to provide refuse collection, ambulance service, street- and traffic-light maintenance, and street paving, for example. Contracts are also used for a wide variety of social services; typically such contracts are with not-for-profit organizations.

And let us remember that it was a private contractor, engaged by Spanish monarchs, who set foot in the New World in 1492.

Extent of Contracting. In 1984 the federal government engaged in more than $20 billion worth of commercial work of the kinds mentioned above: grounds maintenance, custodial, and the like. The Office of Federal Procurement Policy estimated that at least $6 billion worth of these services could be procured from private firms without impairing the missions of the agencies.[5] Of the activities classified as commercial and industrial in the Defense Department—functions such as food service, laundry, airplane and vehicle maintenance, and construction—about a quarter of the total effort as measured in man-years was purchased from the private sector.[6] An estimated $42 billion was spent in 1976 by governments in the United States on purchased services, including both intergovernmental and private contracts.[7] It should be borne in mind that these are all very rough figures, as it is difficult to identify and tabulate the relevant activities on a uniform basis.

TABLE 4.3

PERCENTAGE OF CITIES AND COUNTIES THAT CONTRACT
WITH PRIVATE ORGANIZATIONS TO SUPPLY SERVICES

Service	Number governments reporting	Percentage contracting with:		
		Profit	Neighbor-hood	Non-profit
Public works and transportation				
Residential solid-waste collection	1,376	35	0	0
Commercial solid-waste collection	1,106	44	0	0
Solid-waste disposal	1,223	28	0	2
Street repair	1,643	27	0	1
Street/parking lot cleaning	1,483	9	0	0
Snow plowing/sanding	1,287	14	0	0
Traffic-signal installation/maintenance	1,569	26	0	2
Meter maintenance/collection	640	7	0	0
Tree trimming/planting	1,451	31	1	1
Cemetery administration/maintenance	703	11	1	8
Inspection/code enforcement	1,588	7	0	1
Parking lot/garage operation	780	12	0	2
Bus system operation/maintenance	508	24	1	9
Paratransit system operation/maintenance	560	23	2	21
Airport operation	530	24	0	4
Utility meter reading	1,200	10	0	1
Utility billing	1,243	13	0	1
Street-light operation	1,284	39	0	2
AVERAGE		21	0	3
Public safety				
Crime prevention/patrol	1,660	3	5	2
Police/fire communication	1,684	1	0	3
Fire prevention/suppression	1,516	1	1	3
Emergency medical service	1,333	14	1	10
Ambulance service	1,214	25	1	10
Traffic control/parking enforcement	1,505	1	0	1
Vehicle towing and storage	1,285	80	0	0
AVERAGE		18	1	4
Health and human services				
Sanitary inspection	939	1	0	6
Insect/rodent control	1,037	14	0	5
Animal control	1,482	6	0	9
Animal shelter operation	1,225	13	1	18
Day-care facility operation	436	35	6	37
Child welfare programs	558	5	2	24
Programs for elderly	1,189	4	4	29
Operation of public/elderly housing	602	13	1	18

Service	Number governments reporting	Percentage contracting with: Profit	Neighbor-hood	Non-profit
Health and human services				
Operation/management of hospitals	361	30	1	27
Public health programs	721	8	2	27
Drug/alcohol treatment programs	626	6	4	41
Operation of mental health/retardation programs/facilities	512	7	3	40
AVERAGE		12	2	23
Parks and recreation				
Recreation services	1,444	4	5	13
Operation/maintenance of recreation facilities	1,535	8	3	9
Parks landscaping/maintenance	1,573	9	1	2
Operation of convention center/auditoriums	448	5	1	6
Operation of cultural/arts programs	702	7	8	39
Operation of libraries	1,153	1	1	10
Operation of museums	498	4	3	32
AVERAGE		5	3	16
Support functions				
Building/grounds maintenance	1,672	20	0	1
Building security	1,497	8	0	1
Fleet management/vehicle maintenance				
Heavy equipment	1,643	32	0	0
Emergency vehicles	1,558	31	0	0
All other vehicles	1,631	29	0	0
Data processing	1,466	23	0	2
Legal services	1,608	49	0	2
Payroll	1,720	10	0	1
Tax-bill processing	1,241	11	0	6
Tax assessing	1,038	7	0	4
Delinquent-tax collection	1,213	10	0	3
Secretarial services	1,657	4	0	0
Personnel services	1,663	5	0	1
Labor relations	1,513	23	0	1
Public relations/information	1,545	7	0	2
AVERAGE		18	0	2
GRAND AVERAGE		17	1	9

NOTE: Based on responses to a survey of 1,780 local governments.

SOURCE: Derived from *Rethinking Local Services: Examining Alternative Service Delivery Approaches* (Washington, D.C.: International City Management Association, 1984), table B.

No comprehensive information is available on the total amount of money spent by municipal governments for contract services, but table 4.3 shows the percentage of cities, out of a total survey sample of 1,780 cities, that contract with private organizations for the indicated services. Note that the organizations include for-profit firms, not-for-profit agencies, and neighborhood organizations. The most commonly contracted service is vehicle towing and storage; 80 percent of responding cities use this arrangement. The table indicates that the tangible services associated with public works, safety, administrative support, and health inspection and control are more likely to be obtained from for-profit firms, whereas contracts for cultural and human services are more likely to be with not-for-profit agencies.[8] This pattern may be changing, however, as there is growing interest in competitive contracting for social services from for-profit firms.[9]

A word of explanation may be in order about the entry in table 4.3 for crime prevention and patrol. Typically, this reflects the use of private patrol services in parks, public housing projects, airports, and schools, although private investigative services have been employed to combat organized crime and narcotics distribution.[10]

The average service is contracted out by 26 percent of the responding cities. (Table 4.3 shows 27 percent, due to rounding.) The figure is essentially the same whether it is calculated as a simple or a weighted average. To put it another way, the average responding city contracts 26 percent of its services, in whole or in part, to the private sector. (This assumes that the figures for profit, nonprofit, and neighborhood contracting can be added together; this seems a not unreasonable assumption.) This figure is a useful, summary measure of the extent of municipal privatization by contracting; it is an index that can be monitored and reported periodically.

The roughly comparable figure from a somewhat similar survey in 1973 is 7 percent.[11] Thus, municipal privatization by contracting has grown from 7 to 26 percent between 1973 and 1982, an average, annual, compounded growth rate of 16 percent. This should be treated as a very tenuous estimate.

A further illustration of the extent of contracting is provided by a study of twenty-six municipal services in eighty-four California cities. It was found that city departments produced only 50 percent of these services, while contracts with private firms accounted for 20 percent, and intergovernmental contracts with counties and special districts accounted for 15 percent and 10 percent respectively.[12]

One of the most striking things about table 4.3 is the lengthy and diverse list of services purchased by contract from private firms. No less than 59 services are identified there, yet this list is far from complete. Table 4.4 lists all

TABLE 4.4

CITY AND COUNTY SERVICES PROVIDED CONTRACTUALLY

BY PRIVATE FIRMS

Service

Adoption, air-pollution abatement, airport operation, airport services, alarm-system maintenance, ambulance, animal control, appraisals, architectural, auditorium management, auditing

Beach management, billing and collection, bridge (construction, inspection, and maintenance), building demolition, building rehabilitation, buildings and grounds (janitorial, maintenance, security), building and mechanical inspection, burial of indigents, bus operation, bus-shelter maintenance

Cafeteria and restaurant operation, catch-basin cleaning, cemetery administration, child protection, civil defense communication, clerical, communication maintenance, community center operation, computer operations, consultant services, convention center management, crime laboratory, crime prevention and patrol, custodial

Data entry, data processing, day care, document preparation, drug and alcohol programs

Economic development, election administration, electrical inspection, electric power, elevator inspection, emergency maintenance, environmental services

Family counseling, financial services, fire communication, fire-hydrant maintenance, fire prevention and suppression, flood-control planning, foster-home care

Golf-course operation, graphic arts, guard service

Health inspection, health services, homemaker service, hospital management, hospital services, housing inspection and code enforcement, housing management

Industrial development, insect and rodent control, institutional care, insurance administration, irrigation

Jail and detention, janitorial, juvenile delinquency programs

Labor relations, laboratory, landscaping, laundry, lawn maintenance, leaf collection, legal, legal aid, library operation, licensing

Management consulting, mapping, marina services, median-strip maintenance, mosquito control, moving and storage, museum and cultural

Noise abatement, nursing, nutrition

Office-machine maintenance, opinion polling

Paratransit system operation, park maintenance, parking enforcement, parking lot and garage operation, parking lot cleaning, parking meter servicing, parking ticket processing, patrol, payroll processing, personal services, photographic services, physician services, planning, plumbing inspection, police communication, port and harbor management, printing, prisoner transportation, probation, property acquisition, public administrator services, public health, public relations and information, public works

Records maintenance, recreation services and facility operation, rehabilitation, resource recovery, risk management

School bus, secretarial, security, sewage treatment, sewer maintenance, sidewalk repair, snow (plowing, sanding, removal), social services, soil conservation, solid waste (collection, transfer, disposal), street services (construction, maintenance, sweeping), street lighting (construction and maintenance), surveying

Tax collection (assessing, bill processing, receipt), tennis-court maintenance, test scoring, traffic control (markings, signs, and signal installation and maintenance), training (of government employees), transit management, transportation of elderly and disabled, treasury functions, tree services (planting, pruning, removal)

Utility billing, utility meter reading

Vehicle fleet management, vehicle maintenance, vehicle towing and storage, voter registration

Water-meter reading and maintenance, water-pollution abatement, water supply and distribution, water treatment, weed abatement, welfare

Zoning and subdivision control

the services identified as being provided in communities in the United States by private firms under contract to the local city or county government. This table was compiled by merging information from several surveys and therefore may have some redundant elements described with different wording; nevertheless, it lists some 180 services in all.

An important variant of contracting for service arises when government retains ownership of a facility but contracts with a private firm to operate it. For example, this is sometimes done with wastewater-treatment (i.e., sewage) plants, maintenance garages, airports, and convention centers. Interesting examples of contracting for services can be found abroad. Intercity highways in France are generally privately owned and operated toll roads that are paid for, constructed, and maintained by private firms for a fixed number of years before being turned over to the government.

Most of the cities in Denmark contract with a single private firm for fire and ambulance service; the majority of the population receives protection by this arrangement. About two-thirds of the people in Sweden get their fire-protection services from private enterprises under contract to government.[13] And while Wall Street is cleaned by a government bureaucracy, the streets in Communist Belgrade are cleaned by a worker-owned enterprise that has a contract with the city government.

Broad services generally can be separated into their component subservices, which can be provided through various arrangements. Thus, police services can be separated into police communication, preventive patrol, traffic control, parking enforcement, towing away illegally parked cars, homicide investigation, detention facilities, training courses, police-car maintenance, and so forth.[14] Different components of this large array of services can be provided through a variety of institutional structures in the same city: government service, intergovernmental contracts, contracts with private firms, and voluntary service, for example. This important issue is pursued further in a later section of this chapter.

One final point is that a contract can have a negative price; that is, the private producer could pay the government to perform the service. For example, abandoned automobiles in New York City are picked up by private firms under contract to the city, and, depending on scrap prices, their bids will call for payment either to or from the city. This might also be true for wastepaper collection, or for collection of any other recyclable material.

FRANCHISES

Franchising is another institutional structure used for providing services. An exclusive franchise is an award of monopoly privileges to a private firm to supply a particular service, usually with price regulation by a government agency. Nonexclusive or multiple franchises can also be awarded, as in the case of taxis. In franchise service, as in contract service, government is the arranger and a private organization is the producer of the service; however, the two can be distinguished by the means of payment to the producer. Government (the arranger) pays the producer for contract services, but the consumer pays the producer for franchise service. The relationships among the participants in exclusive and multiple franchise arrangements are illustrated in figures 4.8 and 4.9 respectively.

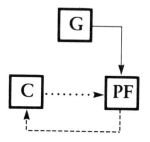

FIGURE 4.8
EXCLUSIVE FRANCHISE, WHERE GOVERNMENT AUTHORIZES
PRIVATE FIRM TO DELIVER SERVICE AND CONSUMER PAYS FIRM

The franchise arrangement is particularly suitable for providing toll goods. Common utilities such as electric power, gas and water distribution, telephone service, and cable television are usually provided as franchise services, and so is bus transportation. Note that many of these services are provided directly by government in some jurisdictions: Local governments own and operate many

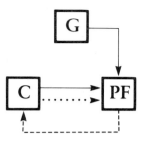

FIGURE 4.9

MULTIPLE FRANCHISE, WHERE GOVERNMENT AND CONSUMER
ARE CO-ARRANGERS

electric plants, water-supply systems, and bus lines, for example, and in An-
chorage, Alaska, telephone service was historically provided by the municipal
government. Concessions on limited-access highways and in parks, stadiums,
airports, and other public properties are also franchises.

Table 4.5 identifies the extent to which franchises are utilized for local
government services.

TABLE 4.5

PERCENTAGE OF CITIES AND COUNTIES THAT FRANCHISE
PRIVATE FIRMS TO SUPPLY SERVICES

Service	Number of governments reporting	Percentage using franchises
Commercial solid-waste collection	1,106	19
Residential solid-waste collection	1,376	15
Utility meter reading	1,200	10
Utility billing	1,243	9
Operation of recreation facilities	1,535	9
Airport operation	530	9
Vehicle towing and storage	1,285	7
Solid-waste disposal	1,233	5
Bus system operation	508	5
Paratransit system operation	560	4
Ambulance service	1,214	4
Auditorium/convention center operation	448	3

NOTE: Based on responses to a survey of 1,780 local governments.

SOURCE: See table 4.2

GRANTS

Toll goods and private goods whose consumption is to be encouraged can be subsidized and provided through two different structural arrangements: *grants* and *vouchers*. Under a grant system, the subsidy is given by government to the producer. The grant may be in the form of money, tax exemption or other tax benefits, low-cost loans, or loan guarantees. The effect of such grants is to reduce the price of the particular good for eligible consumers, who can then go into the marketplace and purchase for themselves from the subsidized producers more than they might otherwise consume.

Under a grant arrangement the producer is a private firm (either profit-making or not), both the government and the consumer are involved as co-arrangers (the government selects certain producers to receive grants, and the consumer chooses the specific producer), and usually both government and the consumer make payments to the producer. This arrangement is depicted in figure 4.10.

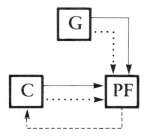

FIGURE 4.10
GRANT ARRANGEMENT, WHERE GOVERNMENT
SUBSIDIZES THE PRODUCER

There are numerous examples of grants in practice. It seems as though every single industry has had some special grant or tax-abatement program tailored for it; subsidies of milk and other farm products are merely the more obvious examples of such programs. Health facilities have also been receiving large grants over a prolonged period of time as a means of making medical care more available and accessible to more people. Other examples are the government-induced provision of low-cost housing by the private housing construction industry, and subsidized mass transit.

Cultural institutions and performing arts groups are the latest beneficiaries of direct government grants, presumably reflecting a collective determination that these goods benefit the public at large and therefore their availability should

77

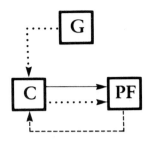

FIGURE 4.11

VOUCHER ARRANGEMENT, WHERE GOVERNMENT SUBSIDIZES THE CONSUMER

be encouraged by subsidies to theater groups, symphony orchestras, opera companies, dance ensembles, and museums.

VOUCHERS

The voucher system is also designed to encourage the consumption of particular goods by a particular class of consumers. Unlike the grant system, which subsidizes the producer and restricts the consumer's choice to the subsidized producers only (if he wishes to avail himself of the subsidy), the voucher system subsidizes the consumer and permits the latter to exercise relatively free choice in the marketplace. Thus, housing vouchers can be contrasted with low-cost housing supplied by grants. The voucher has a certain monetary value, say $100 per month. The consumer can select the housing of his choice, and if the rent is $150 per month, he pays the landlord $50 and gives him the voucher. The landlord takes the voucher, turns it in to the specified government agency, and receives $100 for it.

In voucher systems, as in grant systems, the producer is a private firm, and both government and the consumer pay the producer; but whereas in the grant arrangement both government and the consumer select the producer, in the voucher arrangement the consumer alone makes the choice. This arrangement is shown schematically in figure 4.11. The producer must be authorized by the government to provide the service. Not anyone can turn in housing vouchers to the government and get cash; only legitimate property owners can do so.

Food stamps are another example of a voucher system. Instead of setting up a whole new government-run food-distribution system (with government-run farms, canneries, and grocery stores) to give away food to eligible poor recipients, the latter are supplied with vouchers that they can use in ordinary, existing food stores. The consumer is strongly motivated to shop wisely and look for bargains because his money will then go farther and he can buy more; his behavior as a subsidized consumer should be indistinguishable from that of an unsubsidized consumer. (This can be contrasted with the situation mentioned earlier where government gives away food, virtually as a common-pool good, in school and summer lunch programs. The consumer behaves very differently in those cases and has no motivation to take only the food he will eat.)

A Medicaid or a Medicare enrollment card can be thought of as a voucher for medical service. Instead of having to go to a government hospital for medical care, the cardholder can select the doctor of his choice at any facility (provided the doctor will accept this payment). This is not as good a voucher system as food stamps because there is no incentive for the consumer to seek out a low-cost, good-quality producer; there is no effective upper limit on the cardholder's spending; reimbursement rates are fixed, and if a person finds a doctor who charges less then the maximum, the savings will not accrue to the consumer but to the federal agency that pays the bill. This subject is discussed further in later chapters.

Voucher systems have also been introduced for cultural activities, as an alternative to the grant system. Instead of giving grants to theaters, cultural vouchers are given to individuals to encourage their attendance, and the voucher holder can attend the performance of his choice. The theater accepts the voucher and is reimbursed for it.[15]

At the local government level, vouchers have also been utilized for paratransit service, day care, programs for the elderly, drug treatment programs, and recreation services.[16]

MARKET

The *market system* is the most common of all service arrangements. It is used to provide most private and toll goods in the Western world. The consumer arranges for service and selects the producer, which is a private firm. Government is not involved in the transaction in any significant way, although it may establish service standards. For example, a not uncommon arrangement for refuse collection in small American cities is mandatory private collection, where the municipal government establishes a requirement that all households have their refuse collected at least once a week, let's say, but it is left up to each household to select and pay a private firm to provide this service. Similarly, government can require a plant to clean its effluent stream, but the work can be performed through the marketplace. This arrangement is illustrated in figure 4.12.

Market arrangements are widely used to supply such necessary goods and services as food, water, electricity (and other forms of energy, including oxen), housing, health care, education, transportation, and security in old age.

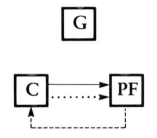

FIGURE 4.12

MARKET ARRANGEMENT, WHERE CONSUMER SELECTS
AND PAYS PRIVATE PRODUCER FOR SERVICE

VOLUNTARY SERVICE

Charitable organizations, through their voluntary efforts, provide a host of human services to people in need. Other voluntary associations perform community services that are provided elsewhere by government agencies; examples of such activities, cited above, include recreation programs, street cleaning, protective patrol, and fire protection by neighborhood associations. In this arrangement, the voluntary mutual-aid association acts as service arranger and either produces the service directly, using its members or employees, or hires and pays a private firm to do the work (see figures 4.13 and 4.14). When a voluntary association engages in the business of supplying private goods, such as a housing or food cooperative, it is no different from a private, nonprofit firm operating in the free market.

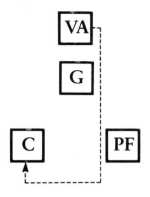

FIGURE 4.13

VOLUNTARY ARRANGEMENT

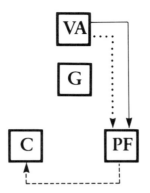

FIGURE 4.14
VOLUNTARY ARRANGEMENT
WITH CONTRACTING

Voluntary efforts by the private sector can handle even major national undertakings, such as the 1984 Olympic Games in Los Angeles, and the $265 million restoration of the Statue of Liberty.

Although such arrangements are widespread, there is little information available as to the precise extent to which they are utilized, except for volunteer fire departments; these constitute more than 90 percent of all fire departments in the United States.[17] (They account for a smaller fraction of all fire-fighters, however, because big-city fire departments are large and have few volunteers.)

SELF-SERVICE

The most basic delivery mode of all is self-help, or *self-service*. Protection against fire and theft is obtained primarily by rudimentary self-service measures, such as extinguishing cigarettes and locking doors. The individual who brings his newspapers to a recycling center, drives to work, bandages a cut, or gives vocational guidance to his child is practicing self-service.

The family as a self-service unit is the original and most efficient department of housing, health, education, welfare, and human services, and it provides a wide range of vital services to its members. In a return to earlier family functions, a minute but increasing number of families, dissatisfied with conventional schools, is braving formidable bureaucratic forces by teaching children at home instead of sending them to school.[18] In Japan, 70 percent of the people over sixty years old live with younger relatives; only 6.3 percent of Americans over sixty do so.[19] Clearly the Japanese have little need for nursing homes and senior citizen housing.

The term *coproduction,* or *coprovision,* is sometimes used to refer to voluntary and to self-service arrangements, and to voluntary citizen contributions of time or money to public agencies[20] (e.g., a volunteer in a county hospital or a donation to a school to buy a computer). Because it attempts to cover too disparate a set of actions, and because the prefix "co" is plainly inappropriate for the self-service arrangement, the word is eschewed here, in favor of the simpler and more descriptive terms employed above. For the sake of completeness, self-service, too, is portrayed schematically, in figure 4.15.

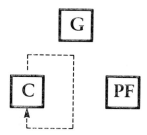

FIGURE 4.15
SELF-SERVICE ARRANGEMENT

ILLUSTRATIVE ARRANGEMENTS FOR COMMON SERVICES
While a particular service is generally provided through one or perhaps several different arrangements in a particular culture or society, some services may be provided under many of the ten arrangements described here. Table 4.6 shows how these arrangements are actually utilized in the United States to provide major local government services. For example, transportation is provided through all ten of the arrangements, refuse collection and education through nine of the ten, and even fire protection, the least versatile (in this respect) of the services illustrated here, is provided through five different arrangements.

Multiple, Hybrid, and Partial Arrangements
The ten organizational arrangements discussed here at length can be thought of as pure structures that can be employed either alone or in combination to provide a service. Specifically, it is possible to make effective use in service delivery of multiple, hybrid, and partial arrangements.

MULTIPLE ARRANGEMENTS
Multiple arrangements can be employed by a jurisdiction for a single service.

For example, in Indianapolis, five different arrangements were utilized for the collection of residential refuse: municipal service, contract service, voluntary service, free market, and self-service.[21] Not only is there nothing necessarily wrong with using multiple structures simultaneously for the same service, but by fostering comparisons and competition among the different service producers, the result may well be superior performance of that activity. This point is pursued further in chapter 8.

HYBRID ARRANGEMENTS

In addition to *multiple* arrangements—the use of more than one arrangement to provide the same service in the same area—there are *hybrid* arrangements. For example, a franchised bus line that receives an operating subsidy (i.e., a grant) from the government represents a hybrid arrangement. The grant arrangement is the most common partner used in hyrid arrangements, and it may be used to subsidize franchise, self-service, market, or voluntary arrangements. A grant may be in be in the form of a direct payment, a low-interest loan, or favorable tax treatment.

PARTIAL ARRANGEMENTS

Partial arrangements are also widely employed. Services are usually comprised of a bundle of separate but coordinated activities, each of which could be supplied separately. Different arrangements could be used for different parts of the service. The result is a comprehensive service that may be part governmental, part contract, part voucher, and part self-service, for example.

The partitioning of a service can be carried out along either operational or functional lines. Operationally, for instance, prison activities include food service, medical service, inmate counseling, education and vocational training, recreation, facility maintenance, security, and industrial work programs. Any or all of these could be, and often are, contracted out, while the main activity of housing and guarding the prisoners is usually carried out by a state corrections agency. The service in this case is part contract and part governmental. (Contracting out of an entire prison operation, privately owned prisons, is a growing phenomenon, as we see in chapter 7). With respect to the activities of a police department, no less than 203 different tasks have been identified.[22]

In the field of bus transportation, the following operational activities can be separated and handled by private contractors, even if the basic service is performed mostly by a public agency: plowing snow from bus routes; towing disabled buses; maintaining buildings; and performing custodial work, body work, brake repairs, transmission repairs, engine repairs, painting, and so on. Again, the result is a combination of arrangements to provide the overall service.

TABLE 4.6

Institutional arrangement	Education	Police protection	Streets and highways	Parks and recreation
Government service	Conventional public schools and state universities	Traditional police department	Municipal highway department	Municipal parks department
Government vending	Local public school accepts out-of-district pupil and is paid by parents	Sponsor pays city for crowd control by police at concert	Circus pays town to clean streets after parade	Private sponsor pays town to clean park after corporate picnic
Intergovern-mental agreement	Pupils from one town attend school in a neighboring town; first town pays the second	Town purchases patrol services from county sheriff	County pays town to clean and plow county roads located in town	City joins special recreation district in the region
Contract	City hires private firm to provide training or to conduct voca-tional education program	City hires a private guard service to pro-tect govern-ment buildings, garages	City hires a private con-tractor to clean, plow, and repair streets	City hires private firm to prune trees and mow grass
Franchise				City authorizes firm to operate city-owned tennis courts and to charge fees
Grant	Private colleges receive grant from the government for every student who attends			
Voucher	Tuition voucher for elementary school, GI Bill, government schol-arships good for any college			

Alternative Arrangements for Providing Goods and Services

Hospitals	Housing	Refuse collection	Transportation
Municipal hospital	Public housing authority	Municipal sanitation department	Public transit authority that runs bus service
		Commercial establishment pays town to pick up its solid waste	Firm hires city bus and driver for a special event
City arranges for residents to be treated at county hospital	Town contracts with county housing authority	City establishes independent solid-waste utility	City is part of regional transportation district
	Housing authority hires private firms for repairs, painting, custodial services	City hires private firm to provide service	School board hires private firm to provide school bus service
		City gives exclusive franchise to private firm to provide service for a fee	Government gives a private firm the exclusive right to provide bus service along a route
Capital construction grant to expand a nonprofit hospital	Government grant to private builder to construct and operate low-income housing	City has user fee for service but subsidizes elderly and low-income households	Government grant to private company to subsidize the acquisition of new buses
Medicare/Medicaid cards permit patients to seek service anywhere	Housing voucher to enable low-income tenants to rent any acceptable, affordable unit		Transportation vouchers that special users (handicapped, elderly) can use for taxis, private cars, etc.

TABLE 4.6

Institutional arrangement	Education	Police protection	Streets and highways	Parks and recreation
Market	Private schools	Banks hire private guards	Local merchant association hires workers to clean commercial street	Commercial tennis courts
Voluntary association	Parochial schools	Block association forms a citizens' crime-watch unit	Homeowners' association arranges to clean and repair local private streets	Tennis club for members
Self-service	Reading books at home, learning from parents	Individual installs locks and alarms and has a weapon	Storeowner cleans street in front of shop	Private tennis courts at home

A service can also be separated along functional lines, and partial contracting can again be employed. For example, a government agency can own the capital facilities required for a service but contract out the service itself. (*Example:* Minneapolis owns vehicle-impoundment lots but contracts out vehicle towing to firms that supply their own tow trucks and labor.) Conversely, an agency can produce the service but rent the privately owned buildings and equipment it needs. Another approach is to have the main-line function run by a government agency but contract for support services such as accounting, printing, legal services, and transportation. Still another approach is to contract only the management of an otherwise governmental service; this is increasingly common for public bus systems and public hospitals. A variant of this is to contract for managing only the support services of a hospital or school, or for managing a physical facility; in effect, the resident manager is a contract department head for the hospital or school administrator.[23]

The three functional areas are ownership, management, and operations. These can be divided between the public and private sectors in eight different ways, as shown in table 4.7. By considering all the different elements of a typically complex "public service," as well as the geographic dispersion of the service, one may arrive at innovative ways to utilize the different arrangements in multiple, hybrid, and partial configurations for different parts of the service. The end result is a larger number of potential service producers and the creation of a competitive climate, a market for public services, that can lead to improved service performance.

Hospitals	Housing	Refuse collection	Transportation
Proprietary (for profit) hospital	Ordinary private housing	Household hires private firm to provide service	Free market for jitneys, private cars for hire
Nonprofit hospital	Housing cooperative	Neighborhood association hires firm to provide service	Carpools, vanpools, commuter buses chartered by groups of suburban neighbors
Accident prevention, self-medication, chicken soup, other traditional cures for common illnesses	Do-it-yourself cabin	Household brings refuse to town disposal site	Driving in one's own car, cycling, walking

TABLE 4.7

FUNCTIONAL DIVISION OF SERVICE ACTIVITIES

	Function		
Ownership	Management	Operation	Description
Public	Public	Public	Typical public system or state-owned enterprise
Public	Private	Public	Management contract (e.g., hiring a private firm to manage a public bus system where buses are publicly owned and workers are public employees)
Public	Private	Private	Management and operations contract (e.g., hiring a private firm to run a county hospital)
Public	Public	Private	Operations contract (e.g., manpower leasing—hiring temporary clerical staff)
Private	Public	Public	Equipment and facility leasing (e.g., a public agency leases vehicles or rents a building)
Private	Private	Private	Typical private system
Private	Public	Private	Government takeover (e.g., in national emergency)
Private	Private	Public	Government-paid workers assigned to a private firm (e.g., as an employment program)

Privatization

In seven of the ten arrangements the private sector is the producer: contract, grant, voucher, franchise, market, voluntary, and self-service. These can be considered private-sector arrangements. But privatization is a dynamic concept and means changing from an arrangement with high government involvement to one with less; correspondingly, it means changing to an arrangement where the private sector plays a more dominant role. Thus, going from a market to a grant arrangement (i.e., introducing a government subsidy) is the opposite of privatization, although the private sector delivers the service in both cases.

Table 4.8 ranks the arrangements in hierarchical order. To *privatize* means to change from one arrangement to another higher on the list. This gives a precise, technical meaning to the definition of privatization in chapter 1. To move in the opposite direction is to nationalize, "governmentalize," "municipalize," "statify," or "deprivatize."

Market, voluntary, and self-service arrangements are the ultimate in privatization and are equivalent on this scale. An intergovernmental agreement is marginally more privatized than the government arrangement because it involves specifying and purchasing a service, which is a step in the direction of a contract or market arrangement. Government vending goes a step further for government relinquishes its role as arranger.

Contracts, grants, and vouchers are ranked as indicated in the table because they involve decreasing government expenditures (government pays the entire cost of a contract, but generally pays only part of the cost under a grant or voucher arrangement) and an increasing role for private choice by citizens. A franchise is next in this progression, ranking just below the market arrange-

TABLE 4.8

RANKING OF ARRANGEMENTS BY DEGREE OF PRIVATIZATION

Arrangement
Market; voluntary; self-service
Franchise
Voucher
Grant
Contract
Government vending
Intergovernmental agreement
Governmental

NOTE: *Privatization* means changing from a lower- to a higher-ranked arrangement.

ment, because government is the arranger and regulator, although it makes no direct expenditures.

From the standpoint of public policy, the principal privatization activity and debate focus on the following transitions:

1. Changing from government to contract, grant, voucher, franchise, voluntary, or market arrangements.

2. Eliminating grants (producer subsidies) in favor of voucher, voluntary, or market arrangements.

3. Denationalizing, a particular form of privatizing that involves selling to the private sector (or giving away to the public or the workers) government-owned enterprises or government-owned assets used in producing goods or services; by extension, this form of privatization also encompasses "demunicipalization" and other forms of "destatification."

4. Recognizing that a particular government-supplied service is a toll or private good and imposing a user charge; if the user is also given a choice between government and a private supplier, this is a change from a government to a government-vending arrangement, and it creates the possibility of a further change to a market arrangement.

5. Deregulating franchises and eliminating other price controls and entry barriers in order to permit the market to respond to people's needs.

These transitions are the most important ones taking place under the umbrella of privatization; each represents a different approach. It is readily apparent that each of these changes creates both winners and losers, and therefore, like all changes, they engender opposition. Chapter 8 describes how to effect these changes, that is, how to privatize. In the meanwhile, the next chapter discusses the advantages and disadvantages of each arrangement, and chapters 6 and 7 present empirical evidence on the effectiveness of privatization and describe numerous applications of this strategy.

Summary

Collective action to supply goods and services requires a government or voluntary group to make decisions about the service to be provided, the level of service, and how to pay for it. Different institutional arrangements are available for supplying goods and services. It is necessary to distinguish between providing or arranging for a service and producing or delivering it. Ten different arrangements can be identified; they differ in the roles played by government, the private sector, and the consumer. Privatization means changing from an

TABLE 4.9

INSTITUTIONAL ARRANGEMENTS FOR PROVIDING PUBLIC SERVICES

Service arrangement	Arranges service	Produces service	Pays producer
Government service	Government	Government	N.A.
Government vending	Consumer	Government	Consumer
Intergovernmental agreement	Government (1)	Government (2)	Government (1)
Contract	Government	Private firm	Government
Franchise (exclusive)	Government	Private firm	Consumer
Franchise (multiple)	Government and consumer	Private firm	Consumer
Grant	Government and consumer	Private firm	Government and consumer
Voucher	Consumer	Private firm	Consumer
Market	Consumer	Private firm	Consumer
Voluntary	Voluntary association	Voluntary association	N.A.
Voluntary with contract	Voluntary association	Private firm	Voluntary association
Self-service	Consumer	Consumer	N.A.

NOTE: Government (1) and Government (2) are two different governments.

arrangement with high government involvement to one with less. The most important privatized arrangements from a policy perspective are the market, contract, voucher, and voluntary arrangements.

The different institutional structures or arrangements for delivering services, and the characteristic identities of producers, arrangers, and payers in each structure, are summarized in table 4.9, which makes it easy to see at a glance how the arrangements differ and how each arrangement is unique with respect to the roles of government, consumers, firms, and voluntary associations. Figure 4.16 assembles the flow diagrams of the arrangements to further facilitate comparison.

The ten basic arrangements can be combined in multiple, hybrid, and partial arrangements, resulting in a rich variety of alternatives for delivering the services that people want.

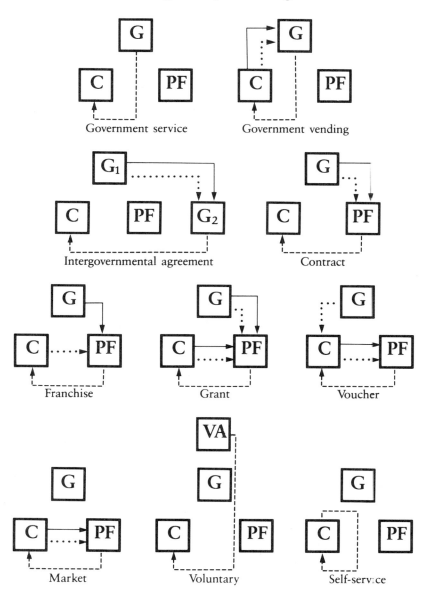

FIGURE 4.16

DIFFERENT SERVICE MODELS, SHOWING FLOW OF AUTHORIZATION
(SOLID LINE), PAYMENT (DOTTED LINE), AND SERVICE DELIVERY
(DASHED LINE) BETWEEN GOVERNMENT (G), VOLUNTARY ASSOCIATION
(VA), PRIVATE FIRM (PF), AND CONSUMER (C)

Notes

1. E.S. Savas, "Public Policy, Systems Analysis, and the Privatization of Public Services," in *Operational Research '84,* ed. J.P. Brans (New York: Elsevier, 1984).

2. E.S. Savas and J.A. Kaiser, *Moscow's City Government* (New York: Praeger, 1985).

3. *The Challenge of Local Governmental Reorganization,* vol. 3 (Washington, D.C.: Advisory Commission on Intergovernmental Relations, February 1974), tables 3.3 and 3.A.

4. Carl F. Valente and Lydia D. Manchester, *Rethinking Local Services: Examining Alternative Delivery Approaches* (Washington, D.C.: International City Management Association, 1974), xiv, xv.

5. Office of Management and Budget, *Enhancing Governmental Productivity through Competition* (Washington, D.C.: Office of Management and Budget, March 1984).

6. U.S. House of Representatives, Subcommittee on Employee Ethics and Utilization, Committee on Post Office and Civil Service, *Hearings on Contracting Out of Jobs and Services,* Serial No. 95-7 (Washington, D.C.: Government Printing Office, 1977), 29.

7. Barbara J. Nelson, "Purchase of Services," in *Productivity Improvement Handbook for State and Local Governments,* ed. George Washnis (New York: Wiley, 1978).

8. See also Donald Fisk, Herbert Kiesling, and Thomas Muller, *Private Provision of Public Services: An Overview* (Washington, D.C.: Urban Institute, May 1978).

9. Harry P. Hatry and Eugene Durman, *Issues in Competitive Contracting for Social Services* (Falls Church, Va.: National Institute of Governmental Purchasing, 1985).

10. See Nelson, "Purchase of Services."

11. John J. Kirlin, John C. Ries, and Sidney Sonenblum, "Alternatives to City Departments," in *Alternatives for Delivering Public Services,* ed. E.S. Savas (Boulder, Colo.: Westview, 1977), 116.

12. Ibid., 120.

13. Robert L. Bish and Robert Warren, "Scale and Monopoly Problems in Urban Government Services," *Urban Affairs Quarterly* 8 (September 1972): 97-120.

14. Elinor Ostrom, Roger B. Parks, and Gordon P. Whitaker, *Patterns of Metropolitan Policing* (Lexington, Mass.: Lexington Books, 1976).

15. Gary Bridge, "Citizen Choice in Public Service: Voucher Systems," in Savas, *Alternatives for Delivering Public Services.*

16. See Valente and Manchester, *Rethinking Local Services,* xv.

17. See Fisk, Kiesling, and Muller, *Private Provision of Public Services.*

18. "Teaching Children at Home," *Time,* 4 December 1978, 78.

19. "Harper's Index," *Harper's,* May 1986, 11.

20. James M. Ferris, "Coprovision: Citizen Time and Money Donations in Public Service Provision," *Public Administration Review* 44, no. 4 (July/August 1984): 324-33.

21. E.S. Savas, *The Organization and Efficiency of Solid Waste Collection* (Lexington, Mass.: Lexington Books, 1977), 34.

22. Marcia Chaiken and Jan Chaiken, "Private Provision of Municipal and County Police Functions" (report by Abt Associates, Cambridge, Mass., for the National Institute of Justice, 1986), appendix tables A1 through A6.

23. Ted Kolderie, "Contracting as an Approach to Management," in *Public Services Redesign Project,* a newsletter of the Hubert H. Humphrey Institute (Minneapolis: University of Minnesota, 1983).

5. An Analysis and Comparison of Alternative Arrangements

We have seen that no fewer than ten institutional arrangements (or structures, or mechanisms) exist for providing services to the public: government service, intergovernmental agreement, contracting, franchise, grant, voucher, market, voluntary, self-service, and government vending. Can each arrangement be used for any service? If not, in what circumstances or for what kinds of services can each be used? What are the relative advantages and disadvantages of each? If more than one arrangement can be used to deliver a particular service, which is best? In what way?

The Nature of Goods and the Choice of Arrangements

Most of these questions can be answered by referring to the intrinsic nature of the service in question. It is clear that private goods can be provided by any arrangement, including voluntary action (i.e., simple charity). In the United States, except for worthy goods, private goods are not generally supplied by government, intergovernmental agreement, contract, or franchise arrangements, although in principle they could be. Indeed, in some countries private goods are routinely supplied by government. For example, in the Soviet Union most retail shops are operated by a municipal agency, and most food is grown on state farms (which accounts for the abysmally poor state of the food supply, most experts agree). In some corrupt regimes exclusive franchises are (unnecessarily) created by governments to supply private goods that are near-necessities; the result is equivalent to government-sanctioned extortion.

BiAS

Toll goods, which are like private goods in that they are subject to exclusion, can be provided through any of the ten arrangements except self-service (because toll goods involve joint consumption; recall the frustrated soul who has the only telephone in the world).

Collective goods can be supplied by government, by intergovernmental agreement, by contract, or by a voluntary arrangement. They cannot be provided through franchises, grants, vouchers, vending, or the marketplace, as these structures all require exclusion to be effective, and collective goods, by definition, do not possess this property. (The reader may recall the lighthouse in chapter 3 as an example of a collective good whose use cannot effectively be denied to any would-be user.)

Goods that are intrinsically common-pool goods are provided by nature, but we saw in chapter 3 that government action can, in effect, create such goods and give them away, in which case government service, intergovernmental agreements, contracts, grants, or vouchers can be used to supply them; free-lunch programs and medical care have been identified previously as falling into this class of government-created common-pool goods. (It should also be recognized that voluntary arrangements can create and supply such goods, as exemplified by a charitable organization that offers food and shelter to the needy.)

The situation is summarized in table 5.1, which shows the different arrangements that can be used to supply each of the different kinds of goods. The table makes it clear that each kind can be provided through more than one institutional arrangement. Note that voluntary action, government service, intergovernmental agreements, and contracts are the only arrangements that can supply all four kinds of goods. Self-service is the most limited arrangement, as one might expect, for it can be used to provide only private goods.

TABLE 5.1

TYPES OF GOODS AND INSTITUTIONAL ARRANGEMENTS
THAT CAN BE USED FOR THEIR DELIVERY

Arrangements	Private goods	Toll goods	Collective goods	Common-pool goods
Government service	x	x	x	x
Government vending	x	x		
Intergovernmental agreement	x	x	x	x
Contract	x	x	x	x
Franchise	x	x		
Grant	x	x		x
Voucher	x	x		x
Market	x	x		
Voluntary	x	x	x	x
Self-service	x			

The next step is to see what further attributes or characteristics of the goods and the arrangements are important in determining the suitability of a particular arrangement for supplying a particular good.

Factors in Evaluating Arrangements

SERVICE SPECIFICITY

Some services can be specified with little ambiguity and little chance of misunderstanding. Other services cannot be specified so precisely and allow much room for reasonable people to differ significantly in their interpretations of what the service entails. Compare, for example, street paving and education. The former can be described in precise engineering terms with detailed technical specifications as to the depth and type of foundation, the thickness and quality of asphalt overlay, provisions for drainage, and so forth. Education cannot be specified in any terms remotely comparable, and so requests to "pave this street" and "educate this child" would produce very different responses from potential service producers. Producers of paving services can proceed to estimate the cost of the work and can submit bids to do it. The service arranger can readily compare bids, and, in due course, he can inspect the work in progress and on completion. He can then state, with relatively little margin for error, that the requested service was or was not performed.

In contrast, producers of educational services, faced with the hypothetical request for proposals to "educate this child," may plausibly design a widely differing range of educational programs, even if the service arranger, prevailed upon to be more specific, goes on to define education as involving reading, writing, and arithmetic. It is not even sufficient to say that the child will be considered educated if he or she can pass a certain examination. The range of information and the kinds of skills that the child should have acquired and will have to demonstrate can ultimately be defined only by reference to a specific curriculum and study materials. If the service arranger goes this far in describing the desired service to potential producers, he is then, in effect, doing nothing more than hiring a teacher.

Because some services can be specified to a much greater degree than others, some arrangements that are feasible for the former are less feasible or infeasible for the latter. Specifiable services permit preparation of intelligible requests for service, submission of proposals that conform with the requests, and evaluation of performance. Services that cannot be specified in detail cannot elicit this series of actions. Services run the full gamut from those that can be specified in great detail to those that can be defined only in rather broad and general terms. The former can readily be provided by any of the arrangements; the latter, in general, cannot. In particular, poorly defined services cannot easily be provided by intergovernmental agreement, by contract, by franchise, or by grant. (An exception occurs if a service is already being performed, in which case a service arranger says, in effect, "I like what you're doing and I'd like to buy some of it too." This is what happens when a school district sends its students to a school in a neighboring district, for instance.)

If a service cannot be specified very well, how can anyone or any arrangement supply it satisfactorily? In particular, how can a government agency or anyone else perform a service satisfactorily if it is not at all clear what the service calls for, and what *satisfactory* means? "Only with difficulty" is the answer. That is, only with close supervision, extensive monitoring, frequent feedback from the consumer to the producer, close coordination between upper and lower echelons of the producing organization, frequent adjustments and corrections, and—in effect—constant negotiation between the consumer and the producer to balance expectations, capabilities, and achievements. These conditions can best be achieved where no third party stands between the consumer and producer, a situation realized when the consumer is the arranger (e.g., food stamps) and also when the arranger is the producer (e.g., police protection). Table 4.9 in the preceding chapter shows that the former circumstance obtains under market and voucher arrangements and the latter under government, voluntary, and self-service arrangements.

Availability of Producers
For some services, many producers are already in existence or can readily be encouraged to enter the field; in other cases, there are few producers and it is difficult to attract more, either because a large capital investment may be needed or because of other barriers to entry. This factor, too, affects the choice of service arrangement, as contract, market, and voucher arrangements will work satisfactorily only if there are relatively many producers from whom to choose. (Chapter 8 discusses how to increase the number of potential producers.)

Efficiency and Effectiveness
The three fundamental criteria of service performance are efficiency, effectiveness, and equity. Equity is discussed later in this chapter; efficiency and effectiveness are examined empirically in depth in the next two chapters, but because they constitute such a dominant issue, they are addressed here as well, on a conceptual basis.

One of the most fundamental determinants of the efficiency and effectiveness of any arrangement is competition; that is, the degree of competition that an arrangement permits will, to a major extent, determine how efficiently that arrangement will supply a service. Competition means that the consumer has a choice, and citizen choice is a revered principle in democratic societies. Provided that there are enough producers to select from, market, contract, and voucher systems are most conducive to fostering competition and thereby achieving economic efficiency.

Franchising, grants, intergovernmental contracting, government vending, and voluntary arrangements permit some degree of competition, although not as great as the aforementioned three. Government service, in contrast, generally operates as an unrivaled monopoly, despite the fact that relatively few such services are natural monopolies. Government bureaus that provide monopoly services behave like unregulated monopolies and are institutionally subject to all the inefficiencies and inadequacies inherent in such a situation. Of course, government monopolies do not maximize profits per se, but they can otherwise take advantage of their position to maximize their budgets or the total remuneration—monetary and nonmonetary—of their managers and employees per unit of work.

For the sake of completeness, it should be noted that self-service is like government service in that neither admits of competition. Both arrangements can be characterized as having a single, monopoly producer—but the effects will be very different for self-service, as the producer and the consumer are one and the same.

SCALE

The scale of a service will generally affect its efficiency. The optimal scale of different services will differ, depending entirely on the technical characteristics of the production process. A one-room schoolhouse with a single teacher handling twelve different grades will not be as effective in providing a desired standard of education as a larger school with more specialized teachers, a library, audiovisual equipment, and the like. Similarly, it is extremely inefficient for a small town with a one-man police force to have a full-time police dispatcher, a spare police car to use when the other is undergoing repair, and a full-time mechanic. At the other end of the scale, a very large police department may require so many coordinators, so many layers of supervisors, and so many reports and file clerks that it, too, is very inefficient. Some intermediate-size department is likely to be most efficient.

Government service is likely to be inefficient because the production unit must, by definition, be the same size as the consumer unit, without regard to the optimal size. Therefore, if the most efficient size for a school system is one that services 50,000 people, then cities with populations of 1,000, 10,000, 100,000 or 1 million would all be inefficient if each had its own school system.

All of the arrangements except government service (and self-service) can achieve economies of scale by allowing the size of the producer to be independent of the size of the arranger, thereby permitting the producer to be the optimal size. Intergovernmental agreements are more flexible than government service in this regard, but they are not as flexible as contract or voucher arrangements, for the producer is limited to the size of either an existing jurisdiction or a new jurisdiction that could be created by aggregating existing ones. Contracting and franchising are quite flexible in their ability to take advantage of scale economies. If the most efficient size of a producer is smaller than the size of the jurisdiction that arranges for the service, then all well and good, for the jurisdiction could divide its territory into two or more separate areas, each of optimal size, ideally. If the jurisdiction is too small, then the franchisee or contractor can nevertheless achieve optimal size by selling its services to other nearby jurisdictions as well. (This is a feasible option even in the case of a franchise service that requires a large capital investment in a geographically circumscribed area, such as water supply or sewage treatment.)

RELATING BENEFITS AND COSTS

Efficiency is more likely to be realized when there is a direct link between paying for the service and realizing its benefits, and the consumer has an economic incentive to shop wisely. Such a link exists only for private and toll goods. Within these classifications, those arrangements that allow a direct relationship between the paying consumer and the service producer—that is, where the consumer pays the producer directly—are market, voucher, grant (in some cases), and franchise arrangements, as these do not involve any third party as an intermediary. For example, the consumer pays the grocer directly with food stamps (a voucher), and the telephone subscriber pays the local telephone company (a franchise). Voluntary service may have this characteristic, as in a cooperative or a country club, for example.

One might say that government service does not interpose an intermediary between the consumer and the producer either, for the taxpayer-consumer pays the producer (government); however, unless a user charge is levied, the link between the act of paying taxes for government service and the act of consuming a particular service is far more attenuated than it is for market, voucher, grant, or franchise arrangements.

RESPONSIVENESS TO CONSUMERS

Direct contact between consumer and producer would be expected to result in more responsive service as well, particularly when the consumer can exercise some choice. This relation exists when the consumer is the arranger, as in market and voucher systems, in voluntary service when no contract is involved, and in arrangements that involve multiple grantees and franchisees. This is obviously true for self-service.

SUSCEPTIBILITY TO FRAUD

At first glance, it appears that several of the arrangements are particularly vulnerable to criminal acts that, in addition to their moral impact on society, increase the cost of service. The award of government contracts, franchises, and grants is obviously susceptible to bribery, collusion, and extortion. Vouchers are vulnerable to a variety of fraudulent schemes, as evidenced by the counterfeiting, theft, sale, and illegal redemption of food stamps.

Opponents of these arrangements cite these weaknesses and point to the apparent superiority of government services (and by implication, intergovernmental agreements) in this respect. Careful reflection blurs this contrast, however, and the issue merits closer scrutiny.

Let us look at the issue of bribery, and its relative, extortion. A would-be contractor might offer a bribe (or a campaign contribution) to a public official to influence the award in his favor, or the official might take the initiative and solicit a payment. Is this reprehensible behavior unique to contract arrangements and the like, or does it occur even in government service? Consider the situation where public-sector employee unions give endorsements, make campaign contributions, and supply campaign workers to favored candidates for office. They can be quite explicit about their expectations when their candidate is elected;[1] they expect—and frequently obtain—a quid pro quo in the form of greater expenditures for the service their union produces, pay raises, more generous retirement plans, or collective bargaining rules that will lead to more favorable outcomes for them during labor negotiations. They may also seek more jobs and agency shops. While such an exchange of favors is legal, one can ask if this differs significantly from a bribe or contribution by a private firm to secure a contract. The result in either case is a higher price paid by the public.

Pension plans can be perverted into rewards from public officials to public employees in return for political support, as was demonstrated in Boston. The son of a former mayor, holding the post of City Clerk, applied for an annual pension of $28,000 because of the emotional damage he claimed he suffered by acting as parliamentarian to the fractious City Council. The city censor applied for a $21,000 yearly disability pension on the grounds that he had been traumatized by two rock concerts he had attended on official duty. "There is no doubt in my mind that the [pension] system was designed . . . to serve the alliance of politicians and public employees," said the city auditor.[2]

Let us consider another villain, the official who tries to extort money from an honest contractor by threatening to delay or deny proper payments to him. Can there be anything analogous to such scurrilous behavior entirely within a pure governmental arrangement? Alas, yes. There have been numerous instances where public officials have extracted money from their employees, demanding kickbacks from the latter's wages in return for allowing them to keep their jobs or obtain promotions.

Yet another form of fraud is collusion, where prospective bidders coordinate their bids in order to keep prices high. How common is such behavior? It is impossible to tell, but if it were widespread, then one might expect the cost of contract services to be higher than the cost of government services. As chapters 6 and 7 reveal in considerable detail, the opposite is usually the case. Moreover, government agencies can often protect themselves and assure competition by competing directly with the private sector for some or all of the work. This strategy is pursued further in chapter 8.

I am familiar with an interesting case worth mentioning here. A city awarded a contract competitively for a particular municipal service and realized net savings of 22 percent per year, along with higher-quality service and greater citizen satisfaction. These improvements were carefully measured and documented by outsiders. A year later, legal proceedings were started because there were allegations of collusive bidding, and, it was averred, the bid price was 10 percent higher than it would have been in the absence of such collusion.

Ponder the irony here. Residents in this city had been paying $100, let's say, for municipal service, and then paid 22 percent less, or $78, for contract service. In the absence of the alleged collusion, the price would have been $71. Significant media attention was directed to the $7 overcharge (the difference between the alleged collusive price and the theoretical market price), but none was paid to the $22 overcharge (the out-of-pocket difference that the public had been paying for years). One can never condone or excuse collusion or any other impropriety in the contracting process; however, one cannot help but be struck by the media's blithe indifference to the larger loss. Clearly, contracting proved to be better than municipal service, and it would have been even better if no collusion had occurred.

This example is not unique. In the reprehensible and much-publicized scandal where New York City officials accepted money in exchange for awarding contracts to collect fines for parking violations, little note was taken of the fact that collections actually increased under the contract;[3] in narrow, economic terms (although not in morality) the city was better off than it had been when a municipal agency was collecting the fines.

As a final dispiriting point, one must acknowledge that embezzling and theft of property by employees occurs in both the public and private sectors.

One may conclude from this discussion that contracts, franchises, and grants, and government service as well, are all subject to various forms of corruption. No arrangement has a monopoly on either virtue or knavery.

ECONOMIC EQUITY

Do the arrangements differ in their ability to provide services to consumers in a fair and equitable manner? Two separate issues can be distinguished here: equity with respect to financial means; and equity with respect to race, religion, or other such characteristics. This section deals with the former and the next section with the latter.

Many people consider the market mechanism to be inherently equitable in that all people are treated equally and (in principle) everyone pays the same amount of money for the same thing. Others consider the market mechanism to be inherently *in*equitable because incomes are distributed unequally and therefore rich people and poor people cannot both buy the same things. Those who make this latter argument equate equity with equality. They view market, voluntary, and franchise arrangements as similarly inequitable, insofar as the ability to obtain service is dependent on income, as in paying for water, electric power, transportation, or recreation. However, the other organized arrangements (i.e., excluding self-service) are alike with respect to this issue. Grants, contracts, intergovernmental contracts, and government service can all be used to dispense services in whatever manner is deemed equitable by the appropriate government body, as can vouchers, which are deliberately designed to equalize access to services.

This is an important point. Many who oppose privatization on the grounds that it is unfair to the poor assume mistakenly that privatization requires a pure market arrangement, and they conjure up the vision of every family, rich and poor alike, having to pay individually to send their toddler off to school, for example. This is not the case at all, as we have seen. Collective goods can be provided by contract and financed by taxes; private goods and toll goods for the needy can be supplied by vouchers; both approaches allow redistribution.

Without expressing a position on the above diametrically opposed views of economic equity, one can make the neutral statement that the arrangements clearly differ in the extent to which they facilitate redistribution of goods and services in the name of equity.

EQUITY FOR MINORITIES

There is another, all-important dimension to the subject of equity besides economic redistribution: equality of treatment without discrimination on grounds of race, color, or creed. Does privatization make any difference to members of minority groups? This question can be divided into two, more focused questions: What is the effect of different arrangements on jobs for minorities, and what is their effect on services for minorities?

Effect on Jobs. Let us begin with the issue of jobs. The federal government and many state and local governments were among the first organizations in the United State to eliminate discriminatory hiring practices. As a result, they tend to have relatively more minority employees, and more of them in higher-paid positions by virtue of promotions and seniority. (In 1980, 27.1 percent of all employed blacks worked for government, compared to 15.9 percent of whites.[4]) At first glance, therefore, it might appear that privatization will cause proportionately more job losses and fewer job opportunities for minority workers.

There is little justification for this fear. In the first place, privatization creates jobs in the private sector, and private firms no less than governments are subject to laws prohibiting discrimination in hiring and can be made to conform to the letter and spirit of the law as closely as state and local governments can. In fact, private firms may be *better* in this respect than the federal government: Congress exempts itself from the laws on equal employment opportunity and does not have to practice "affirmative action" in hiring congressional staff members! In any event, a study of this issue found that minority workers displaced from municipal jobs by privatization were hired by private contractors in about the same proportion as they had been hired by city departments.[5]

In the second place, nondiscriminatory hiring is not always the practice in governments. Many government agencies throughout the world are dominated by particular ethnic, linguistic, religious, or tribal groups; indeed, an individual agency is often considered the private preserve of one group. In the United States this practice is contrary to official policy and is fading, but it can still be observed in older eastern cities. In other countries the practice is often a matter of policy that is understood but is not made explicit. (In Southeast Asia, for example, privatization is viewed as tantamount to "Sinofication" because many private entrepreneurs are ethnically Chinese.)

I observed a case in the United States where a change from municipal to contract service resulted in a fairer distribution of jobs for minorities. The contractor's newly hired workforce closely reflected the city's current demographic composition, whereas the agency's own workforce reflected the composition of an earlier era.

The third and final point with respect to the job issue has to do with entrepreneurial opportunities. Privatization affords ambitious members of minority groups the opportunity to start their own businesses and to prosper. Minority communities in urban areas are particularly well situated in this regard. Many municipal services require only modest amounts of capital and are technologically simple, requiring no professional training. These characteristics are attractive to many potential businessmen and businesswomen in minority communities. These individuals can start firms that would supply municipal services by contract or franchise.

Governmental encouragement of minority entrepreneurship has usually been expressed in the requirement that a certain portion of contracts be set aside and reserved for minority firms or that prime contractors subcontract a certain fraction of their work to minority-owned firms. Despite the laudable intent of such restrictions, namely, to improve the economic condition of minority groups, such "set asides" have been marred by the creation of dummy corporations, paper exchanges of assets, fictitious billing, influence peddling, and other evasions of the spirit if not the letter of such laws. These quota-based methods have been successfully defended before the U.S. Supreme Court, but their constitutional validity has not yet been fully established. Nor have they been very successful so far in achieving their objective.

The opportunity for market-based (instead of quota-based) minority entrepreneurism via privatization was seen and seized by the Bedford-Stuyvesant Restoration Corporation, an economic development unit in a minority community in Brooklyn, New York. The corporation created an indigenous, neighborhood-based, locally owned company to bid for municipal work in the area. However, opposition to any contracting at all came from public employee unions and aborted the plan. Basically, the political power of the latter was greater than that mustered in the minority community.

Despite this local setback, numerous minority entrepreneurs in the United States have started in business through privatization. The trucking industry provides a useful lesson about the business opportunities available to minority entrepreneurs through the marketplace. For many years it was necessary for a would-be trucker to prove beforehand that his entry into the business was a "public necessity and convenience." (Surely the best way to demonstrate this is to allow someone to enter the business and see if he survives!) The effect of such regulation was to keep blacks out of the trucking business, even though in terms of capital and training requirements this is an eminently suitable activity for black entrepreneurs. The situation changed in the early 1980s after trucking deregulation. Modest as it was, deregulation tended to transform this activity from a restricted franchise to a market arrangement, enabling blacks, no longer subject to de facto exclusion, to triple their participation in this industry.[6]

The entrepreneurial opportunities that are inherent in privatization have been recognized in South Africa: An association of black businessmen has enthusiastically embraced the concept and sees it as a means to gain economic strength and become integrated into the economic mainstream, while providing cost-effective services and holding down the size of government.

In summary, job opportunities for members of minority groups appear to be pretty similar regardless of arrangement. In particular, government service seems no better or worse than any other arrangement on this score. Moreover, as explained in chapter 8, no job losses need occur when public services are privatized by contracting.

Effect on Services. Turning to the other part of the main question, do the arrangements differ with respect to level and quality of services to minorities?

This is not merely a hypothetical concern. A court found that the town of Shaw, Mississippi, which had racially segregated neighborhoods, supplied its tax-paid municipal services — street lights, sewers, and paved streets — in a highly discriminatory manner. Whereas the town's population was 60 percent black, (1) all the modern street lamps were in white neighborhoods; (2) 98 percent of all the homes fronting on unpaved streets were occupied by blacks; and (3) 19 percent of black-owned homes were without sewer service, compared to only 1 percent of white-owned homes.[7] All three inequitably distributed services were supplied directly by the local government.

Obviously, a government that discriminates against some of its citizens as a matter of unspoken policy can do so using contracts, grants, vouchers, or any other arrangement in which it has a hand. Sometimes, however, contracting can eliminate bias. For instance, a study I made uncovered the following practice in a city that once had municipal collection of residential waste. When the city agency could not complete its daily collections on time, it sometimes coped by skipping the black neighborhoods, which had relatively little political influence. When the city changed to a contractor, this no longer happened. The contractor methodically completed his assigned daily workload, paying overtime if necessary, and was oblivious to the political strength or weakness of different neighborhoods. (Further discussion of this example appears in chapter 6.)

Like all taxpayers, minority groups have a stake in more efficient use of public funds. Nevertheless, to the extent that minority groups on average have lower than median incomes, they are more dependent on government-provided services than wealthier groups, and they rely more on private goods that have been collectivized. Therefore, any arrangement that results in better quality of service, or in more cost-effective service (which makes more money available to government) is likely to benefit minority groups more. Also, the voucher arrangement is particularly advantageous for low-income minority-group members, because, as explained previously, it gives them greater choice.

In summary, whereas minority groups seem to be served equally well or poorly by any of the different arrangements when it comes to equity in jobs, when it comes to equity in services they are better off with vouchers or with any particularly efficient arrangement. As we see in chapter 6, contracting is generally more efficient than government service.

RESPONSIVENESS TO GOVERNMENT DIRECTION

Public services can be used as a vehicle to advance other governmental purposes, such as regional economic development. The location of military bases in certain favored areas of the country exemplifies this traditional, pork-barrel approach. Government, grant, and contract arrangements are equally responsive to such guidance.

Contrary to what one may think, however, direct government service does not assure effective control or direction by elected officals. Most executives who have served in both government and the private sector are struck — even astonished — at how little control an elected chief executive or an appointed official has over the agency that is under his nominal control. The combination of ossified civil service rules and regulations, powerful public-employee unions, and inflexible traditions rendered immune to change by decades of monopoly power accounts for this effect. It explains much of the frustration encountered by would-be agents of change: the democratically elected or appointed individuals who enter office on platforms that promise reforms.

Private firms can actually be more responsive to public policy than government agencies, for it is generally easier for a public agency to influence the behavior of a private organization than the behavior of another public agency.[8] A number of examples can be cited to support this thesis. City housing inspectors are often better able to persuade private landlords than public housing authorities to correct deficiencies. In fact, a judge placed the Boston Housing Authority (BHA) in receivership and castigated it, accusing it of "gross mismanagement, nonfeasance, incompetence and irresponsibility." He concluded, "If the BHA were a private landlord, it surely would have been driven out of business long ago or its board jailed or most likely both."[9] Similarly, when David Stockman was director of the OMB, he remarked that if the Securities and Exchange Commission had jurisdiction over federal budget documents, members of Congress and the administration "would be in jail."[10] Another example is provided by the Pension Benefit Corporation, the unit within the U.S. Labor Department that guarantees the pension benefits of workers in private firms. The financial condition of this agency is so weak, that is, its contingent liabilities are so large and it is in such an unsound actuarial position, that if it were a private insurance company, a state government would shut it down.

The Tennessee Valley Authority also illustrates this point. It has been notably recalcitrant in reducing its air-polluting emissions despite pressure from environmental control agencies,[11] and it was accused of filing a misleading report to the Nuclear Regulatory Commission about an accident at one of its nuclear generating plants.[12] Similarly, local governments appear to be more successful than private firms in avoiding compliance with state environmental regulations concerning their unsanitary landfills. Perhaps the ultimate example of government agency immunity to the law is provided by two frustrated congressmen. Exasperated by evidence that the Postal Service practiced deceptive advertising with respect to its airmail and special delivery services, and calling it fraud, they asked for an investigation. The Federal Trade Commission declined on the grounds that it cannot investigate another government agency.[13]

Finally, it was a state-owned enterprise that, willfully and deceitfully, grossly violated Norway's own security laws when it sold to the Soviet Union certain high-technology goods used to build quieter submarines.

No definitive conclusion can be drawn from these few anecdotal illustrations; however, one can say that (with the obvious exception of market, voluntary, and self-service arrangements) no arrangement—not even government service—stands out as being significantly more responsive to government direction or control than any other.

The Size of Government

In terms of the number of employees, the size of government is greatest under government service and least under market, franchise, voluntary, and self-service, of course. Contracts, grants, and vouchers result in government expenditures but require relatively few government employees because the latter are needed only to administer the programs and not to produce the services. In addition, if these last three arrangements are more efficient than government service, they would tend to limit government spending, although not as much as franchise, market, voluntary, or self-service arrangements do.

It must be pointed out, however, that vouchers and grants can lead to very large government expenditures even though the number of government employees may be relatively small. Food stamps (vouchers) have cost $30 billion per year, and housing grants have created a $250 billion debt.

A government agency that runs a railroad, sells irrigation water, provides electricity, or is in the middle-class housing business is subject to political pressures to subsidize the activity and spread the cost among nonusers. Rarely can it cancel uneconomical services or dismiss employees, as many nationalized enterprises so clearly demonstrate. The result is often a large cost to the government. Privatization that puts the activity under a market or franchise arrangement reduces these pressures on government spending. (Some private firms were nationalized, however, precisely *because* they became unprofitable; government was persuaded to step in to preserve jobs that had lost their economic justification.)

Comparison of Arrangements

The arrangements clearly differ with respect to various operational characteristics. These differences are summarized in table 5.2. Where the discussion concluded that the arrangements are essentially equivalent with respect to a characteristic, that characteristic is omitted from the table, so that the listing shows only significant differences between arrangements. In the table, a double plus (++) sign (or a blank) appears when the arrangement possesses (or lacks) the indicated characteristic to a significant degree. If the characteristic is present to some degree, or to a minor extent, this fact is denoted by a single plus (+) sign. Unquestionably, there is considerable subjectivity in these ratings.

Having said this, it is nevertheless possible to inspect the table and form some initial impressions. If one merely tabulates the number of pluses—an embarrassingly simplistic approach—the voucher system and the market system stand out with almost unbroken strings of positive attributes; government service, government vending, and intergovernmental agreements have the fewest positive attributes. This is a result of the values implicit in the table; all attributes are weighted equally, and so a different emphasis on redistribution, on efficiency, and on limiting the size of government would produce different outcomes. One can generate other versions of this table by adding other attributes and assigning different weights to the listed attributes, for instance. This is left as an exercise for the reader.

However one tinkers with table 5.2, one can view it in the light of table 5.1 to determine the best arrangement for each of the different types of goods. Market and voucher arrangements are best for private and toll goods, voluntary and voucher arrangements are best for common-pool goods, and voluntary and contract arrangements are best for collective goods, given the ratings in table 5.2.

The relatively high ranking of voluntary arrangements for delivering collective and common-pool goods should come as no surprise. Voluntary arrangements are, after all, a form of self-government and generally offer maximum citizen participation. Democratic government has its roots in a similar voluntary social contract among citizens. Voluntary neighborhood associations can mobilize to provide collective goods that are geographically localized. They can also be organized on the basis of other common interests, such as helping the victims of a particular illness or disability. The matter of voluntary associations is addressed further in chapter 8.

TABLE 5.2
CHARACTERISTICS OF DIFFERENT ARRANGEMENTS

Characteristic	Government service	Government vending	Intergovernmental agreement	Contract	Franchise	Grant	Voucher	Market	Voluntary	Self-service
Handles poorly specified service	++							++	++	++
Requires multiple producers				++			++	++	++	
Promotes efficiency and effectiveness				++	++		++	++		
Achieves economies of scale			+	++	+	++	++	++	+	
Relates costs to benefits		+	+	++	++	++	++	++	++	++
Is responsive to consumer		++	+	++	+	+	++	++	++	++
Is relatively invulnerable to fraud			++						++	++
Facilitates redistribution	++		++	++		++	++		+	
Furthers other purposes	++		+	+	+	+	+	+		
Limits number of government employees			+	++	++	++	++	++	++	++

Characteristics of the Privatization Alternatives

The most prominent mechanisms for privatizing public services that supply collective goods are contracts, voluntary action, and vouchers. (To be precise, vouchers supply private goods that are paid for collectively.) In contrast letting the marketplace take over is the leading mechanism for privatizing nationalized or state-owned enterprises that supply private and toll goods. (See chapter 8 for a discussion of this privatization technique.) It is these three arrangements —contracting, vouchers, and voluntary action—that are most frequently referred to and most often advocated. They merit separate and more detailed discussion as to the pros and cons of each, and the circumstances in which they can be employed.

CONTRACTING

Contracting is feasible and works well under the following set of conditions: (1) the work to be done is specified unambiguously; (2) several potential producers are available, and a competitive climate either exists or can be created and sustained; (3) the government is able to monitor the contractor's performance; and (4) appropriate terms are included in the contract document and enforced.

Of all the privatization options, contracting has engendered the most discussion and heated debate. The battle lends itself readily to ideological posturing and unsubstantiated assertions. The arguments of the advocates for contracting can be summarized as follows:

1. Contracting is more efficient because

    a. It harnesses competitive forces and brings the pressure of the marketplace to bear on inefficient producers.

    b. It permits better management, free of most of the distracting influences that are characteristic of overtly political organizations.

    c. The costs and benefits of managerial decisions are felt more directly by the decision maker, whose own rewards are often directly at stake.

2. Contracting makes it possible for government to take advantage of specialized skills that are lacking in its own workforce; it overcomes obsolete salary limitations and antiquated civil service restrictions.

3. Contracting allows flexibility in adjusting the size of a program up or down in response to changing demand and changing availability of funds.

4. Contracting permits a quicker response to new needs and facilitates experimentation with new programs.

5. Contracting is a way of avoiding large capital outlays; it spreads costs over time at a relatively constant and predictable level.

6. Contracting permits economies of scale regardless of the scale of the government entity involved.

7. Contracting a portion of the work offers a yardstick for comparing costs.

8. Contracting fosters good management because the cost of service is highly visible in the price of the contract, whereas the cost of government service is usually obscured.

9. Contracting can reduce dependence on a single supplier (a government monopoly) and so lessens the vulnerability of the service to strikes, slowdowns, and inept leadership.

10. Contracting creates opportunities for entrepreneurs from minority groups.

11. Contracting limits the size of government, at least in terms of the number of employees.

12. Contracting spurs private-sector research on innovative ways to satisfy society's needs.

In contrast, the advocates of government service, who are often middle managers in government or representatives of government-employee unions, oppose contracting and rebut the above arguments with these rejoinders:

1. Contracting is ultimately more expensive because of
   a. Corrupt practices in awarding contracts.[14]
   b. "Outrageous and pernicious work practices" among private-sector unions.[15]
   c. High profits, whereas government is nonprofit.
   d. The cost of layoffs and unemployment for government workers.
   e. The shortage of qualified suppliers and therefore the lack of competition.
   f. The cost of managing the contract and monitoring contractor performance.
   g. The low marginal cost of expanding government service.
   h. Cost-plus-fixed-fee provisions in some contracts, which provide no incentive for efficiency.
   i. The absence of effective competition in "follow-on" contracts, after government gets out of the business and is at the mercy of the contractor.
2. Contracting nullifies the basic principle of merit employment and subverts laws regarding veterans preference in government employment; it is demoralizing to employees, deprives government of the skills it needs in-house, and therefore is fundamentally debilitating of government capability.

3. Contracting limits the flexibility of government in responding to emergencies.

4. Contracting fosters an undesirable dependence on contractors and leaves the public vulnerable to strikes and slowdowns by the contractor's personnel and to bankruptcy of the firm.

5. Contracting depends on adequately written contracts, which are difficult to draw up, and as a result there is a loss of government accountability and control.

6. Contracting limits the opportunity to realize economies of scale.

7. Entrusting services to private organizations increases the political power of the latter and creates a lobby for more government spending.

8. Contracting will result in disproportionate job losses among members of minority communities, many of whom are government employees.

9. Contracting causes a loss of autonomy of the contractor (e.g., coopting a private, nonprofit social service agency) and thereby decreases the latter's effectiveness in the long run by muting its role as critic and social conscience.

Many of these claims and counterclaims are obviously in direct conflict. The contractor is said to lose his autonomy to government and yet is held to be not accountable to nor under sufficient control of the government. It is claimed both that contracting reaps and that it dissipates economies of scale. It surmounts civil service obstacles and subverts the merit system. It increases and reduces government flexibility. It makes scarce talents available to the government and deprives government of those same talents. It is efficient and inefficient.

Some of the arguments against contracting can be turned around. For example, the above discussion concerning corruption concluded that the problem was symmetrical, affecting both contracting and government service in the same underlying way. As for vulnerability to service disruption, strikes by government employees have the same effect as strikes by private employees. Those who fear a loss of accountability and control under contract service ignore the problem of holding someone accountable in government and ignore the complaint, often voiced by elected officials, that they cannot adequately control government agencies.

Considerable academic attention has been devoted to the theoretical differences in motivation and performance of public and private organizations. Niskanen, Allison, Borcherding, Wolf, Bailis, Downs, Rainey, Meyer, Fitch, Drucker, and Bennett and Johnson are among the many who have considered the matter.[16] One can make a heroic attempt to summarize this literature, as follows:

1. In the public sector there is little incentive to perform efficiently, and management lacks effective control over human and capital resources; in the private sector there generally exist both carrots, in the form of raises and promotions, and sticks, in the form of demotions and firings.

2. Because operating budgets and capital budgets are arrived at through separate processes in the public sector, the opportunity to make tradeoffs between the two is limited; for example, it is more difficult to make coordinated investments in labor-saving equipment.

3. Whereas a private firm generally prospers by satisfying paying customers, a public agency can prosper (i.e., get a bigger budget) even if the customers remain unsatisfied. In fact, paradoxically, sometimes the budget grows even as customer dissatisfaction grows; in this respect a rising crime rate is good for a police department, a housing shortage is good for a housing agency, and an epidemic is good for a health department!

For these reasons, one would expect the private sector to be a more efficient producer of services, and therefore "contracting out" would be better than doing the work "in-house."

Public officials believe that contracting costs less and provides the same or a better quality of service. Surveys of municipal and county officials, in both small and large jurisdictions, reveal these views, which are summarized in table 5.3. About 60 percent of the officials consider contracting to be less costly or no more costly than in-house service, and about 80 percent say it provides better or equal quality of service.

TABLE 5.3

SURVEY OF PUBLIC OFFICIALS' OPINIONS ABOUT CONTRACTING

Opinion	Small jurisdictions[a]	Large jurisdictions[b]
Costs less	40%	41%
Costs same	19	22
Costs more	34	10
Better service	63	33
Same service	14	48
Poorer service	22	15

a. Municipalities with population less than 50,000; N = 89. From Patricia S. Florestano and Stephen B. Gordon, "Public vs. Private: Small Government Contracting with the Private Sector," *Public Administration Review* 40 (January/February 1980): 29-34.

b. Fourteen municipalities and fourteen counties with populations greater than 500,000. From Patricia S. Florestano and Stephen B. Gordon, "Private Provision of Public Services: Contracting by Large Local Governments," *International Journal of Public Administration* 1, no. 3 (1979): 307-27.

Nevertheless, a number of legitimate points, enumerated above, are raised by opponents of contract work, and no matter how persuasive the theoretical analysis or how deep the convictions of public officials, the issue must be resolved by empirical evidence, not by conceptual debate. The next chapter examines the growing body of evidence.

VOUCHERS

Another major privatization technique is the voucher system. As with all arrangements, there are limitations as to how and when to use it. The conditions under which a voucher system will work well can be summarized as follows:

1. There are widespread differences in people's preferences for the service, and these differences are recognized and accepted by the public as legitimate.

2. Individuals have incentives to shop aggressively for the service.

3. Individuals are well informed about market conditions, including the cost and quality of the service and where it may be obtained.

4. There are many competing suppliers of the service, or else start-up costs are low and additional suppliers can readily enter the market if the demand is there.

5. The quality of the service is easily determined by the user.

6. The service is relatively inexpensive and purchased frequently, so the user learns by experience.[17]

The food stamp program is a true voucher system, and it satisfies all these conditions. Medicare and Medicaid fall short of satisfying the last five of these six conditions for the use of vouchers: Consumers have little incentive to shop; they are not well informed about service cost and quality; competition by service providers is conspicuously absent because of regulation by state agencies and medical societies; the quality of service is difficult for consumers to gauge; and the service is purchased infrequently.

Perhaps a better approach to medical care for the indigent is to replace Medicaid "vouchers" with health-insurance vouchers; the latter satisfy the above conditions better than the former. Vouchers that would enable poor people to purchase health insurance offer the prospect of ending the inflationary pressure on health-care costs and bringing them under control.

Other areas where vouchers might be used are in transportation, child care, and legal services. The elderly poor in transit-poor suburbs could be issued vouchers that would be accepted as payment by transportation suppliers such as bus and taxi companies and even private cars. Parents with child-care vouchers could place their children in day-care centers that provided the best combination of price and service. It has been suggested that indigent defendants use vouchers to obtain legal assistance instead of having to rely on either the government's public defender or grant-subsidized legal-aid units; however, this proposed scheme fails to satisfy the conditions listed above.

One of the most promising uses of vouchers is for housing low-income families. As is shown chapter 7, housing vouchers are vastly preferable to public housing (government service) and grants to builders.

Vouchers (i.e., subsidies to consumers) are better than grants (which are subsidies to producers) in that they enhance citizen choice. Some would argue, therefore, that poor people should be given the ultimate voucher (i.e., cash) to strengthen individual choice and responsibility. There is principled opposition to this approach. People have a limited capacity to consume food and shelter, but they have an unlimited capacity to consume money. Therefore, it is easier to control welfare costs for food and shelter than it is to control the cost of unrestricted welfare payments; political pressure would lead to larger allowances, relaxed eligibility requirements, and a growing roster of beneficiaries receiving partial payments for one reason or another. In-kind programs that provide food and shelter are relatively unattractive to the nonpoor and therefore allow more help for the truly needy; people not in need are less likely to try to pass as poor in order to qualify for public housing than to qualify for cash assistance.[18] Moreover, taxpayers are more willing to pay for the necessities of food and shelter for the poor, but are less inclined to trust welfare recipients with unrestricted cash allowances.

Voluntary Action

Privatization can be carried out by relying on voluntary organizations to provide selected goods and services. The organization may be an existing one or may be specifically created to perform the desired activity. In order for individuals to coalesce and form an organization that is willing to do this, there must of course be a commonality of interest sufficient to motivate the people to volunteer their time and money. The community of interest may be geographic, as exemplified by a homeowner or neighborhood association formed to deal with local needs for greater safety, cleaner streets, more recreation, and so forth. Voluntary groups can also come together to provide worthy private goods that deserve to be handled on a collective basis, although the goods may not be localized in a geographic sense. For example, individuals who share similar concerns coalesce to form charitable associations that focus on particular illnesses (e.g., heart, lung, Lou Gehrig's disease, cystic fibrosis) and on specific social problems (e.g., family planning, unwed mothers, adoption, drug abuse). This is privatization by philanthropy.[19]

Existing organizations with a broad purpose may undertake specific services when the need arises. For instance, many religious organizations responded to the plea of New York's mayor for their help in providing food and lodging for some of the city's "street people."

Voluntary organizations can provide services if (1) the need or demand is clear and enduring; (2) enough individuals are motivated to try to satisfy the need; (3) the service is within the technical and material means of the group; and (4) the results are evident to the group and provide psychic rewards and reinforcement.

Summary

The ten institutional arrangements differ in their suitability for providing each of the four classes of goods. Generally speaking, several arrangements are available for supplying each class of goods; collective goods offer the fewest alternatives — only government service, intergovernmental agreement, contract, and voluntary arrangements. Private goods can be supplied by any arrangement.

Many important criteria can be used to evaluate the different arrangements: (1) specificity of the service, (2) availability of producers, (3) efficiency and effectiveness, (4) scale, (5) relationship of costs and benefits, (6) responsiveness to consumers, (7) susceptibility to fraud, (8) economic equity, (9) equity for minorities, (10) responsiveness to government direction, and (11) size of government.

The arrangements differ substantially with respect to this array of important attributes, and no arrangement is ideal. Each has many positive features and lacks others. Many arrangements share each desirable feature. The conclusion to be drawn is that there is generally more than one good way to provide a service; this should be recognized when planning new services or rethinking old ones. A delivery mode should be selected on the basis of reason rather than reflex.

Given these criteria, and the subjective value judgments involved in applying them, one can attempt to rank the different arrangements. For both private and toll goods, the market and voucher arrangements seem best. For common-pool goods, the voluntary and voucher arrangements are best. For collective goods, contract and voluntary arrangements are best.

The most important method for privatizing private and toll goods that are provided by state-owned enterprises is to, first, denationalize the enterprises and, then, allow the market to supply these "nonpublic" goods. On the other hand, the most important arrangements for privatizing "public" services, aside from the market arrangement, are contracting, vouchers, and voluntary action.

Advocates and opponents of "contracting out" each offer a lengthy list of reasons supporting their positions. Theoretical analyses predict that private firms would be more efficient and effective than public agencies, but the debate is best settled on the basis of empirical evidence, which is reviewed in the next part. In any event, certain conditions must be met if contracting is to be a full success.

Likewise, vouchers and voluntary arrangements have many commendable virtues but are also subject to restrictions on their applicability. In other words, there are limits to privatization by any of these means, but then again government provision of goods and services may be even more problematic. It is appropriate then to look at privatization in practice, and compare it with government's performance at the same tasks. This is done in part 3.

Notes

1. E.J. Dionne, Jr., "Unions Awaiting Carey's Quid Pro Quo," *New York Times,* 4 December 1978, B6.

2. Dudley Clendinen, "Problems of Boston Pension System Lead to State and Federal Inquiries," *New York Times,* 21 May 1982, A14.

3. Statement by City Comptroller Harrison J. Goldin in his address at the Privatization Conference, Baruch College, New York, 27 October 1986.

4. *Alternative Service Delivery Systems: Implications for Minority Economic Advancement* (Washington, D.C.: Joint Center for Political Studies, April 1985).

5. Ibid.

6. Walter E. Williams, *The State Against Blacks* (New York: McGraw-Hill, 1982), 113-19.

7. E.S. Savas, "On Equity in Providing Public Services," *Management Science 24,* no. 8 (April 1978): 800-808.

8. James Q. Wilson and Patricia Rachal, "Can the Government Regulate Itself?" *Public Interest,* no. 46 (Winter 1977): 3-14.

9. Michael Knight, "Boston Housing Authority Placed in Receivership," *New York Times,* 26 July 1979, A12.

10. Peter T. Kilborn, "Knowledge Is Clout," *New York Times,* 10 July 1985, A14.

11. Robert F. Durant, Michael R. Fitzgerald, and Larry W. Thomas, "When Government Regulates Itself: The EPA/TVA Air Pollution Control Experience," *Public Administration Review,* no. 43 (May/June 1983): 209-19.

12. Ron Winslow, "TVA Misled U.S. Regulators on Severity of Nuclear Plant Mishap, Staff Study Says," *Wall Street Journal,* 24 August 1984.

13. Ronald Kessler, "The Great Mail Bungle," *Washington Post,* 9 June 1974.

14. *Passing the Bucks: The Contracting Out of Public Services* (Washington, D.C.: American Federation of State, County and Municipal Employees, AFL-CIO, 1983).

15. Joyce Purnick, "Mayor Warns on Union Rules at Javits Center," *New York Times,* 2 November 1985.

16. William Niskanen, Jr., *Bureaucracy and Representative Government* (Chicago:

Aldine/Atherton, 1971); Graham T. Allison, "Public and Private Management: Are They Fundamentally Alike in All Unimportant Respects?" in *Current Issues in Public Administration,* 2d ed., ed. Frederick Lane (New York: St. Martin's, 1982); Thomas E. Borcherding, "Competition, Exclusion and the Optimal Supply of Public Goods," *Journal of Law and Economics* 21 (1978): 111-32; Charles Wolf, Jr., "A Theory of Non-market Failures," *Public Interest,* no. 55 (Spring 1979): 114-33; Lawrence N. Bailis, "Comparative Analysis of the Delivery of Human Services in the Public and Private Sectors," (manuscript, Heller Graduate School, Brandeis University, 1984); Anthony Downs, *Inside Bureaucracy* (Boston: Little, Brown, 1967); Hal Rainey, "Public Agencies and Private Firms: Incentive Structures, Goals and Individual Roles," *Administration and Society,* August 1983, 207-42; Marshall W. Meyer, " 'Bureaucratic' versus 'Profit' Organizations," in *Research in Organizational Behavior,* vol. 4 (Greenwich, Conn.: JAI Press, 1982), 89-125; Lyle C. Fitch, "Increasing the Role of the Private Sector in Providing Public Services," in *Improving the Quality of Urban Management,* ed. Willis D. Hawley and David Rogers (Beverly Hills, Calif.: Sage, 1974), 501-59; Peter F. Drucker, "Managing the Public Service Institution," *Public Interest,* no. 33 (Fall 1973): 43-60; and James T. Bennett and Manuel H. Johnson, "Tax Reduction without Sacrifice: Private-sector Production of Public Services," *Public Finance Quarterly* 8, no. 4 (October 1980): 363-96.

17. Gary Bridge, "Citizen Choice in Public Services: Voucher Systems," in *Alternatives for Delivering Public Services: Toward Improved Performance,* ed. E.S. Savas (Boulder, Colo.: Westview, 1977).

18. David T. Ellwood and Lawrence H. Summers, "Is Welfare Really the Problem?" *Public Interest,* no. 83 (Spring 1986): 57-78.

19. For an extended discussion of this concept, see R.Q. Armington and William D. Ellis, *More: The Rediscovery of American Common Sense* (Chicago: Regnery Gateway, 1986).

PART THREE

Privatization
in Practice

6. Applications in Physical and Commercial Services

The previous chapters demonstrate that many service arrangements exist, each with distinctive attributes, and that there are several kinds of goods, each with characteristics that affect its provision. In brief, there are several ways to provide each of the goods and services that a society wants and needs, and some ways will be better than others. Intense public interest is focused on private-sector alternatives, primarily market, contract, franchise, voucher, and voluntary arrangements. These are the privatization options, where the producer is the private sector instead of government. The privatization debate centers on these arrangements.

This chapter focuses on the delivery of what might be termed the physical amenities of modern life—the maintenance of a clean and adequate water supply, well-cared-for streets and street lighting, efficient transportation and communication systems, and the like. The next chapter turns to the provision of more personal services to the public—for example, decent housing, affordable health care, protection from criminals, and educational opportunities. (This division is admittedly arbitrary.) In both chapters the emphasis is on actual studies and experiences with alternative service-delivery arrangements.

The purpose of these two chapters is threefold:

1. To examine the most authoritative, empirical studies that compare the different arrangements
2. To discuss privatization as it has been or may be applied to various services
3. To describe particularly interesting or thought-provoking examples of privatization

Each chapter is organized by subject area; for example, in this chapter there are sections on street services and transportation, while chapter 7 focuses on private-sector alternatives in housing and social services. Each section includes authoritative comparative studies, reported and potential applications, and anecdotal observations and musings.

The Public Versus Private Debate

The debate about which is better, public or private provision of service, has usually generated more heat than light since the subject was effectively raised as a public policy issue in 1971.[1] Subsequent research and writings in the mid-1970s, by Savas, Poole, and others, resulted in media interest and a counteroffensive from the dominant public-employee union that felt threatened;[2] a similar union in England reacted much the same way several years later.[3] Numerous publications and tracts addressed the subject in the late 1970s and early 1980s. Noteworthy among them were the writings of Rothbard, Poole, Frazier and Olson, Bennett and Johnson, Fisk et al., Hatry, Savas, Spann, Borcherding, and the International City Management Association.[4]

The 1980s saw an explosion of interest in privatization, at both local and national levels in the United States, and in the form of denationalization in Europe and in developing countries. In local governments throughout the United States, the impetus was a result of post-Proposition 13 budgetary pressures and reduced federal grants; also, the concept was actively promoted by the U.S. Department of Housing and Urban Development (where I served as assistant secretary). With respect to federal government activities, the Reagan administration unveiled an ambitious array of privatization proposals in 1985.

The issue of which arrangement is best should properly be addressed as an empirical question, not an ideological or emotional one. There is ample room for values to enter the debate, but surely some light can be shed simply by looking at the available, credible evidence. The relevant criteria to use in comparing arrangements are efficiency, effectiveness, and equity. *Efficiency* refers to the economically appropriate allocation of resources. The most efficient arrangement is the one that produces the greatest output per unit of input, for example, the lowest cost for a given level and quality of service. The most *effective* arrangement is the one whose output most nearly satisfies the need; for example, meeting demands and achieving customer satisfaction, as revealed by low complaint levels. An *equitable* arrangement permits fair distribution of the service.

There are many pitfalls in studying the relative performance of public and private service arrangements. To begin with, one must go beyond individual instances; for example, the claim that contracting is better because Agency A switched from in-house to contract service for custodial work and found it superior can readily be countered by finding and pointing to Agency B, which had the opposite experience. Many of the early references identified above were able to cite only individual, anecdotal experiences because few comprehensive, scientific evaluations had been conducted up to that time. An illustration of this kind of debate is provided by the Reason Foundation in California and the American Federation of State, County and Municipal Employees, who are tireless advocates of opposing positions; the former issues a steady stream of informative newsletters that cite successful instances of privatization,[5] while the latter counters with occasional book-length broadsides that highlight instances of corruption and unsuccessful efforts in contracting.[6]

In a slightly more analytical approach, simple tabulations of public and private examples are frequently offered as evidence of the superiority of one arrangement or another. ("Five cities that contract for such-and-such service have 38 percent lower cost on average than seven cities that provide the service directly.") The problem with this approach is the hidden assumption that all other variables are canceled out and the observed difference resulted only from public or private provision of the service. Generally, many factors affect performance, and some of them may be correlated with the arrangement. For example, if one arrangement is more common in one part of the country than in another, climate and regional wage rates may affect performance, and if they are not explicitly taken into account, their impact would be attributed incorrectly to the arrangement.

Service costs are generally easier to measure than service quality, yet it is imperative that quality be controlled when costs are compared. It is meaningless to point out that one arrangement is more efficient than another without reporting the level and quality of service as well.

The ideal study would begin by carefully defining the service under examination. If it is turf maintenance in a public park, for example, it is necessary to specify which activities are included: seeding, fertilizing, mowing, insect control, fungus control, edging, and so on. A suitably large number of agencies, companies, or communities will be needed in the study if one hopes to arrive at statistically significant findings, and the study sample should be randomly selected from a larger population of eligibles. Performance variables that measure efficiency and effectiveness have to be specified, along with the variables that affect them. On-site data collection that rigorously follows a standard framework is virtually mandatory to avoid serious problems, and sophisticated analysis is necessary in order to distinguish the contribution of each variable and to isolate the unalloyed effect of service arrangement.[7]

Too often, researchers will take the easy way out by collecting and analyzing data that are readily available, rather than undertake the difficult job of obtaining data that are truly desired. This is like the drunk who was crawling around on his hands and knees one night near a lamppost. When asked by a police officer what he was doing, the drunk replied with slurred speech that he was looking for his watch, but then added that he had lost it down the block. The officer asked quizzically, "If you lost it down the block, then why are you looking for it here? Why don't you look there?" Whereupon the drunk replied sagely, "Because there's more light over here." Alas, many researchers rely on data that are easy to find instead of working hard to obtain the data they really should use.

With this understanding about the nature of the evidence, let us now proceed to examine privatization in practice.

Solid-Waste Management

The service studied most extensively and most thoroughly to determine the relative performance of different arrangements is residential solid-waste (or refuse) collection. The evidence is overwhelming and clear: Contract collection is substantially more efficient than municipal collection, and no less effective.

EFFICIENCY

The comparative efficiency of solid-waste collection arrangements has been investigated by detailed, nationwide studies covering the United States, Canada, Switzerland, and Japan, as well as regional studies in Connecticut, California, and the midwestern United States. Nine major studies were conducted by different researchers, some in government and some in academia, over a ten-year span.[8] The results are strikingly consistent and mutually corroborative, as shown in table 6.1. Careful examination of these studies leads one to conclude that municipal collection is about 35 percent more costly than contract collection, although a range from 14 to 124 percent is reported. The single report that found no difference had a relatively small sample size and was restricted geographically to only one county in Missouri.

The most thorough studies (by Savas and Stevens, and by Stevens) carefully included the cities' costs of contract preparation, bidding, monitoring the contractors' performance, contract administration, and the like in the cost of the contract work. Even so, as noted, the cost of municipal collection is about 35 percent greater than the total cost to the city of contract collection.

Moreover, while this is the relevant figure as far as government budgets are concerned, the true difference between the two arrangements is even greater. One should take into account the fact that the cost of contract collection to the city is comprised of administration costs (4.4 percent of the total) and the price of the contract (95.6 percent of the total).[9] The contract price, in turn, includes both profits and taxes, as well as the actual cost of performing the service. That is, private firms generally pay various fees and taxes—local business license, vehicle registration, property taxes, fuel taxes, income taxes—that governments do not. Industry sources in the United States estimate that the sum of all the fees and taxes paid to federal, state, and local governments amounts to 15 percent of revenues. The cost of these taxes is, of course, included in the price charged by the firms. Therefore, when a resident pays government $100 for municipal service, he gets only that service. But when he pays a price of $100 for contract service (via the government as purchasing agent), he receives not only refuse-collection service but also a bonus of $15 worth of other, unidentified government services that the firm, in effect, rebates to the resident via its taxes. When this adjustment is made, one sees that the cost to the resident for municipal service is, in fact, 58 percent greater than contract service.

One more bit of analysis can profitably be carried out. We have discussed the effect of taxes included in the price of contract service; now let us examine the effect of profits. Inspection of the annual reports of several major waste-management firms shows that profits amount to roughly 10 percent of revenues. One can use this figure to make a further calculation, which leads to the conclusion that it costs municipal agencies 88 percent more to perform the work than it costs private firms. To summarize:

1. A municipal budget director has to allocate 35 percent more money for municipal collection than for contract collection of equivalent quality.

2. A resident has to pay 58 percent more for municipal collection than for contract collection, after taking into consideration the tax rebate he receives indirectly from the contractor.

3. It costs the municipal agency 88 percent more to perform the same work; that is, the agency is much less productive.

The reasons why government is significantly less productive are attributed to the use of more men to do the same amount of work, more absences by workers, fewer households served per hour, and less productive vehicles.[10] These findings in the United States are paralleled in Canada.[11]

A powerful illustration of the combined effect on productivity of these factors can be seen in table 6.2, which is based on my study of two similar cities located only 22 miles apart in the New York metropolitan area. The private contractor collected 2.8 times as much waste per worker per day as did the municipal agency.

The four reasons cited above to explain the low productivity of government can be considered immediate causes. The ultimate cause is the absence of competition; when a government agency performs the work directly, it usually acts as a monopoly. When an agency is forced to compete with a contractor, it can be made more productive, and even match the contractor's performance.[12] Chapter 8 discusses how to introduce effective competition.

TABLE 6.1

SUMMARY OF COMPARATIVE STUDIES OF PUBLIC AND

Author	Study site	Date reported	Data period	Number of cities surveyed	Number of cities analyzed	City size
Savas and Stevens	United States	1975	1974	439	315	2,500-720,000
Kemper and Quigley	Connecticut	1976	1972-74	N.R.	101	1,100-158,000
Kitchen	Canada	1976	N.R.	142[a]	48	Over 10,000
Pommerehne and Frey	Switzerland	1977	1970	112	103	5,000-423,000
Collins and Downes	St. Louis County	1977	N.R.	53	53	Under 500-65,000
Petrovic and Jaffee	Midwestern United States	1977	1974	149	83	25,000-180,000
Hamada and Aoki	Japan	1981	1980	N.R.	211	N.R.
McDavid	Canada	1984	1982	N.R.	109	Over 10,000
Stevens	Los Angeles SCSA[d]	1984	1983	20	20	10,000-200,000

NOTE: N.R. = not reported.

SOURCE: Adapted from E.S. Savas, "Public vs. Private Refuse Collection: A Critical Review of the Evidence," *Journal of Urban Analysis* 6 (1979): 1-13.

PRIVATE RESIDENTIAL REFUSE COLLECTION

Means of data collection	Distinguished private and contract collection?	Distinguished collection and disposal costs?	Findings
Visit, phone, mail	Yes	Yes	Cost of municipal collection is 29% to 37% higher than the price of contract collection in cities larger than 50,000 in population; no difference in effectiveness.
Mail, phone	Yes	Yes	"Cost of municipal collection is 14% to 43% higher than the price of contract collection."
Mail, phone	No[b]	N.R.	"Municipally run refuse collection tends to be much more expensive." "Municipalities could economize by contracting out."
Mail	No	N.R.	"Public production of refuse collection seems to be subject to higher average costs than private production."
Visit	Yes	Yes	"No clear pattern emerges."
Visit, mail	Yes	Yes	"Costs . . . tend to be less for a private firm under contract . . . than for a municipally operated system." Cost of municipal collection is 15% higher than the price.
N.R.	Yes[c]	Yes[c]	Municipal collection costs 124% more than contract collection.
Mail, phone	Yes[b]	Yes[c]	Public collection appears to be 40% to 50% more costly than contract collection.
Visit	Yes	Yes	Municipal collection costs 42% more than contract collection; no quality difference.

a. Kitchen reports only that he surveyed all cities over 10,000 in population. There were 142 such cities in 1970.
b. McDavid reports that "nearly all private firms operate via contract"; this may also apply to Kitchen's study.
c. While not stated explicitly, this appears to be the case.
d. Standard Consolidated Statistical Area.

TABLE 6.2

COMPARISON OF MUNICIPAL AND CONTRACT RESIDENTIAL COLLECTION

	City A	City B
Population	70,000	74,000
Area (sq. mi.)	4.3	3.8
Pickups per week	3	3
Pickup location	curb	curb
Arrangement	municipal	contract
Truck shifts per week	63	39
Men per truck	4	2
Man-days per week	237	78
Tons collected per man-day	3.40	9.67
Productivity index	100	284

Thus far in this section, we have been comparing the efficiency of government and contract service. What about market and franchise arrangements? Both are common in the United States, as was indicated in chapter 4. Under the market arrangement, each individual household makes its own arrangement with a private firm. One would expect this cost to be higher than the cost of contract collection because of economies of contiguity and billing costs. The contract firm collects from every household in the area, and this is more efficient—because there are more customers per unit area—than a market arrangement where different firms may collect on the same block. A franchised firm operating in a community with mandatory collection—where every household must subscribe to the service — is like a contract firm (and like a municipal agency, for that matter) in that it realizes these economies of contiguity. Billing costs are a significant cost factor for firms operating under either a franchise or a market system; the cost of sending out bills to each household, and losses resulting from unpaid bills, are not incurred by a contract firm, which receives lump-sum payments from the city in response to a single bill.[13]

EFFECTIVENESS

Contract service is demonstrably more efficient than municipal service, but is it possible that this is achieved because the service is poorer in quality? This question was settled by studying the effectiveness of different service arrangements through a large-scale, nationwide survey of U.S. households. A total of 8,166 telephone interviews were conducted with randomly selected households in eighty-two randomly selected cities. Private collection service, that is, the market arrangement, received the highest evaluation, with 93 percent of respondents rating it good or excellent, compared to 90 percent for municipal service and 89 percent for contract service. From the standpoint of public policy,

"The differences among the three collection arrangements are too small to matter, and . . . the decision as to which arrangement to employ should therefore be based on efficiency."[14]

EQUITY

Contract service is no less equitable than municipal service and may even be more equitable. An important aspect of equity, it will be recalled from chapter 5, refers to fairness of service allocation or delivery. Because contract and municipal service are both paid for by municipal revenues, there is no difference between them on this score. I have experienced the following, however: A municipal agency that cannot meet its daily collection schedule (because of vehicle breakdown or absenteeism—both are relatively common with municipal service[15]) will sometimes handle the matter by postponing collection in the poorer sections of the city; these generally have less political influence and often are minority neighborhoods. This is discriminatory. In contrast, the contractor tends to look at the city merely as a workload to be completed, rather than as a set of political districts to be placated differentially. Moreover, a city generally finds it easier to assure that the contractor completes his daily collection route (and may impose a penalty if he fails to do so) than to order overtime for its own workforce. In fact, municipal agencies are 10 percent more likely to miss a collection than are contract firms.[16]

I can report another personal observation relating to equity, as was already referred to in chapter 5. A city that switched from municipal to contract collection had a residency clause in its contract that was intended to achieve a racial composition in the contractor's workforce that matched the composition of the city's population. This had never been reached in the city's own sanitation department, but it was readily reached by the contractor.

In these two respects, service quality and employment, contract service was observed to be more equitable than governmental service in its effect on minority groups.

ANTICOMPETITIVE BEHAVIOR

No discussion of the private-sector role in waste collection would be complete without discussing illegal behavior in this industry. Numerous instances of such behavior have been reported over many years, particularly in and around several large cities, and each case attracts widespread attention and notoriety.

The issue involves anticompetitive behavior—the allocation of customers or territories among private firms in the waste-hauling business—sometimes with threats or acts of violence against a firm that attempts to compete against an entrenched firm. Such incidents are not restricted to a single ethnic group—

contrary to popular folklore in parts of the United States—nor are they unique to the United States.

The waste industry points out, with considerable justification, that the entire industry is unfairly smeared when a waste hauler breaks the law, whereas illegal acts by bankers, stockbrokers, doctors, and lawyers are treated as isolated incidents, as are price-fixing conspiracies in other businesses.

There is more to it than that. Traditionally, in all cultures, waste removal was a low-status occupation. New workers were recruited primarily from a limited labor pool that consisted of family, friends, and others from the same caste or village. Thus, the work was dominated by untouchables in India, Coptic Christians in Egypt, immigrants from southern Italy in the northeastern United States, Armenian immigrants in southern California, Dutch immigrants in Chicago, Albanians from Yugoslavia in Austria, and Turks in Germany. The resulting tight social network made it easy for members to agree on ways to carry out the arduous and unpleasant work in an amicable, cooperative, noncompetitive manner. Nevertheless, however innocently the sociological pattern may have evolved, the end result can be viewed by an outsider as a conspiracy in restraint of trade.

In the United States, the industry has been changing rapidly, in technology, size, sophistication, and business organization. "Mom and Pop" operations, one-truck firms, and family-owned businesses are disappearing, as are old patterns of association. The industry is rapidly evolving, and in almost all areas of the country it has long since reached the point where its participants are no different from people in other fields of endeavor in terms of obeying the law.

CONCLUSION

Conclusive evidence from a number of authoritative studies shows that the contract arrangement is the most efficient. It is more efficient than free-market service, and substantially more efficient, as effective, and at least as equitable as municipal service. Though government service can be thought of as a permanent monopoly, and the market arrangement as continuous competition, the contract arrangement can be viewed as a temporary monopoly or periodic competition—the two are equivalent—and this is the best arrangement for this service.

The best approach for a city with municipal collection is to divide the city into sections and seek competitive bids for each section *both from private firms and from its own department.* This tactic assures the maximum degree of competition and protects the city against possible collusion by contractors.[17] It can be used by any city with a population greater than 100,000 to create sections of at least 30,000 people; these are large enough to achieve economies of scale in refuse collection.[18]

About 35 percent of cities in the United States were using contract collection for residential refuse in 1982,[19] up from 21 percent in 1975.[20] This is a remarkable growth of two-thirds in just seven years, no doubt attributable to the growing evidence cited above. Contracting for this service is also a growing phenomenon in England, West Germany, South America, and the Middle East.

SOLID-WASTE DISPOSAL

Before leaving the subject of solid waste, one should note the role of the private sector in solid-waste disposal, in addition to collection. Disposal at landfills has long been provided by the private sector, through market and contract arrangements, and by government. Government also owns many disposal facilities (landfills and transfer stations) but contracts for their operation.

A new public service that has emerged at the local level is resource recovery, an innovative disposal technology. Private firms are financing, constructing, and operating these capital-intensive plants in various intricate contract and franchise arrangements with local governments. Unlike collection and conventional disposal, which are gradually being privatized, resource recovery originated in the private sector and is already privatized. Had this technology emerged a decade or two earlier, the facilities might have been routinely government owned and operated. Instead, resource recovery may be the forerunner of other services arising in an era of "less government," an era of privatized public services.

Street Services

Other commonplace, physical services that lend themselves readily to careful measurement are to be found on city streets. As with solid-waste services, mounting evidence shows that privatized arrangements are superior, and as a result more communities are switching to them.

STREET SWEEPING

A careful study in twenty cities found that, per curb mile, the cost of municipal street sweeping was 43 percent greater than the cost of contract sweeping. This is for the same frequency and quality of service (the latter as rated by street-cleanliness surveys), and for similar urban conditions. The difference was attributed to greater productivity by contract crews (i.e., more miles swept per hour), more paid time off for municipal crews, more chiefs and fewer Indians in the municipal government agency, and better equipment maintenance by contractors. Costs incurred by a city to prepare and let contracts, and to monitor the contract work, were properly included in the cost of contract service.[21]

STREET REPAVING

Street repaving, that is, the application of a new asphalt overlay on an existing street, was studied in depth for both municipal and contract arrangements. It was found that the work performed by municipal agencies was 96 percent more costly than the work performed by private firms under contract to cities. Moreover, the quality of the contract work—as determined by examination of the subsequent condition of the surface—was slightly better than the municipal work.

The immediate reason why contractors are almost twice as efficient as municipal agencies is that the former averaged 4,508 tons of asphalt per full-time worker per year, while the latter averaged only a quarter of that, 1,180 tons. This enormous difference more than compensated for the higher wages paid by contractors ($29,049 annually vs. $18,384) and the higher prices they paid for asphalt ($27.58 per ton compared to $23.38 paid by municipalities). The underlying factor behind the contractors' high productivity is the use of larger crews on a job site, more experienced equipment operators, more on-site supervision, more equipment, and better, more expensive equipment.[22]

ROAD CONSTRUCTION AND MAINTENANCE

Road construction and maintenance have been looked at in developing countries, where they are an essential aspect of economic development. A World Bank report states that "experience has demonstrated that building institutional capacities for road maintenance is far more difficult than building roads."[23] The World Bank is trying to encourage countries to place greater reliance on the private sector as the best way to build that institutional capacity.

In the few cases where the true costs of government work were fully recorded, the cost advantages of competitive contracting were evident—the former cost about 60 percent more than the latter. Inefficiences in the management of state road-repair agencies are commonplace. They are top-heavy with professional, administrative, technical, and clerical staff (39 percent of all the workers in one agency, compared to 15 to 20 percent for private firms) and have low utilization rates for expensive major equipment. Salaries are unrealistically low and fail to motivate the staff. Civil service status induces complacency and leads to a reluctance to take risks. Managers are frustrated by restrictions on the freedom to hire and fire, and by the use of employment as a social or political tool. Many governments would rather cover financial losses than liquidate inefficient public enterprises, and so the latter become permanent drains on national budgets.[24]

Problems are not limited to developing countries. A 1984 survey of fifty-five state and local highway officials in the United States by *Roads* magazine disclosed that, by a 2-to-1 ratio, the officials planned to rely more heavily on contractors for road construction and maintenance because they "are convinced that the private contractor can do the job more cost-effectively than public crews and equipment can."[25]

POTHOLE PATROL

As a final cameo on privatization in street repair, let us look at the pothole inspector, who held one of the classic "no-show" patronage jobs in the nineteenth century—typically as a reward for *real* work performed earlier, during an election campaign. Personal financial considerations now are very different, and yesteryear's pothole inspector has given way to today's privatized pothole patrol.

Under a law passed in 1980, a law eagerly sought by the city, New York could no longer be sued for injuries or damages caused by a pothole or broken sidewalk unless the city had been informed previously about the existence of the particular defect. In retrospect, what happened next was inevitable. The city's negligence lawyers, seeing their livelihood threatened, banded together and formed the Big Apple Pothole and Sidewalk Protection Corporation. This civic-spirited new institution has workers who roam the streets and mark the defects they spot on maps that are then formally turned over to the city's Transportation Department! The number of such defects stood at about 750,000 in 1985, which suggests that the lawyers would not soon starve for lack of work.[26]

A moment of reflection is in order. While one can be amused by the transparency of the lawyers' self-interest, the fact remains that their self-interest serves a public purpose. This voluntary arrangement sprang into being to satisfy a public need. The city government, although responsible for maintaining the public thoroughfares, wanted to avoid the consequences of neglecting its responsibility. Thanks to privatization, however, the city was forced at least to weigh the cost of doing its job against the cost of accident claims it must pay to people harmed by its neglect. The lawyers, in pursuit of their private gain, achieve a public benefit—just as Adam Smith foretold.

PRIVATE STREETS

This avenue of thought leads naturally to privatized streets. We have seen that a city government may try to evade its responsibility as the owner of the streets; is there another alternative? Writers of the libertarian school have long advocated private ownership of streets and roads.[27] Private bridges and toll roads were commonplace and still exist. Moreover, in the United States it is possible to find local streets owned by neighborhood associations. In such cases, covenants to deeds usually require that someone buying a piece of property in the area join the homeowners' association and pay dues for street cleaning and repair, snow removal, security patrol, and the like. In St. Louis, numerous local groups formed nonprofit organizations, bought title to their streets, and maintain both the streets and their properties. The stability provided by such ownership gives people the confidence to invest this way. Rothbard offers a provocative scenario in which the streets and sidewalks of Times Square in New York City are owned by a "Times Square Merchants Association." The merchants would be strongly motivated by their self-interest to supply plentiful, courteous, and efficient private police protection, as well as clean and pleasant surroundings, in order to attract and retain customers. The area then would be like a large surburban shopping mall, except that the latter has indoor streets.[28]

This imaginative concept may not be so far-fetched: In New York City it is now possible to create Business Improvement Districts and Special Assessment Districts in which local merchants and/or residents can choose to levy a special tax in the district, to be spent as they see fit on local improvements.

STREET LIGHTING

In most communities in the United States, the street lights are owned and maintained by the local public utility. This is an old and venerable tradition, dating back to the days of Thomas Alva Edison. Indeed, street lighting was often the basis for creating companies to generate electricity, and electric wiring to illuminate streets preceded electric wiring to illuminate building interiors. But the original rationale for street-light ownership and operation by an electric utility company has become outdated. For example, one cannot even contemplate a situation where the local utility owns a lamp *inside* someone's home and sends an employee to replace a burned-out bulb. Yet this is the common practice with respect to the lamp *outside* a person's home, the street lamp on property that belongs to a private or public owner.

The system just described is a contract arrangement, where the local government pays the local electric company for street lighting. More and more communities, however, are discovering economic advantages to partitioning, or unbundling, their street-lighting services — separating ownership, maintenance, and electric power. Specifically, they are buying the lights, contracting with one or more private firms for maintenance, and continuing to buy electric power from the utility under a contract arrangement.

Rigorous studies of the issue have yet to be published, but a major accounting firm that has specialized in this field estimates that cities achieve an annual rate of return of 25 percent when they buy their street lights from the utility, primarily because of their lower costs of capital, reduced maintenance costs, and the elimination of discontinuance fees when they remove lights.[29] (The latter is increasingly commonplace as cities take advantage of new lighting technology and redesign their systems.)

New York City officials are very satisfied with their current system, in which the city owns the lights, private firms under eight separate district contracts maintain them, and the utility supplies the power. Philadelphia has a similar system, but uses only one maintenance contractor. Both cities report declining costs, both in absolute terms and on a per-light basis, since they introduced effective competition for maintenance under this system. Philadelphia estimates that its costs are 30 percent less than they would be if the system were still owned by the local utility company.[30]

From the perspective of city governments, there are many good reasons for assuming full ownership of their street lights, while contracting for maintenance and electric power:

1. The public looks to its municipal officials in all matters concerning street lights; citizen requests and demands for installing, upgrading, repairing, changing, or eliminating street lights are directed at their local government.

2. Municipalities raise taxes to pay for street-lighting service, but they have little control over the service. The public holds local officials accountable, but the latter feel they have too little authority over the service.

3. Municipal ownership leads to lower costs because cities generally have a lower cost of capital than do utilities.

4. With municipal ownership, it is easier for cities and towns to upgrade their systems and to install more energy-efficient lights. It appears that utility-owned lighting systems are often a generation behind in lighting technology; this has sometimes been attributed to a utility's contentment with the status quo, because the utility keeps earning higher revenues both from continued amortization payments for systems installed years ago and from the excess energy consumed by inefficient old lights. Municipal ownership can therefore be considered an energy conservation measure.

5. In addition to the administrative ease of designing and implementing an upgraded system, municipalities that own their lights may be able to achieve lower installation costs by using private contractors.

6. Many cities that own their street lights contract with private firms for maintenance and repairs. I estimate that utility-provided maintenance of utility-owned lights costs about 50 percent more than contract maintenance of municipally owned lights.

7. With the introduction of new lighting that provides more lumens with fewer watts, municipalities are often able to eliminate some light poles as parts

of the city are redeveloped. If the municipality owns the lights, it is not subject to discontinuance fees when it makes these changes.

8. When the municipality owns the light poles, it becomes more feasible administratively to collect damages from motorists whose cars strike the poles.

9. Street-light maintenance can be better integrated with other municipal street services, such as traffic-light maintenance, street signage, and bus-shelter maintenance, particularly as some cities develop computerized data systems to keep track of the location, condition, and servicing of their assorted "street furnishings."

10. The municipality can more easily provide different levels of lighting in different neighborhoods, as requested by the latter, and can charge local property owners accordingly.

11. Municipalities may save money if the cost of energy for street lights is isolated from other charges and is paid for in proportion to its usage. At present there is often little relation between the two because this service is commonly treated as an afterthought by state public utility commissions that approve the rates.

The significance of this new approach to street lighting should be understood in a larger context, for it illustrates a broader principle. A traditional contract service is being separated into its three components. One of the components, ownership of the lights, is being "municipalized." Another component, maintenance, is being contracted out to a new kind of private contractor. The third component, electric power, continues to be provided by the customary contractor. This new and very different institutional arrangement appears to be the best for providing this service. Other services, too, might be improved if they are separated into their component parts and if better arrangements can be instituted for each of them. As I show in chapter 7, a similar process is under way in hospitals.

TRAFFIC-SIGNAL MAINTENANCE

Another public-works function that can be handled by governmental, intergovernmental, or contract arrangements is the maintenance of traffic signals. Which arrangement is best? Twenty cities in California, half with contract and half with municipal maintenance of traffic signals, were studied in 1983. Compared to contractors, municipal agencies do less preventive maintenance, have older systems that take longer to repair, and assign fewer intersections for each repairman to maintain (only forty-three intersections per man, compared to seventy for the contractor). As a result, municipally delivered maintenance is 56 percent more costly than service of the same quality provided by private contractors. (The cost to the municipality of letting and supervising the contract was properly included in the cost of contract service.)[31]

Transportation

Transportation services, historically private or toll goods, offer obvious opportunities for privatization. Considerable movement in this direction is evident, on land and sea, in the air, and in space.

URBAN BUSES

Urban mass transportation was once supplied entirely by market arrangements in the United States, but it was gradually monopolized and "municipalized." Nevertheless, there are enough private bus systems in operation, in the United States and elsewhere, that considerable information is available for comparative studies.

Five studies in the United States, Australia, and England examined the average costs per vehicle mile of comparable public and private urban bus services. Buses were essentially identical in size and amenities. Results were striking and strikingly similar, despite differences in the nations studied, in the researchers, and in the time periods studied (although there may have been some unreported differences in routes): Public costs were 54 to 100 percent greater than private costs. Where private firms in the United States, selected by competitive bidding, were awarded contracts to take over the provision of public transit service, cost reductions of 50 to 60 percent or more were achieved, meaning that, as above, public costs were close to twice the private costs.[32]

Corroboration of these findings comes from another international quarter; analysts from the World Bank conducted an in-depth study of three cities in developing countries that each had similar bus operations in the public and private sectors. They concluded that the cost of government bus service is 68 to 100 percent greater than the cost of private, market-based bus service and that the quality of the private services "is not markedly inferior and [is] usually superior to the public bus operation."[33]

Additional comparisons in the United States are consistent with these findings. A report by the New York State Department of Transportation showed that private buses in Westchester County operated at a cost of $3.18 per mile, whereas a public bus authority in Nassau County, a similar surburban area, had a cost of $4.09 per mile, or 28 percent more. (Informed of the difference, the general manager of the public agency explained, "They don't have the political hacks to take care of, like we do."[34]) According to the Urban Mass Transportation Administration, public bus lines in California provide service at a cost 28 percent higher than comparable private bus lines, and in Phoenix a public bus line has operating costs 163 percent higher than a comparable private bus line.[35]

A limited audit of bus operations in New York City was conducted by the state comptroller. The government bus-operating agency spent 1,518 maintenance hours per bus per year, compared with 1,025 for franchised buses.[36] Unfortunately, no evidence is presented on miles or hours of bus operation or on the number of passengers carried per bus, which could account for differing maintenance needs. Another report from New York shows that public buses generate $16,694 of annual revenues per employee, while the corresponding statistic for comparable private lines in the area charging equivalent fares is $26,279; this means more total employees per passenger for public bus lines.[37] A more recent and detailed report comparing public buses with franchised private buses in New York City is summarized in table 6.3. The public buses had an operating cost per vehicle mile 32 percent greater than that of the private buses, and a 12 percent greater cost per passenger. Moreover, the private buses realized 74 percent more vehicle miles per employee hour.[38]

TABLE 6.3

COMPARISON OF PUBLIC AND PRIVATE BUS OPERATIONS
IN NEW YORK CITY, 1984

	Private	Public
Cost efficiency		
Cost/vehicle mile	$6.16	$8.07
Cost/vehicle hr	$53.17	$62.57
Vehicle mile/employee hr	3.98	2.29
Vehicle hr/employee hr	.46	.30
Service effectiveness		
Passengers/vehicle mile	4.66	5.41
Passengers/vehicle hr	40.24	41.97
Cost effectiveness		
Operating revenues/cost	.67	.60
Cost/passenger	$1.32	$1.49
Passenger revenues/passenger	.85	.60

SOURCE: New York State Department of Transportation, "1985 Report on Transit Operating Performance in New York State," 111-52.

Competitive bidding of contracts to provide fixed-route bus service is likely to lead to particularly efficient operations. There are not many communities in the United States where such bidding (as distinguished from sole-source contracting or negotiated bidding) takes place, but an examination of seventeen bus systems where competitive bidding was introduced showed that public operations had been 40 percent more costly than contract operations.[39]

School buses offer additional opportunities for comparative studies. A large-scale study of 275 school districts in Indiana concluded that publicly owned and operated buses were 12 percent more costly than contracted buses. The authors of the study hypothesize that the difference is relatively small because public and private school buses operate in close proximity, a condition that may lead to competitive pressures.[40] Similarly, a study of school buses in the State of New York found that contract bus costs were lower than the costs of buses operated directly by school boards.[41]

Bus services in the Federal Republic of Germany are operated both by private firms under state contracts and by the state directly. Blankart summarizes the findings and reports that the nationwide average of municipal bus transport costs are 160 percent more per kilometer than the contract price paid to private bus firms for comparable services.[42]

Other studies conclude that public takeovers lead to a 28 percent increase in operating costs per bus-hour, and subsidies result in higher wages and higher costs.[43]

The differences between public and private costs have been attributed to competition, labor costs, management flexibility in decision making, and appropriate scale.

Competition. The effect of competition becomes clear when noncompetitive contracts are compared with competitively bid contracts: The latter are far less costly than the former.[44] This finding tends to confirm the dominant importance of competition, which is in accordance with both theory and common sense.

Labor Costs. With respect to labor, driver costs per vehicle mile were found to be about twice as high for large organizations as for small ones, and also twice as high for large vehicles as for small ones. Therefore, to the extent that public bus services tend to be large and to operate conventional, large buses, this factor helps explain their high cost. High labor costs help explain why Calcutta's public buses are twice as costly as similar private buses: Because of union pressure, the public bus agency employs a whopping 30 employees per bus![45]

The other principal reasons why private buses there make money while public buses lose money, although the fares are the same, is that half the public buses are out of commission at any time, and fare evasion is said to be 25 percent on public buses and negligible on private ones because the employees on the latter are paid a percentage of the revenues.

Another illustration of high public-sector labor costs in mass transit has been unearthed in the New York subways: Token sellers were being paid $21,888 annually while mid-level tellers in banks, whose jobs require substantially higher skills, were earning $11,767.[46]

Management Flexibility. Management in small private bus lines is flexible enough to institute various economical operating policies such as part-time drivers and worker-drivers, conveniently located bus storage, and smaller vehicles.[47] Particularly enlightening is the practical testimony of the general manager of a privatized regional bus line in West Germany that had been spun off from a deficit-ridden public agency:

> We can make decisions faster and move around rolling stock, money, and people in a way that's more flexible than a government enterprise. We make do with a smaller management team and don't have to worry about politicians and lobbyists who affect the fare and scheduling policies of public enterprises. Besides, we are not gagged by the labor regulations covering public employees. [The firm] supplements its earnings by chartering buses for excursions and vacation groups. . . . [B]ehind its competitive edge: much smaller maintenance staffs compared with the excessive and underused work crews of the public companies and much more low-cost initiative and innovation. . . . Flexibility in disposing of used vehicles is another plus. Whereas public enterprises have a fixed life-cycle policy for vehicles, private operations have flexibility to sell off their used units at any time depending on vehicle and market conditions. Greater freedom in establishing wages, fixing fares and bargaining for vehicles and supplies is also cited as a reason behind the competitive advantage of the privatized transportation providers . . . drivers are cross-trained as mechanics and vice versa. When the maintenance staff is fully booked, jobs are contracted to other private service providers.[48]

Scale. The fourth reason for greater private efficiency is the scale of service. There is some evidence that small-scale operators are more efficient than large-scale ones.[49]

One arrangement that is gaining favor distinguishes ownership from operation, and has government owning the buses but contracting with private firms to manage (i.e., to operate) them. Perry examined data on 249 transit agencies in the United States and related their performance (employing twenty-five indicators) to ownership and management arrangements. He concluded that privately owned and managed systems were most efficient, but that publicly owned systems with contract management were no better than those with public management.[50] This might be explained if there is little incentive for efficient operation and if the contract is not competitively awarded, as noted above.

A similar problem arises with subsidized private firms. Subsidies tend to promote inefficient practices.[51] Above-market wages, restrictive work rules, and retention of poorly utilized routes are examples of the inefficiencies promoted by transit subsidies. Another problem is also created by subsidies. In many instances, a state or county authorizes its own bus-operating agency to allocate subsidy moneys, both to itself *and* to its private competitors! Needless to say, this is a serious conflict of interest, for the agency's enlarged power can be used to force private firms out of business.

Roth and Wynne provide fascinating reviews of free-market arrangements for urban transport in less developed countries and contrast their performance with publicly owned urban transport services. They characterize the most successful systems as those that are privately owned, operate in a competitive environment, use small vehicles, involve small firms, and have route associations to facilitate coordination of private operations. They discuss how to overcome the shortcomings of unreliability, poor driving habits, and neglect of weak routes.[52]

Because of the favorable experiences with privatized urban mass transportation, and the theoretical advantages of such systems, the Reagan administration initiated an aggressive program of privatization. State and local government transportation agencies that received operating subsidies were strongly encouraged to experiment with and adopt contract and other private-sector arrangements.

Elevator Transport. At first glance it seems whimsical, and irrelevant to bus transportation, but on a closer look it is instructive to consider the completely private, free-market, highly successful, little noticed, fixed-rail transportation system that logs millions of passenger miles of safe, trouble-free service (this last factor presumably accounts for its being overlooked): the elevator. Let us reflect on some of the factors that make the elevator so satisfactory, and on the lessons it can provide for bus transportation.

The owner selects the number and kind of elevators for his service area (the building). He decides on the routes (which elevators to serve which floors), the number in use, the schedule by time of day, and the allocation of elevators between local and express service. The only role of government is to assure that the system is safe. Perhaps the free-market principles inherent in this vertical system of mass transit can be applied to horizontal systems as well.

A Proposed Surface Transportation Strategy. Drawing on the above experiences, and the insights of Lave[53] and other authorities, one can formulate a strategy to improve urban mass transit in the United States:

1. Remove regulatory obstacles so that the transit field is open to all who can offer service in safe vehicles.

2. Eliminate permanent, exclusive bus and taxi franchises, perhaps to be replaced by route-by-route bidding for the right to provide service for a finite duration.

3. Abandon control over bus and taxi fares, except under contract arrangements where a subsidized fare could be established (fares for taxis, etc., should be posted and readily discernible from afar—for example, by color-coded cabs—but not controlled).

4. Award contracts competitively to private bus, taxi, and jitney firms to serve certain routes or areas at certain times.

5. Issue vouchers to selected service *users* (e.g., schoolchildren, the elderly, and poor people) instead of giving grants (subsidies) to selected service *producers*.

6. Encourage entrepreneurs to enter the marketplace and provide superior services (e.g., express buses, special amenities such as newspapers, coffee, headphones) during rush hours in order to "shave the peak" and reduce the need for money-losing public bus runs.

7. Promote the formation of chartered subscription services and vanpools for commuters, as this also reduces the need for "loss leader" rush-hour runs.

Point 4 requires amplification. Public agencies can cut their costs by contracting with private firms to supply supplementary service during peak periods. This is widely but erroneously believed to be the "cream," and contracting out any of this work to private carriers is vilified as "cream skimming." In fact, peak-period operations are the costliest for a public agency, as it has to buy and maintain enough buses and hire enough full-time drivers to handle the peak load. Far from being a source of enrichment for public mass transit, this "cream" is hazardous to fiscal health. The costly activities at the other extreme of service can also profitably be contracted out to the private sector—the lightly traveled routes, the off-peak periods, and the unprofitable routes that ought to be served because it is in the public interest to do so; private operators can use more appropriate vehicles and less costly labor for this work.

Government should gradually get out of the business of owning, operating, or franchising bus monopolies (or franchising restricted-entry taxi systems) and should instead become a facilitator, coordinator, and purchaser (where necessary) of contractual and market-supplied services, and an inspector and enforcer of vehicle and driver safety. This competitive, deregulated climate can offer better and more responsive service to riders, lower costs, reduce government expenditures, and make for less congestion.

RAILROADS

In the United States, the government-owned freight railroad, Conrail, was privatized in 1987. Initial proposals for accomplishing this were sale to the public, sale to another railroad by negotiation or by open bidding, and sale to the workers. Opposition to the sale stemmed variously from the union's fear of job losses and shippers' fear of price gouging because of reduced competit-ton. The system was ultimately sold to the public for $1.65 billion.

Amtrak is a private passenger railroad that benefits from a generous grant arrangement. It received a federal subsidy of $684 million in 1985 (40 percent of the total cost), or $33 per passenger ride! (Still, that's peanuts compared to British Airways and Air France, the state-owned airlines that once subsidized each passenger on the Concorde to the tune of $900 per trip.) The subsidy is inequitable because the median income of Amtrak passengers was 20 percent higher than the median national income; in other words, the average taxpayer was subsidizing passengers whose incomes were higher than his own.

A principal reason for the high cost of operation is overmanning and the legendary union featherbedding. For example, the work rules require complete crew changes every 150 miles, presumably a relic of the nineteenth century when this constituted a full day's work.[54]

An examination of Amtrak's labor productivity shows profound differences when compared to that of four private railroads. Amtrak work crews that averaged 69 men repaired 182,955 ties, while private firms with 26-man crews repaired 684,338 ties; this is a per-man productivity ratio of 9.9 to 1! A further measure shows that Amtrak removed 71.8 miles of rail using an average crew size of 129, while the comparable figures for the private railways were 344 miles with 77-men crews; the productivity ratio was 8 to 1, again in favor of the private firms. The final reported productivity comparison shows Amtrak surfacing 141.4 miles of track with a 16-man crew, while the private railroads completed 846 miles using an 18-man crew; the corresponding productivity ratio here is 5.3 to 1. Assuming that all other relevant factors were essentially constant, the private firms were vastly more productive than Amtrak when it came to track maintenance work.[55]

Amtrak is not a major factor in intercity transportation; it represents only .25 percent of the total intercity mileage nationally. In 1984 it boarded only 11 million passengers at its twenty-five busiest stations, while airlines boarded 202 million passengers at the twenty-five busiest airports. Three-fourths of the Amtrak stations board fewer than fifty passengers a day.[56]

Attempting to eliminate this drain on the federal budget, the director of the Office of Management and Budget remarked, colorfully, that "without total subsidy termination and the opportunities offered through liquidation of Amtrak's assets, the Federal Government will continue to pour billions of dollars more into the Amtrak mobile money-burning machine."[57] The Reagan administration proposed terminating this grant arrangement, although it recognized that, as currently operated, Amtrak could not compete in the marketplace and would probably become bankrupt. This would be an opportunity to create an efficient railroad along the Northeast Corridor, between Boston, New York, and Washington; it could be subsidized by state and local governments whose areas were served if they found it desirable.

Problems abroad are strikingly similar to those in the United States and can be presumed to have similar roots. Japanese National Railways (JNR), the public railroad, is hamstrung by politicians, unions, and bureaucrats. It has lost its freight traffic, is rapidly losing its passenger traffic, and is deficit-ridden, while private lines employ fewer people, charge lower fares, and make money on routes that almost parallel JNR tracks. For example, JNR employs fifty people at a station in Yokohama, while a private line at the same station employs only twenty-four people, yet carries 60 percent more passengers.[58]

Another comparison can be glimpsed in Greece: Private freight cars are unloaded and turned around in two or three days, which keeps demurrage charges low, while twenty to thirty days is reported to be the typical turnaround time for national railway cars.[59]

In contrast, a study of the Canadian National Railroad (state owned) and the Canadian Pacific Railroad (privately owned) showed no significant difference in efficiency. This was attributable to the fact that the two railroads compete with each other and therefore achieve similar results.[60] This finding reinforces the observations made in connection with solid-waste collection and school-bus transportation, to the effect that competition, not the public or private nature of the service producer, may be the principal determinant of efficiency.

AIRLINES

An interesting comparison has been made between a public and a private trunk airline in Australia. The former is operated by a government agency, whereas the latter operates as a franchise service. Suffice it to say that both airlines are required to fly similar routes, service similar cities, use similar aircraft, and charge equal prices.

Three measures of efficiency were used to compare the airlines: tons of freight and mail carried per employee, passengers carried per employee, and earned revenues per employee. By each measure the private airline displayed greater efficiency, with ten-year means of 204 percent, 122 percent, and 113 percent respectively of the corresponding measures for the public airline. A complete analysis for sixteen consecutive years found that the private airline out-performed the public one in every measure and in every year.[61] (Moreover, the two firms, having exclusive access to these routes, have very high costs — 55 percent higher than the costs of similar airlines in the United States after deregulation.[62]) The reasons for these differences were not explained, however, and it is difficult to generalize from this unique case.

AIR TRAFFIC CONTROL

The air traffic control system in the United States is operated by a federal government agency and is financed mainly by airport and ticket taxes. Poole argues that it is inefficient and technologically backward, an inevitable result of its organizational status as a monopolistic government bureaucracy. He advocates privatization, to be attained by having individual airports (initially, only the small ones) contract with private firms for the service.[63] Many small airports have begun doing this. When this was done at the airport in Farmington, New Mexico, for instance, the costs plummeted from $300,000 to $90,000 a year.[64] The lower cost is not a result of inadequately trained controllers or poor equipment; the controllers are usually very experienced, former federal controllers. The difference lies in the use of flexible work rules, functional equipment, and high employee morale. Indeed, the union strongly supports such privatization, noting that the managerial duties required of controllers at small airports enrich the work and improve morale and performance, in marked contrast to the rigidly bureaucratic conditions in federally operated towers.[65]

What of the lingering feeling that so complex, critical, and interconnected a system as air traffic control, with so many lives at stake, should be operated by a single nationwide organization? On reflection, one realizes that this makes no more sense than requiring that all pilots belong to one airline or that all automobiles be driven by chauffeurs from a single firm that also is responsible for all road markings and traffic signals. All that is needed is a uniform set of conventions covering communication and safety procedures, not a single monolith.

COAST GUARD SERVICES

The U.S. Coast Guard appears to be a military agency and thus as "inherently governmental" as any organization can be. Appearances are deceiving, however; it is mostly a transportation agency. *The President's Private Sector Survey on Cost Control* (also known as the Grace Commission) studied the Coast Guard and concluded that three of its functions should be privatized.[66]

Search-and-rescue activities in situations where no lives were threatened was one area recommended for privatization. It is the most expensive of all

Coast Guard programs, requiring responses to more than 80,000 calls a year, of which about 80 percent are labeled "convenience" and not "emergency" requests. Moreover, 80 percent of the missions are within three miles of the shore and 72 percent involve recreational boats. In view of these facts, about 80 percent of the calls are turned over to a voluntary organization, the Coast Guard Auxiliary. In addition, there is an extensive private-sector towing industry sufficiently equipped to handle many nonemergency search-and-rescue missions. (By way of analogy, vehicles stranded on highways are aided by private towing services, not by a U.S. Army motorized infantry division.) In Denmark, the same private firm that provides road service for stranded motorists also provides air-sea rescue services. The Grace Commission report concludes that the Coast Guard's costs are twelve times greater than those of the private sector when performing the same functions, and it recommends shifting much of the nonemergency search-and-rescue burden to the latter for a first-year savings of $197 million.

Another large Coast Guard program, absorbing about a sixth of the agency's resources, involves short-range aids to navigation: the placing and maintenance of radar beacons, day-markers, buoys, fog signals, lightships, and lighthouses. About 45 percent of all such aids are private aids, typically in the vicinity of marinas, commercial marine facilities, and offshore platforms; this fraction is increasing steadily. Whereas the Coast Guard owns, operates, and maintains the federal navigation aids, its role with respect to the private aids is to review applications, maintain records on approved aids, monitor their performance, and inspect them.

After comparing the work of the Coast Guard and private firms engaged in similar activities, the Grace Commission concluded that a 25 percent cost reduction and a tripling of the utilization rate of certain specialized vessels could be achieved by contracting out, and it recommended doing this for a portion of the Coast Guard's work in buoy tending and in responding to failures of navigational aids.

The final candidate for privatization involves the program for commercial vessel safety. This involves setting and establishing safety standards and personnel standards and inspecting for conformance, investigating accidents, measuring vessels, and issuing documents for vessels. The Coast Guard has begun to use the private sector in measurement and inspection work; the Grace Commission recommends an extension of this effort and estimates that savings of 41 percent could be realized.

SPACE TRANSPORTATION
There is a growing demand for strictly commercial uses of space vehicles, for

communication, manufacturing, and resource management (e.g., specialized photography for purposes of agriculture, forestry, mineral exploration, water management, and weather forecasting). Private firms are ready and willing to go into the launching business and are designing payloads and equipment for commercial functions in space. But there are ominous signs that the National Aeronautics and Space Administration (NASA) is following in the footsteps of the Postal Service in fending off competitors and securing its current monopoly. According to Butler, NASA is adopting arguments used to justify the Synthetic Fuels Corporation and the Clinch River Breeder Reactor ("We admit it's really a commercial project, but it's too expensive and long-range for the private sector to undertake, so we have to do it"—at taxpayers' expense.[67])

NASA's reusable space shuttle, which was "sold" effectively to the taxpayer through superb public relations work and was very glamorous in the eyes of the public until its tragic explosion in 1986, may be inferior to expendable French and Japanese space vehicles for some tasks. These countries are garnering more of the launch business, while China and the Soviet Union have also begun to sell their space services.

The first significant step toward privatization occurred when President Reagan promulgated a policy of auctioning available launch time and shuttle space to the highest bidder, at a price realistically related to the true cost. (Like most conventional government transportation monopolies, NASA had been underpricing its services, thereby tending to keep out competitors, and making up the difference with subsidies from the general taxpayer.) Additional steps advocated by Butler for the federal government are to make existing launch facilities and space technology available to private launch companies, and to sell space vehicles not required for national defense.

Another privatization step involves land remote sensing satellites (LANDSATs), which scan the earth and provide information that is useful to oil companies, crop forecasters, land-use planners, and researchers. In 1985 the Department of Commerce awarded a contract to a firm created by two large aerospace corporations to build and operate LANDSATs and sell data. The government provided a multiyear start-up subsidy for the firm, which receives revenues from its sale of data. The Reagan administration proposed discontinuing the subsidies and allowing the competitive market to determine whether there should be an operational LANDSAT; the government's own data needs are being met by alternative means.[68]

Levine has examined the policy and administration issues involved in the commercialization of space,[69] while Stine warns that space entrepreneurs in the United States are currently stymied by growing regulations that "may mean the U.S. has given away the solar system."[70] Ironically, the space shuttle tragedy forced a reconsideration of NASA's exclusive role and a policy shift toward privatization.

Water Supply and Treatment

WATER SUPPLY

Historically, water supply has been one of the most public of all services, that is, one in which the private sector has been least involved. But it may be a consequence and not a coincidence that in many countries the water supply is both insufficient and unsanitary. In 1980 safe water was available to only 45 percent of the total population of ninety-five developing countries.[71]

Water supply, like the supply of electricity, can be separated into three component services: extraction (or generation), transmission, and distribution to the ultimate consumer. None of these is a natural monopoly, as is most clearly evident in water distribution. Water can be distributed by pipes, but it can also be delivered and sold by water vendors (e.g., bottled Perrier from a gourmet shop in developed countries, and water from a barrel on a donkey-drawn cart in developing countries). Water supply is a toll good, and exclusion is possible even for water from a village standpipe; the water can be dispensed from a coin-operated, metered spigot or a manned kiosk.

An analysis of data from twenty-four private and eighty-eight public water supply systems in the United States concluded that the latter cost about a third more than the former. This was attributed to lower labor productivity and underutilization of capital by the public sector.[72] A subsequent, more careful study, however, found no difference in cost.[73]

In the United States, private water companies serve only about 31 million people; public organizations serve about 180 million, six times as many. (The remainder have private wells.) Hanke contrasts this to the situation in France where private water companies are the major suppliers. The French firms are also dominant internationally in research and development, in equipment manufacture, and in the management and provision of water services.[74] Paris has had a private water system since 1782, when the Perrier family started it.

Two different arrangements are used in France by private water companies. One is a franchise awarded to the low bidder (that is, a low price to be charged to water users) who finances, builds, owns, operates, and maintains all necessary facilities for the duration of the franchise, typically thirty years, and then turns the system over to a public authority.

The second system is like the first except that financing and ownership are by a public body. In terms of the framework presented in chapter 4, the water service is separated into two components, with government service for financing and ownership, and a franchise for the remainder of the water supply system. Hanke does not expand on the relative merits of these two approaches.

A major policy issue in the United States concerns large water projects, particularly in the Southwest. There is a growing realization that enormous waste is encouraged when taxpayers throughout the nation pay for costly water projects that directly benefit local dwellers and local agricultural enterprises. Policy makers are rediscovering the virtues of the marketplace, and environmentalists argue that there is no incentive to conserve water because it is seriously underpriced (users pay only 9 percent of the cost in California's Central Valley) and therefore is used to keep submarginal land in production.[75] Environmentalists were in rare agreement with the Reagan administration about the waste inherent in this entrenched system, and joined with the administration to obtain legislation that required the sharing of costs by localities. (At a meeting of the White House Working Group formed to address this issue, I made the point that if someone wants to grow bananas in the Mojave Desert, he should be free to do so, but clearly he should pay the full price for the water he would need. If this results in too high a selling price for his bananas, he should rethink his agronomic aspirations, not ask for subsidized water.)

WASTEWATER TREATMENT

More than seventy-five communities in the United States contract with private firms to operate and maintain their wastewater-treatment plants. Depending on the available tax incentives, it is sometimes even more attractive economically to have private ownership of the plant, on a sale-leaseback arrangement, for example.[76]

Individual instances of significant savings by contract operation have been reported, such as a New England community that estimated its operating costs to be 25 to 88 percent greater than the contract cost.[77] An Arizona community contracted with a private firm to build and operate a wastewater-treatment plant that would have cost 59 percent more as a completely public enterprise; moreover, the cost of public wastewater treatment is typically 25 to 100 percent greater than private treatment. This reflects inefficiencies in construction and operation, overdesign in conformance with EPA criteria for publicly funded plants, and higher than market wages for construction work that must conform to the Davis-Bacon Act if it receives federal funding.[78]

Electric Power

Several arrangements can be found for electric power generation and distribution systems: regulated franchises; voluntary or cooperative arrangements; and market arrangements with either (1) competing distribution networks (found only in the United States), (2) small, independent systems based on hydroelectric or renewable energy sources, or (3) unregulated monopolies. Generation is sometimes separate from distribution, with the former provided by a private firm while distribution is accomplished by a government enterprise; the private generator sells power to the public grid.[79]

In the United States, 87 percent of electricity users get their power from one of about 200 private companies. The remaining 13 percent, about 32 million people, are served by about 2,200 municipal or state systems.

Several studies compare the cost of public and private electric power, that is, government and franchise service. Unfortunately, some of the studies are flawed, and no single study has effectively addressed the issue comprehensively. (This illustrates the difficulty of conducting good, comparative research on privatization.)

One study found that publicly owned utilities have significantly lower costs than privately owned utilities, but the analysis was faulty because the sample of public power plants included several hydroelectric plants, and these were compared with private plants that burned fuel.[80] Therefore, the difference in findings cannot be attributed entirely to public or private ownership. This study has also been criticized on other methodological grounds.[81]

Another study compared large private utilities with small municipal utilities and found the former to be more efficient; the authors conclude that private firms are better able than local governments to realize economies of scale.[82] This is clearly an important point, but the study does not provide an unambiguous comparison of public and private power for similar market areas. Three other investigations excluded hydroelectric generation and controlled for the effect of size. Their findings indicate that municipal utilities are more efficient than private ones;[83] however, another study attributes the difference to tax exemptions enjoyed by municipalities.[84] (As chapter 8 explains, the apparent savings accruing from tax advantages enjoyed by public agencies are illusory.) To complicate the matter further, Spann concluded that private firms might be more efficient but in any event are no less efficient than municipal utilities, but his study was limited to only a few plants.[85]

In his important study, Hellman found thirty-eight cities in the United States where electric power is provided by competing service producers. In effect, he compared market service with government service and government-regulated franchises and found that free-market arrangements seem to lead to lower prices by private firms than does regulation, although municipal power is still lower. He argues persuasively that competition is better than regulation as a guarantor of inexpensive electricity.[86] Primeaux also studied such communities, in which households have a choice of electricity supplier. Contrary to conventional wisdom about the so-called natural monopoly in electric power supply, and consistent with Hellman's findings, Primeaux concluded that competitive arrangements were more efficient than monopolies (exclusive franchises); the former had an average price 33 percent lower than the latter.[87]

The comptroller general compared 95 federal power plants with 47 private plants of similar size, using 1973-75 data. His report found that private costs were $2.72 per kilowatt-hour compared to $3.29 for the federal plants; in other words, the latter were 21 percent more costly, and had 48 percent more employees per plant.[88] Subsequently, the Grace Commission called attention to the Power Marketing Administration of the Department of Energy, which operates 123 hydroelectric dams and 622 substations and employs 4,900 people. It sells 6 percent of the nation's power; however, its revenues do not repay the investment, its pricing is unsound, and its accounting is undependable. The commission recommended an orderly withdrawal from this business through privatization (or denationalization), to achieve cost savings of $3.5 billion and revenues of $16.3 billion over three years.[89] The 1987 executive budget proposed selling all power generation and transmission facilities at federal dams, while retaining ownership and control over the dams themselves.

DeAlessi summarizes numerous studies in the following way: Compared to private utilities, municipal utilities charge lower prices, spend more on construction, have higher operating costs, show less correlation between costs and marginal revenues, change prices less often, fail to adopt cost-reducing innovations as readily, favor business over residential users, maintain managers in office longer, offer fewer services, and exhibit greater variation in rates of return.[90]

Roth relates the sad story of government's gradual destruction of a private electric company in Caracas, Venezuela. The firm had been a pioneer since its founding in 1895. Despite pressure from the government to raise its rates so that the government's own electric company could charge higher prices, the firm kept its prices low and even gave discounts to slum dwellers. The firm was driven toward bankruptcy in the 1980s when (1) the government failed to pay for power it purchased from the private firm; (2) the firm was forced to pay taxes on the money it was owed but could not collect; and (3) the firm was required to borrow U.S. dollars to invest in additional generating facilities, but the government then devalued the local currency by a factor of three, making it essentially impossible for the firm to repay its foreign loan.[91]

Regulation of franchised firms has also been studied and criticized. Roth cites a Harvard study of regulated electric companies in Latin America; it concluded that the regulatory desire for cheap electricity resulted in low earnings and poor service and that "the effective cost to the economy has often been very high in terms of inconvenience, delay, and damage . . . . Latin America's need is for *more* electricity and not for *cheap* electricity."[92]

It may well be that the proper role for government with respect to electric power is to encourage a private, competitive marketplace, with numerous generating plants using conventional fuels, renewable energy sources, and co-generation facilities producing and selling power into a common grid. Government would set safety and technical standards (e.g., alternating current frequency), and protect consumers who have no choice of suppliers. As Roth states, "The need for it to intervene directly in the generation, transmission, or distribution of electricity, or in its pricing, or in determining who shall and who shall not be allowed to generate electricity, is open to question."[93]

Communications

POSTAL SERVICE

Does the delivery of written messages require a government monopoly? Surely not. While no major study has compared government postal service to other alternatives (because of the absence of a comparable private firm), evidence of the comparative performance of the U.S. Postal Service (USPS) and the private sector is nevertheless accumulating at a rapid rate.

To begin with, it should be understood that the Postal Service is essentially a government agency, despite some changes several years ago that gave it some semblance of independence.

One area where the USPS faces direct competition is in delivering small packages. The United Parcel Service (UPS), with its familiar fleet of brown vehicles, is a private, profit-making, worker-owned enterprise that challenged the USPS parcel-post service head on. The results are striking:

1. UPS rates are generally cheaper.
2. UPS handles more parcels than the Postal Service, 1.96 billion compared to 1.86 billion in 1984.
3. UPS is faster—a parcel mailed by parcel post from Washington to Los Angeles takes more than eight days, or longer than a Pony Express trip from Missouri to California in 1861.
4. The damage rate at UPS is one-fifth that of the Postal Service.
5. UPS insures every parcel up to $100 without an extra charge.
6. UPS keeps a record of each parcel.
7. UPS will pick up parcels from the mailer, for a fee.

8. UPS makes three delivery attempts, compared with one by the Postal Service.

9. UPS earned an after-tax profit of almost $500 million in 1984, whereas the Postal Service lost money on its tax-free parcel-post business.[94]

USPS was the first to introduce an electronic mail service, but it was a disaster, with a loss of more than a dollar on every letter it delivered. Meanwhile, a similar service by a private company, Federal Express, quickly overtook the USPS service, even without the benefit of a subsidy.[95] Additional evidence as to the inefficiency of the Postal Service comes from the General Accounting Office, which found that USPS janitors are paid more than twice as much as contract personnel doing the same work.[96]

Another direct comparison between the USPS and private contractors is provided by the Grace Commission. It costs the USPS an average of 24 cents per dollar of revenue to operate a postal window, compared to a tenth of that, 2.8 cents, in post offices operated by private contractors for the USPS in Arizona.[97] The General Accounting Office estimated that $125 million to $150 million could be saved annually if the USPS replaced 7,000 of its limited-service offices with community post offices operated by private contractors. This would extend the current contract efforts of the USPS: Nearly all intercity mail is currently transported by contractors, and almost 5,000 delivery routes are handled by private carriers under contract. The latter step is saving up to two-thirds of the normal costs.[98]

The principal reason for the relative inefficiency of the Postal Service is its monopoly with respect to letter mail, a monopoly it defends like a lioness guarding her cubs. Indeed, it was quick to protect its territory against the depradations of Cub Scouts who tried to raise money by delivering Christmas cards.[99]

Even more alarming to the USPS is the House & Senate Delivery Service, a private firm that delivers unaddressed, identical letters to each senator and congressman in Washington within a half-day of pickup (*free* pickup if the sender is within about nine miles of the Capitol), for only 5 cents a letter — 8 cents if the letter is addressed. This is at least twice as fast as USPS and only about one-fourth the price. Alas, it is illegal to provide such inexpensive service, and the businessman can be fined and jailed for doing so.[100]

The monopoly has been attacked both theoretically and practically.[101] The postal monopoly statutes were questioned by President Reagan as being contrary to the public interest because they lead to higher rates and poorer service. Private courier services have proliferated, exploiting ambiguities as to what constitutes a "letter" in terms of the statutes.[102] For example, UPS promises next-day delivery between any two addresses in the nation, a service that the

USPS does not offer. Periodicals are switching to private delivery; for example, *Better Homes & Gardens* said it paid only 10 cents a copy compared to 16.5 cents if it were to use the Postal Service.[103] Third-class mail, which consists mostly of advertisements, is being replaced to a significant extent by newspaper inserts—some 20 billion pieces are being delivered by conventional, private, newspaper delivery services. The ultimate indignity was suffered by the Postal Service when the General Services Administration urged all federal agencies to reduce their mail costs by using commercial carriers for parcels.[104]

"Cream skimming!" is the accusation hurled by advocates of the monopoly at those who would privatize postal services. That is, while the private sector, under contract or franchise arrangements, could provide some services at much lower than current average costs, this would skim the easy-to-provide services from the system and leave the costly rural services, for instance, without the cross-subsidies that keep them going today. This need not be the case. One could subsidize an efficient rural service directly, and this would be less expensive than maintaining an inefficient service in the entire country. Instead of using general taxes for this purpose, however, Butler shrewdly proposes a tax to be levied on mail carried by private firms. This would keep the cross-subsidy within the industry, and because the subsidy costs would be borne by particular firms and their customers instead of general and anonymous taxpayers, one would expect strong and well-organized pressure groups to form and to lobby to keep the subsidy low.[105] (As was pointed out in chapter 2, it is almost impossible to get general taxpayers to lobby against a particular expenditure—they do not have enough at stake, and therefore costs rise almost inexorably.)

A postal rate commissioner proposed introducing competition by gradually contracting out individual rural routes, and he envisioned contracts or franchises being awarded separately to the lowest bidders for the processing, delivery, and retail functions in each city. Ultimately, the federal role could shrink to that of a regulator, purchasing agent, and provider of subsidies for service to high-cost areas.[106]

TELECOMMUNICATION

A government monopoly is not necessary to deliver messages and parcels; is it necessary for electronic communication? Little formal research has been conducted to compare public and private telecommunication services, but two points can be made. Telephone service in developing countries is almost always government provided, and this results in low levels of ownership and usage as a consequence of decisions based on politics instead of consumer demand. The political desire is for uniform rates and access in both rural and urban areas, despite the vastly different costs incurred. Therefore, given the scarcity of funds available to developing nations, the rate of telephone installation is limited by the high cost of rural installation, to the detriment of the nation as a whole.[107]

The second point is illustrated by government telecommunication in France. The post and telegraph monopoly allows only its own products to be connected to its lines, with the result that telephone-answering machines cost three times as much as they do in the United States, and telephones with ten-number memories cost four times as much.

The government bureaucracy's basic self-interest was revealed clearly by the postmaster general of the United Kingdom in 1882 when he argued successfully that the government should take over the rapidly growing telephone system in order to prevent a decline in its telegraph revenues.[108] It is not clear whether he intended to stifle the new invention or merely appropriate its revenues.

In Japan, the public telephone company was transformed into a private one in 1985. There were several reasons for this step. In the first place, advances in microelectronics made possible new telecommunication products and services, which can best be brought to market by competitive, profit-driven companies. Second, the privatization of British Telecommunications and the breakup of AT&T in the United States, which offered the promise of greater innovation, threatened to leave Nippon Telephone and Telegraph a backward system. The third reason was the growing political pressure, as in Europe and North and South America, for paring the size of government.[109]

Commercial and Administrative Activities

Deep within the innards of every government, various prosaic activities are going on. They lack the high visibility of services delivered directly to the citizenry, such as collecting trash, supplying water, and operating buses, but they are the chores necessary for maintaining the metabolism of any large organization and carrying out bureaucratic housekeeping. A list of such activities, loosely called commercial and administrative activities, appears in table 6.4; it is condensed from a lengthier list issued by the Office of Management and Budget to encourage contracting out in the federal government.[110] In 1984 an unsuccessful attempt was made in the Congress to prohibit the federal government from engaging in such commercial activities.

These activities are extensive. Based on a 1981 survey of federal agencies, the Office of Federal Procurement Policy (OFPP) estimated that at least $6 billion in annual operating costs, $3 billion in capital investments, and 226,000 employees (mostly blue collar, and constituting about 10 percent of the federal civilian workforce), were devoted to these commercial activities.[111]

TABLE 6.4

EXAMPLES OF COMMERCIAL AND ADMINISTRATIVE

ACTIVITIES IN GOVERNMENT

Audiovisual and Printing Services
Photography and photographic processing; printing, reproduction, and binding; film and videotape production; microfilming; art and graphic services; maintenance of audiovisual equipment; management and operation of audiovisual facilities

Automatic Data Processing
Facility management; equipment installation and operation; systems engineering, analysis, and design; programming; key punching, data entry, and data transmission

Food Services
Operation of cafeterias, kitchens, bakeries, and vending machines

Health Services
Medical, hospital, and nursing care; physical examination; manufacturing and fitting of glasses and hearing aids; medical and dental laboratories; dietary and veterinary services

Office Services
Stenographic, secretarial, typing, word processing, mail and messenger, translation, training, material and supplies management, payroll and financial services, insurance, debt collection, advertising, public relations, library operations, and real property management

Maintenance and Miscellaneous Services
Carpentry, plumbing, electrical, painting, air conditioning, custodial and janitorial, office-machine repair, laundry, bus service

Actually, these estimates are significantly understated, for the $6 billion figure excludes many commercial activities in the Defense Department (DOD) and in Veterans Administration (VA) hospitals, and many "white-collar" activities. If these were included, the cost would be $10 to $15 billion annually. The OFPP estimates that about $2 to $3 billion of the total could be saved if agencies aggressively compared the cost of public and private provision and instituted competitive bidding to purchase these services—of the same quality—from private firms. A separate study by the Congressional Budget Office (CBO) is generally consistent with the OFPP figures.[112]

It is not necessary, however, to rely on OFPP and CBO estimates. Detailed information has become available from DOD about its experience with contracting for commercial services (as distinguished from military procurement). In response to a legislated requirement, DOD analyzed the performance of outside contractors on all 235 contracts on which work started during the two-year period that began on 1 October 1980. If no competitive contracting had been considered, the cost of the in-house commercial work by government employees would have been 38 percent greater than the actual cost (to the government) of the same work performed by private contractors.[113] The analysis was conducted after each contract had been in effect for at least one full year, so the comparison was based on actual operations. The cost of the contract work properly includes the cost of government-furnished property used by the contractor, transition costs, and the cost of contract supervision and administration.

It is worth noting that the mere threat of competition from the private sector brought about a 7 percent reduction in the cost of in-house services, even if no outside contract was ultimately awarded. In 45 percent of the cases where a study was conducted to see if substantial savings could be achieved by contracting, it was decided to retain the work in-house; the aforementioned 7 percent cost reduction contributed to the decision. One cannot conclude that all in-house work is 38 percent more costly than contract work; that figure applies only to the activities actually contracted out, namely, those in 55 percent of the studies. Presumably the studies were not conducted at random; they must have been directed at activities that seemed to offer the greatest potential for improvement by contracting out. Therefore, it would be incorrect to assert that the current cost of *all* such activities in government is 38 percent greater than it would be if they were contracted out; it is true only of those that *were* contracted out. This finding serves to reinforce the recommendation that all activities be examined to see if contracting can reduce their cost. At the least, one should be able to capture improvements just by raising the question (or posing the threat, as some would perceive it).

Los Angeles County also reported the results of its contracts for a variety of services: auditing, transportation, travel, parking revenue collection, secretarial, custodial, physical examinations for employees, embalming, microfilming, automobile liability claims management, data conversion, paramedic equipment repair, dietary, medical records transcription, laundry, and laboratory testing. From 1979 through 1984 a total of 193 contracts were awarded for these 16 services, at a cost of $54.96 million, and the savings amounted to $24.75 million. In other words, the in-house work cost 45 percent more than the contract work.[114]

In 6 of the 193 cases, the contract work turned out to be more costly than the in-house work; this is properly reflected in the totals. In other cases, contractors were able to increase revenues for the county by better management (e.g., of parking facilities); these benefits are *not* included in the figures cited here, but are important to bear in mind when contracting is contemplated.

CUSTODIAL SERVICES

Custodial services are ubiquitous and are frequently performed by contractors. The evidence strongly supports this arrangement.

The most definitive comparison of governmental and contract arrangements for cleaning services in public buildings was carried out by Stevens. In a detailed study of twenty cities, half with contracts and half with in-house workers, she determined that the cost in cities with municipal service was 73 percent greater than in cities with contract service, after controlling for the floor area to be cleaned, the specific cleaning tasks carried out, and the resulting cleanliness. Stevens attributes the contractor's lower cost to lower wages and fringe benefits, greater use of part-time workers, scheduling more of the work during nonbusiness hours, using more equipment, and achieving lower absentee rates.[115]

Schools in New York City were examined by the city comptroller, who concluded that large sums of money were wasted on custodial services. Changing to outside contractors at five schools brought about savings of 13.4 percent and provided a yardstick for evaluating the efficiency of custodial services in the other schools. The comptroller went on to recommend a gradual expansion of the number of schools using outside contractors for such work.[116]

Information is also available on custodial services in Germany. Blankart reports that office cleaning by the federal post office administration is 42 percent to 66 percent more expensive than contracting out and that the cost when government cleans its offices in Hamburg ranges from 1.4 to 5 times as much as contract cleaning;[117] Pommerehne summarizes a number of West German studies, which found that public costs exceeded private costs by 50 percent for printing work, 85 percent for laundries, 100 percent for automobile repairs, 50 to 150 percent for floor cleaning, 20 percent for building construction, and 160 percent for bus operations.[118]

TREE MAINTENANCE

Most communities exercise responsibility for maintaining trees on streets and in public parks; the activities include planting, spraying, pruning, and removing fallen trees. These functions can be and often are contracted to private firms. In Detroit, after a study showed that private firms could do the work at one-third the unit cost of the city agency, they were given part of the responsibility for trimming healthy trees and removing dead and diseased trees from city streets.[119]

A much more comprehensive study compared public and contract performance of this highly labor-intensive work,[120] and used professional arborists to measure the quality of tree care, as the quality level is related to cost. Municipal tree maintenance was 37 percent more costly than contract service, even though the quality of work was indistinguishable. A full quarter of the cost of contract work, as calculated, was the cost of municipal overhead, contract letting, and performance monitoring.

The reasons for the difference in cost for equivalent work were that municipal workers had somewhat higher wages and fringe benefits, had more days off with pay, had more seniority, were more unionized, and had more layers of supervision over them; their supervisors had little flexibility in hiring and firing, their agencies were less likely to be responsible for maintaining their own equipment, and their work was not scheduled as efficiently as contractors scheduled their work. For example, contractors recognize and take advantage of the seasonality of this activity, whereas cities generally do not.[121]

TURF MAINTENANCE

When governments own as many acres of land as they do, it is inevitable that they will have a lot of grass that needs mowing, weeding, fertilizing, reseeding, and aerating; it is located in parks, on median strips on highways, alongside roads, and in areas surrounding public buildings. The typical choice facing government is to do the work in-house or contract it out, although in some cases voluntary community organizations have assumed this responsibility for neighborhood parks and other local grassy areas.

A detailed and sophisticated econometric analysis compared public and contract arrangements for this function. All costs were considered, including depreciation of equipment and the costs of awarding, letting, and overseeing contracts. The quality of work was rated visually, in terms of color, coverage, extent of weeds, height, and edging. After controlling for scale (number of acres mowed), number of activities performed (aerating, etc.), and quality, it was found that municipal service was 40 percent more expensive than contract work. Moreover, the quality of the contract work was better than the municipal work, although not significantly so. The reasons for higher public costs are higher salaries and fringe benefits for public employees—in part at least attributed to the fact that they are older and have worked longer in this activity—lower productivity per worker, greater absenteeism (including more paid vacations, holidays, and sick leave), and less flexible supervision.[122]

This finding illustrates one of the inherent defects in the system of tenured civil service. In order to facilitate supposedly objective testing for hiring and promotion, jobs are very narrowly defined. As a result, public employees achieve tenure and often spend their entire working lives in collecting trash or mowing grass or other similar chores. Their wages increase with longevity, but their productivity can be expected to decline with age and with the increasing boredom of simple, repetitive, manual labor. In the private sector, workers are generally not engaged (or trapped) in these occupations as lifelong careers; such labor is usually viewed as a young man's job, an initial activity that one is expected to outgrow. Quite apart from the demonstrated efficiency of this approach, it is also much better for the individual in terms of personal growth and job satisfaction.

GROUNDS MAINTENANCE

Since 1979, the County of Los Angeles has been pursuing a program of prudent privatization and carefully keeping track of the relative costs of similar work by county personnel and by contractors. One area with a sufficient number of cases to permit meaningful comparisons between the two arrangements is grounds maintenance. Between 1980 and 1984, county agencies awarded fifty-three contracts for such work. Examination of the data shows that the work performed by county agencies had cost 84 percent more than it did after it was contracted out, $8.8 million compared to $4.8 million. The data were self-reported by county agencies and might therefore be suspected of inflated managerial claims, but they were reviewed by the auditor-controller of the County of Los Angeles, an independently elected official, which gives the findings substantial credence.[123]

PAYROLL PROCESSING

One of the most thorough comparative studies of public and contract arrangements for administrative functions was carried out by Stevens.[124] She examined twenty cities, half of which used contractors while the other half did the work in-house. Contrary to most such studies, no differences were found in either cost or quality (error rate and speed of processing) between government and contractor work. The explanation is simple. Payroll processing was defined to include timekeeping, preparing payroll transmittal forms, processing data on computers, and printing and distributing checks. The role of the contractor was restricted merely to processing data and printing checks. Indeed, payments to the contractor averaged only 31 percent of total payroll processing costs in the contract cities; most of the work even in these cities was performed by city personnel, and therefore it should come as no surprise that municipal costs and contract costs were effectively equal in this analysis: Contract costs constituted mostly municipal costs!

DEBT COLLECTION

The General Accounting Office examined debt collection in federal agencies and recommended that the government improve its performance in this area by adopting the practices of commercial firms. A federal agency spent $8.72 to maintain and pursue collection of an account from the time it was determined to be delinquent until the debt was collected, written off, or referred for legal action; a commercial firm spent less than $3.50 for the same function. Also, firms found it cost effective to pursue collection to the point of seeking court judgments on debts as small as $25 (in 1978), but the federal government generally did not go this far on debts smaller than $600. Moreover, whereas private firms reached this point in only five months, the government normally took a year or more. In other words, private debt-collection firms were faster, more efficient, and more persistent.[125]

PROPERTY ASSESSMENT

As noted in chapter 4, assessment of real property is commonly carried out by private firms for local governments, particularly when a community is undergoing comprehensive reassessment in a relatively short period. Ohio requires such work to be done by the private sector, and the work there was studied by the International Association of Assessing Officers. The quality of assessment in Ohio, as measured by the difference between assessed value and actual sales prices for single-family homes, was the best of all states, and the cost of assessment was only half the national average.[126] (It should be recognized, however, that the small difference noted may reflect state policy rather than the superiority of private assessment.)

OTHER ACTIVITIES

Laundry services are required for prisons, hospitals, and many other institutions. A study by the General Accounting Office of government laundry and dry cleaning in federal installations showed that in seven of sixteen cases the cost of in-house operation was greater than the cost of comparable contract service. Thus, in the majority of cases, in-house service was at least as efficient as a contractor would be. However, a representative of a private laundry complained that he was unable to find out what the laundering requirements were so that he could prepare a sensible bid to do the work; all he was told was that 246,584 pieces had to be done, and it was impossible for him to learn how many pieces had to be washed, how many to be pressed, and how many, such as towels, merely had to be fluffed dry without ironing.[127]

In New York City, a car illegally parked in certain areas is subject to being towed away, whereupon a substantial towing fee as well as a parking ticket must be paid by the owner to reclaim his car. The towing was done by a special unit of the police department, at an estimated cost of $65 per car. Part of the work was subsequently put up for bids, and a contract was awarded to the low bidder, whose price was only $30 per car. The second lowest bid was also much lower than the city's cost, $34.75 per car.[128]

San Francisco hired a private accounting firm to perform some of the work of its Budget Bureau and saved $102,000 annually.[129] Detroit hired a private firm to process parking tickets (which carry fines of $15), at a cost of $1.80 per ticket, after calculating that it cost $26 per ticket when the city did the work.[130]

Another administrative activity performed by private firms under contract to government is conducting background checks on job applicants. This was described as a temporary solution to reduce a large backlog. The government pays only $500 per case for the contract work, compared to $1,200 per case when the work is done by government employees in the personnel office. The affected government union asserts that the quality of the work is lower, however.[131]

State-Owned Property

PUBLIC LAND

The federal government owns 32 percent of the total land area of the United States, or more than a million square miles; this corresponds to the entire land area east of the Mississippi River plus Texas. Less than a tenth of this land is in national parks; most of it is forests, grazing land, or wilderness.

Forests. The federal government owns more than 90 million acres of commercial timberland, an area equal to Japan in size; in ten states it owns more than half the commercial timberland. Various scholars advocate privatization of these lands on grounds of efficiency, effectiveness, and conservation. Empirical evidence indicates greater private efficiency: Commercial forests managed by the U.S. Forest Service have a negative cash flow of about $1 billion a year, whereas private timber firms typically generate positive cash flows.[132] Corroboration comes from a study in Germany that compared the management of public and private forests over a six-year period. In terms of net operating revenue, the public forests operated at a loss of 30 Deutschmarks per hectare, whereas the private forests showed a gain of 15 Deutschmarks per hectare.[133] Moreover, the same area of forest yielding the same amount of wood can be operated by one foreman and nine workers by a private firm, compared with two foremen and twenty workers in a public forest.[134]

These indicative reports may not be sufficiently robust to make the case altogether, and there is still a need for an evaluative comparison of the actual performance of political and market-based decision making in circumstances that are similar with respect to resources allocated and outputs produced.[135] Nevertheless, a growing number of theoretical analyses make a persuasive case for less reliance on government ownership of forests—with its attendant politically based decisions—and more on private ownership, with its market-based decisions. The former is held to be less efficient than the latter for three broad reasons: (1) Government ownership leads to costly lobbying efforts to influence the decisions; (2) even if they are paragons in terms of professionalism and public spirit, government bureaucrats are handicapped in their decision making by the absence of market information and tend to be captured by those regulated; and (3) private owners will be harmed if they make uneconomic decisions about their property, whereas government employees are generally shielded from this corrective force. Government ownership often leads to poorly defined property rights; lack of enforcement of those rights; and either a tragedy of the commons or wholesale plunder by settlers, lumbermen, or government officials. (Destruction of a public park by a similar process is noted in chapter 7.) In the absence of clearly defined and enforced property rights, and the concomitant rewards for proper management, the stage is set for wanton harvesting of timber and no reforestation. Those who take the trees cannot exclude others, they have no claim to future timber, and therefore have no incentive to practice efficient forestry.[136]

The list of poor policies applied to public forests is a lengthy one: prohibiting the export of logs from government forests, reserving a portion of public timber for sale at bargain prices to small businesses, expanding federal agencies by propagating myths of timber shortages, following inappropriate timber-harvesting schedules and bidding procedures, selling timber below cost, losing money by failing to consider the net present value of bids for the timber (the government, in effect, allows buyers to fatten their trees at public expense by letting them grow in the public forest instead of clearing them out so that a new crop can be planted), ignoring the new sciences of forest management and forestry economics, incorrectly dealing with fishing rights and with subsurface mineral recovery, and following a rigid mixed-use policy instead of specializing, where appropriate, so that recreational uses, mining, and timbering can be separated.

A consequence of this mismanagement is uncertainty and instability in timber supply, which has fostered migration of the forestry industry from the Pacific Northwest, where the industry is highly dependent on government forests, to the South where private timberlands predominate. The timber industry has gradually changed from an extractive one to an agricultural one, but government policies have been oblivious to this transformation.[137]

Rangeland. A case similar to that for forests can be made for privatizing government-owned, commercial grazing lands, which amount to 155 million acres, an area the size of France, Belgium, and Switzerland combined. This land generates negative cash flows of about $100 million annually, whereas comparable private rangeland normally is profitable.[138] The major impediment to privatization is the current user, who in effect has complete use of it for only the token price of a grazing permit. (Ranchers pay only $1.35 per head of cattle a month, whereas fees on private lands range from $3 to $7.[139]) Why buy it if one can use it for next to nothing? Hanke describes how to calculate the value of this land and offers a method of selling it that may be politically feasible.[140] This is a situation where the benefits are rather clearly individual and the good in question is not a collective one. It is difficult to argue for public ownership but even more difficult to privatize this property, or even to raise the fees, because of political opposition from beneficiaries of the current system.[141]

It has been argued that wilderness lands should be given outright to environmental groups such as the Sierra Club and the Audubon Society so that the groups would balance their innate desire to block development against the opportunity to allow development that would generate revenues for them that they could then use to acquire more wilderness land.[142]

Petroleum Reserves. The U.S. government finds itself in the business of owning and operating two oil fields (including the infamous Teapot Dome). It sells the oil and gas on the open market, but to meet emergency national needs it relies on the Strategic Petroleum Reserve (SPR), a stored supply of petroleum that has already been extracted from the ground. It can pump oil thirty times faster from the SPR than from its oil fields, and therefore the former is a much better emergency reserve than the latter. Running an oil field is a commercial, not a governmental, activity and can probably be run more efficiently by private owners; therefore the Reagan administration proposed selling the oil fields in a competitive process.[143]

PUBLIC INFRASTRUCTURE

A wide variety of facilities are collectively referred to as *public infrastructure* or *public works.* They include streets, highways, bridges, tunnels, airports, port facilities, waterways, water supply and distribution systems, wastewater collection and treatment systems, resource recovery plants, and public buildings such as schools, prisons, and offices.

There is growing interest in private provision of such facilities, based on the premise that "creative financing" techniques, coupled with the greater efficiency of the private sector, can significantly reduce the net cost to the public of such facilities.

As long as large federal subsidies were available to state and local governments for such infrastructure, it was always less costly to the user community to take advantage of the subsidies, as these generally overwhelmed any advantage that private-sector efficiency could offer. As federal subsidies decreased, however, and as new tax laws provided incentives for public-private partnerships to address infrastructure needs, an array of complex arrangements was created for this purpose. Although no definitive evaluation of completed projects and no clear comparisons with traditional public works projects have yet been reported, this approach, understandably, has gained the enthusiastic approval of investment bankers, accountants, construction firms, and local officials.

The sale-leaseback arrangement is one common technique, which typically involves the following steps:

1. A government unit issues tax-free industrial bonds to raise capital.
2. It lends the proceeds to a private party.
3. The private party uses the loan and adds private equity to purchase an asset from the government unit.
4. The private party leases the asset back to the government unit, which makes periodic payments to the private party.
5. The private party usually operates and maintains the asset, under a contract with the government unit.
6. On expiration of the lease, the government unit can exercise an option to purchase the asset.

The entire arrangement is highly dependent on the tax treatment of the various complicated transactions and has been criticized as a scheme to evade state constitutional limitations on public spending. Also, inasmuch as buyers of tax-free bonds tend to be upper-income individuals, a significant "tax expenditure" results.

The same facility can be provided by the private sector in a straightforward manner. Given 1984 construction costs, financing charges, and tax laws, it was calculated that private provision of water and wastewater services, for example, usually leads to a lower cost than public provision.[144]

Hanke provides guidelines for selling surplus government facilities, which he defines as assets that do not yield an appropriate rate of return. He describes a bidding procedure that will yield the information needed to make that calculation.[145] He warns, however, that in government there is a bureaucratic bias toward hoarding assets, as there are no carrying charges or rents paid for them.

The assets are considered free, for nothing has to be given up to retain them. There is a further bias against selling such assets as the revenues usually go to another agency, whereas the selling agency faces reductions in both its personnel and its budget.

Bennathan and Wishart discuss the roles of public and private enterprises in owning and operating port facilities in developing countries. While they lament the fact that empirical data are lacking, their carefully reasoned article concludes that technical changes in port operations have strengthened the case for substantially unfettered private control of port facilities, even in countries with few ports.[146]

State-Owned Enterprises

When government sells private or toll goods, it is engaged in a state-owned enterprise (SOE). By comparison with other countries, the United States has relatively few SOEs. Nevertheless, some of them came under the scrutiny of the Reagan administration, which initiated a major effort to sell or otherwise privatize them. They include regional electric power systems; a freight railroad; portions of the U.S. Postal Service; the two major airports in the Washington metropolitan area; the Federal Housing Administration; a large portfolio of loans to students, farmers, and businesses; and a number of insurance programs.[147]

Several insurance programs were proposed as candidates for privatization; this would involve changing from government to grant arrangements or from grant to market arrangements. For example, the Federal Crop Insurance Corporation (FCIC) subsidizes crop insurance for farmers, through reinsuring private companies. The subsidy distorts the true cost of production, return on investment, and land values; moreover, it encourages farmers to farm marginal lands. The administration proposed charging insurance companies for the services of FCIC and gradually phasing out the program, thus allowing private insurance companies to sell, and farmers to purchase, insurance on an actuarially sound basis.[148]

The Export-Import Bank provides direct loans, loan guarantees, and insurance to assist U.S. exporters in meeting competition that is supported by foreign official export subsidies. An interest-rate subsidy was proposed as a substitute for direct loans.[149]

The Overseas Private Investment Corporation (OPIC) is a government corporation that promotes economic development in friendly developing countries by insuring U.S. investment in those countries against political risks such as expropriation, currency inconvertibility, and loss resulting from political violence, and by providing guarantees and direct loans to help finance U.S. investment. The Reagan administration proposed privatizing OPIC, taking into consideration the appropriate role of the federal government in the political risk insurance market, the growth of a private insurance market, and a similar insurance program of the World Bank. The goal of privatization is to ensure an efficient market for political risk insurance that will support market-oriented development in Third World countries.[150]

A variety of other insurance and loan programs would be reduced or terminated, including those for small businesses, community development, farm housing, home mortgages, rural electrification, ship construction, college tuition, and railroad rehabilitation. In effect, market arrangements would replace the current grant system.[151] At present, the effect of government loans and loan insurance is to create preferred classes of borrowers and thereby "crowd out" market-rate borrowing that benefits the economy as a whole in a neutral manner.

SOEs are common outside the United States. Also called government corporations, public corporations, public enterprises, and parastatals, they make automobiles, run airlines, refine petroleum, own and operate utilities (e.g., electric, gas, water, and telephone systems), and engage in innumerable other businesses that are also routinely found in the private sector. Such enterprises may have once been private but were nationalized, or they may have been created from the outset as government enterprises, as happened in many developing countries. The extent to which major industries in different nations are run as state enterprises is shown in figure 6.1.

The classic problem of SOEs is their monopoly status. Instead of facing the marketplace, their managers look to the state to provide financing, guarantee loans, buy products, protect markets, minimize competition, and otherwise subsidize inefficiencies. A further problem of proliferating state enterprises is incoherence: According to one student of the subject, the situation grows so complicated that officials who should know what is going on do not, and the state becomes essentially unmanageable.[152]

One of the major arguments used to justify nationalization or the perpetuation of historically state-owned enterprises is that this is necessary for guiding the economy: "seizing the commanding heights of the economy." But a nation does not have to own its major industries in order to influence the economy, any more than it has to buy its citizens in the slave market in order to govern them.

Disenchantment with nationalized and state-owned enterprises is widespread. As a result, denationalization, a particular form of privatization, is proceeding rapidly in both developed and less developed nations,[153] whatever the reigning politico-ideological persuasion. ("We are all capitalists now," mourned one state economic planner.)

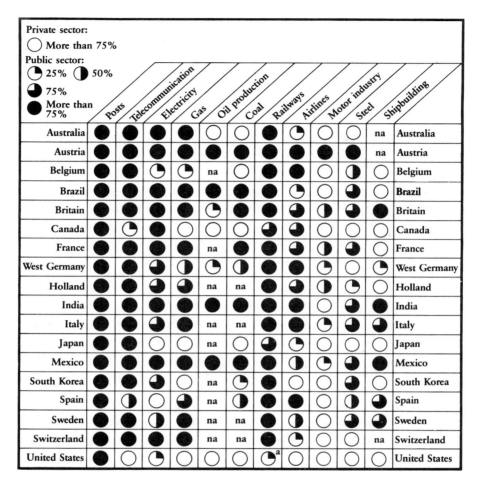

FIGURE 6.1

EXTENT OF STATE-OWNED ENTERPRISES, BY COUNTRY (1980)

SOURCE: *The Economist*, 4 January 1986, 72. Reproduced with permission.
a. Includes Conrail.

NOTE: Extensive denationalization has taken place in Britain since 1980.

Developing countries that cumulatively spent billions of dollars in foreign aid to create SOEs realized their mistake and are rapidly privatizing them, or at least talking about doing so.[154] In retrospect, the error of the developing countries was understandable.

> The European powers had run their colonies mainly through governmental bureaucracies [and promoted the economic interests of their own private firms] but allowed little or no development of large-scale indigenous businesses. It was natural, therefore, for the newly independent countries to regard bureaucracies as symbols of political maturity and [large-scale] private enterprises as instruments of economic exploitation. The former colonists, meanwhile, felt a responsibility to help with "institution building" and channeled their aid to the public sector.[155]

The range of denationalization activities is very broad. In the United Kingdom, Prime Minister Margaret Thatcher initiated a major privatization effort, resulting in divestiture of numerous state-owned industrial enterprises.[156] The government sold off all or part of its holdings in the aerospace industry, automobiles, telecommunication, radio, chemicals, oil, ferries, and hotels, among others. (For the first seven enterprises, profits rose 49 percent to record heights after privatization. Four hundred thousand jobs, or about 2 percent of all jobs in the country, were transferred from the public to the private sector.[157])

Mexico, which expanded the number of its state-owned, nonfinancial enterprises from 175 to 520 between 1960 and 1980, began to reverse the process and sold its hotel and automobile businesses. Argentina appointed a Minister of Privatization, as did Canada. Japan took the first steps to privatize its telephone, tobacco, airline, and railroad enterprises. Brazil, where the number of state enterprises quintupled between 1960 and 1980, began selling, divesting, or closing some of its 20,000 federally owned companies and official bodies. Spain, with a stake in 747 industrial companies in 1983, lost more than $2.8 billion and incurred debts of $36 billion, prompting the country to sell its textile, travel, tourist, truck, and automobile businesses. Italy sold shares in its food, telephone, electronics, aerospace, and pipeline-laying companies and its largest bank. The Philippine government put up for sale its resort hotels, bulk-cargo ships, cement plants, poultry farm, soybean and other food-processing plants, textile mill, copper mine, pulp and paper mills, plywood plant, shoe factory, jade-processing plant, and plastics plants. The trend is evident in countries on every continent, but a limiting factor in the pace of privatization is the shortage of local capital.[158]

Nowhere has privatization advanced as dramatically as in China after Mao Zedong's demise. One billion people living in a totally collectivized state were suddenly exposed to privatization. Farming communes were disbanded and most farmland was returned to private ownership, with the result that food production skyrocketed. Some manufacturing and services are also being privatized, reducing the degree of centralized economic control and laying the foundation for major changes in China's world role in the twenty-first century.

Even the Soviet Union has belatedly discovered the virtues of the marketplace and private enterprise, as it desperately tries to forestall further slippage toward Third World economic status.

Miscellaneous and Prospective Applications

Weather Forecasting

Many private firms offer specialized weather predictions for their clients, and in 1978 rivalry between private weather forecasters and the U.S. Weather Service broke into the open. Based on a sample of three snowstorms (inadequate for statistical purposes but sufficient for starting a fight), one of which was correctly predicted by a private service four days before the government predicted it, the private sector claimed credit for superior performance. A public official whose agency contracted with a private weather service explained that "when you're depending on the U.S. Weather Service, they put it [the forecast] out on their time, at their convenience, on their schedule—they're not working for us. In other words, with [the private contractor], we're the boss."[159]

Bennett and DiLorenzo report that contracting out of weather forecasts at Washington's National Airport resulted in cost savings of 36 percent (i.e., the public costs were 56 percent higher). The contract terms provided incentives for accurate forecasts by reducing the payments for poor forecasts.[160] More research is needed before any definitive conclusions can be drawn.

Bank Deposit Insurance

The federal government and some state governments in the United States guarantee savings deposits in banks and in savings and loan associations. This kind of insurance is only about fifty years old and is rarely found in other countries; for example, it does not exist in Switzerland, which is famous for its cautious approach to financial matters.

The problem with government-supplied insurance is that it is not actuarially sound, premiums are not related to risks, and risky investments are encouraged because government will foot the bill if a bank fails.

There is a successful private bank-insurance company that insures sixty-eight savings institutions in four states. It exercises much closer oversight and disciplinary powers than do federal or state insurance agencies, it requires more reserves, charges variable premiums depending on the risks taken by the bank, is more flexible, and has never experienced a failure, in sharp contrast to the state and federal agencies.[161] Although this successful example is a tiny one, private insurance is not likely to grow as long as government agencies dominate the field and can use public funds to cover losses incurred by mismanaged and undersupervised banks. This is a complex area that cannot be treated adequately here, but the concept is important enough to merit greater attention.

BANKING

In many countries, banks are nationalized, and one can ask how such banks compare to private banks. Davies examined government and private banks in Australia and found that managers of government banks hold a higher proportion of their assets in low-risk and low-paying investments than do their private counterparts. Furthermore, they arrange easier, less arduous business lives, monitor and organize work and workers less effectively than do private managers, and have larger staffs. The result is substantially higher costs in government banks and a significantly lower rate of return on sales and on capital than in private banks.[162]

MONEY SUPPLY

Among the most hallowed of national government functions is the control of money. Can this basic activity be privatized? That is, apart from contracting with private mints or printers to produce coins or paper currency, can and should the private sector issue money? An active group of economists, spearheaded by Nobel Laureates Friedrich A. Hayek and Milton Friedman, argues that monetary policy should be shaped by competitive market forces rather than government central banks; in effect, they propose to denationalize money, an iconoclastic concept that challenges (recently) established custom. They do not question government's right to issue money but its *exclusive* right to do so and to force people to use it and accept it at a particular price. Hayek reasons that with other currencies in circulation, it would be more difficult for a central bank to inflate the money supply. Competition between private issuers of brand-name money would lead to better money, just as competition in other markets leads to better products. This is certainly a provocative notion.[163]

Conclusion

Scientifically rigorous comparisons of the relative efficiency and effectiveness of alternative arrangements for service delivery require a large sample size and special-purpose, on-site data collection, using a standard framework to measure inputs and outputs. Such research is difficult, time-consuming, and costly. (For example, the comprehensive, nationwide examination of solid-waste collection carried out by Savas[164] cost almost $2 million.) In contrast, analysis of routine data, such as that found in government budgets and government-mandated reports that private organizations are sometimes required to file, is superficially enticing, as data collection costs are then small in comparison to on-site data collection costs. Such analyses are likely to be inadequate, however, if they do not allow sufficient control of all the other variables that one would like to hold constant or otherwise adjust for, and this is necessary in order to isolate the effect of arrangement alone.

Only some of the studies cited in this chapter satisfy these stringent standards; additional rigorous research is surely in order. Nevertheless, the evidence from the definitive studies, coupled with the other suggestive, if not conclusive, findings reported here, and supported theoretically and pragmatically by the obvious virtues of competition, lead one to conclude that the private sector generally can deliver so-called public services more efficiently and more effectively than government can, particularly when the latter has a monopoly.

In the next chapter we discuss alternative arrangements for a different set of services — those related more closely to the personal safety, health, and well-being of the citizenry.

Notes

1. E.S. Savas, "Municipal Monopoly," *Harper's,* December 1971, 55-60.

2. E.S. Savas, "Municipal Monopolies versus Competition in Delivering Urban Services," in *Improving the Quality of Urban Management,* ed. Willis D. Hawley and David Rogers (Beverly Hills, Calif.: Sage, 1974), 473-500; idem, ed., *Alternatives for Delivering Public Services* (Boulder, Colo.: Westview, 1977); idem, *The Organization and Efficiency of Solid Waste Collection* (Lexington, Mass.: Heath, 1977). See also Robert W. Poole, Jr., *Cut Local Taxes without Reducing Essential Services* (Santa Barbara, Calif.: Reason Press, 1976); John D. Hanrahan, *Government for Sale: Contracting Out, the New Patronage* (Washington, D.C.: American Federation of State, County, and Municipal Employees, 1977).

3. *Improve Public Services: Shut Out Contractors* (London: National Union of Public Employees, 1982).

4. Murray N. Rothbard, *For a New Liberty: The Libertarian Manifesto* (New York: Collier Macmillan, 1978); Robert W. Poole, Jr., *Cutting Back City Hall* (New York: Universe Books, 1980); Mark Frazier and Walter Olson, eds., *More for Less* (Washington, D.C.: Taxpayers' Foundation, 1980); James T. Bennett and Manuel H. Johnson, *Better Government at Half the Price: Private Production of Public Services* (Ottawa, Ill.: Caroline House, 1981); Donald Fisk, Herbert Kiesling, and Thomas Muller, *Private Provision of Public Services: An Overview* (Washington, D.C.: Urban Institute, 1978); Harry P. Hatry, *A Review of Private Approaches for Delivery of Public Services*

(Washington, D.C.: Urban Institute, 1983); E.S. Savas, *Privatizing the Public Sector* (Chatham, N.J.: Chatham House, 1982); Robert M. Spann, "Public versus Private Provision of Governmental Services," in *Budgets and Bureaucrats: The Sources of Government Growth,* ed. Thomas E. Borcherding (Durham: Duke University Press, 1977); Thomas E. Borcherding, "Toward a Positive Theory of Public Sector Supply Arrangements," in *Crown Corporations in Canada: The Calculus of Instrument Choice,* ed. J.R.S. Prichard (Scarborough, Ont.: Butterworth, 1983); International City Management Association, "Issues in Contracting for Public Services from the Private Sector," May 1982; "Alternative Approaches for Delivering Public Services," October 1982; and "Rethinking Public Services," October 1982 (Washington, D.C.).

5. See *Fiscal Watchdog,* a regular newsletter on privatization, and *Reason* magazine, both published by the Reason Foundation of Santa Monica, Calif. See also *Urban Innovation Abroad,* a newsletter of the Academy for State and Local Government, Washington, D.C., that reports privatization news from outside the United States.

6. *Passing the Bucks: The Contracting Out of Public Services* (Washington, D.C.: American Federation of State, County, and Municipal Employees, AFL-CIO, 1983).

7. E.S. Savas, "How Much Do Government Services Really Cost?" *Urban Affairs Quarterly* 15, no. 1 (September 1979): 23-41.

8. E.S. Savas, "Public versus Private Refuse Collection: A Critical Review of the Evidence," *Journal of Urban Analysis* 6 (1979): 1-13; K. Hamada and S. Aoki, " 'Spinning Off' in Japan: The Upsurge in Privatization," in *Cutback Management: A Trinational Perspective,* ed. G.G. Wynne (New Brunswick, N.J.: Transaction Books, 1983); James C. McDavid, "The Canadian Experience with Privatizing Residential Solid Waste Collection Services," *Public Administration Review* 45 (1985): 602-8; Barbara J. Stevens, "Comparing Public- and Private-Sector Productive Efficiency: An Analysis of Eight Activities," *National Productivity Review,* Autumn 1984, 395-406.

9. Barbara J. Stevens, *Delivering Municipal Services Efficiently: A Comparison of Municipal and Private Service Delivery* (Washington, D.C.: Office of Policy Development and Research, Department of Housing and Urban Development, June 1984).

10. E.S. Savas, "Policy Analysis for Local Government: Public versus Private Refuse Collection," *Policy Analysis* 3, no. 1 (Winter 1977): 49-74; Barbara J. Stevens, "Service Arrangement and the Cost of Refuse Collection," in Savas, *Organization and Efficiency,* 121-38; idem, *Delivering Municipal Services.*

11. McDavid, "Canadian Experience."

12. E.S. Savas, "An Empirical Study of Competition in Municipal Service Delivery," *Public Administration Review* 37 (1977): 717-24.

13. Savas, "Policy Analysis."

14. "Customers Rate Refuse Service," *Waste Age* 12 (November 1981): 82-88. This article is based on Donald Sexton, "Effectiveness, Equity and Responsiveness of Solid Waste Collection Services," Center for Government Studies, Graduate School of Business, Columbia University, 1979.

15. Stevens, *Delivering Municipal Services,* 182.

16. "Customers Rate Refuse Service."

17. Savas, "An Empirical Study"; idem, "Intracity Competition between Public and Private Service Delivery," *Public Administration Review* 41 (1981): 46-52.

18. Stevens, "Service Arrangement."

19. Carl F. Valente and Lydia D. Manchester, *Rethinking Local Services: Exam-*

ining Alternative Delivery Approaches (Washington, D.C.: International City Management Association, March 1984), 4.

20. Savas, *Organization and Efficiency,* 51.

21. Stevens, *Delivering Municipal Services,* 26-80.

22. Ibid., 312-69.

23. *The Road Maintenance Problem and International Assistance* (Washington, D.C.: World Bank, December 1981), foreword.

24. *The Construction Industry: Issues and Strategies in Developing Countries* (Washngton, D.C.: World Bank, 1984), 35-36. See also Clell Harral, Ernesto Henriod, and Peter Graziano, *An Appraisal of Highway Maintenance by Contract in Developing Countries,* 2d ed. (Washington, D.C.: World Bank, 1985).

25. "ROADS Public Fleet Survey," *Roads* 22, no. 12 (December 1984): 16-19.

26. "Pothole Patrol," *New York Times,* 21 July 1985.

27. For example, see Rothbard, *For a New Liberty,* 201-14; and William D. Burt, *Local Problems, Libertarian Solutions* (Washington, D.C.: Libertarian Party, 1979). See also Robert W. Poole, Jr., "Public Works," in Frazier and Olson, *More for Less.*

28. Rothbard, *For a New Liberty,* 201-2.

29. Scott Burns of Touche, Ross & Co., New York, personal communication.

30. Based on my communication with officials in New York and Philadelphia.

31. Stevens, *Delivering Municipal Services,* 290.

32. Edward K. Morlok and Philip A. Viton, "The Comparative Costs of Public and Private Providers of Mass Transit," in *Urban Transit,* ed. C.A. Lave (San Francisco: Pacific Institute, 1985), 233-54.

33. Charles Feibel and A.A. Walters, *Ownership and Efficiency in Urban Buses,* Staff Working Paper no. 371 (Washington, D.C.: World Bank, 1980).

34. Christopher Conte, "Resurgence of Private Participation in Urban Mass Transit Stirs Debate," *Wall Street Journal,* 27 November 1984.

35. Martin Tolchin, "Private Concerns Gaining Foothold in Public Transit," *New York Times,* 29 April 1985.

36. Office of the Comptroller, State of New York, *Summary of Audit Reports on New York City Transit Authority Operations,* Report No. NY-Auth-6-76, 1976.

37. Steve H. Hanke, "Privatization: Theory, Evidence, and Implementation," in *Control of Federal Spending,* ed. C. Lowell Harriss, *Proceedings of the Academy of Political Science* 35, no. 4 (New York, 1985): 101-13.

38. An analysis by Sigurd Grava and Elliot Sclar, publication pending, based on data from *1985 Report on Transit Operating Performance in New York State,* New York State Department of Transportation, 111-52.

39. Edward K. Morlok and Frederick A. Moseley, *Potential Savings from Competitive Contracting of Bus Transit,* Report R-UP9951-86-1, University of Pennsylvania Civil Engineering Department, 16 April 1986.

40. Robert A. McGuire and T. Norman Van Cott, "Public versus Private Economic Activity: A New Look at School Bus Transportation," *Public Choice* 43 (1984): 25-43.

41. New York State Legislative Commission on Expenditure Review, *Pupil Transportation Programs,* 30 January 1978.

42. Charles B. Blankart, "Bureaucratic Problems in Public Choice: Why Do Public Goods Still Remain Public?" in *Public Finance and Public Choice,* ed. K.W. Roskamp (Paris: Cujas, 1979).

43. Morlok and Viton, "Comparative Costs."

44. Ibid.

45. Gabriel Roth and George G. Wynne, *Free Enterprise Urban Transportation* (New Brunswick, N.J.: Transaction Books, 1982), 14.

46. Robert W. Poole, Jr. "Transit Systems," in *This Way Up: The Local Official's Handbook for Privatization and Contracting Out,* ed. Raymond Q. Armington and William D. Ellis (Chicago: Regnery, 1984), 20-47.

47. Morlok and Viton, "Comparative Costs."

48. Quotation from Reinhard Stuettgen, reported in *Urban Transportation Abroad* 8, no. 2 (Summer 1985).

49. A.A. Walters, *Cost and Scale of Bus Services,* Staff Working Paper no. 325 (Washington, D.C.: World Bank, 1979); see also Morlok and Viton, "Comparative Costs."

50. James L. Perry, *Organizational Form and Transit Performance: A Research Review and Empirical Analysis* (Irvine, Calif: Institute of Transportation Studies, University of California, September 1984). See also James L. Perry and Timlynn T. Babitsky, "Comparative Performance in Urban Bus Transit: Assessing Privatization Strategies," *Public Administration Review* 46 (1986): 57-66.

51. Poole, "Transit Systems."

52. Gabriel Roth, *Private Provision of Public Services in Developing Countries* (New York: Oxford University Press, 1987); Roth and Wynne, *Free Enterprise Urban Transportation.*

53. Charles A. Lave, "The Private Challenge to Public Transportation—An Overview," in *Urban Transit,* 1-30.

54. Christopher Conte and Daniel Machalaba, "Amtrak May Have to Drop Some Weight to Survive," *Wall Street Journal,* 8 May 1985.

55. James T. Bennett and T.J. DiLorenzo, "Public Employee Unions and the Privatization of 'Public' Services," *Journal of Labor Research* 4 (Winter 1983): 33-45. See also Hanke, "Privatization."

56. Office of Management and Budget, *Major Policy Initiatives, Fiscal Year 1987* (Washington, D.C.: Government Printing Office, 1986),: 45-46.

57. Reginald Stuart, "Stockman Presses Senators to End Amtrak Subsidy," *New York Times,* 30 April 1985.

58. Peter F. Drucker, "Beyond the Bell Breakup," *Public Interest* 77 (Fall 1984): 3-27. See also Susan Chira, "Japan Railways: Sleek but Troubled," *New York Times,* 26 November 1984.

59. Demetrios Panagiotakopoulos, University of Thrace, Greece; private communication.

60. George W. Downs and Patrick D. Larkey, *The Search for Government Efficiency* (Philadelphia: Temple University Press, 1986), 37-38.

61. David G. Davies, "The Efficiency of Public versus Private Firms, the Case of Australia's Two Airlines," *Journal of Law and Economics* 14, no. 1 (April 1971): 149-65; idem, "Property Rights and Economic Efficiency—The Australian Airlines Revisited," *Journal of Law and Economics* 20, no. 1 (April 1977): 223-26.

62. Michael J. Kirby, "Airline Economies of Scale and Australian Domestic Air Transport Policy," in *Property Rights, Regulation and Efficiency: A Further Comment on Australia's Two Airline Policy,* ed. Michael J. Kirby and Robert P. Albon (Canberra: Australian National University Press, 1984).

63. Robert W. Poole, Jr., "Towards Safer Skies," in *Instead of Regulation,* ed. R.W. Poole, Jr. (Lexington, Mass.: Heath, 1982).

64. Breton R. Schrender, "Some Small Airports Hiring Firms to Provide Air-Traffic Controllers," *Wall Street Journal,* 24 March 1982.

65. Larry Phillips, "Time to Change Our Stalling Air Traffic Control System," *Wall Street Journal,* 5 July 1984.

66. "Privatizing Selected Coast Guard Services," in *Report on Privatization, President's Private Sector Survey on Cost Control* (Washington, D.C.: Government Printing Office, 1983), 18-197. See also Philip E. Fixler, Jr., *Privatizing Coast Guard Services* (Washington, D.C.: Citizens for a Sound Economy, 1985).

67. Ibid., 128-32; see also "Privatization of National Space Transportation System," in *Report on Privatization,* 72-87.

68. Office of Management and Budget, *Major Policy Initiatives,* 47-48.

69. Arthur L. Levine, "Commercialization of Space: Policy and Administration Issues," *Public Administration Review* 45 (1985): 562-69.

70. G. Harry Stine, "Closing the Door to Space Development," *Wall Street Journal,* 17 July 1985.

71. Roth, *Private Provision of Public Services.*

72. W.M. Crain and A. Zardkoohi, "A Test of the Property-Rights Theory of the Firm: Water Utilities in the United States," *Journal of Law and Economics* 21 (October 1978): 395-408.

73. Susan Feigenbaum and Ronald Teeples, *Public versus Private Water Delivery: A Hedonic Cost Approach* (Claremont, Calif.: Claremont Graduate School, June 1982).

74. Steve H. Hanke, *On Privatizing Water and Wastewater Services* (Baltimore: Johns Hopkins University Press, 1982).

75. Robert Lindsey, "Arid West Realizing Water Is a Salable Crop," *New York Times,* 10 June 1985; idem, "Irrigation Policy Assailed on Coast," *New York Times,* 22 August 1985. See also Terry L. Anderson, ed., *Water Rights: Scarce Resource Allocation, Bureaucracy, and the Environment* (San Francisco: Pacific Institute, 1984).

76. Harvey Goldman and Sandra Mokuvos, *The Privatization Book* (New York: Arthur Young, 1984).

77. Richard J. Girouard and David L. Phillips, "Contract Operations Save Over $1 Million," *Public Works* 116, no. 4 (April 1985).

78. Hanke, "Privatization," 110.

79. Roth, *Private Provision of Public Services.*

80. R.A. Meyer, "Publicly Owned vs. Privately Owned Utilities: A Policy Choice," *Review of Economics and Statistics* 7, no. 4 (1975): 391-99.

81. P.C. Mann and J.L. Mikesell, "Ownership and Water Systems Operations," *Water Works Bulletin,* October 1976; see also Feigenbaum and Teeples, "Public versus Private Water Delivery."

82. R.L. Wallace and P.E. Junk, "Economic Inefficiency of Small Municipal Electric Generating Systems," *Land Economics* 46 (February 1970): 98-104.

83. James A. Yunker, "Economic Performance of Public and Private Enterprise: The Case of U.S. Electric Utilities," *Journal of Economics and Business* 28 (Fall 1975): 60-67; and Richard Hellman, *Government Competition in the Electric Utility Industry* (New York: Praeger, 1972). See also Leland G. Neuberg, "Two Issues in the Municipal Ownership of Electric Power Distribution Systems," *Bell Journal of Economics* 8, no. 1

(Spring 1977): 303-23.

84. Sam Peltzman, "Pricing in Public and Private Enterprises: Electric Utilities in the United States," *Journal of Law and Economics* 14 (April 1971): 109-47.

85. Spann, "Public versus Private Provision."

86. Hellman, *Government Competition.*

87. Walter J. Primeaux, Jr., "Estimation of the Price Effects of Competition: The Case of Electricity," *Resources and Energy* 7 (1985): 325-40.

88. U.S. General Accounting Office, *Increased Productivity Can Lead to Lower Costs at Federal Hydroelectric Plants,* report by the Comptroller General of the United States (Washington, D.C.: Government Printing Office, 29 May 1979).

89. *War on Waste, President's Private Sector Survey on Cost Control* (New York: Macmillan, 1984), 437; Office of Management and Budget, *Major Policy Initiatives,* 25-26.

90. Louis DeAlessi, "An Economic Analysis of Government Ownership and Regulation: Theory and the Evidence from the Electric Power Industry," *Public Choice* 19 (Fall 1974): 1-42.

91. Roth, *Private Provision of Public Services.*

92. Ibid.

93. Ibid.

94. See Ronald Kessler, "The Great Mail Bungle," *Washington Post,* 12 June 1974; Henry Scott-Stokes, "UPS Shines in Yule Package Service," *New York Times,* 10 December 1977; and Ernest Holsendolph, "Mails Losing Package Business," *New York Times,* 30 May 1977.

95. Stuart M. Butler, *Privatizing Federal Spending: A Strategy to Reduce the Deficit* (New York: Universe Books, 1985), 125.

96. U.S. General Accounting Office, *The Post Office Can Substantially Reduce Its Cleaning Costs,* report by the Comptroller General of the United States, AFMD-83-23 (Washington, D.C.: Government Printing Office, 1982).

97. Hanke, "Privatization," 108.

98. U.S. General Accounting Office, *Replacing Post Offices with Alternative Services,* report by the Comptroller General of the United States, GGD-82-99 (Washington, D.C.: Government Printing Office, 1982).

99. Butler, *Privatizing Federal Spending,* 125.

100. Jack Shafer, "A Private Firm Plays Post Office to Congress," *Wall Street Journal,* 19 February 1985.

101. John Haldi, *Postal Monopoly: An Assessment of the Private Express Statutes* (Washington, D.C.: American Enterprise Institute, 1974).

102. Ted Vaden, "Soaring Costs Cloud Postal Service Future," *Congressional Quarterly Weekly Report* 34 (20 March 1976): 627-33; Ernest Holsendolph, "Should U.S. Postal Office Continue as a Monopoly?" *New York Times,* 3 February 1976; idem, "Mail Service Competition Rising," *New York Times,* 18 April 1976, 31; Cynthia Jabs, "And Deliver Us from the Post Office," *New York Times,* 4 July 1976, sec. 3, p. 2; Philip H. Dougherty, "Alternatives to the Postal Service," *New York Times,* 2 February 1978, D11; "Deliverer Facing Action as Flouter of Postal Law," *New York Times,* 18 April 1976, 31; "Mailman Vows He'll Fight On," *Chicago Tribune,* 17 August 1976, sec. 4, p. 13; "Court Stops Mrs. Brennan's Postal Service," *New York Times,* 6 August 1978; and Michael S. Larsky, "Alternative Delivery: Is the Postal Service Really Necessary?" *Folio* 2 (February 1973): 34-40.

103. Phyllis Berman, "Do We Really Need the Postal Service?" *Forbes,* 11 June 1979, 47-49.

104. "Agencies Told to Skip Postal Service," *Washington Post,* 21 May 1976.

105. Butler, *Privatizing Federal Spending,* 126.

106. Ibid., 127.

107. Roth, *Private Provision of Public Services.*

108. Ibid.

109. Christopher J. Chipello, "Privatization May Open Japan's Telecommunication Market," *Wall Street Journal,* 1 April 1985.

110. *Examples of Commercial Activities,* Attachment A of Circular A-76 (rev.) (Washington, D.C.: Office of Management and Budget, 4 August 1983).

111. *Enhancing Governmental Productivity through Competition: Targeting for Annual Savings of One Billion Dollars by 1988* (Washington, D.C.: Office of Management and Budget, Office of Federal Procurement Policy, March 1984).

112. *Contracting Out for Federal Support Services: Potential Savings and Budgetary Impacts* (Washington, D.C.: Congressional Budget Office, October 1982).

113. *Enhancing Governmental Productivity,* 13-14. Careful analysis is needed to glean this figure from the reported data. The in-house cost estimate, revised to allow for salaries in the comparable time period, was 7 percent less than the actual cost of the in-house work before competitive contracting was considered. The latter cost was 38 percent greater than the actual contract costs (line 6 in table 1 of the reference).

114. Data were kindly provided by the Office of the Chief Administrative Officer of Los Angeles County.

115. Barbara J. Stevens, *Delivering Municipal Services,* 81-140.

116. Charles Kaiser, "Custodial Services in the Schools Termed Wasteful by Goldin," *New York Times,* 24 January 1977, 45.

117. Blankart, "Bureaucratic Problems."

118. Werner W. Pommerehne and Friedrick Schneider, *Private or Public Production: A European Perspective* (Aarhus, Denmark: Institute of Economics, University of Aarhus, 1985), 12-15; see also Philip E. Fixler, Jr., *Germany's Privatization Push,* Fiscal Watchdog no. 95, Local Government Center (Santa Monica, Calif.: Reason Foundation, September 1984).

119. Frederick O'R. Hayes, *Productivity in Local Government* (Lexington, Mass.: Heath, 1977), 43.

120. Stevens, *Delivering Municipal Services,* 429-500.

121. Ibid.

122. Ibid., 370-428.

123. I am grateful to Lynn Bayer, of the Chief Administrative Officer's staff, for providing data for this analysis.

124. Stevens, *Delivering Municipal Services,* 204-59.

125. U.S. General Accounting Office, *The Government Can Be More Productive in Collecting Its Debts by Following Commercial Practices,* report by the Comptroller General of the United States, FGMSD-78-59 (Washington, D.C.: Government Printing Office, 23 February 1979).

126. Poole, *Cutting Back City Hall,* 164.

127. John Contney, Statement, U.S. House of Representatives, *Hearings on Contracting Out of Jobs and Services, Part II, Subcommittee on Employee Ethics and Utiliz-*

ation, Committee on Post Office and Civil Service, Serial no. 95-29 (Washington, D.C.: Government Printing Office, 1977), 74-75.

128. Charles Kaiser, "Private Towaways," *New York Times,* 4 September 1976.

129. "City of San Francisco Contracts Out Budget Bureau Services and Saves $$," *Newsletter, Municipal Finance Officers Association* 54, no. (16 February 1972): 2.

130. Susan Tompor, "For Fast Cash, Cities Pursue Illegal Parkers," *Wall Street Journal,* 23 July 1981, 25.

131. Martin Tolchin, "U.S. Hires Private Concerns to Check Job Seekers," *New York Times,* 1 February 1986, 54.

132. Hanke, "Privatization," 106.

133. Blankart, "Bureaucratic Problems."

134. Pommerehne and Schneider, *Private or Public Production,* 14.

135. B. Delworth Gardner, "Foreword," in *Forestlands: Public and Private,* ed. Robert T. Deacon and M. Bruce Johnson (San Francisco: Pacific Institute, 1985), xxii.

136. Robert T. Deacon and M. Bruce Johnson, "Introduction," in Deacon and Johnson, eds., *Forestlands,* 1-22.

137. Ibid.

138. Hanke, "Privatization," 106.

139. Philip Shabecoff, "Rise in Federal Grazing Fees Is Sought by Wildlife Group," *New York Times,* 31 December 1985.

140. Steve H. Hanke, "Land Policy," in *Agenda '83,* ed. Richard N. Holwill (Washington, D.C.: Heritage Foundation, 1983), 181-91.

141. Frank J. Popper, "The Timely End of the Sagebrush Rebellion," *Public Interest,* no. 76 (Summer 1984): 61-73.

142. Richard L. Stroup and John Baden, *Natural Resources: Bureaucratic Myths and Environmental Management* (San Francisco: Pacific Institute, 1983); see also Butler, *Privatizing Federal Spending,* 82-91.

143. Office of Management and Budget, *Major Policy Initiatives,* 27-28.

144. Goldman and Mokuvos, *The Privatization Book;* and Steve H. Hanke, *On Privatizing Urban Infrastructure* (Washington, D.C.: Office of Policy Development and Research, Department of Housing and Urban Development, April 1983).

145. Ibid.; see also Hanke, "Land Policy."

146. Esra Bennathan and Jennifer Wishart, *Private and Public Enterprise in the Ports of Developing Countries,* Working Paper (Washington, D.C.: World Bank, 1982).

147. Office of Management and Budget, *Major Policy Initiatives,* 23-48, 159-60.

148. Ibid., 43-44.

149. Ibid., 39-40.

150. Ibid., 41-42.

151. Ibid., 153-60.

152. Ira Sharkansky, *Wither the State?* (Chatham, N.J.: Chatham House, 1979), 7-10.

153. "Privatization—Everybody's Doing It, Differently," *Economist* 3 (January 1986): 71-86; and Peter Young, *Privatization around the Globe* (Dallas: National Center for Policy Analysis, 1986).

154. Anatole Kaletsky, "Everywhere the State Is in Retreat," *Financial Times* (London), 2 August 1985.

155. Ibid.

156. "Privatization," *Economist.*

157. Peter Young, "Privatization in Great Britain," *Government Union Review* 7, no. 2 (Spring 1986): 1-22.

158. "Privatization," *Economist.*

159. Gregory Jaynes, "Public versus Private Weatherman," *New York Times,* 15 February 1978. See also J. T. Bennett and M. T. Johnson, *Federal Government Growth, 1959-78: Theory and Empirical Evidence* (New York: International Center for Economic Policy Studies, 1980).

160. Bennett and DiLorenzo, "Public Employee Unions," 39.

161. Catherine England, "Private Deposit Insurance That's Worked," *Wall Street Journal,* 18 June 1985; see also Martin Tolchin, "Private Insurance for Banks Debated," *New York Times,* 11 June 1985.

162. David G. Davies, "Property Rights and Economic Behavior in Private and Government Enterprises: The Case of Australia's Banking System" (manuscript, Duke University, August 1978).

163. Friedrich A. Hayek, *Denationalization of Money* (London: Institute for Economic Affairs, 1976).

164. Savas, *Organization and Efficiency.*

7. Applications in Protective and Human Services

Perhaps the most fundamental reason why government evolved was to assure the safety of its citizens. The security of the populace, whether locally through police and prisons or globally through national defense, is a most basic responsibility of government. Other responsibilities have been added throughout the nation's history, and today it is assumed that government must play a large role with respect to the health, education, and general well-being of the citizenry. This chapter examines alternative service-delivery arrangements for the "human services" the public wants and needs.

Public Safety

Public safety is the ultimate collective good and the most basic responsibility entrusted to the state. Nonetheless, even in this area privatized arrangements can be found. This section addresses policing, fire protection, and prisons. National defense is discussed in the following section.

POLICING

Basic protection is provided by self-service to some degree; for example, households and businesses employ individual protective measures such as locks, bars, gates, safes, and burglar alarms. The mainstay of public safety, however, is an organized security force.

Security forces may be public or private. Public agencies are traditional police departments that patrol their home communities, but they can also serve nearby communities under intergovernmental contractual arrangements; county police and sheriffs often sell their services in this manner. Private firms may be hired by individuals, businesses, and governments to guard particular buildings and properties, but they can also be hired by neighborhood associations and governments to patrol the streets and perform most police functions.[1]

Intergovernmental contracting for police service has been examined and was found to improve overall efficiency. It allows small cities to exploit economies of scale by purchasing services from large-scale producers; it preserves local autonomy; and it imposes competitive pressure on the producer. This pressure arises because (1) producers, typically county sheriff departments, must generate and make available detailed cost data to their customers, namely, purchasing cities and residents of unincorporated areas; and (2) each purchasing city poses the threat of starting its own police department. The observed result of the competitive pressure is that urban county sheriff departments that supply services on contract are more cost efficient than departments that have no contract operation.[2]

Turning to purely private policing, one must begin by noting that guards in the private security industry outnumber law-enforcement officers, with 680,000 of the former compared to 580,000 of the latter. Moreover, expenditures in 1980 for private security forces in the United States were $21.7 billion, compared to $13.8 billion for public police forces, and government agencies paid an estimated $3.3 billion to private security companies for their services.[3]

The growth of private policing can be seen in villages that cater to the wealthy; these are the modern equivalents of medieval walled cities.[4] But private policing is also evident in middle-class communities, where families pay up to $150 a year for around-the-clock patrols.[5] Indeed, a survey of New York City residents revealed that 69 percent of the people either pay for private security or say that they would pay up to $120 a year for it, whereas only 59 percent believed that more police officers on foot patrol would help reduce crime a lot.[6] Competition among private firms is strong, and often there is competition among public police departments that want to grow by selling their services to small towns that do not have their own force. A senior police official acknowledges the increasing preference among middle-income and upper-income families for private security services and fears that public police departments will be undersold: "I can see the day when an entrepreneur will come along and say I can police the Bronx for $50 million less and do a better job."[7] If that were indeed to happen, no doubt there would be widespread rejoicing.

Private guards were used to guard equipment and property within Boston's City Hall, instead of using regular city police for this purpose. The U.S. General Services Administration makes extensive use of contract guard services, using them to supply 41 percent of its needs.[8] Private security firms conduct passenger and baggage screening at airports, protect stores against shoplifters, and provide security at banks and hotels, generally working in close coordination with local police departments.[9]

Only a few communities in the United States contract with private firms for all their police work. A widely reported example is Reminderville, Ohio, a small town of two thousand people located between Cleveland and Akron.

The private firm was started by a retired police chief from a nearby town and was awarded the contract when the county sheriff, who had been providing contract service, raised his price to $180,000 a year. For exactly half the price, the private firm provides twice as many patrol cars and has a six-minute emergency response, compared to forty-five minutes for the sheriff.[10]

Because municipal contracts for private policing are so rare in the United States, no meaningful comparative studies have been reported. In Switzerland, the practice is more common. Thirty villages and townships there contract with Securitas, a private company, and achieve substantial savings, according to the Swiss Association of Towns and Townships, although no analysis is available to support that assertion. Contracts typically involve foot and vehicle patrol, building security checks, and nightly closing checks of bars and restaurants.[11]

Guard services, as distinguished from street patrol, lend themselves to comparative studies. Los Angeles County awarded thirty-six contracts for security services from 1980 to 1984; county data show that the cost was 34 percent greater when the work was performed by county personnel. The same caveat noted in the discussion of grounds maintenance (see chapter 6) applies here: No information was available concerning the level and quality of service before and after contracting out.

Legitimate concerns can be raised about the level of training of private guards, who are sometimes hired at the minimum wage and sent out on the job with no training and minimal instructions. With brand-name firms, however, this problem may be no worse than the problem of errant police officers. In the meanwhile, it would appear that the best way to deal with the issue is through appropriate contract specifications and performance monitoring.

When voluntary neighborhood patrols, and private guard services engaged by neighborhood groups, began to proliferate in the late 1960s, some concern was expressed that they would deteriorate into vigilante squads. These fears proved unfounded. Indeed, in many communities the police came to look favorably on crime-watch programs and voluntary citizen street patrols.

FIRE PROTECTION

Fire protection is another vital service provided by public agencies, private firms, and volunteers. Two major studies, one in Denmark and one in Canada, compared the efficiency of the public and private arrangements.

In Denmark, the Falck company provides fire protection to almost half the population. Started in 1906 as a private salvage corps, the firm began providing motorized fire protection by contract to rural areas and then expanded to towns and cities. In 1983 the firm had 6,000 employees and 130 stations staffed around the clock. Besides fire protection, it operates emergency ambulances (including helicopter ambulances), does road towing (mostly for private subscribers), and provides water rescue service.

The costs of fire protection in 241 Danish municipalities were analyzed using a multivariable regression model, and the cost difference between private and public service was found to be "next to incredible." The cost of the former was 46.3 kroner per capita, versus 131.9 for the latter; that is, the public service was almost three times as expensive as contract service. If the analysis is conducted only for the 22 largest municipalities, the result is even more one-sided. The difference is attributed to three factors: (1) economies of scale (municipal fire departments are constrained to function at whatever size their jurisdiction happens to be); (2) competition from alternative suppliers (if Falck were not competitive, it would be pushed out of the market); and (3) separation of the arranger (the articulator of demand) from the producer. When these two are the same, the study's author warns, bureaucratic imperialism can overcome the forces for austerity, and he quotes a candid fire chief to that effect: ". . . a dynamic fire chief . . . will naturally try to make the fire department grow to satisfy his ambitions as a leader and to have deputies to do the work in the department which he dislikes himself."[12]

In Canada, fire protection was studied in 104 municipalities with populations greater than 10,000. Unlike Denmark, Canada has few if any private fire-fighting firms, and so the study focused on all-volunteer, paid, and mixed departments. The cost of all-paid, municipal fire departments was about a third higher than the cost of departments that had both volunteers and paid firefighters, but the effectiveness of the two (as measured by property losses) was no different. The fact that such mixed departments are so common in Canada, the authors of the study observe, indicates that many municipalities have discovered for themselves the advantages of mixing volunteers and paid firefighters, without the loss of service quality sometimes associated with all-volunteer departments.[13] A study of cities in the United States came to similar conclusions.[14]

Fire protection in American cities was provided exclusively by private firms and volunteers in the nineteenth century, but municipalization started in 1853 as cities grew, and the private firms became extinct. Now, private fire departments are enjoying a renaissance, with seventeen of them operating in fourteen states; they even have their own trade association. The pioneer in the industry, founded in 1948 in Scottdale, Arizona, is the Rural/Metro Fire Department. Serving 20 percent of Arizona's population, and operating fifty fire departments in five states, the firm was studied and its costs compared to those of paid, volunteer, and mixed fire departments in forty-nine cities.[15] The sample was large enough to permit isolation of the various cost determinants and project what the costs would be in Scottsdale if it had one of the other service arrangements. It was concluded that the cost of contract fire protection in Scottsdale was only 53 percent of the estimated cost of supplying the service by a government agency; that is, the latter would be 89 percent more costly.

In addition to the economic comparison, observers of the firm in Arizona comment admiringly on the highly innovative and imaginative developments introduced there, including robot firefighting equipment, high-visibility paint on fire trucks, high-capacity hose, and creative staffing patterns.[16] Moreover, the effectiveness of Rural/Metro and other private fire departments, as rated by insurance companies, is about the same as municipal fire departments.[17] The founder of Rural/Metro presents data showing the cost of private service to be about half the national average.[18]

The high costs of municipal fire departments, particularly for labor, are legendary. In Oakland, California, benefits are 79 percent of salaries, and the total annual cost of salary and fringe benefits for a fireman with four years of service is $61,392.[19] When a small midwestern city tried to reduce the cost of its fire department, all the firefighters resigned, then they audaciously tried to recall a councilman, abolish the city-manager form of government, and capture a majority of seats on the city council. The effort failed badly.[20] Efforts to hire private fire companies arouse strong passions.[21]

Judging from the available information, the best approach for most communities of small-to-average size is a fire department that has some full-time paid professionals and relies on volunteers who work at other jobs in the community and can be summoned by pager directly to the fire. When not responding to alarms, the paid firefighters should be spending virtually all their time on fire prevention efforts, inspecting premises in coordination with "civilians" in the buildings department. Given the strong traditions of conventional city fire departments and their resistance to change, attempts to introduce volunteers, to merge police and fire departments, to hire a private firm, or to cut back the existing department will be met with fierce opposition.

PRISONS

In the United States there is a growing demand for incarceration of criminals, but the supply of prison space is not keeping pace, at least not at the current price. Prisons are overcrowded; the cost of prison construction and operation is high; and the public does not want to pay the price, although it demands that criminals be locked up. These conditions are ripe for competition and for new suppliers to come forth, and that is what privatization of prisons represents.[22]

The private sector can perform several distinct functions with respect to prisons: (1) finance and construct prisons; (2) operate facilities for juveniles;

(3) operate facilities for adults; (4) provide work for prisoners; and (5) provide specific contractual services to prisons, for example, health care and vocational education for inmates and training for staff.

Public interest is focused on the role of private firms in the first three areas, the construction and operation of various kinds of prisons. Private organizations, particularly not-for-profit ones, have long operated halfway houses for offenders, but now they are operating the detention facilities themselves, including a medium-security prison for convicted adult felons. Maximum-security prisons as well are being planned by private, for-profit firms. In 1985, some two dozen adult prisons were being built or were operated by private firms. Most of them were for illegal aliens and protective-custody prisoners. In a dramatic proposal, however, the Corrections Corporation of America offered to take over and operate the entire prison system of Tennessee. It proposed a ninety-nine-year lease, offered to pay the state $100 million, and promised to spend another $150 million on capital improvements, including construction of two new maximum-security prisons. In return, the state would pay them on a per diem basis for each of the roughly seven thousand prisoners. The proposal was declined, but a great deal of attention was drawn to this bold concept.

The interest in prison privatization stems from the perceived efficiency in operation, speed in construction, and flexibility in innovation of the private sector. Public costs are said to be some 20 to 40 percent greater, but the data are flimsy: Public costs omit various factors, and private costs may or may not cover the cost of construction of new facilities, and so the institutions are not comparable.[23] The definitive study of relative costs remains to be carried out, as the sample size grows and as uniform cost frameworks are constructed.

Contract services in *existing* prisons are already extensive. Fifty-two agencies in thirty-eight states had about $200 million worth of contracts with private firms for thirty-two different kinds of services. The agencies reported that contract services were more cost effective than they could provide. Advantages outweighed disadvantages, and most agencies planned to expand their use of contracts for specific services; 22 percent even indicated that they would consider contracting out the operation of entire facilities.[24]

The private-sector advantage in speed and flexibility of construction seems supportable. Private financing and construction is attractive to state governments in part because it permits them to evade voter approval of bond issues: Typically, the state does not have to raise the capital to build the prison; the private sector builds the prison with private financing and operates it, while the state makes annual payments to the owner under a lease-purchase contract. This feature can save time and money for state governments, although an eyebrow could be raised about it inasmuch as it bypasses direct approval by the voters. Logan provides several illustrations of the speed and flexibility of private firms in responding to government requests for more prison space. He also derives arguments from the general concepts of privatization to support the proposition that commercial prisons could save taxpayers money without mistreating prisoners or allowing unacceptable prison conditions to develop.[25]

Concern is nevertheless being expressed, mostly by civil libertarians and correction officers and officials, about the movement toward private prisons. The issues raised include basic constitutional questions about the right of private individuals to deprive someone of his freedom. Advocates of privatization respond that only the state has a right to imprison someone, but surely not only the state can run a prison in a fair, humane, and efficient manner. (In fact, state prisons are hardly paragons: In 1986 no less than thirty-three states were under court orders to correct the miserable conditions in their prisons.[26]) Legitimate issues that will have to be sorted out are contractual standards for inmate care and staff training, and guidelines for punishment and the use of force within the private prison, although this issue remains no different for state prisons. Authority and liability will have to be carefully and clearly allocated between public and private agents. Some think it immoral to profit by imprisoning people, but this is no more immoral than paying police officers to capture felons or paying physicians to save lives.

Some opponents of privatization worry that private firms would lobby for more and longer prison sentences and less use of probation, parole, and halfway houses. One reply to this concern is that such action would demonstrate responsiveness to the public, which is demanding longer sentences to keep criminals off the streets. Another counter to this concern is that it does not occur today, although prison officials, guards, and their unions could presumably behave in that manner for the same reason, namely, aggrandizement of their organizations. Finally, one can look by analogy at day-care centers: Private contractors in that business are not notably active in encouraging higher birthrates and opposing birth control and abortion. Nevertheless, it is possible for a prospending coalition to emerge over time and to hamper elected officials; the matter deserves attention when and if prison privatization is widespread.

Prison work is an area where private prisons may be able to make a truly significant contribution, creating factories with fences instead of warehouses with walls, in the words of former Chief Justice Warren E. Burger. Of course, care must be taken to avoid a modern replica of the old system of leasing prisoners to farms, where they worked for next to nothing.

Legislative and political barriers to private prisons and prison work (including some union opposition) will have to be overcome. The critical need is to define clearly the respective roles of the public agency and the contractor, to develop quality standards, and to monitor the performance of the contracted work. Satisfying the last requirement could involve a gamut of activities, from examining the contractor's records and conducting on-site inspections to the use of temporarily imprisoned undercover agents and sophisticated opinion surveys among inmates. Recidivists might be particularly in demand as interview subjects if they had been previously imprisoned elsewhere, as they could offer the perspective of a comparison shopper.

National Defense

MILITARY PROCUREMENT

About one-quarter of the U.S. defense budget is for weapons procurement, and almost all of that is done by contracting with the private sector. The results do not always add luster to this arrangement. In the mid-1980s, there was an unending series of disclosures about cost overruns for weapon systems, high prices for standard spare parts, and large expenditures for such mundane items as coffeepots and ashtrays. These unfortunate experiences have been cited as arguments against contracting, although the alternative is not clear.

The problem is that the contracting is done with insufficient competition and inadequate testing of the delivered products. A public-spending coalition has developed between contractors and military officials, with the Congress willingly coopted by military spending plans in every state. Overly close relationships have developed, and some defense contractors—those with assured futures as sole-source suppliers—are more like government agencies than private enterprises in the marketplace. This is a potential hazard of contracting in general: the emergence of a spending alliance between buyer and seller.[27] This does not imply venality or corruption, but simply enthusiastic agreement that it would be nice to have, for example, a hi-tech, rapid-fire, purple cannon with tank treads and tailfins that fires multiple laser beams simultaneously to shoot down bullets before they strike.

To protect against such occurrences requires good contract management. Careful preparation of contract specifications for necessary systems is the first step, and truly competitive bidding must be encouraged and rewarded. Rigorous acceptance testing of the delivered systems is indispensable and should be carried out by an independent unit, not by the unit that wants the system.

In the section on commercial services (see chapter 6), we saw that the Defense Department (DOD) does substantially better in contracting for commercial services than for weapons systems.

SHIP MAINTENANCE

Ship maintenance is a function necessary for both public (e.g., U.S. Navy) and private vessels. The indications are that private-sector maintenance is more efficient than public-sector maintenance. The General Accounting Office (GAO) studied naval support vessels and compared them to similar commercial ships. The naval ships were at sea only 20 percent of the time, whereas the commercial ships were at sea two to three times as much, and therefore would be expected to undergo more maintenance. Nevertheless, the annual cost of maintaining the naval ships was five times as much, $2 million versus $400,000 per ship. Moreover, the commercial vessels are out of service for only 11 to 31 days a year, compared to 30 to 68 days for the typical naval support ship. Finally, the GAO discovered that whereas the *largest* crew it found on a commercial ship numbered 46, the *smallest* crew size on a naval support ship was 92, exactly twice the complement.[28]

MILITARY BASE SUPPORT

To a significant degree, base support services at military installations are obtained by contract. Bennett and DiLorenzo compared contract with in-house costs and report data on facility maintenance, vehicle maintenance, aircraft maintenance, custodial services, food services, laundry and dry cleaning, housing services, and base operations. When it was conducted in-house, the work cost $266 million, 18 percent more than the contract cost.[29]

These findings are consistent with more limited earlier reports. The GAO examined support services at domestic military installations and concluded that at twenty-two of the twenty-seven bases the services would have been less costly — by $3.7 million — if the work had been done by contractors. As a result, the GAO recommended more extensive contracting of such activities. Also, a RAND study compared support services at two similar air force bases in the Southwest. As measured by the availability of parts and planes, the one serviced by air force civilian employees had lower quality and less responsive support than the one serviced by a contractor, while using 35 percent more manpower and costing 15 percent more than the latter.[30] Hanke provides additional corroborative details on this issue.[31]

Health Care

Because of the rapid rise in the cost of health care — it represented 11 percent of GNP in the United States in 1984, the highest of any industrial nation — profound changes have taken place in the institutional arrangements used to provide this vital service. For-profit hospital chains have taken over both private voluntary hospitals and public hospitals, market-responsive urgent-care centers are drawing patients away from hospitals and physicians' offices, office surgery is supplanting some in-patient hospital treatment, the management of entire hospitals is being contracted out, hospital activities have been dissected and parts have been contracted out, kidney dialysis centers have sprung up, home care by contractors is shortening hospital stays, health maintenance organizations (HMOs) contract to keep people healthy instead of merely treating them when they are sick, and hospitals are integrating backward by selling health insurance. In addition, Medicare and Medicaid reimbursement policies are changing, both for patients and for hospitals. Emerging from this turbulence may be a system of brand-name medical care, a potentially welcome development. Besides all these changes, the importance of self-service is being recognized as people learn to eat better, exercise more, and smoke less.

This section discusses privatization as it relates to general, Veterans Administration (VA), and military hospitals, to ambulance service, to nursing homes, to health insurance (including Medicare), and to family planning.

General Hospitals

Hospital corporations have grown rapidly as they buy, lease, or assume management of public hospitals and voluntary hospitals. This phenomenon is a result of a change in philosophy. Hospital care was originally viewed as doing good, more or less an eleemosynary duty rather than an economic activity, and therefore somehow exempt from the constraint of limited resources. To providers who always put compassion over cost, treating health care as a commodity was unthinkable. Nevertheless, as the universal applicability of economic laws pressed home and costs rose through the roof, for-profit hospitals that could provide good care at reasonable cost became more widely accepted, and thus the hospital "business" and the health-care "industry" were born. Former Secretary of Health, Education, and Welfare Joseph A. Califano, Jr., long an advocate of a major government role in health care, and of strong government controls on medical costs, came to realize that "the key to health care cost containment rests in an aroused private sector . . . in an awakened, varied, competitive world of business purchasers [of health insurance] insisting on high-quality care at much lower cost."[32]

Competition is now burgeoning—and apparently working. Hospitals compete to become "favored providers" in the health-insurance plans of large employers. For-profit hospital chains, which took over 180 public hospitals between the late 1970s and 1984, and had about 20 percent of all hospital beds in the country, compete intensively with one another. They face further competitive cost pressure from firms that provide contract management of specific services within public and voluntary hospitals. A survey showed that more than five thousand individual hospital departments were being managed by eighty-four outside contractors. The most commonly contracted functions were, in descending order, housekeeping, food service, emergency room, plant operations and maintenance, respiratory therapy, pharmacy, laundry, and data processing.[33] As with many services, it is possible to separate hospital service into its individual components and utilize different arrangements for the different components.

The expected advantages of for-profit hospitals compared to public and voluntary hospitals are (1) the ability to raise money for physical modernization and new technology (because, unlike public hospitals, they do not require voter approval to issue bonds, and, unlike individual voluntary hospitals, they have greater access to capital markets); (2) greater efficiency through streamlined staffing, computerization, and bulk purchasing; (3) the ability to attract new physicians; and (4) the flexibility to provide new services.

There is some dispute as to the relative cost of public, private, and voluntary hospitals. Studies based on data reported to state agencies in California, Texas, and Florida indicate that investor-owned hospital chains had costs up to 8 percent higher than comparable figures for nonprofit hospitals. A closer look reveals, however, that while cost *per patient day* is higher in investor-owned hospitals, costs *per admission* are essentially comparable, reflecting shorter overall stays for the investor-owned hospitals, despite similar patient characteristics.[34] Moreover, an examination of the data reveals that total *revenues* (collected from patients *and* contributors) per patient day and per admission were *greater* for voluntary, not-for-profit hospitals than for investor-owned hospitals; as a result, and contrary to the expectations of some, after-tax profit was actually *higher* for the not-for-profit than the for-profit hospitals.[35] A comprehensive study by the National Academy of Sciences compared for-profit and private, not-for-profit hospitals. It found no difference in the quality of care, but found that the former had costs ranging up to 10 percent higher than the latter, reflecting in part taxes and the need to amortize more recent capital investments.[36] But taxes paid by for-profit hospitals should be considered a rebate to the public and should be subtracted from the raw cost figures; also, more recent investment means newer facilities and more modern equipment, so the two kinds of hospitals are not fully equivalent. (Admittedly, this is an "input" rather than an "output" measure of performance.) The effect of making these two adjustments would be to reduce, and possibly even reverse, the small cost differential.

A more fundamental point bears mentioning. Any analysis based on data filed in response to routine government reporting requirements must be viewed with deep reservation because of the extreme variability of assumptions and accounting procedures, particularly for public institutions.[37] A definitive study is still needed.

In the meanwhile, individual case studies showing both successes and failures have been reported.[38] Many local officials favor privatization of their public hospitals because it eliminates a deficit-ridden activity and leads to upgrading of the physical plant and equipment—and therefore presumably to better health care for the community—at no cost to the government. Finally, one limited report is available comparing particular departments in voluntary and municipal hospitals. The New York State Comptroller's office studied the relative productivity of X-ray technology units and darkroom developing units in the two kinds of nonprofit hospitals, voluntary and municipal. The study found that productivity was 33 percent greater for the voluntary hospital's X-ray unit, and developing costs were 84 percent greater for the municipal darkroom unit.[39]

Fear has been expressed that when teaching hospitals are purchased by for-profit chains, the research and teaching functions will be slighted in favor of returning profits to investors. A priori, this fear seems groundless. A major hospital chain would invest in a teaching and research facility for the same reason that AT&T and IBM invest in Bell Laboratories and the Watson Research Center, namely, to attract the best people, develop the best procedures, maintain industry leadership, and sustain profits for a long time into the future. The complaint seems myopic, as though from people ignorant of other areas of endeavor who see medical care as a unique calling that cannot be compared with any other activities that satisfy human needs.

When a hospital, public or voluntary, is privatized, an important concern is to assure the continued availability of medical care for the indigent and for patients who require costly, labor-intensive care. In some states there are people not poor enough to be eligible for Medicaid but too poor to pay their hospital bills. Accusations are made and rebutted about how medical indigents are treated by for-profit hospitals with reports of both good and bad instances. A study of the matter by a neutral party found that hospital chains and voluntary hospitals provided about the same amount of free care to the poor, about 4 percent of their gross revenues.[40] One approach that works well has been to create a fund for treating indigent patients, with contributions into the fund coming from the private hospital and from state, county, or local government. According to the classification scheme in chapter 4, this would be considered a grant arrangement (a subsidy to the producer). Compared to a voucher, a grant has the virtue of relative ease of administration. Moreover, by directing the subsidy toward a particular hospital, a grant serves to ration health care and minimize the cost to government because government avoids subsidizing every eligible person in the jurisdiction. Whether this is good or bad public policy is debatable.

Given the general superiority of vouchers to consumers over grants to producers, isn't there a way to use vouchers for medical care? It should be understood that Medicare and Medicaid enrollment cards are not really vouchers; they are essentially open-ended credit cards that the holder can use freely, knowing that (except for a token co-payment) the bills will be mailed elsewhere. In chapter 5 we saw that vouchers, even if they were capped in value, like food stamps or housing vouchers, cannot work well to purchase medical care directly. They have been proposed, however, to enable poor people to purchase health insurance; this is a promising approach for subsidizing medical care for the needy without driving up costs the way Medicare and Medicaid have done.

VETERANS ADMINISTRATION HOSPITALS

Other comparisons of public and private hospitals are available. The Grace Commission conducted an intensive examination of Veterans Administration (VA) hospitals. It found the VA system to be highly inefficient by many measures, compared to either not-for-profit or for-profit private hospitals. To begin with, construction costs per bed ranged from $153,000 to $320,000 for the VA, compared to $97,000 to $140,000 for nonprofit hospitals. Moreover, for similar-size construction programs, the VA had sixteen times as many employees on its construction administration staff as did the Hospital Corporation of America, the largest private hospital system. Operating costs were also higher: 78 percent higher for medical care and 48 percent higher for surgical care than in nonprofit hospitals affiliated with medical schools. The VA asserts that its patient mix is different, but after adjustment, the data still show VA costs to be higher by 16 percent.[41]

Contributing to the higher cost is a much longer length of stay, an average of 27.3 days in 1981, compared to 7.2 days in private hospitals. It is not clear how much of the extra stay is caused by medical reasons as opposed to bureaucratic efforts to keep the beds filled. Another cost factor is inventory levels that are 33 to 50 percent higher than typical levels in private hospitals. The VA's procurement of supplies is also relatively inefficient; it obtains only 58 percent through national contracts (the rest by local purchases), compared to about 80 percent as the corresponding figure for private hospital systems. This suggests that the VA is foregoing economies of scale in purchasing.

To summarize, while these comparative figures are suggestive rather than conclusive, they led the commission to recommend that the VA phase out construction of hospitals and contract out hospital management services to the private sector on a trial basis. Doing this would yield cost savings of $1.4 billion over three years.[42]

MILITARY HOSPITALS

Arguably the most monopolistic health-care system in the United States is that of the military. For all practical puposes, personnel on active duty and their dependents are restricted to using military hospitals. The results are not re-assuring. A series of scandalous revelations showed failure to investigate physicians' references before admitting them to hospital staffs, impostors, malpractice, incompetent doctors with abnormally high death rates when they operated, and twice as many childbirth complications as the national average. The situation got so bad that the Pentagon announced it would contract with private-sector physicians to monitor the performance of government physicians in these government hospitals.[43] There seems to be no alternative other than retaining and improving this hospital system. Nevertheless, these unfortunate experiences should be a rude awakening to those who assume, unthinkingly, that public monopolies can always be trusted to perform in the public interest.

AMBULANCE SERVICE

Ambulance service is comprised of several major functions: emergency medical treatment on-site, emergency transportation to a hospital, and nonemergency transportation to or from a hospital. A survey of cities in the United States showed that 25 percent of them contracted with private firms for ambulance service, and 11 percent contracted with not-for-profit agencies and neighborhood organizations (see table 4.3). The practice is growing, and there are more than eight hundred private ambulance companies in the United States, with annual revenues of more than $1.5 billion.[44] (This figure includes revenues from contracts and from market-based, nonemergency transportation of individuals.)

The reason for the growth in contracting is a reduction in cost: Contractors are less expensive than conventional municipal emergency ambulance services because the latter often dispatch a fire truck with six men, only one of whom has paramedic training. The authoritative comparative study of this service remains to be carried out, however.

NURSING HOMES

As the population ages, more people than ever before will need care in nursing homes. How do the different kinds compare? A study by the National Center for Health Statistics showed that not-for-profit nursing homes, both public and voluntary, charge 13 percent more than the for-profit homes. The latter seem to achieve their superior results by maintaining a higher bed occupancy rate and managing with fewer employees per bed, yet the fraction of residents discharged alive (an admittedly crude measure of quality or effectiveness) is the same as other nursing homes. One cannot rule out the possibility, however, that patients in government-run homes were sicker when admitted. It is possible that nonprofit homes provided more or better services, notes the economist responsible for the study, but "they may simply be a little less efficient."[45]

In a study of nursing homes operated by the VA, the average cost per patient day was found to be 83 percent higher than the cost of comparable care for similar patients placed by the VA in privately operated, community nursing homes.[46] Furthermore, this comparison was biased against the private facilities because the cost of real estate, buildings, and equipment was not included in the figures for the VA-operated nursing homes, whereas it was included in the contract price charged by the private institutions. Another study examined construction costs and found that the average construction cost per bed was $61,500 for the VA, almost four times as high as the private cost (for-profit and not-for-profit) of $15,900.[47]

A study in Minnesota examined 118 nursing homes to see if quality differences could be found between the different arrangements. Differences were found in only four of ninety-six quality variables: Private profit-making nursing homes had more patients per room but a greater variety of physician specialties and more therapeutic services than government and voluntary (private nonprofit) nursing homes, even though they had fewer registered nurses per licensed practical nurse than the voluntary institutions.[48]

HEALTH INSURANCE ADMINISTRATION

The relative efficiency of public and private administration of health insurance has also been examined. It was found that after adjustment to assure comparability of functions, the processing cost per claim in two consecutive years was 35 percent and 18 percent greater for public than for private administration. Four reasons are offered to explain the difference: (1) competition in the private sector, which provides pressure for greater efficiency; (2) higher compensation in the public sector, ranging from 16 to 47 percent higher than corresponding jobs in the private sector; (3) incentives for private managers to maximize efficiency in the private sector, in contrast with budget-maximizing and seniority-rewarding practices among public managers; and (4) greater administrative complexity in the public sector because the work of the public administrators includes not only claims processing but also extra administrative work associated with government efforts to control medical costs.[49]

A study of for-profit and nonprofit insurance companies under contract with the Social Security Administration to process Medicare and Medicaid claims revealed that the for-profit firms did the work faster and had a lower error rate.[50]

MEDICARE
Many important issues can be raised about the equity of Medicare, the federal government's program for medical care for the elderly, but Goodman and Rahn make the particularly interesting observation that Medicare discriminates against those who have below-average life expectancies. This little-noticed feature particularly affects blacks, who are overrepresented among Medicare payers and underrepresented among Medicare beneficiaries. A black male at birth has a life expectancy of 64.8 years, which is to say that although he will pay Medicare taxes throughout his entire working life, he can expect to die two months before he becomes eligible for benefits. Goodman and Rahn recommend a policy that would enable the elderly to provide for a larger portion of their medical expenses rather than impose more taxes on the less affluent working-age population. Specifically they propose privatization of Medicare, through the creation of individual health-bank accounts for retirement. Workers would be given tax incentives to establish IRA-like accounts that would be used to pay for health insurance and other medical expenses in retirement.[51]

FAMILY PLANNING
Population control programs in Bangladesh and Sri Lanka by a private, voluntary agency using social marketing techniques in the marketplace appear to be twice and five times as effective, respectively, as prior efforts by local government agencies in these countries.[52] Such programs are reported to be the most cost effective and quickly accomplished means of distributing family planning information in developing countries and to have achieved significant increases in contraceptive usage.

Housing and Urban Development
Government has been heavily involved in housing and urban development, with its primary activities in (1) housing the poor; (2) encouraging homeownership; (3) regulating the location, construction, and price of housing; and (4) urban economic development. Advocates of privatization want to create a housing sector that functions in an open environment with minimal government participation and with an emphasis on individual freedom of choice. Accordingly, housing aid to the poor ought to take the form of consumer-oriented housing vouchers that augment the household's purchasing power and thereby enable it to make its own housing decisions. With respect to encouraging homeowner-

ship, privatization means increasing the viability of conventional mortgage institutions, attracting other lenders into the mortgage market, and redirecting government credit agencies so that they complement rather than compete with the private market in housing finance. Finally, proponents of privatization in housing call for reducing or removing unnecessary legal and regulatory barriers in order to increase the affordability and availability of housing.

What is the best role for government, and for the private sector, in satisfying the need for shelter? What are the effects of current government programs, and what benefits are offered by privatized arrangements?

LOW-INCOME HOUSING

The vast majority of people in the United States obtain their housing in the marketplace, as buyers or renters. But because housing is considered a worthy good, government has attempted in various ways to provide better housing for low-income households. The principal approaches have been grants of various kinds to builders to lower the price of housing, vouchers to the poor to enable them to obtain better housing in the marketplace than they could otherwise afford, and government housing (i.e., public housing). The following discussion addresses these alternative arrangements for low-income housing. The proper starting point in choosing among them is a correct diagnosis of the problem.

The Housing Problem. An overview of housing conditions in the United States is provided by figure 7.1, which shows a continuing improvement in the housing stock. The amount of dilapidated housing, for example, declined to a small fraction of the total and was no longer measured after 1970. Overcrowding (more than one person per room) declined substantially, from 20 percent of all households in 1940 to 3.5 percent in 1983; severe overcrowding decreased to .8 percent in that period. Housing quality increased so that only 2.4 percent of all units lacked plumbing by 1983.[53]

What, then, is the housing problem of the poor? First, we must be clear about what it is *not*. There is not a general housing shortage. In 1985, the national vacancy rate was 6.8 percent, the highest in eighteen years. The absorption rate—the rate at which new units are rented—fell in 1984 to the lowest rate in at least fifteen years; only 67 percent of new rental units were rented within three months of completion.[54] Nor is the problem generally one of homelessness, for low-income households are rarely homeless. Shopping-bag ladies, derelicts, and other unfortunates who live on the streets surely constitute a problem, and a human tragedy, but theirs is more than a problem of housing: About half are drug addicts, alcoholics, or mentally ill and require supervision or appropriate institutionalization.[55] Many of the others have been thrown out of

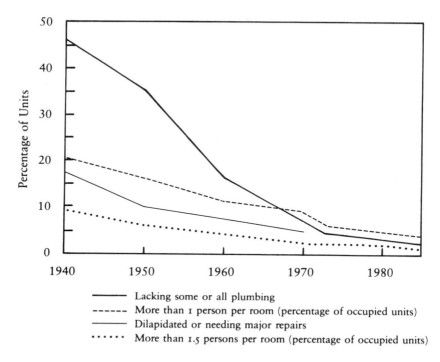

FIGURE 7.1

THE IMPROVEMENT IN MEASURES OF ADEQUATE HOUSING

NOTE: Data for "dilapidated" are not reported after 1970. Compiled from data that were supplied by the U.S. Department of Commerce, Bureau of the Census.

the house by their families and former friends because of their antisocial be-havior.

The housing problems of low-income households are affordability (many pay a large portion of their incomes for rent) and quality (many live in sub-standard housing).[56] Based on 1980 data, about 40 percent of all unassisted, low-income households (those below 50 percent of the median family income in their local area) live in standard housing, but pay more than 30 percent of their incomes for it. Another 5 percent live in standard housing that is within their means. About another 35 percent live in substandard housing that can be repaired and brought up to standard for a relatively small amount of money. This means that about four out of five unassisted, low-income, renter house-holds either have no housing problem or their housing problems can be ad-dressed with payments that help pay the rent or induce the landlord or tenant to make minor repairs.

Construction Grants versus Vouchers. Recognizing that the problems are affordability and quality, not a physical shortage of housing, it becomes clear that the emphasis between 1940 and 1980 on new construction as the principal form of housing assistance—whether as public housing or as grant-assisted private housing—is no longer appropriate. Instead of subsidizing builders, with grants, we should be subsidizing low-income tenants, with vouchers. Despite the political appeal of construction programs, today they are a solution to the wrong problem. They are wasteful; unfair; and often destructive to families, buildings, and neighborhoods.

Let us examine each of these assertions. The programs are wasteful because it costs 2.9 times as much to house a needy family by building a new unit as to use vouchers: On the basis of net present value, vouchers cost $53 per month for thirty years ($19,000), whereas new construction costs $153 per month ($55,000) to house the same family over the same thirty years. Thus, about three times as many needy families can be housed for the same amount of money and it is unconscionable not to do so.[57] (Incidentally, this is one of the few authoritative comparisons of vouchers and grants.) The programs are unfair because people who are ineligible for housing assistance but who cannot afford to live in new units themselves resent paying taxes to provide new units for others. Finally, the programs are destructive because buildings that are, in effect, labeled *For Poor People Only* frequently become warehouses for troubled families. The result is often contagious delinquent behavior and family disintegration, vandalism of buildings to the point of uninhabitability, and neighborhood deterioration.

An additional shortcoming of the grant system was highlighted in New York City: "Unexplained fires" were much more likely to occur in buildings whose owners eventually received government renovation subsidies, according to a study by the Arson Strike Force. The implication of the report was that burning a building often made it eligible for attractive government grants.[58]

Given these considerations, the best arrangement is a voucher program. Tenants get a subsidy, based on their income, family structure, and housing costs in the area, to apply toward rent in the housing unit of their choice. As a family's income goes up, its subsidy goes down. If tenants can find bargains that meet quality standards, they can keep the savings from the lower rent; this is a shopping incentive that keeps costs low. If tenants are willing to pay the extra amount themselves, they can rent units at higher rent levels. Thus, families, not government agencies, can decide where to live and what portion of their incomes to spend on housing; they have freedom of choice.

This voucher system was adopted by President Reagan and became the principal low-income housing initiative of his administration. (At the time, I

PART THREE: PRIVATIZATION IN PRACTICE

was serving as assistant secretary in the Department of Housing and Urban Development.) Congress approved the program reluctantly, and it was not until 1985 that the program was under way. (There was a strong desire on the part of housing developers, lawyers, and builders to continue the old system of subsidies for producers; a good explanation of Congress's delay in adopting this program of subsidies for tenants is that successful developers make larger campaign contributions than poor renters do.)

The basic features of this voucher system were well tested for over ten years in the experimental housing allowance program. The cost of this massive experiment, about $160 million, made it one of the largest social experiments in history. The experiment was well studied, with more than three hundred reports produced. It demonstrated that the voucher system is flexible enough to remedy both the affordability and the adequacy problems, and is much more cost effective than other low-income housing programs, meaning that more people can be helped by the same amount of money.[59]

Some advocates of aggressive government programs to improve the housing of low-income households were disappointed to learn from the experiment that a significant fraction of the eligible poor people were uninterested in receiving money to improve their housing quality; the results suggest that the housing-quality standards were too high and that better housing was not a very high priority of the poor.[60] In short, poor households wanted less housing than government bureaucrats thought they should have.

Public Housing. Public housing is an expensive and often trouble-ridden approach to housing low-income households. The construction cost of an average unit of public housing is only 10 percent lower than the median price of a new house (although the latter offers much more for the money) and is 25 percent greater than the cost of comparable private housing. The total subsidy is large enough so that if it were given in cash directly to the tenants, it would lift virtually all of them out of poverty.[61]

Many public housing projects, particularly in smaller communities, are trouble-free, but one-fifth of all public housing is officially labeled by the federal housing agency as *troubled*. Public housing was stigmatized—and its problems symbolized—by the razing of the notorious Pruitt-Igoe houses in St. Louis only fifteen years after they were built because they had become dangerous, vacant, and vandalized.

Judging by the experience in Great Britain, public housing seems an attractive candidate for privatizing. In the first six years after being granted "the right to buy," 13 percent of public housing tenants purchased their units, at discounts of up to 50 percent—depending on how long they had occupied them.

Pirie and Butler describe the process and the resulting change in attitude and even voting behavior of the new homeowners: They switched from Labour to Conservative in significant numbers.[62] The trend toward purchasing is continuing, and the reasons are the age-old ones: a desire to own, to have greater control over one's home, to keep pace with inflation, and to leave something to one's children.

It appears impossible to replicate the British experience successfully in the United States. More than a third of Britons but less than 2 percent of Americans live in public housing, and whereas the former have an average family income very close to the national median, the latter have an average income that is only 28 percent of the national median. An additional difference is that more of the public housing in Great Britain consists of single-family dwellings, which are easy to sell, whereas in the United States relatively more of the units are in multifamily buildings. For these reasons, it is unlikely that more than 2 percent of public housing units could be sold to tenants, although the Department of Housing and Urban Development started a program to encourage such sales.

Tenant-management associations have been proposed as a means of increasing tenants' skills in homeownership, as an interim step to full private ownership. These associations would take over the management of public housing projects and reduce costs by involving the tenants; this has already been done in several instances.[63]

Tenant management is one form of privatization of public housing; another form is contract management by for-profit firms, analogous to the contract management of hospitals discussed in the preceding section. A limited study was made of nineteen public housing authorities that used contract management, comparing them with similar authorities that managed their own projects. No significant differences in either cost or performance were found between the two arrangements, except for the specialized case of public housing projects for the elderly in urban areas; there the performance was the same, but contract management was 28 percent more costly.[64]

One idea suggested for existing public housing in the United States is to give vouchers to current residents. The value of the voucher would be equal to the current annual subsidy per unit. Like any other voucher recipient, the resident would be free to use his or her voucher to find better housing. Conversely, any voucher holder could use it to rent a unit in public housing. The effect would be to integrate public housing into the local housing market, and to give freedom of choice to tenants who are now trapped — in effect, *institutionalized* — in public housing and have no chance to move. Public housing would no doubt lose some of its clientele, just as county and municipal hospitals lost theirs when low-income families were granted, through Medicaid, greater freedom of choice in health care.

Government has attempted in other ways, some of them comical in retrospect, to provide housing assistance. For example, federal funds have been used to pay for clinics that solemnly advise tenants of the importance of paying their rents and teach them the virtues of household budgeting so that they are able to do so. In another instance, an enterprising mayor in a town in New York obtained a subsidy from the Department of Housing and Urban Development to paint the exteriors of eligible homes in his community. Apparently, someone decided that a well-painted house is a collective good and merits a public subsidy.[65] Presumably the collective good involved is that a passerby who happens to glance in that direction will have a beautiful experience instead of having his aesthetic sense assailed by a house that is not freshly painted. But what if the color is not to his liking? Why not a collective decision on acceptable and desired colors? By the same reasoning that implicitly pronounces house painting to be a collective good, why not more attractive clothing, modish hairstyling, and face lifts for all, at collective expense?

Despite all these government efforts in behalf of low-income housing, it is the private sector that developed the first truly low-cost housing in history: the manufactured home.[66] Nine-tenths of low-priced homes, which constitute a third of the total market, are manufactured homes. In short, the free market has produced an innovative solution — the best solution so far — to the problem of building low-cost housing. If local governments were to adopt more reasonable zoning and building codes, it is safe to predict that the manufactured-home industry would grow and develop, attract capital, conduct the research necessary to improve its products further, and design and build attractive communities of salable houses.

HOMEOWNERSHIP

The federal government in the United States is heavily engaged in various programs to encourage homeownership. About 65 percent of Americans own their own homes, a higher percentage than in any other industrialized nation. (The figure is higher in undeveloped countries, where people build and own their huts and rental housing is not an established custom.)

By many conventional measures, the federal government does more for middle-income and upper-income homeowners than for low-income households, with various programs of direct loans, housing finance, mortgage insurance, and tax benefits.[67] Treating mortgage interest as a deductible expense for income tax purposes is a subsidy to homeowners, relatively few of whom have low incomes; this amounted to a "tax expenditure" of $25 billion in 1985, plus another $11 billion from the deductibility of property taxes and the exclusion of interest on state and local housing bonds issued to finance owner-occupied homes.[68]

Another principal program that benefits homebuyers is mortgage insurance through the Federal Housing Administration (FHA), Farmers Home Administration, and Veterans Administration. The program insures mortgages made by private lenders, but in doing so it competes with the private mortgage-insurance industry (which has about 31 percent of the market, more than twice that of FHA). Homebuyers with incomes above $40,000 account for 25 percent of FHA's business, while buyers of vacation homes and investors account for 8 percent. Up to $90,000 of insurance can be obtained, which is substantially higher than the median price of a new home. In other words, this is primarily a middle-class subsidy. Moreover, the beneficiaries are arbitrarily chosen, in essence. The marketplace can easily serve this need and can do it more fairly. The Reagan administration prepared a plan to privatize the program by selling it to the private sector; in the meantime, it sought to increase the user fees and target the program toward lower-income households by making it available only for principal residences — not vacation or investment properties — and only for households with incomes below $40,000.[69] (The median household income at the time was about $25,000.)

HOUSING REGULATIONS

The third major area of government involvement in housing is in the regulation of housing. In an attempt to balance the interests of property owners, the community, and prospective residents, state and local governments have imposed a growing array of regulations on land use and on development and construction. At the same time, consumer, environmental, and energy movements resulted in a proliferation of federal government regulations that also, directly or indirectly, affect housing costs. A newer form of local regulation is the growing practice of extracting fees from developers for the "privilege" of building housing in response to market demands.

Three presidential commissions, from 1968 to 1982, have warned about the abuses possible through exclusionary zoning (large-lot requirements, exclusion of multiple dwellings and mobile homes, imposition of minimum house-size requirements), subdivision requirements, and building codes that fail to take advantage of new construction technology. The end result of excessive and misused regulation is reduced housing choices, constrained production, lowered productivity, and increased prices — as much as 25 percent of the final sales price in some localities.[70] In 1982 the President's Commission on Housing made a series of recommendations to reduce the burden imposed by overregulation.[71]

Another area of regulation is rent control, whose avowed intent is to keep rents low. Yet, both the theory and the evidence are overwhelmingly against this as a viable approach,[72] and no less than three Nobel Prize winners in economics—Gunnar Myrdal, Friedrich A. Hayek, and Milton Friedman, covering the widest possible range of social philosophies—have declaimed against it.[73] In brief, rent control produces a shortage of housing, which inevitably harms the poor. This occurs because cheap, existing units are overconsumed, and new ones are not built. Depending on how rent control is administered, (1) it leads to terrible inequities among families in equivalent housing; (2) the poor frequently subsidize the rich; and (3) young couples are discriminated against in favor of the middle-aged.

The inequities arise because two families may be living in adjacent, identical units in the same building but one pays much less than the other because it has been living there longer. If the newer tenant has a much lower income than the other, than he is subsidizing the wealthier one. Finally, the long-term resident—who may be an "empty nester" who no longer needs as much space—benefits from a low, controlled rent, while the young couple with young children has to pay more for a smaller unit. (Ironically, one of the few virtues of rent control is that because of the housing shortage it creates, owners are in a better position to pick and choose among the tenants they will accept, thereby more readily permitting them to exclude misfits, troublemakers, and vandals!) The principal beneficiaries of rent control are the political leaders who support it, for they garner more votes from tenants than from landlords.

With respect to zoning, since 1916 local governments in the United States have been able to decide what uses can be made of privately owned land within their boundaries. Ruled constitutional by the U.S. Supreme Court in 1926, zoning decisions have spawned unending challenges and bitter political disputes. Zoning serves the same protective purpose as membership in a local homeowners' association and has the effect of creating collective property rights. Therefore, it should be possible to supplant litigation-inducing government zoning with market-oriented private alternatives.[74]

Zoning rights have been sold and transferred, for instance, as compensation to the owners of Grand Central Station in exchange for its designation by New York City as an unalterable landmark. One could go a step further and allow a neighborhood to form an association and bargain with someone who wants to build a fast-food restaurant or a high-rise condominium in an area of one-family homes. The neighborhood association would weigh the benefits, monetary and otherwise, of the proposed structure against its aesthetic and other attributes. There are many enticing features to this novel approach, as well as the inevitable problems of arriving at a binding neighborhood position, the rights of renters vis-à-vis property owners, and so forth, but this could be a mechanism for re-creating a sense of community as well as establishing more flexible and satisfactory controls on land use.

ENTERPRISE ZONES

Local governments in the United States try in various ways to promote economic development in their communities and eliminate urban blight. Often these efforts involve condemnation of property, land clearance, sale to selected developers on concessionary terms, government grants, and other favorable treatment to encourage the construction, occupancy, and operation of job-creating plants, offices, and retail centers, and to build new housing. In the United States, the urban renewal program and the Model Cities program attempted to counter urban decay by doing all these things, and by introducing a profusion of anti-poverty, job-training, social welfare, and community programs. The results were not conspicuously successful, to put it charitably. *The President's National Urban Policy Report* (1982) reviewed several major urban programs and concluded that good intentions do not necessarily result in improved urban conditions.[75] Government programs for inner cities did not bring about a general revival.[76]

These conventional urban policies were not restricted to the United States, and neither were their disappointing results. In England these experiences led a socialist, academic, urban planner, Peter Hall, to observe that the planned sector had stifled the market sector, and he advocated a policy by which selected inner-city sites would be thrown open to pretty much unbridled free-market initiatives, with the aim of re-creating the economic climate of Hong Kong in the 1950s and 1960s.[77]

In time, these radical ideas emerged as *enterprise zones* in England and the United States. When he proposed legislation to establish such zones, President Reagan said:

> Enterprise Zones are based on an entirely fresh approach for promoting economic growth in the inner cities. The old approach relied on heavy government subsidies and central planning. . . . The Enterprise Zone approach would remove government barriers, freeing individuals to create, produce and earn their own wages and profits. In its basic thrust, Enterprise Zones are the direct opposite of the Model Cities Program of the 1960s.[78]

Congress did not pass federal legislation for enterprise zones, but thirty-two states passed legislation adopting the concept. More than fourteen hundred zones had been designated where various provisions to reduce taxes and unnecessary regulations went into effect. Preliminary indications are that tens of thousands of jobs were saved or created, and that more than $1 billion were invested.[79] It is inherently difficult, however, to measure the effect of such programs and estimate what might have occurred in their absence. The definitive study of this promising, privatized approach to urban development remains to be carried out.

Social Services

Social services are typically provided by government agencies, voluntary charities, private firms in the marketplace, and government contracts with private agencies — usually not-for-profit organizations, but increasingly for-profit firms.

There is a dearth of systematically collected, empirical data comparing the different service arrangements. Until this shortage is remedied, one will have to look piecemeal at studies that are suggestive rather than conclusive. For example, the New York State Commission on the Quality of Care for the Mentally Disabled concluded after a two-year study that state-run community residences provided worse care and were 55 percent more expensive than those run by private voluntary agencies. The median annual costs per resident were $43,093 and $27,876 respectively.[80]

Another study focused not on efficiency but solely on issues of equity and quality of service. Do private agencies under contract exercise selectivity in their choice of clients, leaving public agencies to handle those more difficult to treat? No significant differences in characteristics were found between clients served by public or voluntary agencies. The latter, moreover, offered a broader range of services to their clients than did the former; this was true of both "hard" services (e.g., transportation and day care) and "soft" services (e.g., counseling). Contracting results in more aid per tax dollar simply because most voluntary agencies receive private contributions that defray some of their costs, enabling the government agency in effect to get a discount when it purchases the service.[81]

A well-respected, private, voluntary group claims that its small, community-based shelters for the homeless are far more cost effective than the large public shelters, as well as more acceptable to the surrounding community, and it argues for more government contracts with private voluntary agencies for this purpose. It cites figures of $8.90 a day for a newly renovated private room in the voluntary shelter, versus $27 a day for a dormitory-style bed in the public shelter.[82] Although this analysis is from an interested party, it cannot be dismissed out of hand.

Most public funds for social services are spent on contracts with private organizations. Traditionally, contracting with not-for-profit voluntary organizations was done on a negotiated basis rather than through competitive means. It was thought unseemly for religious agencies and United Way charities to compete for contracts to provide child care, foster homes, services for the disabled and the retarded, care for the elderly, aid to battered wives and children, and the like. Indeed, many states have legislation that prohibits for-profit firms from competing with not-for-profit social service agencies and exempts social services from the competitive bidding requirements that apply to all other government contractors. Other than a traditional bias, there is little reason for such strictures, and increasingly there is competitive bidding for such services, with all providers eligible to compete.[83]

Some government agencies, however, failed to realize the potential benefits of competitive contracting for social services. They imposed excessive layers of supervision over contracts and line-item control over contract items. Not surprisingly, they found few providers. They stifled innovation by burdensome regulation and were negligent in monitoring contractor performance. Moreover, they accepted cost savings at the expense of service quality, although the latter is a legitimate managerial tradeoff if done consciously.[84] Some would say that it is as difficult for government officials to contract wisely and well in this field as it is to manage a government social service agency directly. If so, then voucher and voluntary arrangements should be preferred.

Contracting for social services raises another issue. Just as defense contractors form coalitions with procurement officials and legislators, and the coalitions jointly press for higher spending, analogous public spending coalitions have emerged in the social service area, comprised of not-for-profit contractors, clients, and advocates—both in public office and on the outside. Behaving like any other coalition, but presumably sanctified by its purity of motive, this coalition succeeded in driving up spending and erecting regulatory barriers that ostensibly "uphold standards"—whose main effect is to suppress competition by keeping out traditional service providers.[85]

As a result, in Washington, D.C., the annual cost of maintaining a child in an institution is $12,775 compared to only $3,306 in a foster family; 70 percent of the public funds spent on foster care is for professional salaries and administration, and only 30 percent is spent directly on the object of the care—the child.[86] Professional service providers crowd out and displace lower-cost, alternative providers that may be at least as good but lack politico-professional clout. Ministers and relatives have been replaced by costly Community Mental Health Centers and their credentialed staffs.

Woodson makes a persuasive case in advocating a voluntary rather than a contract arrangement for many social services, relying more on "mediating structures"—religious institutions, ethnic groups, families, neighborhood associations, and other voluntary community institutions.[87] Rigorous evidence as to the effectiveness of this arrangement is lacking, but an arresting illustration is provided by the House of Umoja, a home for former street-gang members in Philadelphia: The recidivism rate of ex-offenders at Umoja was just 3 percent, compared with up to 87 percent at some public "correctional" facilities.[88]

Social services are private goods, and vouchers can be used to supply them. Vouchers have all the advantages discussed in chapter 5 and in the section in this chapter on housing assistance. They give the client freedom of choice and thus empower him, whereas contracts and grants to service providers impose coercive monopolies on the poor—if they want help, there is only one provider to go to. (This problem is more troublesome with private goods, which are individually consumed, than with collective goods: A poor individual is far more dependent on the social worker, who can control the basic necessities of his or her daily life, than on a fire department.) Vouchers can be used not only for food, housing, and health care but also for home care,[89] vocational education, employment training, day care, and in place of unemployment insurance (an unemployed worker can give his valuable voucher to someone who will hire and train him). But there is organized opposition to vouchers, primarily from service providers who see their own welfare and that of their clients as inseparable. A different concern with the voucher arrangement is that under political pressure the eligibility standards can be relaxed and the value of the voucher increased, so that more and more people become eligible and costs skyrocket; this happened with food stamps, as then Budget Director David Stockman cautioned at the meeting where housing vouchers were first proposed to President Reagan.

With respect to voluntary and market arrangements for social services, no doubt these would expand and replace some direct government activities and contract arrangements if regulations whose principal effects are to suppress competition were pruned, and if taxes were reduced (e.g., total tax exemption for families below the poverty level and higher exemptions for children), thereby letting families spend their own money to satisfy their needs as they define them.

Day Care

Child-care services for working parents are as old as families. The need for such care in the United States is obvious when one considers that in 1984, 52 percent of all mothers with children under age six were working (outside the home), and 48 percent of all children under age six had working mothers. Not surprisingly, a variety of institutional arrangements has evolved to satisfy this age-old need. According to the Census Bureau, 31 percent of working mothers have their young children cared for at home, 40 percent in another home, 15 percent at group day-care centers, 9 percent at work, and 5 percent in other ways. Numerous institutional arrangements are in use. There are publicly funded day-care centers (contract arrangement), and private, not-for-profit centers subsidized by the government (grant arrangements). Self-service via grandparents and other relatives is commonplace and universal. Vouchers have been used by Hennepin County in Minnesota.[90] The marketplace offers a rich variety: private centers (both for-profit and not-for-profit); babysitters, nursemaids, and governesses; and employers who, to attract and retain workers, offer on-site centers, vouchers, discount arrangements with private providers, and cafeteria-style benefit plans that include day care.[91] (Employer-sponsored day care dates back to the Civil War in the United States.)

At the request of the Finance Committee of the U.S. Senate, the comptroller general compared the cost of federally funded day-care centers with the cost of comparable private centers.[92] The results are shown in table 7.1, and they are striking. The federally funded programs (grant and contract arrangements) are more expensive than the private ones (market and voluntary arrangements). Moreover, the for-profit ones are less costly than the not-for-profit ones.

TABLE 7.1

MONTHLY COST PER CHILD FOR DAY-CARE CENTERS

Program Type	Cost
Federally funded	
Not-for-profit	$188
For-profit	120
Not federally funded	
Not-for-profit	118
For-profit	102

SOURCE: Comptroller General of the United States, letter to U.S. Senate Committee on Finance, 25 September 1979.

The federally funded programs are more costly because they have higher ratios of teachers and aides to children, employ more workers who do not provide care directly, pay higher wages, and offer additional services. The study concluded, however, that the high staffing ratios increased the costs without increasing the quality and that reducing the staff-to-child ratio would reduce costs without harming the children's development. Interestingly, these findings are independently corroborated by an analysis that shows the cost per child went up in private centers when subsidized children were placed there, as a result of (1) quality improvements, (2) increases in wages, and (3) replacement of donated goods and services by purchased goods and services.[93] In other words, cost inflation to government levels and withdrawal of voluntary contributions accounted for much of the increase in cost.

The biggest impediment to low-cost day care is regulation: facility standards sometimes copied from children's hospitals, lofty credential requirements, and zoning ordinances that inhibit or prohibit home-based day care in residential areas. (!) Woodson quotes an irate day-care operator who testified before a zoning board in Washington, D.C.: "You're telling us we cannot operate a day care facility in a residentially zoned middle-class neighborhood with a large number of working mothers, but we can operate a center in a commercial zone between two topless bars."[94]

Taken together, the standards are so demanding that virtually all Americans can be described as having been raised in substandard circumstances.

SOCIAL SECURITY

Social security refers to the system for providing income to retired working people. The subject of numerous analyses and campaign promises, the system in the United States periodically teeters on the brink of actuarial unsoundness and has to be rescued. Until the 1950s, grown children were generally responsible for their aging parents, and most of them accepted the responsibility, as children have done since prehistoric times. But in some cases they did not. To save the pride of the elderly who did not want to ask their children for help, or who were childless, the law was changed and adults were no longer required to aid their parents. Legislation weakened the prevailing ethic. The result is that today (except for certain ethnic groups in which the ethical sense of duty is still strong) grown children provide little direct aid to their parents, even if the children are relatively affluent. It has become government's duty. (The elderly have been nationalized, so to speak.) The irony of it all, of course, is that working adults continue to support their aged parents, but they now do so impersonally, anonymously, and indirectly through the government by paying social security taxes.

The current system was analyzed in detail by Ferrara, who points out that the payroll tax may have to be raised from the current 14 percent to about 35 percent in order to pay all the benefits promised to those currently entering the workforce. He further notes that those now starting their careers, regardless of their prospective lifetime earnings, would receive much higher retirement benefits if they could invest such amounts privately at market rates. He offers a carefully wrought model for a privatized system, which in essence would separate the welfare function of social security from the retirement income function and would satisfy each of the two needs separately.[95] The latter function would be handled by compulsory contributions to individual retirement accounts. Changing the social security system is fraught with political danger, however, and therefore attention has been given to devising a viable strategy for implementing this thoughtful plan.[96]

DISPUTE RESOLUTION

Disputes or disagreements are a normal feature of interpersonal relations, and most of them are resolved informally, either by the disputants alone or with the intervention of parents, relatives, friends, neighbors, teachers, ministers, business associates, and so forth. In addition to these self-service and voluntary arrangements for dispute resolution, the marketplace provides arbitration services, and so does government, through civil courts.

As the quality of the government service declines — in terms of speed and convenience — because of clogged courts, people increasingly are turning to private services to resolve private disputes. *Alternative dispute resolution* (ADR) is the formal term used to describe this approach, known colloquially as "rent-a-judge." With seventy thousand civil cases backlogged in a California court, and with a median delay of fifty months, more and more disputants agree to hire retired judges for $500 to $750 a day to conduct quick and discreet trials.[97] Not only is this quicker and more convenient — particularly important advantages in commercial cases — but it is also cheaper because fewer hours of legal work are needed; the cost of litigation in civil court often exceeds the damages paid. Moreover, when the issues are technically complex, litigants can choose a retired judge who is a specialist in the area.

The criticisms voiced about this growing practice are curious. One is that only those who can afford it can utilize this approach. But what is wrong with that? Only those who can afford to buy food do so directly; others use food stamps. Should everyone be forced to rely on food stamps? Why should public funds be used to pay for judges, clerks, and courthouses, and why should jurors lose time and wages to settle a grievance between a real-estate developer and a builder, or between a corporate defendant and its insurance company? Baseball leagues pay private umpires for conceptually similar services, and even governments and their employee unions hire labor mediators and arbitrators to resolve conflicts between them. By definition, private disputes have no public consequences and therefore do not require collective action.

The other principal criticism of private dispute resolution, voiced by the media and by civil-liberties groups, is that the proceedings are closed to the press and the public. This argument seems extraordinarily weak, and is self-serving with respect to the media, for it implies that no disagreement is private and that all should be exposed to public view by the press. Does the public have a right to watch people fight? Why not complain that in the 90 to 95 percent of court cases resolved privately before coming to trial, the public is similarly deprived of its spectacles?

With respect to misdemeanors and felonies, a related form of privatization is occurring, and for reasons similar to those involving civil cases. Neighborhood justice centers and community dispute resolution committees are handling cases referred by the courts on complaints ranging from neighborhood squabbles about loose dogs and loud radios to assault and battery and petty theft between neighbors. Mediators at the centers are lay people from all walks of life, who receive training for this role. They seek to help parties arrive at written agreements, with hearings held promptly, informally, confidentially, and at sufficient length to get at the underlying causes of the dispute.[98]

Legitimate concerns have been raised about the emergence of a second-class justice system for the poor, and critics point to instances where judges relegate cases of domestic violence to neighborhood centers for resolution, instead of to criminal courts for adjudication. Privatized justice for civil cases seems sensible enough and logically consistent with long tradition; however, the jury is still out on using this approach for criminal cases.

Legal Aid

A study of legal aid services revealed that poor defendants thought privately retained lawyers (market arrangement) did the best job and court-appointed lawyers (contract service) were inferior. The legal community rated the quality equal, however, and an analysis of conviction and imprisonment rates supported their view: Private and contract lawyers did just as well for their clients; in fact, the small differences found favored the contract (court-appointed) lawyers.[99]

Education

There is considerable discussion in the United States about the quality of elementary and secondary education. Surveys and studies attest to a mood of dissatisfaction, and they document the shortcomings. Suggested reforms include higher teacher salaries, merit pay, designation of master teachers, less emphasis on pedagogical credentials and more on subject-matter expertise, bigger school budgets, magnet schools, greater business involvement in the curriculum, back to basics, more discipline in the classroom, and greater parental choice of schools for their children. The growing chorus for this last approach accounts for the growing interest in vouchers and in tax credits for tuition paid to private schools, as both would help parents afford nonpublic schools.

Roth provides a fascinating historical and contemporary look at public and private education in developing countries, a look that lends perspective on the issue.[100] As early as the beginning of civilization on the Indian subcontinent, the Aryans required at least eight years of broad schooling for every child; this was done as a matter of religious practice, not state legislation. In fact, it was the British who brought government fully into the education picture in India, and it was for political reasons, namely, to control the curriculum. The vulnerability of public schools to government whim can be seen in the perversion of public schools that occurred in Uganda during the odious dictatorship of Idi Amin. Schools had to purchase all their supplies from a central office and had to pay in advance, even though often the supplies were never delivered. (Except for the extortionary payment in advance, this is a familiar lament in large public school systems in the United States!) In Malta, in 1973, the government imposed politically mandated changes in the public schools, which caused a large-scale withdrawal of children from those schools and an influx into private schools. The government relentlessly sought to recapture the children by freezing the fees the private schools could charge, in 1982, and abolishing fees in 1984. By thus starving the private schools, the government hopes to force all Maltese children into state-controlled schools.

The Soviet Union allows school-age children to accompany their parents when the latter are assigned to live abroad only if there is a Soviet government school they can attend in the area; the basic policy is that the Soviet child's thinking is to be guided along approved channels and is not to be exposed to other concepts. Note the difference with Japanese children temporarily living abroad: They generally attend local schools full-time and then after school or on weekends go to specially established Japanese schools to study the language, history, and culture of their native land.

The United States has not been completely spared of heavy-handed attempts to control education. A 1922 Oregon law, subsequently overturned by the U.S. Supreme Court, outlawed all private schools and compelled all children to attend government schools. The motive force behind the passage of this law was the Ku Klux Klan, with its fear of foreign influences.[101]

Several arrangements are used for education in the United States and many variants have been proposed with the objective of giving parents greater choice. There are public schools and private schools—the latter operating in the educational marketplace as for-profit or nonprofit, religious or secular institutions. There is self-service education (some 250,000 children, most of them disabled, are educated at home; this is allowed in thirty-eight states).[102] There is education through intergovernmental agreements, where children in one jurisdiction go to schools in another and the sending unit pays the receiving one. A suburban family that prefers the public school in a nearby town over its own can send its children there and pay tuition privately. There are voucher arrangements that have been utilized on an experimental basis, loans or grants for private education, and contracts with private firms for education.

The introduction of more competition and the enhancement of parental choice in schooling increasingly is seen to be an essential lever for improving education. Typically, at present, a child is assigned to a particular public school, and the parents have no choice in the matter unless they want to place the child in a private school, in which case they have a very wide choice limited only by cost and distance (and any selection criteria the school may have for the children it accepts — bright, slow, artistic, athletic, science oriented, from prominent families, from alumni, and so on). If a family chooses to use a private school, as 10 to 15 percent do, it must pay tuition, but it receives no rebate on its taxes, even though it saves money for the public school system. In effect, the family pays twice: once in tuition for the school it wants, and once in taxes for the school it shuns.

To correct this inequity, two different approaches have been proposed: vouchers and tuition tax credits. Under a fullblown voucher system, a child's parents would receive a voucher and could send their child to the school of their choice, public or private; they would give the voucher to the school, which would turn it in to the issuing jurisdiction and receive money for it. A more restricted voucher plan would limit the choice to public schools.

President Reagan endorsed the voucher concept for remedial education. He submitted a legislative proposal that was known as The Equity and Choice Act (TEACH — an apt acronym). It would give educational vouchers to parents of children selected to receive compensatory educational services. (Almost 5 million children participated in the existing nonvoucher program in 1983-84.) Under TEACH, parents might choose to have their child attend the compensatory program operated by the local school district or could use the voucher to pay for tuition or compensatory education in a private school or at a public school other than the one to which the child is assigned. A voucher could be used at any nonprofit school that does not discriminate on the basis of race, color, or national origin. This proposal would expand the range of choices available to disadvantaged families and give them some of the educational options already available to more affluent families. It would increase parental involvement, thereby improving the quality of education, and it would promote competition among schools to meet the needs of disadvantaged children.[103]

Voucher plans have been attacked by teacher groups, who fear for their jobs, and their opposition is so strong that ultimate acceptance cannot be assumed. Voucher advocates also have fears: They fear that if their system were adopted, legislation, regulation, and bureaucratization of private schools might someday follow and would so transform the schools that they would resemble today's public schools.[104] This happened with the voucherlike system in the Netherlands. Private schools, which are fully state financed, are regulated as to inputs, for example, teacher salaries and curriculum. Equality with the public schools is achieved, but at the expense of the very choice that the system was intended to ensure.[105]

Another approach to remedying the above-mentioned inequity, enhancing competition and expanding parental choice, is the tuition tax credit. Advocated by President Reagan, Senator Daniel Patrick Moynihan,[106] and many others, it permits parents to take a dollar-for-dollar reduction in their taxes, up to a certain limit, for tuition paid in private schools. There is no problem of separation of church and state if parents use such a credit to send children to church-affiliated private schools. A tuition tax-deduction measure in Minnesota withstood the highest level of judicial scrutiny when Justice Rehnquist stated for the Supreme Court that a tax deduction "to defray the cost of educational expenses incurred by parents—regardless of the type of schools their children attend . . . serves [the] purpose of ensuring that the state's citizenry is well educated."[107]

The case for vouchers and tuition tax credits is significantly bolstered by James Coleman's second famous education study, which found that private high schools, including Catholic schools, provide a better education than public high schools and are less segregated as well.[108]

Kolderie offers a stimulating discussion of ways to expand choice and thereby bring the benefits of competition to bear on education.[109] "Choice, not assignment" is the unspoken watchword of this movement. In essence, one can devise numerous ways to introduce competition and choice both from the "buyer's side" (the parents) and the "seller's side" (the school). Parents can be allowed to send their child to any school in the district or to a school in another district, or to a private school. In the first two cases, the parents' own school district would transfer funds accordingly, including any state aid to which the district is entitled. In other words, as the toddler goes off to school, he would be carrying, in a manner of speaking, a little sack containing tax-levy funds for his chosen school. This inevitably means that the sack of funds will *not* go to a school he is *not* attending, not even the public school nearest his home.

Whether intradistrict or interdistrict, this profound change would end the current monopolistic practices of most school systems. When restricted to public schools, this approach is simply an open-enrollment program, but one with adverse consequences for any school that cannot attract enough pupils to stay in business, for it would no longer be allowed to compel enrollment of the neighborhood children—to impress them into its service, so to speak. By way of contrast, the few existing, intradistrict, open-enrollment programs tend to be rather feeble in practice: The school that is shunned rarely loses much of its budget (and may even be rewarded with more money, to improve itself), and the school that gains a good reputation is rarely expanded—its waiting list is lengthened instead.

In many instances, parents withdraw their child from their own school district and send him or her to a neighboring one; however, they have to pay individually just as if they were sending the child to a private school. The tuition tax credit could apply to this situation as well. In 1984 Minnesota enacted legislation to facilitate interdistrict enrollment. Either allowing public funds to accompany the child, as described above, or a tuition tax credit would enhance choice and promote healthy competition, with the objective being to produce better and better schools. The end result, in effect, is a voucher system because the parents are the arrangers.

From the seller's side, that is, the school system, it can increase its appeal by contracting out for teaching some courses or for educating some kinds of students. For example, colleges could be hired to run programs for gifted children, private firms for vocational education and driver training, and special private schools for handicapped children. In fact, New York City followed this approach and offers some comparative evidence on the relative efficiency of in-house and contract work. It educates handicapped children both directly, in public schools, and by contract, in private schools. The city comptroller compared the two approaches and found that the per pupil cost in public schools was slightly greater than in private schools. The public and private costs were $4,785 and $4,512 respectively for the nonseverely handicapped, and $6,196 and $4,730 for the severely handicapped.[110] In a bold proposal, Boston University offered to operate the troubled Boston public schools under a contractual arrangement. One should recall, however, that performance contracts between schools and private firms were not notably successful.[111]

Another approach can be followed, particularly if enrollments are low in some grades: A school district can arrange to buy its educational needs from another district under an intergovernmental contract. Or entrepreneurial teachers and administrators can form a group teaching practice, in the manner of a group medical practice. They can then contract with a school district to teach a subject or grade, or, in a more ambitious step, they can assume complete managerial responsibility for an entire school and strive to attract a growing clientele by the excellence of the education they offer.

Of course, contracting some of the support functions in a school can be accomplished, such as the custodial, building and grounds maintenance, cafeteria, medical, and data processing activities.

Unlike most services, it is not necessary to privatize education, strictly speaking, in order to introduce competition. It can be achieved by allowing parents to choose among public schools, provided the schools offer the diversity that comes only with sufficient autonomy and independence. It may well be, however, that only competition from private schools, via vouchers and tuition tax credits, can bring about the necessary diversity among public schools within a single district, as in large cities.

Critics of vouchers and tuition tax credits raise several arguments. One criticism is that these approaches would destroy public schools. Several points can be made in rebuttal: (1) What is important is that education be universal and offered without charge, not the public or private character of the teacher's employer; (2) if a school is doing a poor job, it should go out of business; the adjective "public" in its name *should* not grant it immunity to the consequences of incompetence; and (3) the competition from private schools may actually *save* the public schools if it succeeds in waking them from their torpor.[112]

A second criticism of parental choice is the familiar cream-skimming argument; that is, the private schools would skim the best students, and the public schools, with the leavings, would be a dumping ground. This argument can be turned around. A vigorously competitive environment can be expected to create schools with specialized "market niches," including schools for children with discipline problems. Besides, should gifted students be deprived of the opportunity to develop their innate abilities to the fullest and instead used merely to enrich the environment of others?

A third criticism is that private schools promote segregation. On the contrary, as noted, Coleman found that private schools are less segregated than public ones (because so many suburban public schools are highly segregated).[113] This corroborates and expands on an earlier study in California, which found that private Catholic schools have a higher population (40 percent) of minority pupils than do public schools.[114] Levine and Doyle report that for many inner-city black families, few of whom are Catholic, the Catholic schools are an affordable alternative to unsatisfactory public schools. (Gallup polls show inner-city blacks to be the most dissatisfied with urban public schools.) Enrollment figures reveal that Catholic schools are responding to this demand.[115] More generally, it is remarkable that so many poor, inner-city blacks scrimp and save to enroll their children in neighborhood-based private schools.[116] A survey showed that people making less than $15,000 a year were more than twice as likely as those making more than $25,000 to say they would use a $500 tuition tax credit. Similarly, blacks and Hispanics are twice as likely as whites to utilize such a credit.[117] The explanation is probably that low-income minority groups located in large cities are more dependent on monolithic public schools, which they find unsatisfactory, than higher-income whites, who often can find a satisfactory school by choosing an appropriate, small, suburban community in which to live. This means that low-income families and minority groups constitute an important constituency for vouchers and tuition tax credits.

A fourth criticism is that if many more children attend independent private schools, we soon will have a nation of adults who lack any common educational background, and may even lack basic exposure to the nation's history and its basic democratic values. This putative shortcoming is easy to avoid. State education authorities can require certain common curriculum elements at a minimum, and should administer common achievement examinations to all students. The results of the examinations would serve at least three purposes: (1) They would inform parents about their child's progress; (2) they would be used for accreditation; and (3) properly summarized, they would help parents assess and choose schools for their children. No doubt, rating services would spring up in time, providing parents with an analysis of educational institutions, a hybrid of *Lovejoy's College Guide* and *Consumer Reports*.

To summarize the discussion, one can have *universal* education without *public* schools and *market-oriented competition* in education without charging parents a *user fee* for their child's schooling. As long as every child attends school, at common expense financed by general taxes, the public interest would be satisfied.

Recreation and Leisure

Recreation is an individual or toll good, although many kinds of facilities, by tradition, are owned and operated by public agencies. Examples are swimming pools, beaches, golf courses, tennis courts, parks, athletic fields, and marinas. Museums, libraries, zoos, opera houses, and concert halls may be governmental but are often provided at least in part by private voluntary organizations. Unlike police services, an almost classic collective good, these leisure and recreation services are toll goods, and each is enjoyed by only a segment of the populace.

It is evident from these characteristics that government, franchise, contract, voucher, and voluntary arrangements could be used to provide these goods. Unfortunately, there seems to be no definitive study of the relative performance of these different arrangements, but some interesting individual cases illustrate at least the applicability of alternative arrangements.

The use of franchises for public golf and tennis courts is growing rapidly, impelled by budget stringency at the local government level, and it is politically palatable because these activities are viewed by the public at large as pursuits of the wealthy. Municipal and county golf courses have been turned over to private operators who maintain and run them, and generally pay a percentage of gross receipts and a guaranteed minimum annual income. The government's objective in doing this is to improve maintenance, increase revenues, reduce costs, and keep the courses open to the public. An experiment with one course in New York City showed that better management by a private operator led to about a 21 percent increase in attendance and revenues, and city officials decided to franchise almost all the municipal golf courses.[118]

A novel hybrid arrangement was developed to rescue Bryant Park, the classic park behind the New York Public Library, on Fifth Avenue. Under conventional municipal operation, the nine-acre park gradually became the preserve of assorted drug addicts, pushers, vagrants, and muggers. In desperation, the city turned to the private sector to manage the park, contracting with a voluntary organization created for the purpose. The latter, in turn, plans to award a franchise to a private restaurateur to build and operate a major restaurant in the park. Revenues from the food service will help pay for reconstruction, plantings, maintenance, and security. The resulting arrangement is a promising hybrid of government, voluntary, and franchise elements.

Perhaps the most famous urban park in the world is Central Park, also in New York City. Its slow physical deterioration led to the formation of several private groups devoted to its restoration. These voluntary associations coalesced into a single influential body that entered into a contractual arrangement with the city's Parks Department. The private group raises funds for the park and pays for a park manager who is stationed in the park, assigns priorities, allocates resources, and in effect oversees the work of civil service employees. This hybrid government-voluntary arrangement has been successful and was transplanted to other major parks in New York City.

Theorists from the property rights school argue that public ownership of land (or any other tangible asset) inevitably means diffuse responsibility and no permanent concern for using it wisely, caring for it, and preserving it for future use. Aristotle warned of this propensity: that which is shared in common by the greatest number has the least care bestowed on it; that is, it becomes a common-pool good. Hardin's observation on the tragedy of the commons makes the same point: Grazing land is destroyed because it is free and therefore overused.[119] New York City's experiences with its parks and recreational facilities confirm this prediction.

Anderson and Shaw tell the sad tale of a major urban park, Ravenna Park in Seattle, that was destroyed by public ownership. Late in the nineteenth century, the park was assembled privately as a preserve of giant fir trees. It was opened to the public and attracted 8,000 to 10,000 visitors a day, at a fee that would be the equivalent of $3 today. After twenty-five years, the city condemned the property and took it over as a public park. Then, within fourteen years, all the giant firs were gone, apparently cut down and sold illicitly by park employees. Today it is a high-crime area with a concrete tennis court where once stood the largest tree, one with a twenty-foot diameter. Whereas the private owners recognized the latent public demand for a park preserve, and found it profitable to create the park and treat it well, when the public owned it, the public employees—who had no true ownership rights and therefore no long-term stake in it—found it profitable in the short-term to convert the trees into firewood.[120]

Private ownership continues to preserve potential parkland. When the Department of the Interior was seeking suitable land for a national park that would feature tallgrass prairie, it realized that its own landholdings were inferior in condition to land maintained by private owners.

Of course, few public employees are as venal as those in Ravenna Park, and an exemplary counterexample can be found in California. When severe budget cuts threatened the survival of a public park and recreation agency, two employees left and started their own business. They contracted to provide an even broader range of recreation programs (a 20 percent increase in offerings and a 30 percent increase in participation) at a lower cost.[121]

This example can be used to support the above argument about property rights: When the employees founded their firm, they acquired a long-term stake in the success of their enterprise and delivered more cost-effective services than the public agency could. The reported successes of contracting out led the Department of the Interior to issue a guidebook for the purpose.[122]

Poole offers a number of examples of voluntary associations that "adopted" parks and otherwise assumed neglected governmental responsibilities with respect to parks and recreation activities.[123]

Vouchers can be used to supply recreational services, just as they can be employed for other individual or toll goods. In New York City culture vouchers were distributed to low-income residents through community organizations, and they entitled the bearer to attend any of eight museums. Voucher programs in culture-rich New York also were aimed at theaters, dance programs, and other performing arts.[124] These efforts seemed to succeed in expanding the horizons of the voucher recipients and enlarging the audience for specialized cultural institutions.

The city of South Barwon in Australia, with a population of forty thousand, has operated a modest system of recreation vouchers since 1976.[125] About 12 percent of the city's parks and recreation budget is allocated to vouchers, and every year each taxpayer receives a voucher and a list of the 150 organizations authorized to receive vouchers. The organizations are extraordinarily diverse and include clubs devoted to photography, croquet, astronomy, life saving, drama, go-cart racing, ceramics, and scouting. In effect, the voucher recipient makes a contribution to the club of his or her choice, and this eliminates political pressure on city officials to support this or that activity. The scheme was opposed by those entrenched interests (e.g., cricket and field hockey) that had benefited traditionally from their favored status. Among the problems encountered was that of defining "recreation"; more and more community service groups (such as Coast Guard volunteers, an ambulance brigade, and the Red Cross) were declared eligible, and a growing fraction of vouchers was being turned in to such groups. Promotional efforts by groups to obtain vouchers from residents were viewed as a mixed blessing; they created greater awareness of the choices available, but promotion came to dominate the activities of some groups and displaced their initial goals.

A moment's reflection raises some very serious questions about this entire scheme. In essence, people pay property taxes and receive vouchers that they then contribute to the association of their choice. Why go through this roundabout and unnecessarily indirect and inefficient process? Why not levy a smaller tax and let people contribute entirely on their own initiative? In the New York example, the vouchers were clearly and sensibly aimed at low-income residents; in the Australian case, they are aimed at property owners, surely a middle- and upper-income group. It is not at all clear what public purpose is served by this curious procedure.

Sports Arenas and Stadiums

An interesting study sheds light on the comparative performance of publicly and privately owned sports arenas and stadiums. The study encompassed all thirty-eight arenas used since 1953 either as home courts for National Basketball Association teams or as home ice for National Hockey League teams. The average inflation-adjusted cost per seat (AIACPS) to construct a privately owned arena was $1,333, compared to $1,946 for a publicly owned one; the difference is statistically significant at the 5 percent level, even though there is no significant difference in the capacities of the two kinds of arenas. Moreover, the privately owned arenas were used an average of 254 days per year, compared to 197 days for the publicly owned ones. An additional comparison showed that the private facilities had better ratios of parking spaces to seats (neither too much nor too little).

The same study also examined the fifty-eight stadiums used by major league baseball or football teams since 1953. The AIACPS for stadium construction was $422 and $1,023 for the private and public facilities respectively (a finding significant at the .1 percent level), utilization was insignificantly different, and private stadiums had more appropriate ratios of parking space.[126]

A final point of comparison deals with team loyalty. Between 1970 and 1985, there were twenty-two franchise moves in the major leagues. Only two of them involved a team leaving a privately owned facility. The private facility implies an economic commitment to the community, whereas a tenant in a publicly owned stadium finds it a convenient base from which to shop for a better deal elsewhere. No wonder losing communities have been agitating for legislation to interfere with a team's right to move; in retrospect, perhaps the stadium should not have been built at public expense.

CONVENTION CENTERS
Convention centers, civic centers, auditoriums, theaters, arenas, and stadiums are toll goods that can be supplied by the private sector and are not natural monopolies. For example, in the absence of government action a consortium of businesses in visitor-oriented industries would probably be formed to finance, construct, own, and operate a convention center. According to this reasoning, such facilities should not be built with public funds. Nevertheless, many convention centers were built by cities eagerly competing for the convention trade, and contract management has been suggested for them.

One might expect a private operator to function better in this competitive climate, applying imaginative and sophisticated marketing techniques, free to negotiate "deals" to attract major conventions, and able to respond rapidly and efficiently to urgent needs with a flexible, private-sector workforce. Public agencies are seriously and innately handicapped in all these respects. In contrast, advocates of public management fear that a private operator would tend to emphasize entertainment extravaganzas (e.g., rock-music concerts) that draw mostly local residents rather than national and international conventions that draw out-of-towners who stay for several days and patronize hotels, restaurants, shops, and theaters. In other words, the former attraction benefits the center primarily, while the latter benefits many other businesses as well; indeed, this is presumably why a convention center is a civic undertaking rather than a private one.

The fear of private management seems unfounded. It is not difficult to write into the contract specifications some terms about the number (or fraction) of national conventions to be held, or the number of out-of-town convention registrants to be drawn. Simple sample surveys of attendees would suffice to monitor the contractor's performance on this score. In sum, contracting for private management of a convention center is not at all unreasonable on its face and seems like a promising option for communities that, wisely or not, have built such complex, publicly owned facilities.

Conclusion

Privatization has been successfully applied to public safety, national defense, health care, housing and urban development, social services, education, and recreation. Comparative studies of public and private provision of these services are generally not as robust as those discussed in the preceding chapter, and more research would be useful. (When one considers the huge sums spent on health care, education, and social services, it is dismaying that so little effort has been devoted to sound research on the effect of service arrangements in these areas.) Nevertheless, the available evidence tends to confirm the conclusion reached there, namely that the private sector performs so-called public services more efficiently and effectively than government usually can. Statisticians and econometricians can argue about homotheticity, heteroskedasticity, and other arcane features of the mathematical analyses, but as a matter of public policy the case for *prudent* privatization is very strong.

Because it is difficult to draw up detailed specifications for human services such as health, housing, education, and social services, privatization by contracting (except for certain components of the service) may not work as well as other alternatives, particularly voucher, voluntary, and market arrangements.

We have seen that privatization encompasses a variety of approaches and can be applied in many different ways to improve the functioning of society. To privatize an existing activity, however, is no simple matter. The next chapter describes how to go about it.

Notes

1. Marcia Chaiken and Jan Chaiken, *Private Provision of Municipal and County Police Functions,* a report prepared for the National Institute of Justice (Cambridge, Mass.: Abt Associates, 1986).

2. Stephen L. Mehay and Rodolfo A. Gonzalez, "Economic Incentives under Contract Supply of Local Government Services," *Public Choice* 46 (1985): 79-86.

3. William C. Cunningham and Todd Taylor, "The Hallcrest Report: Private Security and Police in America," in *Crime and Protection in America,* ed. Daniel Ford (Washington, D.C.: National Institute of Justice, 1985).

4. "Some Rich Towns Being Walled Off," *New York Times,* 27 June 1983.

5. "Private Security Patrols on Rise in City's Middle-Class Areas," *New York Times,* 18 September 1983.

6. Robert D. McFadden, "Poll Indicates Half of New Yorkers See Crime as City's Chief Problem," *New York Times,* 14 January 1985.

7. Kathleen Teltsch, "Private Guard Forces Feared as Drain on Money for Police," *New York Times,* 29 January 1984.

8. Tom L. Peyton, Jr., "Standards for Public Building Maintenance," *APWA Reporter* 44, no. 10 (October 1977): 28-29.

9. James K. Stewart, "Public Safety and Private Police," *Public Administration Review* 45 (November 1985): 758-65.

10. Theodore Gage, "Cops, Inc.," *Reason* 14, no. 7 (November 1982): 23-28.

11. Ibid.

12. Ole P. Kristensen, "Public versus Private Provision of Governmental Services: The Case of Danish Fire Protection Services," *Urban Studies* 20 (1983): 1-9.

13. James C. McDavid and Evelyn Butler, *Fire Services in Canadian Municipalities* (Victoria, B.C.: School of Public Administration, University of Victoria, 1984).

14. Lois A. MacGillivray, *Evaluating the Organization of Service Delivery: Fire,* technical report (Washington, D.C.: National Technical Information Service, 1982).

15. Roger S. Ahlbrandt, Jr., *Municipal Fire Protection Services: Comparison of Alternative Organizational Forms* (Beverly Hills, Calif.: Sage, 1973), 45.

16. Mark Frazier, "Scottsdale Slashes Spending," *Reader's Digest,* February 1978.

17. Martin Tolchin, "Localities Shift to Private Firefighters," *New York Times,* 28 July 1985.

18. Lou Witzeman, "The Fire Department Goes Private," in *This Way Up: The Local Official's Handbook for Privatization and Contracting Out,* ed. R.Q. Armington and William D. Ellis (Chicago: Regnery, 1984), 65-92.

19. Neal R. Peirce, "Cities Sound Alarm over Firefighters' Benefits," *National Journal,* 20 July 1985, 1698.

20. Ibid.

21. Howell Raines, "Officials Face Possible Ouster for Cutting Back Jobs," *New York Times,* 9 February 1979.

22. Charles H. Logan and Sharla P. Rausch, "Punish and Profit: The Emergence of Private Enterprise Prisons," *Justice Quarterly* 2, no. 3 (September 1985): 303-18; and Charles H. Logan, "Competition in the Prison Business," *Freeman,* August 1985, 469-78. See also Joan Mullen, "Corrections and the Private Sector," *Research in Brief* (Washington, D.C.: National Institute of Justice, March 1985).

23. Logan and Rausch, "Punish and Profit."

24. Camille G. Camp and George M. Camp, *Private Sector Involvement in Prison Services* (Washington, D.C.: National Institute of Corrections, February 1984).

25. Logan and Rausch, "Punish and Profit."

26. *Newsweek,* 6 October 1986, 48.

27. Stuart M. Butler, *Privatizing Federal Spending: A Strategy to Reduce the Deficit* (New York: Universe Books, 1985), 136-42.

28. James T. Bennett and Manuel H. Johnson, *Better Government at Half the Price: Private Production of Public Services* (Ottawa, Ill.: Caroline House, 1981), 53-54.

29. James T. Bennett and T.J. DiLorenzo, "Public Employee Unions and the Privatization of 'Public' Services," *Journal of Labor Research* 4 (Winter 1983): 41-42.

30. Edward C. Lesson, Statement, U.S. House of Representatives, *Hearings on Contracting Out of Jobs and Services, Part II, Subcommittee on Employee Ethics and*

Utilization, Committee on Post Office and Civil Service, Serial no. 95-29 (Washington, D.C.: Government Printing Office, 1977), 153.

31. Steve H. Hanke, "Privatization: Theory, Evidence, and Implementation," in *Control of Federal Spending,* ed. C. Lowell Harriss, Proceedings of the Academy of Political Science 35, no. (1985): 10-13.

32. David E. Rosenbaum, "Chrysler Program Saves Millions in Health Costs," *New York Times,* 29 April 1985; see also Joseph A. Califano, Jr., "A Revolution Looms in American Health," *New York Times,* 25 March 1986.

33. Linda Punch, "Contract Management Companies Manage Growth Rate of 13.3 Percent," *Modern Healthcare,* 15 August 1984, 45-52.

34. Lawrence S. Lewin, Robert A. Derzon, and Rhea Margulies, "Investor-Owneds and Nonprofits Differ in Economic Performance," *Hospitals* 55, no. 13 (1981): 52-58.

35. Robert V. Pattison and Hallie M. Katz, "Investor-Owned and Not-for-Profit Hospitals," *New England Journal of Medicine* 309 (11 August 1983): 347-53; and Frank A. Sloan and Robert A. Vraciu, "Investor-Owned and Not-For-Profit Hospitals: Addressing Some Issues," *Health Affairs,* Spring 1983, 25-37.

36. *For-Profit Enterprise in Health Care* (Washington, D.C.: National Academy of Sciences, 1986).

37. E.S. Savas, "How Much Do Government Services Really Cost?" *Urban Affairs Quarterly* 15, no. 1 (September 1979): 23-41.

38. Michael D. Bromberg and Mark J. Brand, "Privatization of Hospitals," in Armington and Ellis, eds., *This Way Up;* and Martin Tolchin, "Impact of Profits on Hospitals Argued," *New York Times,* 26 January 1985.

39. Glenn Fowler, "Audit Compares City and Private X-Ray Units," *New York Times,* 11 October 1981.

40. Martin Tolchin, "As Companies Buy Hospitals, Treatment of Poor Is Debated," *New York Times,* 25 January 1985.

41. Hanke, "Privatization," 106.

42. J. Peter Grace, *War on Waste* (New York: Macmillan, 1984), 487.

43. "Records of Military Hospitals Faulted in Audits by Services," *New York Times,* 12 February 1985; "Pentagon Adopts Steps to Improve Quality of Military Medical Care," *New York Times,* 10 June 1985; and "Quality Military Medicine to Be Reviewed by Civilians," *New York Times,* 1 February 1986.

44. Pamela G. Hollie, "Ambulances Go Private," *New York Times,* 25 May 1986.

45. *An Overview of Nursing Home Characteristics: Provisional Data from the 1977 National Nursing Home Survey,* Advance Data no. 35 (Washington, D.C.: U.S. Department of Health, Education, and Welfare, Public Health Service, National Center for Health Statistics, 6 September 1978).

46. Cotton M. Lindsay, *Veterans Administration Hospitals* (Washington, D.C.: American Enterprise Institute, 1975), 11. See also "Veterans Administration Hospital Management," in *Report on Privatization,* 88-121.

47. Hanke, "Privatization," 106.

48. Robert M. Spann, "Public versus Private Provision of Governmental Services," *Budgets and Bureaucrats: The Sources of Government Growth,* ed. Thomas E. Borcherding (Durham: Duke University Press, 1977).

49. William Hsiao, "Public versus Private Administration of Health Insurance: A Study in Relative Economic Efficiency," *Inquiry* 15 (December 1978): 379-87.

50. H.E. French III, "Health Insurance: Private, Mutuals or Governments," in *Proceedings of the Seminar on the Economics of Nonproprietary Organizations,* ed. K.W. Clarkson and D.L. Martin (Greenwich, Conn.: JAI Press, 1980).

51. John Goodman and Richard W. Rahn, "Salvaging Medicare with an IRA," *Wall Street Journal,* 20 March 1984.

52. Robert L. Ciszewski, *Contraceptive Marketing Program in Bangladesh Doubles Number Practicing Birth Control* (New York: Population Services International, 20 September 1978); and John Davies and Terrence D.J. Lavis, "Measuring the Effectiveness of Contraceptive Marketing Programs: Preethi in Sri Lanka," *Studies in Family Planning* 8, no. 4 (April 1977): 82-90.

53. *Report of the President's Commission on Housing* (Washington, D.C.: Government Printing Office, 1982), 4-6; 1983 data from Office of Policy Development and Research, Department of Housing and Urban Development.

54. Office of Management and Budget, *Major Policy Initiatives, Fiscal Year 1987* (Washington, D.C.: Government Printing Office, 1986), 33-35.

55. *Report of the Secretary on the Homeless and Emergency Shelters* (Washington, D.C.: Office of Policy Development and Research, Department of Housing and Urban Development, May 1984).

56. *President's Commission on Housing,* 9-15.

57. Ibid., xxiii. See also *The Long-Term Costs of Lower-Income Housing Assistance Programs* (Washington, D.C.: Congressional Budget Office, 1981); James E. Wallace et al., *Participation and Benefits in the Urban Section 8 Program: New Construction and Existing Housing* (Cambridge, Mass.: Abt Associates, January 1981); Office of Management and Budget, *Major Policy Initiatives;* similar findings were reported in West Germany for corresponding programs; for example, see Stephen K. Mayo and Jörn Barnbrock, *Rental Housing Subsidy Programs in Germany and the U.S.: A Comparative Program Evaluation* (Cambridge, Mass.: Abt Associates, September 1980). This section relies heavily on numerous reports and analyses in which I was involved while serving as assistant secretary for policy development and research in the Department of Housing and Urban Development from 1981 to 1983.

58. Maurice Carroll, "A Pattern of Fires Cited in Subsidized Buildings," *New York Times,* 3 September 1983.

59. *President's Commission on Housing,* 17-22; Ira S. Lowry, *Experimenting with Housing Allowances, Executive Summary,* R-2880-HUD (Washington, D.C.: Department of Housing and Urban Development, April 1982); and Raymond J. Struyck and Mark Bendick, Jr., eds., *Housing Vouchers for the Poor* (Washington, D.C.: Urban Institute Press, 1981).

60. Katharine L. Bradbury and Anthony Downs, eds., *Do Housing Allowances Work?* (Washington, D.C.: Brookings Institution, 1981), 399-403.

61. John C. Weicher, *Housing: Federal Policies and Programs* (Washington, D.C.: American Enterprise Institute, 1980).

62. Madsen Pirie, *Dismantling the State* (Dallas: National Center for Policy Analysis, 1985), 69-71; idem, "Buying Out of Socialism," *Reason* 17 (January 1986): 23-27; and Butler, *Privatizing Federal Spending,* 68-70.

63. Butler, *Privatizing Federal Spending,* 71-72. See also Robert Woodson, *Tenant Control of Public Housing: An Economic Opportunity* (Washington, D.C.: National Forum Foundation, 1985).

64. *Public Housing Authority Experience with Private Management: A Comparative Study* (Washington, D.C.: Office of Policy Development and Research, Department of Housing and Urban Development, May 1983).

65. "Subsidized Paint," *New York Times,* 21 April 1979, 26.

66. Peter F. Drucker, "Can the Businessman Meet Our Social Needs?" *Saturday Review,* April 1973.

67. *President's Commission on Housing,* 157-73.

68. Office of Management and Budget, *Tax Expenditures* (Washington, D.C.: Government Printing Office, February 1986), G38.

69. Office of Management and Budget, *Major Policy Initiatives,* 38.

70. *President's Commission on Housing,* 180.

71. Ibid., 223-37.

72. Walter Block and Edgar Olsen, eds., *Rent Control: Myths and Realities* (Vancouver, B.C.: Fraser Institute, 1981); and Peter D. Salins, *The Ecology of Housing Destruction* (New York: New York University Press, 1980).

73. F.A. Hayek, Milton Friedman, et al., *Rent Control: A Popular Paradox* (Vancouver, B.C.: Fraser Institute, 1975).

74. Robert H. Nelson, *Zoning and Property Rights* (Cambridge, Mass.: MIT Press, 1977); see also "A Breath of Free Markets in Zoning," *Wall Street Journal,* 22 May 1985.

75. *The President's National Urban Policy Report* (Washington, D.C.: Department of Housing and Urban Development, 1982), 46.

76. Stuart M. Butler, *Enterprise Zones: Greenlining the Inner Cities* (New York: Universe Books, 1981), 24-74.

77. Ibid., 95-97.

78. President Ronald Reagan, Message to the Congress, 23 March 1982. I helped prepare this message while serving as assistant secretary for policy development and research, Department of Housing and Urban Development.

79. *Enterprise Zone Update* (Washington, D.C.: Department of Housing and Urban Development, 22 April 1985).

80. Ronald Smothers, "State-Run Residences for Retarded Reported Inferior and More Costly," *New York Times,* 29 August 1982.

81. Margaret Gibelman, "Are Clients Served Better When Services Are Purchased?" *Public Welfare,* Fall 1981, 26-33.

82. J. Biber, "Small Shelters Are Cost-Effective," *New York Times,* 17 March 1984.

83. Harry P. Hatry and Eugene Durman, *Issues in Competitive Contracting for Social Services* (Falls Church, Va.: National Institute of Governmental Purchasing, 1985).

84. This is my interpretation of the facts presented by Mark Schlesinger, Robert A. Dorwart, and Richard T. Pulice, "Competitive Bidding and States' Purchase of Services," *Journal of Policy Analysis and Management* 5, no. 2 (Winter 1986): 245-63.

85. Butler, *Privatizing Federal Spending,* 92-119.

86. Ibid., 102.

87. Robert L. Woodson, "The Importance of Neighborhood Organizations in Meeting Human Needs" and "Child Welfare Policy," in *Meeting Human Needs: Toward a New Public Philosophy,* ed. Jack A. Meyer (Washington, D.C.: American Enterprise Institute, 1982), 132-52 and 455-65. See also Peter L. Berger and Richard John Neuhaus, *To Empower People: The Role of Mediating Structures in Public Policy* (Washington, D.C.: American Enterprise Institute, 1977).

88. Butler, *Privatizing Federal Spending,* 110.

89. For a proposal on home health-care vouchers, see Amitai Etzioni, *Statement for Hearing on Proprietary Health Care, U.S. Senate Special Committee on Aging,* 28 October 1975; for job-training, see Burt Schorr, "Retraining Programs Offer Some an Escape from Dying Industries," *Wall Street Journal,* 8 June 1983; for a discussion of employment vouchers, see Lawrence H. Summers, "Employment Incentives," *New York Times,* 3 August 1983.

90. Ted Kolderie, *Public Services Redesign Project* (Minneapolis: Humphrey Institute, University of Minnesota, 15 November 1982).

91. Dana Friedman, *Corporate Financial Assistance for Child Care,* Research Bulletin no. 177 (New York: Conference Board, 1985).

92. U.S. General Accounting Office, *Report on National Day Care Study,* report by the Comptroller General of the United States (Washington, D.C.: Government Printing Office, 1979); see also letter from the comptroller general to the U.S. Senate Committee on Finance, File No. FGMSD-79-48 (910360), 25 September 1979.

93. Michael Krashinsky, "The Cost of Day Care in Public Programs," *National Tax Journal* 31, no. 4 (December 1978): 363-72.

94. R.L. Woodson, "Day Care," in Armington and Ellis, eds., *This Way Up,* 149-63.

95. Peter J. Ferrara, "Expand IRAs to Social Security," *Wall Street Journal,* 7 December 1984; idem, "Social Security Reform: The Super IRA," in *Beyond the Status Quo,* ed. David Boaz and Edward H. Crane (Washington, D.C.: Cato Institute, 1985), 51-74; idem, *Social Security: The Inherent Contradiction* (Washington, D.C.: Cato Institute, 1980). See also John C. Goodman, "Opting Out of Social Security: Why It Works in Other Countries," in *Privatization* (Dallas, Tex.: National Center for Policy Analysis, 1985), 79-86.

96. Butler, *Privatizing Federal Spending,* 143-65.

97. "Retired Judges Hired to Decide Lawsuits in Private," *New York Times,* 26 October 1980. See also Bowie K. Kuhn, "Privatized Justice Deserves a Trial," *Wall Street Journal,* 18 June 1985; Martin Tolchin, "Private Courts with Binding Rulings Draw Interest and Some Challenges," *New York Times,* 12 May 1985.

98. Martin Tolchin, "When the Justice System Is Put under Contract," *New York Times,* 4 August 1985.

99. Robert Hermann, Eric Single, and John Boston, *Counsel for the Poor: Criminal Defense in Urban America* (Lexington, Mass.: Lexington Books, 1977).

100. Gabriel Roth, *Private Provision of Public Services in Developing Countries* (New York: Oxford University Press, 1987).

101. *Pierce v. Society of Sisters* (1925); see also Murray N. Rothbard, *For a New Liberty* (New York: Macmillan, 1978), 126.

102. Jane Wollman, "Teaching at Home with Help of Computers," *New York Times,* 9 February 1984.

103. Office of Management and Budget, *Major Policy Initiatives,* 31-32.

104. Arthur E. Wise and Linda Darling-Hammond, *Education by Voucher: Private Choice and the Public Interest,* paper no. P-6838 (Santa Monica, Calif.: Rand Corporation, December 1982).

105. Estelle James, "Benefits and Costs of Privatized Public Services: Lessons from the Dutch Educational System," *Comparative Education Review* 28, no. 4 (November 1984): 605-24.

106. Daniel Patrick Moynihan, "Government and the Ruin of Private Education," *Harper's,* April 1978, 28-38.

107. *Mueller v. Allen,* 77 L. Ed.2d 721, 728 (1983).

108. James Coleman, Thomas Hoffer, and Sally Kilgore, *High School Achievement* (New York: Basic Books, 1982).

109. Ted Kolderie, *Two Alternate Routes to the Improvement of Education: Part II, Public Services Redesign Project* (Minneapolis: Humphrey Institute, University of Minnesota, May 1984). See also his related article in the July 1985 issue.

110. *Policy Analysis of the Cost and Financing of Special Education to Handicapped Children in New York City* (New York: Office of the Comptroller, 22 May 1978).

111. Polly Carpenter and George Hall, *Case Studies in Educational Performance Contracting: Conclusions and Implications,* report no. R-900/1-HEW (Santa Monica, Calif.: Rand Corporation, December 1971).

112. Clint Bolick, "Solving the Education Crisis: Market Alternatives and Parental Choice," in *Beyond the Status Quo,* ed. David Boaz and Edward H. Crane (Washington, D.C.: Cato Institute, 1985), 207-21.

113. Coleman et al., *High School Achievement.*

114. John E. Coons and Joseph Kul, "Schools: What's Happening to Local Control?" *Taxing and Spending* 1, no. 1 (October-November 1978): 39.

115. Marsha Levine and Denis P. Doyle, "Private Meets Public: An Examination of Contemporary Education," in *Meeting Human Needs,* ed. Jack A. Meyer (Washington, D.C.: American Enterprise Institute, 1982), 286-87.

116. Butler, *Privatizing Federal Spending,* 109; see also Bolick, "Solving the Education Crisis," 211-12.

117. "Trustbusting Education," *Wall Street Journal,* 13 February 1985; see also Thomas A. Johnson, "Black-Run Private Schools Lure Growing Numbers in New York," *New York Times,* 5 April 1980, 1.

118. Office of the Mayor, City of New York, release no. 23-80, 24 January 1980.

119. Garrett Hardin, "The Tragedy of the Commons," *Science* 62 (13 December 1968): 1243-48.

120. Terry L. Anderson and Jane S. Shaw, "Grass Isn't Always Greener in a Public Park," *Wall Street Journal,* 28 May 1985.

121. Reinhart Knudsen, "Recreation for Hire," *Sacramento Union,* 5 March 1981; see also *Leisurelines* 6, no. 8 (California Park and Recreation Society, October 1980).

122. Heritage Conservation and Recreation Service, *Contract Services Handbook* (Washington, D.C.: Department of the Interior, October 1979).

123. Robert W. Poole, Jr., *Cutting Back City Hall* (New York: Universe Books, 1980), 101-2.

124. Gary Bridge, "Citizen Choice in Public Service: Voucher Systems," in *Alternatives for Delivering Public Services: Toward Improved Performance,* ed. E.S. Savas (Boulder, Colo.: Westview, 1977), 51-110.

125. John L. Crompton, "Recreation Vouchers: A Case Study in Administrative Innovation and Citizen Participation," *Public Administration Review* 43, no. 6 (November/December 1983): 537-46.

126. Dean Baim, *Comparison of Privately and Publicly Owned Sports Arenas and Stadiums* (Chicago: Heartland Institute, 1985).

PART FOUR

Toward Successful Privatization

8. How to Privatize

How does a conscientious public official who wants to privatize in order to improve both government and the condition of society go about doing it? Four broad, interrelated, and mutually reinforcing strategies may be followed for this purpose:

1. Government should encourage the marketplace and voluntary organizations to supply goods and services that it now provides. This is *load shedding,* the partial or complete withdrawal of government from an activity. Load shedding can be carried out by divestiture, default, accommodation, and by the gradual replacement of government activity with market and voluntary activity. Denationalization of state-owned enterprises, by divestiture or other means, is an important aspect of load shedding.

2. Where continued government involvement in an activity is necessary, government's role should be reduced by devolution, that is, making greater use of the private sector through vouchers, franchises, and contracts. In addition, programs should be moved to lower levels of government, to be financed and administered closer to the people being served.

3. User charges should be levied wherever possible, to make the true cost of government services more evident and thereby stimulate interest in alternative arrangements.

4. Competition should be introduced and promoted wherever possible, and government monopolies should be broken up. Deregulation is a useful tool for accomplishing this.

Long-term, incrementalist tactics are needed to implement a privatization strategy, with a research and public relations effort to press for privatization, tax reforms to encourage it, legislation to allow it, and strong coalitions of stakeholders — some newly converted — to support it. It may also be necessary to erode antiprivatization coalitions, for example, by selling or giving shares to workers of an enterprise that is to be denationalized[1]. It must always be borne in mind that privatization is more a *political* than an *economic* act.

Load Shedding

The extensive collectivization of goods heretofore considered private goods, such as education, health care, housing, and various social services, has accomplished much but has failed to achieve reasonable expectations and has been very costly. It is time to pursue other paths toward the desired objective of social well-being. Specifically, government's overly dominant role in supplying some goods should be diminished gradually to achieve a better balance with private institutions. A reduction in government's role should go hand in hand with an increased supply of these goods through other arrangements.

For example, many social and health services redefined as collective and common-pool goods, which account for much of the growth in government expenditures, are already being delivered through the marketplace, and that mechanism can be strengthened. Private firms typically provide such fringe benefits to their employees as pensions and subsidized life, health, and unemployment insurance. Increasingly they provide day-care benefits, education programs for employees, and tuition assistance. With reduced government involvement in such services, the list of employer-provided fringe benefits could be extended even further while utilizing nongovernmental service-delivery arrangements. The cost of this expanded fringe-benefit package would be offset by lower taxes. Ideally, employees should be free to choose either these fringe benefits or cash, but changes in the tax laws will be needed to avoid penalizing employees who take advantage of the option to "cash in" their fringe benefits. The growth of individual retirement accounts (IRAs) is an example of successful privatization of old-age security fostered by favorable tax treatment.

Day care is a promising candidate for load shedding. Since time immemorial, parents have arranged for relatives, friends, and neighbors to care for their children; and parents have taken into consideration the character and qualities of individuals to whom they have entrusted their children and the surroundings in which their children have been placed.

In recent years, however, day care has become the object of increasing government involvement and financing. The result has been an increasingly complex web of legal restrictions as to who can provide the service, the number and kind of personnel who must be in attendance, the nature of the facilities, and so forth. The statement of an incredulous and indignant day-care operator to a zoning board (cited in chapter 7) is worth repeating here: "You're telling us we cannot operate a day-care facility in a residentially zoned middle-class neighborhood with a large number of working mothers, but we can operate a center in a commercial zone between two topless bars?"[2] The bizarre result of all the restrictions, however well intended, is that most families and homes today would not be classified by government as suitable for child care.

Government withdrawal from established services will not be easy, for a new political consensus must be achieved to replace the one that brought about government entry in the first place. Nevertheless, discontent with government services suggests that such a consensus may emerge.

This need not involve a bruising battle between opposing ideologies. All that is needed is appropriate encouragement of forces already at work and producing movement, however modest, in the desired direction. Recent evidence concerning the extent to which working adults care for their elderly relatives is instructive. A study of employees in a large insurance company showed that 28 percent of the full-time employees over the age of thirty provided regular care for elderly relatives and friends; they devoted an average of 10.2 hours per week to such care, and 42 percent of the caregivers had daily contact with the elder.[3] The remarkable aspect of this finding is that this traditional pattern of family care persists and is adhered to even by people holding full-time jobs outside the home. To the extent that this practice can be rewarded, made easier, and encouraged by government behavior, the demand for more government provision of such care will be obviated.

A very different example is offered by the municipal tennis courts in New York City. Their poor condition led many players to abandon city facilities in favor of private ones, and ultimately the city of New York decided to lease its courts to private operators, that is, to switch from municipal to franchise service.

Gradual or partial load shedding also could be carried out for a whole range of other recreational activities, such as golf and swimming. Facilities that are publicly owned could be sold to private bidders and operated as ordinary private businesses, selling their services to the public at large or functioning as nonprofit membership organizations that are prohibited from engaging in discriminatory practices. The rationale for doing so is that these specialized recreational pursuits are classical toll goods, exclusion of nonpayers is possible, and the benefits accrue directly to the users with little spillover to society at large. There is little reason for government to provide these goods at collective expense, and every reason for the *aficionados* to band together for mutual enjoyment under their own rules and at their own expense.

Load shedding or transfer by default occurs when the public finds the government service inadequate or unsatisfactory, and the private sector steps in to fill the void and satisfy the need. The growth of private tennis facilities and private policing are examples of this process. Legislation may be needed to facilitate this movement. For example, some states grant campus police and other private security personnel the power of arrest and give them jurisdiction on public streets in the vicinity of their employer's property.

Load shedding by accommodation occurs through informal cooperation between government and private-sector providers. This happens when the latter relieve the former of a function the public agency would rather not perform. For example, private companies provide security inside shelters for the homeless, a relatively unpleasant task, but regular police officers respond expeditiously to calls for help from such private guards.[4]

We are seeing the phenomenon of load shedding by default in public education in large cities. Even parents of limited means have been withdrawing their children from the public schools in droves and enrolling them in private schools. This reduction in demand invites load shedding. Policies that would treat this trend as an opportunity are discussed later in this chapter.

Load shedding can also take place through the voluntary formation of geographic collective units, in both urban and suburban communities. Virtually unnoticed, a new, very local level of government is emerging in the United States: the condominium. It has great potential. Ranging in size from a single building to a large community, condominiums, neighborhood organizations, and civic associations—we can call them voluntary *microcollectives*—already provide an array of collective goods. They can assume even greater responsibility—for social services, cleaning and maintaining local streets and parks, removing snow, collecting refuse, and operating volunteer ambulance, fire, and patrol services. Such organizations can forge a desperately needed sense of community and can restore citizenship skills atrophied from disuse, skills without which a democracy cannot long survive.

Such units can best be formed in established communities that have well-defined geographic boundaries, are relatively homogeneous in terms of income, and have shared values with respect to the services to be provided through this mechanism. Local leadership is necessary, as is an encouraging posture by the local government. The latter can mean giving tax rebates to residents in areas that forego city services. This poses a minor administrative problem for the local government, but many communities do this, including Houston and Kansas City. Another device to encourage the creation and assure the viability of such self-governing associations is to grant them taxing authority as special assessment districts. New York State has such legislation. A detailed discussion of the virtues of special districts is provided by Hawkins.[5]

In this light, one sees that while government has been growing, load shedding also has been proceeding—without overt political struggles—as a minor countercurrent. The demand for certain collective goods has exceeded the ability of government to supply them at a suitable price, particularly in cities that have been experiencing fiscal stress and high costs of public services. Many municipal services declined in quantity and quality to the point where exasperated citizens formed organizations to supplement the municipal service. In New York City, for example, citizen safety patrols were organized, and groups of neighborhood merchants formed associations to take on tasks such as cleaning sidewalks and streets and maintaining greenery. Other groups were created to undertake maintenance and restoration work in Central Park and elsewhere. In London and Seattle, similar local efforts are encouraged by policies that permit city governments to contract with voluntary groups to assume this responsibility at a cost that is far lower than the city would pay for municipal service. From the standpoint of these voluntary associations, they obtain the services they want, custom-tailored to their specific local needs and preferences; they exert a direct influence over the quality of their surroundings and pay less than they would otherwise.

An important attribute of such microcollectives, besides honing the citizenship skills of their members, is that the latter have an opportunity to contribute their labor instead of their money. In the days of a barter economy, people could pay their taxes in specie such as grain and livestock. In a market economy they must pay cash. Load shedding to voluntary associations restores to the taxpayer the choice of paying in kind—with his labor. "Off the books" earnings would then have their counterpart in "off the books" tax payments, that is, payments in kind for collective goods.

Organized charities are reclaiming their traditional direct role in helping the poor and the afflicted, after slipping gradually over many years into the role of lobbyists distinguished mainly by their lofty moral purpose. Is government needed as the middleman, collecting taxes and distributing them for charitable purposes either directly to the needy or to charitable institutions? In the United States there was an enormous growth in charitable giving by individuals after 1982. Americans gave more (and volunteered more) than at any time in the nation's past. This occurred despite dire predictions that giving would decline sharply because a change in tax laws made contributions much more costly (two-thirds more costly for someone in the top tax bracket). Instead, charitable gifts burgeoned because of lower inflation, higher disposable incomes, and in response to President Reagan's promotion of privatization and his emphasis on private, humane efforts in behalf of the needy. Similarly, when New York's Mayor Koch made a plea for the city's churches to provide food and shelter for "street people," there was a heartening response. As always, private individuals, prompted by moral considerations and acting through voluntary charitable associations, proved able and willing to help those less fortunate than themselves and thereby assumed a portion of the social burden amassed by government.

In the late 1960s, social problems were aggregated and shifted to the highest and most distant level of government, where they were found to be unmanageable even with the involvement of the best minds and leaders. The original emphasis on self-help and community effort gave way to a large and paternalistic welfare apparatus, which saw recipients as helpless victims rather than as citizens needing assistance. Social reforms often made matters worse for the intended beneficiaries, the poor and minorities, as Charles Murray demonstrated in *Losing Ground*.[6] In retrospect, the problem of the so-called permanent underclass ("transgenerational welfare dependence") may be *cratogenic,* that is, created by the state.

Such problems cannot be addressed without the participation of local citizens, who ultimately have both the responsibility and the resources, and who will benefit most from the well-being of their neighbors. The state lacks the critical power of suggestion that a neighbor or local clergyman can have. State power is limited, paradoxically, because it can only issue orders. By contrast, a priest can suggest that an alcoholic getting support from the church also get counseling and clean up his act; he may be entitled to help, but he must also assume the social obligations of citizenship, as Lawrence Mead points out so convincingly.[7] A localized system allows fine-grained judgments based on personal knowledge about an individual and his changing circumstances.

The situation was articulated very well by Goodman and Stroup:

> Entitlement programs for welfare are structured so that benefits are granted solely on the basis of personal circumstances. Applicants do not have to give the reasons for their circumstances, nor are they required to explain how they plan to change them in the future. They don't even have to show a willingness to change. In the AFDC program, for example, the requirements for eligibility essentially amount to: (1) low income, (2) very few assets, (3) dependent children, (4) no man in the household. Anyone satisfying these requirements is entitled to benefits. And the word entitlement means "right"— benefits cannot be withdrawn simply because the recipient refuses to modify behavior.
>
> The philosophy of the private sector is quite different. Because of the emphasis on a behavioral approach to the problem of poverty, our best private charities do not view the giving of assistance as a "duty" or the receipt of assistance as a "right." Instead, charitable assistance is viewed as a tool which can be used intelligently, not only to provide relief but to change behavior. At many private charities, for example, the level of assistance varies considerably from individual to individual. Private agencies usually reserve the right to reduce the level of assistance or withdraw assistance altogether if recipients do not show behavioral changes.[8]

Building on this insight, Goodman and Stroup advocate "privatizing the welfare state" by allowing taxpayers to allocate up to a third of their federal income taxes to private charities; for every dollar allocated in this manner, the federal government would be required to reduce its proverty budget by one dollar.[9]

Growing recognition of the potential of "mediating structures" is evident in dealing with the alarming rise in births among unmarried black teenagers. The initial, reflexive reaction among many policy advocates was to call for a government program to "solve the problem." That approach—offered more out of habit than conviction—has stalled because people are realizing that government programs, no matter how well intended and well financed, are essentially unavailing for this kind of problem. Creative local initiatives, informal person-to-person efforts, local role models, and intracommunity pressures are more likely to be effective than bureaucrats following federal guidelines. Leaders in the black community recognize this.[10]

The problem grew in severity at the same time that sex education became widespread, and contraceptives and abortion became legalized, widely accepted, readily available, safe, and cheap. Surely births among teenagers cannot be due to ignorance about birth control; therefore, more instruction and more clinics are not the answer.

What societal institution *is* most capable of providing the detailed, long-term attention and the concern, love, care, support, guidance, admonition, restriction, control, and punishment necessary to reduce teenage pregnancy and yet do so in a way that is acceptable to society and consistent with our values? *Answer:* The family; certainly not a government agency.[11]

Centralized, government-based programs are not only of questionable effectiveness, they may be dangerous as well. They run the risk, however small, of someday being transformed into abhorrent, Draconian "final solutions," such as sterilization. If this seems far-fetched, consider the reports of forced abortions in China, the result of a firm-handed government effort to reduce the birthrate.

Government did not always occupy a dominant position in the area of welfare. Its role as a supplement to private charity was articulated by President Thiers of France in the mid-nineteenth century:

> Some general diseases, affecting an entire social class, must be treated by the collective charity of everybody, in fact, by public assistance. But it is important that this virtue, when it changes from individual to collective, retains its virtuous character, which is to remain spontaneous, voluntary, and free. It must not become a constraint. Therefore, there must be public charity, to complete the private or religious charity, acting where some good remains to be done.[12]

The challenge facing governments at the end of the twentieth century is to strike a better balance between state and private charity, bearing in mind the great value to society of having its members behave as willing philanthropists (defined as "those who love their fellowmen, and exert themselves for their well-being") instead of reluctant taxpayers.

To summarize, alternative arrangements have emerged to supply services that the government arrangement was not supplying satisfactorily. To implement load shedding, then, can involve no more than a no-growth policy for government and natural growth for the alternative arrangements. Limiting devices such as Proposition 13, spending caps, budget cuts, revenue cuts, revenue limitations, and mandatory balanced budgets all facilitate this process. Inflation can actually help to the extent that limitations are imposed in absolute dollar amounts. More vigorous pursuit of load shedding involves promoting the growth of alternative arrangements by offering tax reduction and tax credits, issuing vouchers, conferring assessment authority on microcollectives, contracting with local citizen groups, deregulating, and encouraging private charity.

A systematic review of government-supplied goods and services, to see which ones can revert, admittedly with much effort, to private or toll goods, and which collective goods might be supplied by voluntary arrangements, might be criticized on the grounds that the ax will fall on the poor, for they benefit from government action. This need not be the case. In the first place, the poor could be served even better by the marketplace if they were given vouchers. Second, it is primarily the broad middle class that both pays for government programs and is the main beneficiary, although this is not to say that the process is therefore fair. In the main, taxes are taken from powerless, middle-class *individuals* and given to organized, middle-class *groups*. Government intervenes to create a carefully crafted set of beneficiaries—be they tobacco growers, veterans, construction workers, day-care users, the elderly, the auto industry, or lawyers—while absorbing a substantial portion of the tax dollar to pay for the expense of considering and identifying potential beneficiaries and figuring out how to direct taxpayers' money to them. Government revenues go in part to pay for the expense of making and executing decisions about redistributing the remainder of the revenues back to middle-class taxpayers in the form of government-produced services. The taxpayer would be better off if he were free to keep more of his income and decide for himself what to buy with it and how to help the needy; instead, he must lobby as a member of a group to get back merely a portion of his money, and get it in a less satisfying, less useful, and possibly unwanted form—all the while being expected to feel grateful for the beneficence of his elected representatives.

Deregulation is another means of expanding the role of the marketplace. Consider the issue of building codes touched on in an earlier chapter. Building codes are imposed by local governments with the intent of assuring public safety. Unfortunately, their unintended consequences often are to force residents to pay for costly and archaic construction techniques, featherbedding, and corrupt inspectors. The National Commission on Neighborhoods found that building codes in the United States add significantly to the cost of rehabilitation and recommended features of the system used in France: a code for safety-related matters; performance-based guidelines for construction; and liability of contractors for building components and construction.[13]

If this were done in the United States, one could anticipate that, as in France, safe construction would be enforced by the marketplace as builders purchase insurance to protect themselves against claims, insurance companies hire inspection firms, and banks make building loans preferentially to insured builders.[14] The end result would be greater reliance on proven market mechanisms.

An example of successful privatization brought about by deregulation can be found in Somalia. The government-owned corporation that had a monopoly in the distribution of agricultural products saw its market share plummet from 100 percent to less than 5 percent within three years after private entrepreneurs were allowed to buy and sell farm products.[15]

Load Shedding by Denationalization

The divestiture of state-owned enterprises (SOEs) and assets is called *denationalization*. This is conceptually straightforward, although far from effortless, and is going on throughout the world, as chapter 6 notes.

Divestiture is not the only route to shedding the functions of an SOE, however. It can also be accomplished by what we might call "the withering away of the state," with thanks to Karl Marx for providing the phrase whose use in this context is surely beyond his wildest nightmare. (In the hindsight of history, this scenario seems more likely than his.)

Consider the instance of a Third World city which has an SOE with an exclusive monopoly to provide intracity bus service, but which has private jitneys (using ordinary sedans) that carry two-thirds of all paying passengers. The country also has private bus companies that provide intercity and charter service, and transport school children. Further, the SOE's bus fleet is old and is comprised of vehicles that are too large for the purpose.

The government's desire to privatize this activity can be accomplished either by selling the SOE (with its old and inefficient buses) or by deregulating entry and allowing the existing transport industry (private jitney and bus operators) to expand and gradually displace the SOE, using more appropriate vans and small buses. The SOE would wither away and de facto load shedding will have occurred. (The country involved still has visions, however, of raising cash by selling the SOE's assets through formal divestiture of the intact operating entity.)

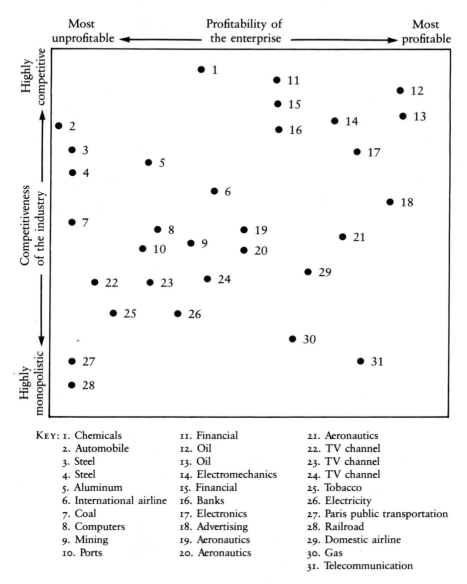

KEY:
1. Chemicals
2. Automobile
3. Steel
4. Steel
5. Aluminum
6. International airline
7. Coal
8. Computers
9. Mining
10. Ports

11. Financial
12. Oil
13. Oil
14. Electromechanics
15. Financial
16. Banks
17. Electronics
18. Advertising
19. Aeronautics
20. Aeronautics

21. Aeronautics
22. TV channel
23. TV channel
24. TV channel
25. Tobacco
26. TV channel
27. Paris public transportation
28. Railroad
29. Domestic airline
30. Gas
31. Telecommunication

FIGURE 8.1

CHARACTERISTICS OF PARTICULAR STATE-OWNED
ENTERPRISES IN FRANCE

SOURCE: Adapted from B. Jacquillat, *Désétatiser* (Paris: Éditions Robert Laffont, 1985), 138. The key identifies the industry to which each numbered enterprise belongs.

Returning to the more common approach to denationalization, divestiture, a useful strategic framework for denationalization is offered by Jacquillat.[16] Government enterprises are classified according to their profitability and to the extent that they have competitors in their industry. The result is shown in figure 8.1, which displays the status of state-owned enterprises in France.

The enterprises in the upper-right quadrant are profitable and have many competitors; therefore, they would be easy to denationalize by selling them off. They can attract investors because they earn profits but are not monopolies and so do not pose legal or economic problems for the buyers.

Sale of the operationally intact entity can be made to another firm, a group of investors, the firm's own managers or employees, the firm's customers, or the public at large through a stock offering.[17] If, for political reasons, the time is not yet ripe to sell off a state enterprise in its entirety, it may be possible to create a constituency by selling some shares to the public and thereby reducing the level of state ownership. As long as government retains control, however, partial divestiture is not true privatization; it is simply a means of raising capital.

In contrast to profitable enterprises, consider the organizations located in the lower-left quadrant of figure 8.1. They lose money despite their monopoly status, presumably because they are forced to operate under price controls or because there is little demand for their products. Without a significant change in their policy environment, they are unlikely sale candidates.

Unprofitable enterprises in competitive industries (the upper-left quadrant in figure 8.1) could be denationalized in whole or in part by selling profitable segments or subsidiaries to private firms. Alternatively, they can be given away to the employees or to the public; if all else fails, they can be liquidated. (Liquidation can be considered a form of privatization inasmuch as it restores assets to a more productive use in the marketplace, and ends the need for subsidies.)

A prolonged and bitter political debate in Canada focused on the proposed sale of an enterprise owned by a provincial government, the British Columbia Resources Investment Corporation. In order to block the sale, opponents questioned the proposed sale price. The dilemma faced by the proponents was that if the price was too low, they would be accused of giving away the people's patrimony; if it was too high, the sale would not be consummated. In a stroke of political genius, the provincial premier reasoned that since, in the final analysis, the corporation belonged to the people, it could be given away to them! Despite its complexity, this bold step was carried out successfully.[18]

Returning finally to figure 8.1, the ideal strategy for denationalizing the monopolistic, profitable enterprises in the lower-right quadrant is to deregulate the industry, allow competition, and ultimately sell the assets to the newly formed private enterprises. Where permanent monopoly status seems likely for a profitable enterprise in the lower-right quadrant, regulation by government may be needed to prevent price gouging after privatization. But regulation would be unnecessary if the private monopoly were owned by its users. For example, a rural electric, water, or telephone company owned cooperatively by its subscribers is self-regulating because if it were to charge excessively high prices, the profits would go right back to the customer-owners. So, privatization of profitable monopolies by selling them to the users is a promising approach.

Another approach to selling such monopolies is to auction them at a price equal to the appraised (or replacement) value of their capital assets plus the highest bid for the percentage of annual profits that will be paid to the government making the sale. Because part of the profits will be recouped by government, some measure of self-regulation can be expected to prevail.

These strategies are broadly applicable. For instance, at the national level they apply to the U.S. Postal Service (see chapter 6), and at the local level they apply to public buses. In developing countries, the strategies are applicable to the many government enterprises that so often burden their national economies.

The foregoing discussion emphasizes economic factors in choosing among candidates for privatization. Profitability and competitive status, however, are not the only factors to consider. Privatization of an SOE is fundamentally a political act, and therefore commitment from the very top of the government is essential for success. Moreover, commitment is needed not merely to divestment of a particular SOE, but, more important, to a policy environment that allows market forces to prevail in the sector where the newly privatized entity operates. If the entity is to be sheltered, little will be gained by privatization.

The policy environment necessary for successful privatization includes the following elements: market-based prices without price controls or subsidies, no government-erected barriers to entry by competitors, prompt and fair enforcement of contracts, equal application of all laws and controls, equal access by all to credit and foreign exchange, elimination of protectionism, no preferential loans, market-based interest rates, freedom to hire and fire, and the abandonment of any other policies that would hinder entry by lower-cost, more efficient competitors.[19]

Sometimes governments envision denationalization or divestment as a straightforward process of identifying the largest white elephant in their portfolio (the one losing the most money), announcing their intention to sell it, and finding a suitable buyer at an acceptable price. Nothing could be farther from the truth. Divestment can be a long, slow, arduous process, and only if this is understood at the outset, and if full advantage is taken of successful experiences elsewhere, is the process likely to be accelerated and a favorable outcome achieved.

Among the major factors that influence the selection of SOEs to denationalize, and the means of doing so, are the following:

1. Is it the purpose of privatization to obtain immediate income or foreign exchange? Reduce expenditures? Improve efficiency and responsiveness of operations? Encourage industrial development? Encourage foreign investment or loans? Encourage entrepreneurs? Punish political opponents? Pursue a free-market philosophy?

2. The business climate.

3. The commercial viability of the SOE.

4. The availability of local or international capital (including ethnicity of potential local buyers).

5. The availability of managerial and technical skills.

6. National prestige (e.g., a national-flag airline).

7. The nature and extent of labor displacement (including ethnic, racial, linguistic, or tribal impact).

8. And, above all, the political implications, risks, and side effects for the ruling group.

A country's initial effort at divestiture should be handled so as to assure success. The first SOE to be privatized should be an attractive one with the best prospects for new investors.

It must be understood that true divestiture involves (1) a genuine risk of financial loss for new investors/owners if their enterprise is poorly managed; (2) the possibility of profit commensurate with risks if the enterprise is well managed; and (3) profits that are genuine, based on free-market competition rather than government favoritism or protectionism. The new owners of a former SOE, and the managers they employ, must have freedom to take timely actions in response to competitive conditions, including restructuring the firm, changing products and prices, changing lines of activity, expanding some activities and closing down others, using subcontractors, making employment and compensation decisions, and making decisions concerning suppliers, engineering, financing, investment, and innovation.

Divesture can be partial; however, anything less than 50 percent may bring in cash but bring none of the other expected benefits of privatization because control will remain in the hands of the state. When government has sold more than half ownership, it sometimes retains crucial control by means of a "golden share." For example, government's minority share may include special veto power over a particularly crucial decision, such as sale to a foreign firm.

Another approach to protecting the public interest under partial divestiture is to separate beforehand functions of the SOE that are to be retained by government (e.g., quality-control standards for food products), while turning over the market function to the private sector (e.g., the purchase and sale of agricultural products that are currently under the control of a state marketing monopoly). Partial and hybrid privatization can also be carried out by contracting out some of the functions, as discussed in chapter 4.

Enterprises must be reasonably valued in the eyes of the investor; that is, he must be able to anticipate a profit on his investment. The country must be prepared to accept this approach to valuation, not what the SOE cost the government or some inflated notion of the value of the assets.

Partial privatization can be very profitable both for the government and the initial investors. For example, in Britain the government sold just over half the Cable and Wireless Company for £182 million, but two years later it sold another quarter for £263 million; in other words, the stock had tripled in value.[20]

Privatization should spread the wealth. Wealthy local investors must support privatization, but it is important to recognize the benefits of broader ownership and capital markets. Privatization by divestiture must not result in crony capitalism. Creative techniques should be employed to encourage widespread public ownership even by small shareholders, which may require concessionary prices for them (note the analogous sale of public housing in Great Britain, in chapter 7), or even giving them shares gratis (note the British Columbian example above). Similarly, employee ownership should be encouraged so that employees become stockholders interested in the success of the enterprise after privatization. Shares could be sold at a discount to employees, including managers, and in the extreme case of a money-losing SOE, if sale to a buyer or the public is impossible, the SOE could be given to its workers. (This was done with Britain's cross-channel hovercraft ferry service, and the workers managed to turn it into a profitable private enterprise.[21]) The denationalization strategy in Great Britain placed great emphasis on worker participation, in part to make denationalization irreversible by making renationalization difficult under a new government. The policy was successful in that more than 90 percent of the workers bought shares in many of the denationalized SOEs.[22]

A critical issue associated with divestiture in developing countries is who is allowed to buy the SOEs. For various political and social reasons, many such countries exclude certain groups from purchasing SOEs, especially foreign businesses, multinational corporations, and local entrepreneurs of particular minority groups. There is concern that these potential buyers, who may already own or control a large share of the country's economy, will further increase their control. Advocates of economic development through free markets argue that no potential buyers should be excluded on the basis of race, nationality, or economic position. Moreover, foreign investors can be valuable because they are generally less tolerant of cronyism and other inefficiencies.

The question of who shall be allowed to buy is largely irrelevant in industrial countries, where the major issues are building a constituency for sale, overcoming political opposition to the sale, and utilizing the appropriate sale mechanism. Whether the country is developed or developing, any strategy for privatization by divestment must take into account the groups whose interests may be harmed. These may include labor groups and current managers of the SOE; bureaucrats whose positions and power may be eliminated; groups that favor public enterprises as a matter of political philosophy; local private enterprises that will face more vigorous competition; and other enterprises, public or private, that have favored relationships with the SOE. A divestment program must identify these opposing groups and have a strategy for dealing with them. A successful strategy is one that leads to more winners than losers.

Limited-Government Arrangements

Where load shedding to the market or to voluntary organizations is not currently possible, a second broad strategy for privatizing is available: making greater use of arrangements in which government plays a more limited role in service delivery. That is, institutional arrangements should be chosen so that government is involved in only a minimal way. By this rule, one would prefer the market arrangement for private goods (e.g., housing), the franchise arrangement for toll goods (e.g., bus service), and the contract arrangement for collective goods (e.g., waste collection and disposal). If it is decided that the cost of a service is to be paid collectively, then a government subsidy through a grant or voucher system is preferred over direct government service. Table 4.6 in chapter 4 ranks the arrangements in terms of their degree of privatization.

A firm believer in citizen choice might argue against the paternalism of choice-directing grants and vouchers and might call instead for a negative income tax, thereby providing poor citizens with both the wherewithal and the freedom to purchase the goods they desire. But, self-appointed protectors of the public interest are likely to find that poor people's preferences are insufficiently refined and their expenditures thoughtlessly shortsighted; the money would be spent in ways unacceptable to the providers of the money—taxpayers and bureaucrats—and there would be strong pressure to appoint guardians to establish family budgets and supervise spending. The result may well be even larger and costlier government.

The preferred rankings of alternative institutional arrangements, for each type of good, appear in table 8.1, which is consistent with table 4.6. The basic

TABLE 8.1

RANKING OF INSTITUTIONAL ARRANGEMENTS TO REDUCE
GOVERNMENT EXPENDITURES, BY TYPE OF GOOD

Arrangement	Private goods	Toll goods	Collective goods	Common-pool goods
Self-service	1			
Voluntary		1	1	1
Market	2	2		
Franchise		3		
Voucher	3	4		2
Grant	3	4		2
Contract		6	2	4
Government vending		7		
Intergovernmental agreement		8	3	5
Government service		9	4	6

NOTE: The highest ranking is 1.

principle used to produce these rankings is simply the relative size of government expenditures: the lower the cost to be paid out of taxes, the higher the ranking.

User Charges

The third privatization strategy identified at the outset of this chapter is to impose user charges wherever practicable or to link spending programs directly to taxes levied for that purpose. This should be done for all private and toll goods provided directly by government, by intergovernmental agreement, and by contract arrangements. Moreover, the user charge should be equal to the full cost of service. The fundamental purpose of the user charge in the context of promoting privatization is not to raise money (the usual reason why governments levy such charges) but to reveal fully the true cost of service. This creates the opportunity to make comparisons with other arrangements and devise alternatives.

It may be argued that a user charge is antithetical to the basic idea of privatization, for it is merely another method for collecting funds to be expended by government. This is faulty and shortsighted reasoning. A service financed by a user charge should be compared to a service financed by taxes, both of which are provided by the same delivery arrangement. The cost of the latter is obscured, but the cost of the former is highly visible. If hidden sub-

248

sidies for government-produced services are prohibited, and the full cost of service is charged to the user, citizens will start looking for alternatives if they feel the service is not worth the price.

This situation arose in St. Paul, Minnesota, when both the city and the private sector sold residential refuse-collection service. The city's price was 26 percent higher than that of most private firms, and it lost virtually all its customers except for senior citizens and welfare recipients, who were eligible to receive city service at half price.

It is somewhat surprising that user charges are not used more widely for government services in the United States, as they are elsewhere. One might expect that toll goods, such as refuse collection in densely populated cities, would be paid for entirely out of taxes in socialist countries and in Western European countries ruled by social democrats. Surprisingly, that is not the case. In Vienna, Belgrade, and Moscow, citizens pay a monthly charge for that service, whereas in the United States this is rare; San Francisco is one of the few large cities where residents pay a fee for this service.

User fees that are too low or that represent merely token payments result in profligate use and squandering of resources. This is amply illustrated by the experiences with federally supplied water and hydropower in the western United States. State-run businesses are prone to political pressures that lead to inefficiency because they are rarely able to drop uneconomical activities or dismiss unnecessary employees; the result is a demand for subsidies to mask the high costs. Raising the user fees to cover the costs, or conversely, ending the subsidy, is the first step toward privatization, which is a means toward the end of satisfying people's demands more cost effectively.

Political leaders seem to find irresistible the notion of eliminating user charges and providing a service "free" to their constituents, that is, paying for it out of taxes that are hidden from view. Consider the allegory of the engineer, the economist, and the state senator sitting in a rowboat near New York City's George Washington Bridge and observing the rush-hour traffic. The engineer wants to enlarge the bridge to relieve congestion. The economist wants to increase the existing toll and introduce time-of-day pricing to reduce peak-hour usage. But the state senator starts drafting a bill to eliminate the toll altogether, and anticipates with barely concealed glee the boundless gratitude that all those motorists will feel toward him at election time.

What is the likelihood that user charges will become more commonplace? Very good. Proposition 13 in California, tax limitations elsewhere, and "spending caps" in various jurisdictions are resulting in greater use of such charges, for they are not taxes and are generally outside the purview of these revenue-limiting devices.

There are administrative costs involved in collecting user charges; for example, procedures for billing and for handling delinquent accounts must be established. Furthermore, while the charge is theoretically applicable to all private and toll goods, it is more appropriate for some than for others. Consider water supply and refuse collection as contrasting examples. Water can be turned off to a delinquent account with no harm to the neighbors, but a similar sanction involving refuse collection would result in a neighborhood nuisance. User charges work best when the service involves no external side effects on others and exclusion is a relatively simple matter, as in turning off gas or water, prohibiting a delinquent borrower from checking another book out of the public library, or denying bus service to someone who does not pay the fare.

Gaining political acceptance for any new charge is always a problem, of course, but the more clearly the service is a private or a toll good, with individual, identifiable beneficiaries, and the more that service is permitted to deteriorate because of underfinancing, the more acceptable a user charge becomes, like an increase in mass-transit fares.

The Reagan administration made a strong effort to increase user fees so as to recover actual government costs. It proposed increases in fees for recreational use of national forests and parks, meat and poultry inspections, Coast Guard services, harbor and inland-waterway use, premiums for the Pension Benefit Guarantee program, the sale of timber and minerals, enriching uranium sold to electric utilities, and for IRS services such as providing private letter rulings, issuing determination letters, and collecting back taxes.[23] It also proposed to establish a fee for ocean sportfishing. The discussion in chapter 3 is relevant here: Fish in the sea are common-pool goods, but they are being depleted by overfishing. That is, marine fisheries are an exhaustible resource and must be managed; such management can be considered as somewhere between a toll good and a collective good, which must be paid for. Establishing a sportfishing fee is one means of paying for this service. Alternatively, as discussed in chapter 6, one could establish an auction market to achieve the same end.

Competition

Waste in government will not yield to preaching, indignation, or finger-pointing at villains (although this sometimes helps, temporarily!). The forces of competition must be brought to bear, to overcome the monopoly mechanisms we have unwittingly introduced in public services. The failure to understand the distinction between *providing* for a service and *producing* the service has led to a curious reliance on monopolies for delivering public services. How strange. We vigorously oppose monopolies in the private sector and enforce laws to break up monopolies and conspiracies that would restrain competition; we know that the public interest suffers without the goad of competition and in the absence of alternative choices. But in the public sector, perversely, we have often chosen monopoly and prohibited competition in the mistaken belief that competition constitutes wasteful duplication. We labor under the enormous delusion that total reliance on a single supplier is the best way to assure satisfactory delivery of vital public services if the supplier is the government itself.

Hence, in improving government services, the emphasis has been on better public administration, preservice education, in-service training, civil service reform, budgeting reforms, computers, quantitative methods, reorganization, organizational development, sensitivity training, incentive systems, productivity programs, joint labor-management committees, and the like. All of these are desirable, but they fail to identify, let alone address, the underlying, structural problem of government monopoly, which is the dominant factor responsible for malperformance of government services.

Introducing competition requires a conscious strategy of creating alternatives and fostering a receptive climate and mental attitude in favor of giving options to the citizen-consumers of public services.[24] Service-delivery options are essential. Total dependence on a single supplier, whether a government agency or a private firm, is dangerous. Without choice and flexibility, the consumer of public services, the citizen, is subject to endless exploitation and victimization. He and his government should have a chance to shop around, for when choice is replaced by compulsion, the fundamental relationship between citizens and public employees is altered; the latter are no longer public *servants*.

The existence of public-service options provides a form of insurance; if several organizations are delivering the same service and one fails or is subject to too many work stoppages, or is inefficient or ineffective or unresponsive or unsatisfactory or too expensive, the public can turn to another supplier. Furthermore, separating the decision about supplying a service—what kind, what quality, how much—from the actual production process gives the citizen-consumer greater leverage and liberates him from the control of a single bureaucracy that determines what service he will get, how much of it he will consume, how it will be produced, and how much he will pay for it.

Such monopoly power has important consequences. When a service is financed by taxes without pricing and without citizen choice, there is no effective way to determine the level of popular support for the service except in the very long term. Ordinarily, customers who have a choice will seek out producers who will tailor their services to satisfy their customers' different needs. Citizens denied the right to choose one alternative over another cannot indicate their preferences to shape the service, and the ballot box is a poor substitute for communicating program preferences. In the absence of citizen choice, so-called public servants have a captive market and little incentive to heed their putative customers. Control of the service depends instead on the relative political power of the interested parties.

Competition can be fostered between different producers within the same or different institutional arrangements. For example, a civilian advisory board has called for competitive analysis of intelligence information to reduce the monopolistic role of the Central Intelligence Agency in this function. The French government, unwilling to end the state monopoly of television, nevertheless responded to complaints about its "incompetent, flippant, disjointed and criminally wasteful" Office of French Radio and Television with a decision to establish each of the three channels as a completely independent, competing, government institution.[25] Subsequently, two private franchises were awarded as well, and plans were made to privatize one of the three state stations.[26]

A refreshing and thought-provoking example of a deliberate effort to stimulate intergovernmental competition comes from Yugoslavia. The city fathers of Ljubljana, the capital of Slovenia, desired the services of city planners and solicited formal bids not only from the city planning agency of their city but also from the city planning agency of Zagreb, the capital of the neighboring Croatian Republic. An American observer there at the time remarked that he had never seen city employees anywhere work as hard as Ljubljana's city planners, who wanted desperately to avoid the humiliation of having their city's work contracted out to their professional and regional rivals.[27]

Competition is at work in the United States in intergovernmental agreements when a county sheriff who provides police services to a local community recognizes that the community can form its own police department and thus he tries harder to provide cost-effective services.

Nowhere is the problem of monopoly more serious and competition more needed than in education. Primary and secondary education is the largest function of state and local government, as measured by the size of the budget and the number of employees. In large cities, most students are below the national average in reading and mathematics, and the dropout rate is high. Teachers attribute the problem to conditions in the home. Parents blame uncaring or incompetent teachers. The education establishment wants more money spent on the problem. No one has a certain prescription for teaching inner-city children.

What should you do when you do not know what to do? *Answer:* Do many different things. Nature's incessant experimentation with mutations enables species to evolve, adapt, and survive despite drastic environmental changes; some of these "experiments" turn out to be better suited to the new surroundings than the original mode and ultimately replace it. Similarly, a variety of educational approaches should be encouraged to see which ones can prove themselves fit and able to educate the city's children. Today's monolithic public school system is inadequate, yet it cannot effectively facilitate broad experimentation or tolerate alternative pedagogical approaches. Diversity has never been the strong suit of government. The education of millions of children is stunted and the effort of many dedicated teachers is wasted by the traditional and blind insistence on a government education monopoly. "Education which truly meets the needs of the public can be achieved only by allowing the public free choice to sample, judge, and individually vote for the education they choose."[28]

The government monopoly is particularly stifling in that, for the most part, pupils must attend a particular school; generally they are not free even to attend another school within the monopoly. Clearly such a policy is designed for the administrative convenience of the school system rather than the educational advantage of the child. A better approach to the problem, using vouchers or tuition tax credits, is discussed in chapter 7.

A comparison of ancient Athens and Sparta with respect to education monopolies is instructive. In Sparta there was no scope for parental choice. The state's responsibility went so far as to remove children from their homes and place them in schools designed to shape them in the Spartan mold. By contrast, in democratic Athens education was the responsibility of the parents and subject to parental choice and control. Schools were private, often owned by the teachers. The state's role was to specify minimal standards and provide military training. Rather than destroy the family, as in Sparta, Athens preserved it as a means of developing and reshaping personality and gave it responsibility for education. Athenians understood that this was vital in promoting a healthy sense of involvement in the community.[29] In terms of American values, the Athenian ideal is much to be preferred over the Spartan.

A new form of private schooling is beginning to appear at the edges of traditional public schools. For-profit learning centers are springing up, where children are tutored after their regular classes. Tutoring is hardly a new concept, but doing it under a corporate form of organization, as a business, dates only to 1979. It is related to the commercial enterprises that prepare students to take Scholastic Aptitude Tests. The latter business aims mostly at high school juniors and seniors, whereas commercial tutoring concerns market their services mostly to upper elementary and junior high school pupils. Both represent private-sector initiatives to improve educational performance.

The private sector has long had a large role in adult or continuing education: Business and industry spend more than $30 billion a year on educating and training employees, a figure that compares favorably with the annual expenditures of the nation's public colleges and universities. Increasingly, firms offer accredited courses and even grant degrees. The largest private employer in the United States, AT&T, before it was broken up, spent $1.1 billion on education, and on any given day 3 percent of its employees were in class.[30] It would not be a giant step for some firms to move fully into adult education, by opening enrollment to the public at large.

Private education programs have their flaws too. In New York City, the numerous proprietary schools that offer training to would-be barbers, beauticians, computer programmers, cashiers, secretaries, truck drivers, and other job seekers are sometimes accused of flagrant abuses; they are charged with enrolling students who are incapable of doing the work and failing to find jobs for them. Nevertheless, when political powers forced an open-admissions program on the city's own university, the latter also accepted students unable to do the work, as was demonstrated by the high failure rate.[31] Moreover, one wonders whether the placement results of proprietary schools are any worse than those of public vocational schools. One has to suspect the motives of those who would impose rigid and nearly fatal restrictions on proprietary schools that charge tuition, ostensibly to protect individuals from wasting their *private* funds, while ignoring similar shortcomings in the public schools that result in a waste of *public* funds. Again, the focus of concern should not be whether private education has faults—of course it does—but how it compares with public education today.

Another matter comes to mind: the proper extent of compulsory education. Too many older teenagers are forced, against their wills, to enroll in schools—I say "enroll" advisedly, for many of them rarely attend, and truant officers are ineffective in getting them to do so. When they do attend, they are the principal causes of violence and disruption in schools, so their presence results in less total education taking place than if they were absent. In effect, schools are used to keep troublemakers in the classroom and off the streets—surely an inappropriate function. Why force someone to consume a good he does not want and which costs a lot to produce? Permitting students to end their formal schooling at an earlier age is likely to lead to improved education for those who choose to continue, while opening up to the dropouts—a less pejorative term will be needed—opportunities for on-the-job training at public (via vouchers) or private (via wages) expense. The latter choice will require a more realistic minimum wage to be applied to such apprentices, who are not yet fully productive workers. Remedial education opportunities should be available for them when and if, as adults, they desire to resume classroom learning.

While vouchers continue the practice of tax-paid schooling so that families do not pay individually for this good however private it may be, there is one circumstance where a user charge has been imposed for education below the college level. Tuition-charging summer school programs sprang up throughout California after Proposition 13 caused a shutdown of what was called the world's largest babysitting service: the summer program in public schools that was free for everyone. It was finally recognized that summer programs cost money, relatively few children need academic help during the summer, and the vast majority of families can afford to pay a fee for recreation and enrichment programs to occupy their children during the vacation period.[32]

Contracting for Services

As illustrated in chapter 4, many services can be procured by contract from the private sector, a process that offers the best opportunity to introduce and institutionalize competition.

In the United States, both the public at large and public officials have gradually accepted the idea that under the proper circumstances contracting results in better and cheaper public services (e.g., see table 5.3). This growing conviction is a result of the studies reviewed in chapters 6 and 7, reinforced by numerous, widespread experiences and observations. Despite this intellectual acceptance, however, and despite the growth rate of contracting and the availability of useful guidelines for all the steps involved in contracting,[33] no stampede in this direction is evident, for the decision to contract is not made easily.

DECIDING TO CONTRACT

In no sense is the decision to contract an admission of failure or an abdication of government's responsibility, although opponents may try to block the decision by claiming that it is. The experience in waste management is instructive, for contracting and other forms of privatization are well advanced there and are being extended. This does not mean that government is abandoning its concern for solid-waste management; on the contrary, its involvement is growing. But increasingly governments turn to the private sector for collecting waste efficiently and effectively; for disposing of wastes at sophisticated, environmentally sound landfills; for extracting energy and recyclables from the waste stream in technologically advanced resource recovery facilities; and for treating hazardous wastes. The public sector retains its responsibility but exercises it in a superior manner by calling on the specialized skills of the private sector and taking advantage of its strengths.

In order for a unit of government to adopt and implement privatization by contracting, four conditions must generally be satisfied (see also chapter 5):

1. The government unit is under serious fiscal stress.

2. Significant monetary savings are achievable by contracting, with no reduction in quality or level of service.

3. Contracting is politically feasible, in view of the power of the service constituency—the affected employees and other beneficiaries.

4. Some precipitating event makes it impossible to continue with the status quo.

The first three factors have been examined closely,[34] but in my experience the fourth factor is indispensable to successful implementation of contracting. The mere availability of large and much-needed savings by privatizing is necessary but by no means sufficient to assure adoption of this approach. (In some circumstances, it may not even be necessary!) Generally, some other factor must be present that elected officials can seize as an opportunity to create the political consensus that makes privatization feasible. (Alternatively, and equivalently, they can use the precipitating factor as an excuse, claiming that it has forced privatization on them.)

Precipitating events often originate at higher levels or in other branches of government. For example, a state agency may threaten a county hospital with loss of accreditation because of poor conditions in the hospital. A court may order the closure of a municipal landfill because it presents an environmental hazard. These actions necessitate responses by the affected government unit, and privatization—of the hospital or the solid-waste management activity—may be the best option, or the path of least resistance.

Similar events that demand action, often culminating in privatization, are employee strikes that, if they arouse strong public indignation, practically call for contracting out. In an interesting variation of this theme, St. Louis took the step of contracting its municipal hospital after the physicians, who were themselves on contract from the local university medical school, went on strike in part because the civil servants neglected or refused to perform their patient-care functions, thereby forcing the responsible physicians to work as orderlies. When the city contracted out, the nonmedical staff were employees of the private firm, and the problem was eliminated.

Yet another kind of event that often precipitates privatization is the sudden need for a large and unanticipated capital expenditure, for facilities or equipment. A new hospital, prison, water-supply system, wastewater-treatment plant, truck fleet, sanitary landfill, or large computer system are all examples of such capital needs; a government may resort to privatization of the service instead of raising taxes or borrowing money to build the facility or buy the equipment required for continued in-house service.

If all these conditions are satisfied, then it is likely that a decision to privatize will be made. It is not automatic, however, and a strong internal champion of the idea has to carry the argument and sell the idea. That person may be a legislator, often with business experience in the private sector, an elected chief executive who is a resourceful leader, or a budget director or professional public administrator. Rarely does the head of the affected department take the lead in promoting privatization in his or her agency. On the contrary, persons in such positions are often to be found either leading the opposition or quietly sabotaging any effort to privatize.

The principal opposition to privatization, understandably, comes from employee organizations. It takes the form of public demonstrations, media campaigns, lawsuits, extracting campaign promises from candidates that they will not contract for services, negotiating anticontracting clauses into labor agreements, and hinting darkly at corrupt practices.

Lawsuits aimed at blocking contracts on the grounds that they violate civil service statutes have been rejected in numerous court cases. Other legal challenges are possible, based on labor contracts, or on any one of myriad other grounds.

Labor agreements handle contracting in several different ways: (1) It is not mentioned and is assumed to be an inherent right of management; (2) it is explicitly mentioned as a management right; (3) it is mentioned as a management right with certain restrictions, typically, that no layoffs occur; or (4) it is prohibited.[35]

Contracting is seen as a profound threat by government-employee unions. Ironically, the contractor's private employees are themselves often unionized, and so from the overall perspective of the union movement, the losses of some union leaders are balanced by the gains of others. Nevertheless, contracting is such a threat to the affected union that allegations of corruption are likely to be hurled in the heat of battle to sway the media and the public. This is the strongest argument available to the unions. A publication issued by the American Federation of State, County, and Municipal Employees, despite its strident tone and obvious self-interest, performs a public service by describing numerous instances of corruption in contracting.[36] Corruption is not to be tolerated, and the best defense against it is effective competition. By drawing attention to the problem, unions exert pressure on public officials to adopt good and honest procurement practices. Unfortunately, in many countries corruption in contracting is commonplace.

In the face of opposition, proponents of contracting have to develop coalitions in support of privatization.[37] They can be amalgams of neighborhood groups dissatisfied with poor services, civic associations seeking better government, disgruntled taxpayers, trade associations of private-sector providers, and business groups. Associations of minority businessman can be particularly effective because privatization, particularly of municipal services, offers entrepreneurial opportunities uniquely suited for their members, as noted in chapter 5.

Success bears the seeds of its own destruction, however; if contracting is instituted and then carried out over a prolonged period in an increasingly casual and undisciplined manner, there is a danger that the erstwhile reform coalition will deteriorate into nothing more than a lobby in favor of more government spending. If that were to occur, the situation would be indistinguishable from the earlier evil.

The thorniest problem in contracting an existing activity is what to do with the redundant government employees. This issue must be faced and resolved at the outset. The most successful approach minimizes the number who will lose jobs; it involves a hiring freeze, transfers, training, attrition, and jobs with the contractor. First, government imposes a hiring freeze on all positions, in any agency, that could be filled by personnel currently performing work that is to be contracted. Then, as normal attrition occurs, employees are trained and transferred into the openings. Finally, it is not unusual to require the contractor, as a condition of the contract, to fill his openings by offering jobs first to the affected employees before recruiting elsewhere. (Once hired, such employees have no special privileges, job security, or seniority.)

This discussion of the factors to consider when deciding to contract should not be viewed with dismay, nor should the would-be privatizer be daunted by it. This decision process was examined in a series of case studies and it was found that contracting occurred with surprising ease; political leaders were readily able to overcome the resistance to change.[38]

COMPARING COSTS

As mentioned above, one of the essential conditions for contracting is a large potential for cost savings. Therefore, a feasibility study to compare the costs of government and contract service is necessary. A reliable cost comparison is not as easy to make as it might appear, for there are some serious errors that must be avoided.

Common Errors. The first and most flagrant fallacy is that "government can do it cheaper because it doesn't make a profit." This incantation is supposed to ward off privatization and was intoned even by the Speaker of the U.S. House of Representatives.[39] Unfortunately, the phrase reveals a serious degree of economic ignorance. The quest for profits leads to greater efficiency, and the resulting gain to the public far offsets the profit. The studies reviewed in chapters 6 and 7 repeatedly show that the price of for-profit contract work is substantially lower than the cost of non-profit, in-house work.

Another common error in determining the cost of in-house government service is excessive reliance on published budgets. The problem with budget documents is that they are not designed as cost-accounting reports but merely reflect established conventions and bookkeeping practices. A detailed examination of the matter, covering sixty-eight jurisdictions, revealed that the true cost of a government service, measured properly using valid cost-accounting procedures, was 30 percent greater than the cost nominally ascribed to that service in the formal budget. Given the magnitude of this misperception, incorrect conclusions will often result from analyses that rely on budgets to compare the cost of government and contract services; the cards are likely to be stacked in favor of the government producer, unless the comparison is carried out correctly.[40]

The principal factors responsible for understating the cost of government-produced services are the following:

1. Capital expenditures for facilities, vehicles, and other equipment do not appear in conventional operating budgets.

2. Interest costs on capital expenditures are rarely allocated to the operating activity that incurs them.

3. Costs of supplies, such as fuel for vehicles, are often included in budgets of supporting agencies instead of the operating agency; the same is true of maintenance labor.

4. Fringe benefits, including pension contributions, are often entered in an overhead category.

5. If pension funds are underfunded, the government has incurred a liability that it will someday have to pay, even though it makes no provision for this in the current budget.

6. The cost of labor borrowed from other agencies or hired seasonally may not be attributed to the activity being studied.

7. The costs of operating and maintaining any buildings used in carrying out the activity are often neglected.

8. The opportunity cost of land and buildings used by the agency should be charged to the activity; foregone property tax should be included here.

9. The cost of premiums paid for liability and fire insurance, or the cost of claims paid under a program of self-insurance, should be apportioned to the activity.

10. Overhead costs of executive and staff agencies should also be apportioned correctly to the activity being evaluated as a candidate for contracting.[41]

These factors must all be taken into consideration when determining the full cost of a government service.

When comparing the cost of in-house and contract work, one has to recognize that overhead costs are not likely to change much on privatization, for although the costs of personnel administration and payroll processing will decline, there will be legal costs involved in preparing contracts and administrative costs in conducting the bidding process, evaluating bids, and awarding the contract. Operational costs will also be incurred to monitor the performance of the contractor; in my experience, the cost of systematic and thorough monitoring typically ranges from 2 to 7 percent of the contract price.

Yet another frequent error, often made by government employees arguing against contracting, is to estimate the cost of producing a single unit of the activity and then to extrapolate it. I witnessed this, for example, in connection with a city's proposal to contract for street-sign installation. The supervisor of the city agency, who opposed the plan, estimated that it required only ten minutes to install each sign and calculated the labor cost for ten minutes and the cost of the sign materials, which came to a total of $15.27 per sign, compared to a contractor's bid of $30 per sign.

The supervisor's implicit assumption was that 12,000 signs a year were installed (6 per hour times 2,000 hours per year). In fact only 2,000 signs were being installed annually by his unit (an average of 1 sign per hour), and the true cost for materials and direct labor alone were $46.57 per sign. Thus, instead of the contractor's price being twice the in-house price, it was one-third less. Rigorous analysis is needed to guard against such errors; a useful primer and worksheets for calculating in-house costs are available.[42]

The true cost of service emerged as a major point of contention in efforts to contract more federal government functions. Before 1976, for the purpose of comparing government to contract costs, the total cost of retirement benefits for federal employees was considered to be 7 percent of gross pay. This unbelievably low figure was recalculated in 1976, and was found to be 24.7 percent of gross pay. Federal employees fought vigorously against this realistic guideline and actually succeeded a year later in getting this figure (but not their benefits, of course!) reduced to 14.1 percent of gross wages; later it was raised to 20.4 percent and in the 1979 and 1983 guidelines it was 26 percent.[43]

In order to limit the potential for contracting federal functions, a representative of the civil servants ingeniously noted that the Social Security Administration is seriously underfunded and therefore, since additional social security costs will ultimately be incurred by the government when workers retire from the private sector, this amount should be added to the price of the contract for the purpose of making comparisons between government and contract work. He also

asked that the cost of unemployment compensation for discharged federal workers be added to the contract price, but failed to note that, correspondingly,
unemployment compensation would end for any workers hired by the private
sector to perform the contract work; presumably these costs and savings balance
out each other. He made the excellent recommendation, however, that a competitive cost analysis be performed and made public for every proposed contract.[44]

Opponents of contracting also tried to insert into the guidelines additional
restrictions, whose net effect was to impose cumbersome bureaucratic barriers
and thereby discourage managers in government agencies from undertaking
any effort to contract for service. For example, they called for the creation of
a central agency to oversee all proposed contracts and the preparation of social-
impact statements for each proposal.[45]

The federal guidelines set a savings threshold: Contracting should be done
only if the expected savings exceed 10 percent of the personnel-related costs
of performing the work in-house. At the same time, agencies that wished to
assume functions performed by a contractor would have to demonstrate that
they could save at least 10 percent on personnel costs and 25 percent on the
cost of facilities and materials that the government would have to begin providing. Agencies were further required to take into consideration the federal
taxes paid by a contractor; these constituted a rebate, in effect, and led to a
lower net cost to the government than the stated bid.

Tax Treatment. The proper treatment of taxes is an important point and
the source of many errors. It is worth reviewing here. Private firms pay many
taxes and fees that government agencies do not. Sometimes those who oppose
contracting will exclaim triumphantly that the agency's cost is lower precisely
because it does not have to pay taxes. This is shoddy thinking. If the firm does
not collect taxes and pass them along to government, the public will inevitably
have to pay those same taxes through another tax collector; the people's total
taxes will not decline merely because the work is retained in-house, although
that is the logical implication of the faulty reasoning. Taxes and fees paid by
a contractor to all government units constitute a rebate to the public and should
properly be subtracted from his price in order to arrive at a figure that can
be compared correctly with the cost of the government service. (The only grain
of truth in the otherwise fallacious reasoning is that some of the firm's taxes,
the federal ones, are rebated to taxpayers throughout the country instead of
going only to local ones. This makes a difference in the thinking of the contracting agency if it is a state or local government unit because it means that
taxpayers elsewhere subsidize the local in-house service. As contracting becomes
more widespread, however, this loophole dwindles in significance.)

Low-Ball Bids. Much concern is expressed about "low-ball bids," that is, a very low bid submitted by a contractor whose intention is to win the award, make the government dependent on him, and then raise his price drastically when it is time to renew the contract. This is a troubling scenario, and may occur from time to time, but the empirical evidence shows that it is not common, and in any event a good defense is readily at hand.

The low-ball theory is refuted by all the findings of the detailed scientific studies reviewed in chapter 6. When contract prices were determined in those studies, a few of the contracts no doubt were first-time ones and therefore subject to low-ball pricing according to this theory, but most were well into their second, third, fourth, and even more advanced cycle of contracting and thus would have experienced the drastic increases predicted by the theory. After all, in any randomly drawn sample of contracts, as in a large-scale study I did,[46] only a few contracts will be new ones. But the studies show that contract prices on average are substantially lower than government in-house costs. How can this be if most of the contracts have matured into the post-low-ball stage? The theory is plainly inconsistent with the facts and cannot be generally true.

Having demonstrated that low-balling is not a pervasive problem, we must nevertheless address the possibility of it happening in a particular instance. A moment's reflection shows that low-balling can occur only if the bidder is confident that once he wins the contract, he will have no future competitor. The contracting agency can thwart this hope by the simple expedient of fostering competition, as discussed in the next section. If the nature of the service is such that a private monopoly is unavoidably created on contracting, the agency can make sure that it is only a temporary one and that it remains contestible in the future. Once a contract is awarded, of course, the incumbent becomes familiar with the work and may naturally gain a competitive advantage over a future competitor. The agency can minimize even this legitimate advantage, and reduce the height of this entry barrier to future bidders, by making available to them in the subsequent round of bidding as much useful operational information as possible, such as work plans and schedules, manning levels, output measurements, and performance data.

FOSTERING COMPETITION

The most important single attribute of contracting is that when properly done, it creates and institutionalizes competition, which is the underlying factor that encourages better performance.

True competitive bidding, when there are multiple suppliers who desire to do the job, is the preferred mechanism in most cases. At times, however, when it is difficult to disqualify marginally competent bidders, it may be best to negotiate bids with a handful of clearly eligible contractors. This may also be the best approach for contracting prisons, hospitals, social services, and professional services. State laws differ in their requirements for formal competitive bidding, depending on the nature of the service. Interestingly enough, there is some empirical evidence that negotiated and competitive bids do not differ in price.[47]

One of the barriers to contracting for services is a shortage of prospective suppliers. This is a major problem in developing countries but is not unknown in industrial nations either. Sometimes this is merely an excuse to avoid changing the comfortable status quo.

One reason why the number of potential suppliers is sometimes low is the dilatory behavior of some governments in paying their bills. Consider a city that, over the past century, constructed an elaborate, time-consuming, costly, bureaucratic system of checks and balances designed to assure that it received fair value in its purchases and was protected against corruption in contracting for supplies and equipment. The consequence, however, is a long delay in securing bids, ordering goods, and paying bills. Requests are prepared and sent to bidders on an approved list. Sealed bids are received and analyzed, contracts are awarded, purchase orders are prepared and issued, goods are received, several different agencies check to see that the right goods are delivered in good condition to the right place at the right time, payment is authorized after a proper invoice is received and then cross-checked, and finally a check for payment is grudgingly issued by the city treasury many months later.

The result of all this red tape is that many potential vendors refuse to do business with the city, while those who do deal with it have to charge higher prices to make up for their additional costs and trouble. Thus, a strategy intended to increase competition and reduce the cost of goods has precisely the opposite effect of reducing competition and increasing costs.

For any service that is contracted, the ideal is to have many competing suppliers. One way to attract many bidders, in the case of a service that is geographically dispersed, is to divide the contract area into small zones, with each zone large enough to allow economies of scale. If the service does not permit geographic subdivision, it may be divisible into small functional units; clerical work and data processing can be segmented in this manner. The policy should be to offer many small contracts, if possible; give a long lead time to bidders; give lots of publicity to the bid; give enough information to bidders; award enough contracts both to avoid excessive reliance on a single supplier and to permit a significant fraction of the bidders to succeed in their quest, thereby encouraging the losers to try again next time; stagger the contracts so that some of them are awarded every year and bidders' interest is sustained; establish a

low upper limit on the number of contracts that any one bidder may be awarded at one time; and handle problems and pay bills promptly to keep suppliers
interested in holding on to the business.

Competition can be sharpened even further when the public and private
sectors both deliver the same service in the same jurisdiction; that is, when
multiple arrangements are utilized. In such cases the results are likely to be
particularly beneficial to the public. For example, Montreal, Minneapolis, Phoenix, New Orleans, Kansas City, Newark, and Oklahoma City have such systems for residential refuse collection. They employ contracts with private firms
to service several districts of the city and a municipal department to service
the remainder. In effect, the city agency bids against the private firms. This
growing practice has come to be called *contracting in*. The resulting competition has been successful in producing operating efficiencies and costs that are
remarkably low by national standards. In Minneapolis, city officials assiduously
cultivated a competitive climate and, by pointing to the superior practices of
the private crews, were able to get the city crews to adopt similar practices and
ultimately to match the private performance.[48]

The government agency should be invited to submit a bid just like any
other bidder, but care must be taken to assure full pricing; this requires an a
priori determination of fringe benefits and overhead percentages. It is generally necessary to use an independent auditor to verify the validity of the agency's
bid and assure that there is no cross-subsidization.

I am familiar with a case where the city agency was selling its container-
ized commercial refuse-collection service to local businesses, in competition
with private firms. It was temporarily successful because its prices were lower;
however, its cost was higher than the price it charged, and private firms had
to pay disposal fees at the municipal landfill, while the city agency did not.
Moreover, private firms had to pay various other taxes and fees from which
the city was exempt. The competition was manifestly unfair, and the residents
as a whole were subsidizing the agency's customers. Indeed, the city was accused of discriminatory and predatory pricing.

When fair competition is taking place, the performance of the public agency can serve as a yardstick to measure the performance of the private agency,
and vice versa. If the private sector shows signs that its competitive spirit is
waning, government can expand the size and scope of its unit's work and reduce
the size of the contract correspondingly. In fact, the threat of greatly reducing
the role of either the public or private producer is a most effective check on
both, as is the ability to use one to intervene on an emergency basis to do the
work of the other if the latter is unable or unwilling to perform (e.g., because
of strikes or equipment malfunction). Montreal has developed this to a fine

art and has a well-defined rate schedule to cover the cost of municipal intervention if a contractor fails to collect refuse or clear snow on schedule in its assigned area. The plausible threat of municipal intervention, and the occasional need to do so—for a day or two every couple of years—has been sufficient to guarantee excellent performance by the city's fifty-odd contractors, while the fact that the municipal agency does only 10 percent of the work means that the city can readily have a contractor substitute for the city agency if necessary.

The practice of competitive bidding by government agencies has been introduced effectively in the United Kingdom. Major improvements have been realized in road maintenance since legislation in 1981 required road-repair agencies to compete with private firms, to maintain separate accounts of income and expenditures, and to achieve a prescribed rate of return on the capital equipment they employ.[49]

Poole presents an intriguing scenario of a fictitious city in California that, over twenty years, gradually contracted out all its services.[50] It started with a contract for private fire protection after the city experienced a serious fire while its firemen were on strike. Following a grand jury indictment of the police chief, in Poole's vivid tale, the city entered into a contract with the county sheriff for police services. In short order thereafter, street, park, and vehicle maintenance were contracted to private firms, followed by building inspection, sewage treatment, and water supply. Then a private guard service replaced the county sheriff. Next, the city sold off its docks, beaches, and parking lots to private operators and its parks to local neighborhood associations. Finally, City Hall itself was sold, and the remaining three employees rented a small office to oversee and manage the contracts. (They had to charge for the time they spent with the incredulous researchers and outside officials who swarmed in to see how the city achieved such a low per capita cost and such a high growth rate with full employment.) This fictitious example is not so far-fetched: La Mirada, California, a city of forty thousand people, contracts out more than sixty essential services, and has only fifty-five employees.[51]

There is ample room for competition for the plethora of commercial activities that the federal government workforce performs. In 1982 the Congressional Budget Office estimated that about $7 billion annually of in-house commercial work could be contracted out to the private sector, with a shift of 165,000 jobs and annual savings of $870 million.[52] A more recent estimate by the Office of Management and Budget indicates that up to $15 billion of works could be contracted out, with annual savings of $2 billion to $3 billion.[53]

Government service has the characteristic of a permanent monopoly, while contract service can be thought of as a system of periodic competition, and the free market offers permanent competition. In refuse collection there is strong reason to prefer contract collection instead of municipal collection or free-market private collection; the former is significantly more efficient than the latter two, which are equally inefficient,[54] as discussed in chapter 6. Contrary to one's initial expectation, the reason why the market arrangement, which features continuous competition, is inferior to the contract system, which is characterized by periodic competition or temporary monopoly, is that (1) it is inefficient to have several different trucks from several different firms collecting from residences on the same street, and (2) it is more costly for a private firm to bill each individual residential customer than to bill a single government agency. The contract collector is awarded, in effect, a temporary monopoly to service every house in the area, but the contract is of limited duration, typically two or three years, and is awarded competitively. Unlike a city agency, the contractor who wins the award has no assurance that he will continue to do the work forever; he cannot become complacent and must aim for continued or improved efficiency and effective service if he is to win in the next competition. (It must be emphasized that the relative ranking of market and contract arrangements noted here applies to a particular service for the indicated reasons and cannot be generalized.)

One final point must be made here, a caveat. Contracting is not synonymous with competition. Often social services are contracted to not-for-profit private organizations, including religious ones, without competitive bidding, essentially on a quota basis. However well-meaning the institution, this practice is not likely to lead to the most efficient and effective provision of care to those who cannot help themselves. On the other hand, efforts to establish competitive bidding for social services encountered numerous problems, as noted in chapter 7.[55]

Specifying Contract Terms

To purchase services requires careful preparation of contract specifications, which must be expressed in ordinary language. As Lave points out, if many suppliers are to be encouraged to bid, they must not be confronted with massive and impenetrable documents that require legions of lawyers and accountants to comprehend. Many potential bidders can do the job well enough, but are relatively small and lack the sophisticated bureaucratic apparatus government agencies assume to be universal.[56] A contractor cannot respond intelligently to a poorly drawn request for bids, and if he does, subsequent misunderstandings are inevitable. The instance was cited in chapter 6 where a federal government facility that ostensibly sought to contract its laundry operation did not know how many pieces had to be ironed and could not inform prospective bidders.

But some agencies go too far and prepare specifications that go beyond stating performance requirements and specify in detail just how the contractor should carry out the work. For example, some misguided specifications for public works contracts call for particular kinds of vehicles to be used, the number of men to work on each truck, the wages to be paid, and the union to be recognized. In another instance (municipal parking garage operation in Cincinnati), bid specifications stated that "a bidder must agree to employ City personnel in their present positions at present pay rates and provide a comparable benefits package for a minimum of two years." Considering that the term of the contract was only three years and that labor is the overwhelming cost component in this activity, no savings could possibly be achieved. Clearly, such specifications transgress the bounds of management prerogatives and obviate the entire purpose of contracting for service—which is sometimes the underlying intention of those who draw up such self-defeating contracts! This is one of the barriers to contracting for service—setting specifications whose hidden purpose or ultimate effect is to make contract service as costly as government service, thereby eliminating the incentive to change.

Outright sabotage can also be carried out, for example, by planting a time bomb in the specifications. I know of one such instance: A department head in New Orleans, reluctant to contract but ordered to do so, wrote service specifications for a lower level of service than the community was used to. The winning bidder, naturally enough, started providing service at the level called for in the contract. A public uproar ensued, much to the consternation of the unsuspecting contractor, to the embarrassment of the elected officials, and to the satisfaction of the vengeful department head—who was on the verge of retirement anyway.

Other obstacles to contracting include the difficulty of writing specifications for some services and possible legal restrictions with respect to matching funds. For example, a local government that receives a federal matching grant for a program may wish to use city overhead expenditures as part of its matching contribution. This may or may not be acceptable to federal auditors if the service is contracted to a private organization.

"Hard" services, those involving tangible and visible physical results, are generally easier to write specifications for than the kind of "soft" services provided by social workers to clients. But even the former can be difficult to do. For example, whereas street paving is a good candidate for competitive contracting, repair of potholes is not as good. The reason is that information on the location and frequency of pothole occurrence, and on the expected life of repaved streets, is virtually nonexistent in most cities. How, then, can one write specifications for such work? A contractor cannot respond sensibly to a specification that calls for "the repair of all potholes that may occur on a given street" nor to a broader specification "to maintain a given street free of potholes," for in the latter case he cannot intelligently weigh the tradeoffs of repaving the entire street or repairing individual potholes. Finally, because it is technically difficult to identify particular potholes, letting a contract on a "per pothole" basis is inviting trouble.

On the other side of the coin, it is relatively easy to write proprietary specifications that favor a particular bidder and hence there is an opening for corrupt practices.

Marlin offers illustrative specifications for sixty-five different municipal services.[57] The specifications briefly identify both quantity and quality factors, and typical outputs. The listing goes awry, however, by suggesting that input resources should be included in the specifications; government agencies should focus on ouputs and leave the configuration of input resources to the contractor in order to allow creativity and innovation in service delivery.

Contracting for a service that requires long-lived capital assets presents a problem, although not an insuperable one. How will someone who has been awarded a contract for three years amortize a facility he had to build that has a twenty-year life? The most direct approach would be to set the term of the contract equal to the life of the assets. This approach is tantamount to granting a long-term monopoly, however, and has little to commend it. Another approach is to recognize that the asset can be depreciated over time, has a value at any point in time, and can be sold to the new service producer if the original one is unsuccessful in bidding for a successor contract. Yet another approach is to have the government own the long-lived asset and lease it to the successful bidder at a price stated in the request for bids. This could be done for buses, garages, restaurants and service stations on turnpikes, and facilities for concessions in parks and stadiums.

Contracting that involves private construction and ownership of complex facilities, such as resource-recovery plants, wastewater-treatment plants, and prisons, presents intricate problems in several domains: legal,[58] including the antitrust field,[59] financial,[60] and insurance.[61] These require careful consideration to avoid lengthy delays and unanticipated consequences.

To assure serious bidding and effective contract performance, it is common to require bid bonds and performance bonds. The former is forfeited if the bidder declines the award, and the latter is forfeited if the contractor defaults during the contract period. Increasingly, certified checks submitted with the bids are replacing bid bonds. As for a performance bond, its size should not be set at a punitively high level, which simply increases the cost of the contract unnecessarily; it should be sufficient merely to defray the cost of making other arrangements to have the work done.[62] Besides, an unnecessarily large bond has the undesirable effect of screening out small contractors. A performance bond is best thought of as an insurance policy whose premium is ultimately paid by the contracting authority.

As to the type of the contract, there are several alternative ways to provide incentives for good performance and to handle uncertainties. Cost-plus-fixed-fee is at one end of the spectrum of contract types, and firm-fixed-price-with-incentives is at the other.[63] The former appears at first glance to lead to minimal price but has no incentive to encourage efficiency and much disincentive; thus there is little to commend it. A firm fixed price, with an incentive for superior performance, seems better. Depending on the particular service, unit pricing or an hourly rate may be appropriate. The former makes sense for replacing lamps in street and traffic lights, at so much per lamp, and an hourly rate may be best for snow removal work, for example.

An interesting payment mode has been proposed to encourage effective informal cooperation between a government agency and a contractor working on a complex, one-of-a-kind, first-time project: an extra fee awarded to the contractor based on a unilateral judgment about the contractor's performance by the government buyer.[64] This could invite corruption, however.

CONDUCTING THE BIDDING PROCESS
The bidding procedure will influence the number and quality of bidders who will participate. In addition to the factors discussed above, the following guidelines can be recommended to public officials:

1. Make sure the bid specifications contain no ambiguous, contradictory, or erroneous provisions.

2. Avoid unnecessarily restrictive provisions that eliminate or discriminate against potentially qualified bidders.

3. Advertise the request for bids as broadly as is reasonable, being sure to go well beyond the minimal requirement of placing a legal notice in a particular newspaper; use vendor lists drawn from trade associations, telephone directories, industry publications, experiences of other jurisdictions, and the like. Mail individual notices to firms on the list.

4. Allow enough time between the announcement date and the date the bids are due to allow preparation of responsible bids.

5. Hold a bidders' conference to answer the questions of prospective bidders. If this is the first time a service is being contracted, hold a planning conference of prospective bidders to help shape a request that is sure to attract bids.

6. Avoid asking for too many bid prices. If many bid combinations are called for (e.g., price for one year, price for two years, price for three years), it is likely that there will be several "low bidders" and perhaps one for each pricing combination. Selecting the low bidder in this circumstance leaves too much room for favoritism and improper influence, and tends to discredit the process. Astute bidders will generally spot this possibility and may not bother participating.

7. Avoid rejecting competitive bids on inappropriate grounds, and then negotiating with one of the bidders. This damages the credibility of future requests for bids from the offending jurisdiction.

8. Avoid rebidding if one of the bidders is deficient in his response (e.g., omits a required document). If any bids that are in full conformance with the bid request are disclosed, an award should be made. To do otherwise is manifestly unfair and would encourage bidders to do this deliberately in order to see what others have bid.

9. In the request for bids, announce when the award will be made. Allow sufficient time between the date of award and the contract starting date to allow the winner to mobilize for the work.

MONITORING THE CONTRACT

Contracting requires contract monitoring, that is, a systematic procedure to monitor the performance of the contractor and compare it to that specified in the contract. Sometimes agencies contract for a service and use carefully drawn performance specifications but fail to monitor the work and essentially abdicate their role. New York City before 1980, for example, had stringent performance standards for its street-light maintenance contractor, to the effect that all lights had to be restored to working order within ten days of being reported or a daily penalty charge would be levied. This was an eminently sensible standard, but unfortunately the city kept no records and had no idea whether the standard was being met. Since then, the city has followed a much better approach, with computerized tracking of all reported light outages and random checking in the field, coupled with an arrangement whereby the city is divided into eight roughly equal-size zones (equal in terms of the number of street lights) with no more than two zones awarded per contractor.

Service monitoring can consist of complaint monitoring, citizen surveys, field observations, and examination of the contractor's work records, as well as periodic cost comparisons if several contractors are involved or if part of the work is being performed in-house.

Some activities lend themselves readily to citizen monitoring; residential refuse collection and traffic-light repairs are examples. Poor service is reflected immediately in complaints, and the crucial aspect of contract monitoring in this instance is to make sure that complaints are directed to the government agency, not to the contractor. If this is done, good performance records can be compiled easily and inexpensively. Nevertheless, some agencies are oblivious to this opportunity and advertise the contractor's telephone number for complaints instead of the agency's; they think they are being efficient by eliminating the middle man who relays the complaint from the citizen to the contractor, but this is shortsighted.

Citizen surveys have been developed as a useful tool for monitoring satisfaction with public services. Hatry has written extensively on this issue and has designed suitable survey instruments for the purpose.[65]

Other monitoring techniques are surprise field inspections (e.g., of social service institutions) and scheduled field inspections (e.g., at critical points in construction projects). Other contract services are best monitored by periodically sampling and evaluating the cleanliness of janitorial services, quality of tree pruning, timeliness of bus service, and the condition of repaved roads, for example.

Newark, New Jersey, utilized a combination of these methods in order to compare the performance of municipal waste collection in one part of the city with contract collection in another, similar part. City costs were analyzed both for the in-house service and for the contract work, and the costs of the city's complaint handling and contract monitoring were included. Citizen opinion surveys were conducted, both by random telephone calls and by mail-back questionnaires distributed on selected blocks. Street cleanliness was measured by trained observers, using photographic scales, and both municipal and private crews were followed discreetly and their work performance observed and tabulated directly.

Contract monitoring requires careful planning beforehand as to what and how to measure, suitable training of inspectors, and appropriate recordkeeping and analysis. Retired persons and housewives are particularly good for inspection work, some of which may not require full-time employees.[66]

Unless the contract is monitored and administered well, there is a long-term danger that the competitive factor will be weakened and the contract service will degenerate into a private monopoly, which would be no improvement over a public one.

Owners of firms have been known to get together with their employees and demand an increase in the contract price to pay for "unanticipated" wage increases, under the threat of a strike. A private-sector union sometimes serves as the vehicle for assuring noncompetitive practices and conspiratorial, collusive bidding. The best defense against such occurrences and against collusive bidding is to have part of the work done by a government agency and part by contractors.

Summary

Four broad strategies are available to implement privatization: load shedding, adopting arrangements that have minimal government involvement, instituting user charges, and introducing competition. These are mutually reinforcing and can be blended together. A decline in the quantity or quality of service leads some citizens to seek out or devise alternatives to supply more adequate service. This invites load shedding. Numerous institutions are available to take up the slack and assume some of the responsibilities that have accrued to governments. Denationalization of state-owned enterprises, for example, by divestment, is another form of load shedding.

User charges, and government spending programs linked directly to taxes used to finance them, make the cost of programs more visible and invite comparisons of costs and benefits, thereby encouraging alternatives to government services.

Contracting and vouchers promote competition and can be employed in concert with load shedding. Competition is the key to achieving better and more cost-effective public services; a monopolistic arrangement, whether governmental or private, is an invitation to poor performance.

Contracting can occur if four conditions are satisfied: (1) The government is under fiscal stress; (2) large cost savings are likely; (3) the act is politically feasible; and (4) a precipitating event upsets the status quo and requires change. The major opposition to any form of privatization comes from public-employee unions, and their strongest argument is the fear of corruption. Skilled political leaders can generally create coalitions to overcome unreasonable opposition and have developed techniques for tempering the impact on employees affected by contracting.

The comparison of in-house and contract costs must be carried out astutely, as there are many pitfalls for the unwary. Low-ball bids are not a common occurrence, but in any event they are easy to guard against.

Various techniques can be used to induce potential suppliers of services to enter the competition, and "contracting in" can supplement "contracting out." The former term refers to the growing practice of having government agencies bid for the work on a fair and equitable basis against private contractors. Dividing the work among several contractors and an in-house unit, where feasible, assures effective competition, knowledgeable contract supervision, defense against possible collusion, and certainty of service.

Contract specifications must be prepared with care because they will affect the number and quality of bids. They can also be manipulated to undermine a decision to contract or to favor a particular bidder. Bidding procedures will affect the outcome, for better or worse.

Once a contract is in effect, performance must be monitored systematically. Techniques suitable for this purpose include complaint monitoring, citizen surveys, field observations and measurements, and examination of records.

Privatization is well established. There is ample experience in making and implementing the decision to privatize, and a large body of practical knowledge has been developed to help government officials and give them confidence in taking this step.

Notes

1. For another formulation of this prescription, see Stuart M. Butler, *Privatizing Federal Spending: A Strategy to Eliminate the Deficit* (New York: Universe Books, 1985).

2. Robert L. Woodson, "Day Care," in *This Way Up: The Local Official's Handbook for Privatization and Contracting Out,* ed. R.Q. Armington and William D. Ellis (Chicago: Regnery, 1984), 159.

3. Glenn Collins, "Many in Work Force Care for Elderly Kin," *New York Times,* 6 January 1986, B5.

4. Marcia Chaiken and Jan Chaiken, *Private Provision of Municipal and County Police Functions* (Cambridge, Mass.: Abt Associates, 1986), 5-7. A report prepared for the National Institute of Justice.

5. Robert B. Hawkins, Jr., "Special Districts and Urban Services," in *The Delivery of Urban Services,* ed. Elinor Ostrom (Beverly Hills, Calif.: Sage, 1976), 171-88.

6. Charles Murray, *Losing Ground: American Social Policy, 1950-1980* (New York: Basic Books, 1984).

7. Lawrence M. Mead, *Beyond Entitlement: The Social Obligations of Citizenship* (New York: Macmillan, 1986). See also Gregory A. Fossedal, "The Second War on Poverty," *American Spectator* 19 (February 1986): 14-18; and Ralph Segalman, "Welfare and Dependency in Switzerland," *Public Interest,* no. 82 (Winter 1986): 106-21.

8. John C. Goodman and Michael D. Stroup, *Privatizing the Welfare State,* NCPA Policy Report no. 123 (Dallas: National Center for Policy Analysis, June 1986), 18.

9. Ibid.

10. Glenn C. Loury, "The Moral Quandary of the Black Community," *Public Interest,* no. 79 (Spring 1985): 9-22.

11. Kathleen Teltsch, "Teen-age Mothers Get Aid in Study," *New York Times,* 19 May 1985, 27.

12. Jacques Rigaudiat, *"Deux cent ans d'histoire"* (Two Hundred Years of History), *Cahiers Francais,* March/April 1984, 10-17.

13. Personal communication from John McClaughry, 1980.

14. Robert W. Poole, Jr., "Rethinking Building Codes," *Fiscal Watchdog,* no. 29 (Santa Barbara, Calif.: Local Government Center, March 1979).

15. Charles Taylor, "Policy Environments and Privatization," *Proceedings of the AID Conference on Privatization* (Washington, D.C.: Agency for International Development, February 1986).

16. Bertrand Jacquillat, *Désétatiser* (Paris: Éditions Robert Laffont, 1985), 138.

17. Madsen Pirie, *Dismantling the State: The Theory and Practice of Privatization* (Dallas: National Center for Policy Analysis, 1985).

18. T.M. Ohashi and T.P. Roth, *Privatization Theory and Practice* (Vancouver, B.C.: Fraser Institute, 1980), 3-105.

19. This section draws upon miscellaneous memoranda prepared by the U.S. Agency for International Development and its consultant, the Center for Privatization.

20. Peter Young, "Privatization in Great Britain," *Government Union Review* 7, no. 2 (Spring 1986): 1-23.

21. Ibid. See also Pirie, *Dismantling the State,* 50.

22. Young, "Privatization in Great Britain."

23. Office of Management and Budget, *Major Policy Initiatives, Fiscal Year 1987* (Washington, D.C.: Government Printing Office, 1986), 71-90.

24. For further discussion of these ideas, see the publications of Public Service Options, Minneapolis, Minn., and those of the Public Services Redesign Project at the Hubert H. Humphrey Institute, University of Minnesota, Minneapolis.

25. Nan Robertson, "France Divides State TV Network into Rival Units," *New York Times,* 4 July 1974.

26. "En Garde: The Battle of French Television Has Begun," *Business Week,* 24 February 1986, 50.

27. E.S. Savas, "Municipal Monopolies versus Competition in Delivering Urban Services," in *Improving the Quality of Urban Management,* ed. Willis D. Hawley and David Rogers (Beverly Hills, Calif.: Sage, 1974), 473-500.

28. William D. Burt, *Local Problems, Libertarian Solutions* (Washington, D.C.: Libertarian Party, 1978).

29. Richard E. Wagner, "American Education and the Economics of Caring," in *Parents, Teachers and Children: Prospects for Choice in American Education* (San Francisco: Institute for Contemporary Studies, 1977).

30. Gene I. Maeroff, "Business Is Cutting into the Market," *New York Times,* 30 August 1981, sec. 12, p. 1.

31. Edward B. Fiske, "Schools for Profit," *New York Times,* 26 July 1979, B1; "State Seeks Tighter Control of Vocational Education," *New York Times,* 27 July 1979, B1; "Playing Politics with Public Money," *New York Times,* editorial, 7 November 1980.

32. Robert W. Poole, Jr., "Toward Free Public Education," *Fiscal Watchdog,* no. 33 (Santa Barbara, Calif.: Local Government Center, July 1979).

33. H. Edward Wesemann, *Contracting For City Services* (Pittsburgh: Innovations Press, 1981); and John T. Marlin, *Contracting Municipal Services: A Guide For Purchase from the Private Sector* (New York: Wiley, 1984).

34. James M. Ferris, "The Decision to Contract Out: An Empirical Analysis" (manuscript, School of Public Administration, University of Southern California, 1985).

35. Wesemann, *Contracting for City Services,* 87-92.

36. *Passing the Bucks: The Contracting Out of Public Services* (Washington, D.C.: American Federation of State, County, and Municipal Employees, AFL-CIO, 1983). For a strongly ideological attack on privatization, see Dexter Whitfield, *Making It Public:*

Evidence and Action against Privatization (London: Pluto Press, 1983); this is part of the series Arguments for Socialism.

37. Butler, *Privatizing Federal Spending,* 57-62, 108-19, 155-65.

38. Eileen B. Berenyi, "Privatization of Residential Refuse Collection Services: A Study of Institutional Change," *Urban Interest* 3, no. 1 (Spring 1981): 30-42.

39. Martin Tolchin, "Congress Wary on Plan to Sell Assets," *New York Times,* 6 February 1986, B16.

40. E.S. Savas, "How Much Do Government Services Really Cost? *Urban Affairs Quarterly* 15, no. 1 (September 1979): 23-42.

41. Ibid.

42. Wesemann, *Contracting for City Services,* 35-47.

43. U.S. Office of Management and Budget, Circular A-76 (Washington, D.C., 29 March 1979).

44. James M. Pierce, Statement, U.S. House of Representatives, *Hearings on Contracting Out of Jobs and Services, Subcommittee on Employee Ethics and Utilization, Committee on Post Office and Civil Service,* Serial no. 95-7 (Washington, D.C.: Government Printing Office, 1977), 41-43.

45. Ibid.

46. E.S. Savas, *The Organization and Efficiency of Solid Waste Collection* (Lexington, Mass.: Heath, 1977).

47. Franklin R. Edwards and Barbara J. Stevens, "The Provision of Municipal Sanitation Services by Private Firms: An Empirical Analysis of the Efficiency of Alternative Market Structures and Regulatory Arrangements," *Journal of Industrial Economics* 27, no. 2 (December 1978): 133-47.

48. E.S. Savas, "An Empirical Study of Competition in Municipal Service Delivery," *Public Administration Review* 37, no. 6 (November/December 1977): 717-24.

49. Brian E. Cox, *Evaluation of the U.K. System of Incentives for Efficiency in Road Maintenance Organisation and Possible Lessons for Developing Countries,* Report to the Transportation Department (Washington, D.C.: World Bank, 31 October 1985).

50. Robert W. Poole, Jr., "Looking Back: How City Hall Withered," in *Cutting Back City Hall* (New York: Universe Books, 1980).

51. "La Mirada: A City with a Different View," *Government Executive Magazine,* May 1981, 47-48.

52. *Contracting Out for Federal Support Services: Potential Savings and Budgetary Impacts* (Washington, D.C.: Congressional Budget Office, October 1982).

53. *Enhancing Governmental Productivity through Competition: Targeting for Annual Savings of One Billion Dollars by 1988,* A Progress Report on OMB Circular No. A-76 (Washington, D.C.: Office of Federal Procurement Policy, Office of Management and Budget, March 1984).

54. E.S. Savas, "Policy Analysis for Local Government: Public versus Private Refuse Collection," *Policy Analysis* 3, no. 1 (Winter 1977): 49-74.

55. Mark Schlesinger, Robert A. Dorwart, and Richard D. Pulice, "Competitive Bidding and States' Purchase of Services," *Journal of Policy Analysis and Management* 5, no. 2 (Winter 1986): 245-63.

56. Charles A. Lave, "The Private Challenge to Public Transportation—An Overview," in *Urban Transit: The Private Challenge to Public Transportation,* ed. Charles A. Lave (San Francisco: Pacific Institute, 1985), 16.

57. Marlin, *Contracting Municipal Services,* 46-49.

58. James C. Dobbs, "Rebuilding America: Legal Issues Confronting Privatization," *Privatization Review* 1 (Summer 1985): 28-38.

59. Stephen Chapple, "Privatization of Pollution Control Financing: Antitrust Implications," *Privatization Review* 1 (Summer 1985): 48-59.

60. Harvey Goldman and Sandra Mokuvos, "Financing: Privatization from a Banker's Perspective," *Privatization Review* 1 (Summer 1985): 39-47.

61. Lawrence Dlugos and Howard B. Whitmore, "Lessons Learned from Resource Recovery: Insuring Privatization Projects," *Privatization Review* 1 (Summer 1985): 16-23.

62. Bennett C. Jaffee, "Contracts for Residential Refuse Collection," in *Organization and Efficiency of Solid Waste Collection,* ed. E.S. Savas (Lexington, Mass.: Heath, 1977), 153-68.

63. James L. Mercer and Edwin H. Koester, *Public Management Systems* (New York: AMACOM, 1978), 177-85.

64. Raymond G. Hunt, "Award Fee Contracting as a J-Model Alternative to Revitalize Federal Program Management," *Public Administration Review* 45 (September/October 1985): 586-92.

65. Harry P. Hatry et al., *How Effective Are Your Community Services? Procedures for Monitoring the Effectiveness of Municipal Services* (Washington, D.C.: Urban Institute, 1977); see also Kenneth Webb and Harry P. Hatry, *Obtaining Citizen Feedback: The Application of Citizen Surveys to Local Governments* (Washington, D.C.: Urban Institute, 1973).

66. Wesemann, *Contracting for City Services,* 83.

9. Problems with Privatization

Privatization is no panacea, and it presents its own problems. Some of the problems arise from the basic concept, some arise because it is difficult to satisfy the conditions that are necessary for privatization to succeed, and still other problems appear during implementation.

Problems That Arise from the Concept

The very word *privatization* unfortunately summons forth images from a deep reservoir and causes misunderstanding, premature polarization, and shrill arguments that are beside the point more often than not. Some read into the word a plot to restore a completely free market, with overtones of dog eat dog, exploitation of the weakest, and survival of the fittest. Others interpret the word as an attack on government and the things government has been doing; direct beneficiaries of government programs, including employees, may therefore defend their self-interest by attacking privatization. Still others are provoked by the term because they see it as an attack on the ideals they cherish. *Public* to them denotes brotherhood, sharing, and community, and they mistakenly interpret *private* to mean the negation of these important values.

Numerous public officials throughout the world have told me, in great frustration, that they wished another word could be found. Indeed, the euphemism *productivity enhancement* was employed early in the Reagan administration to minimize reflexive employee opposition, and *alternative service delivery* is the term of art often used in municipal government circles in the United States. In fact, I devised this term specifically for that audience as a circumlocution to avoid using *privatization*.[1]

Another problem with privatization is the motivation of some of its advocates. They seize upon privatization as an excuse or mechanism to eliminate worthy goods, arguing that these are private goods (see chapter 3) and therefore should not be provided by collective means; the marketplace should be relied on to supply such goods. To the public at large, this appears to be a mean-spirited, uncaring, callous attack on society's unfortunates.

In contrast, some advocates for the needy ascribe this attitude to anyone who endorses privatized arrangements for public services. They do so mostly out of ignorance. Discussions in earlier chapters should have made it clear by now that the decision about what goods to supply at collective expense is quite separate from the decision about what arrangement to use to deliver the goods. The poor can benefit greatly by privatization, as has been shown repeatedly. Vouchers, for example, can provide more benefits, greater dignity, more choice, and a greater sense of personal responsibility. Indeed, the legitimate societal aspirations once thought attainable only by big government have proven elusive and might be achieved by smaller but better government, through privatization. Privatization can be profoundly compassionate and humane.

Here is a fundamental paradox: Privatization as a *means* can be employed effectively even by the welfare state, but privatization as an *end* is inimical to the welfare state. Thus, even socialist governments (e.g., USSR and China in the mid-1980s) turned to privatization as a pragmatic way to improve their economies and thereby raise their people's standard of living; but to anachronistic socialists who continue to exalt the role of the state, privatization is an anathema.

This same paradox also explains why some proponents of privatization berate other proponents: Those who believe in much less government want to encourage only market, voluntary, and self-service arrangements, and will often challenge privatizers who also advocate contract, voucher, and franchise arrangements, which involve a substantial role for government. To the former, only the withdrawal of government and the sale of government assets count as *real* privatization; contracting hardly merits inclusion within the same concept. My earlier writings were sometimes attacked for this very reason.

An analogous semantic phenomenon can be found in countries with strong socialist traditions. Because contracting out is commonplace even in these settings, it is not seen as a form of privatization by the guardians of the flame. This selective blindness permits them to preserve their ideological purity and remain eternally vigilant against what they consider "real" privatization, that is, denationalization.

Necessary Conditions for Successful Privatization

Chapters 5 and 8 identified the characteristics of privatization alternatives and the techniques for putting them into practice. What is necessary here is to stress again that certain conditions must be satisfied if privatization is to be successful. Each privatized arrangement has its own set of conditions. The major ones are listed in table 9.1 for the principal privatized arrangements.

TABLE 9.1

NECESSARY CONDITIONS FOR SUCCESSFUL PRIVATIZATION

	Privatized arrangement				
	Franchise	Contract	Voucher	Market	Voluntary
Type of good	Private or toll		Private, toll, or common-pool	Private or toll	
Number of suppliers		Many	Many	Many	
Specifications		Must be well specified			
Information			Consumer informed about cost, quality, suppliers	Consumer informed about cost, quality, suppliers	
Other	"Natural monopoly"		Shopping incentive	Shopping incentive	Clear and enduring need; commonality of interest; opportunity for tangible accomplishment

To the extent that the conditions are not satisfied, the privatized arrangement will not be fully satisfactory. For example, the motivation for voluntary action may be lacking if there is not a common perception of need and an obviously feasible joint approach. Similarly, the conditions for an effective voucher system may not exist and perhaps cannot be created. It was shown in chapter 5 that Medicare and Medicaid are not satisfactory voucher systems for health care because they fail to satisfy the necessary conditions.

The importance of initial conditions is most evident with contracting, where the service under consideration must be well specified. If detailed contract specifications cannot be written, the contractor cannot be expected to conform, and the agency cannot monitor the contractor's performance.

This is the principal distinction between "hard" and "soft" services, that is, engineering-type services (public works, etc.) and human services (child care, mental health counseling, etc.). The former are relatively easy to specify in detail, the latter are more difficult (but far from impossible). This accounts for most of the reported problems in contracting for human services.[2]

Services are intended to achieve certain results, and these can be considered as lying along a continuum, from highly to poorly specifiable. The ideal contract specifies the desired result, which can be and is monitored. For instance, a contract for traffic-light maintenance might specify that all malfunctioning lights must be repaired within four hours after being reported, with a penalty to be paid for tardy work. A contract for data entry can specify an upper limit on the error rate. Such services are easy to buy through contracts. But for services at the other end of the spectrum, the results are more difficult to quantify. What is the output of a geriatric day-care facility or a center that provides family counseling to prevent child or wife abuse?

Because their outputs are relatively difficult to quantify, contracts for such services often resort to input measures as surrogates for the outputs. Thus the emphasis turns to staffing ratios, the number of personnel with certain training, conformance to building codes, the adequacy of smoke alarms, and the like; that is, the contractor's performance is evaluated according to his adherence to rules, not to his output. But this stifles innovation. The comparative advantage of private firms lies in their ability to innovate, not in obedience to rules. Hence, one might not expect them to be markedly superior to public agencies in providing services where the contracts are heavily laden with production rules.[3] Thus, a street-sweeping firm is rewarded in the marketplace for finding a new, more efficient way to remove litter from city streets, not for its adherence to rules concerning the width of its brooms and the strength of the men who wield them.

It follows that a service characterized by relatively intangible outputs may not be a good candidate for privatization by contracting unless it has the potential to be improved significantly by innovative approaches. But then, one can never tell where innovation may strike; prisons may have this potential, and therefore experiments with private prisons offer much promise. Perhaps the best rule of thumb is to encourage experimental privatization of any "public" service that is currently unsatisfactory.

Implementation Obstacles

Privatizing an existing government function may not be a simple matter. The legitimate concerns of current providers and beneficiaries have to be addressed, and any unfounded fears must be dispelled. Opponents of the change must be placated or circumvented, converts must be gained, and coalitions to support the change must be assembled.

Each step toward privatization is subject to significant problems. Imposing user charges, often a first step, is fraught with political obstacles because of the profound economic impact on the beneficiaries: They must pay for a service previously paid for by their fellow citizens through taxes. Nowhere is this more evident than in the opposition by yacht owners to fees for using the inland waterways of the United States, and in the opposition in western states to paying for their water.

There is similiar opposition to another privatization step, deregulating franchises and allowing market forces to rule. A well-known example is the successful effort by the taxi industry in New York City to block any increase in the number of authorized taxicabs; the total has been fixed at 11,787 since the mid-1930s. Public sentiment against deregulation is often fanned by confusing economic regulation with safety regulation. To continue with the taxicab illustration, one can have free entry into the field (and even free pricing) while nevertheless mandating safety inspections, insurance, and driver-related safety matters: competence, identification cards, and character checks.

Economic deregulation may be politically unattractive in other ways. For example, cross-subsidization favors some groups at the expense of others. Politicians are rarely willing to abandon such a handy instrument, therefore the scope of politically feasible deregulation has been limited.[4]

Privatizing by changing from grants to vouchers encounters comparable political opposition. When the Reagan administration scaled back grants to builders and introduced housing vouchers, both builders and politicians who enjoy presiding at cornerstone layings and ribbon cuttings were unhappy.

Voluntary arrangements can be inhibited by legal problems. There is growing interest in ride sharing, especially vanpooling by co-workers, but the practice is currently consigned to a legal no-man's land. The passengers and driver may have been identified, the vehicle selected, the vehicle expenses calculated, the routes and fares determined, and the vanpool rules established; but the liability, taxes, insurance, applicable wage-and-hour standards, and other important features, depend on whose name is on the vehicle title. A totally different body of law applies—ranging from lease law to common-carrier law to labor law—depending on whether the vehicle belongs to the employer of the vanpool group, the local transit authority, a leasing firm, the driver, or a corporation specifically created for the purpose by the vanpool group. Legislation has been suggested to cut through this legal thicket.[5]

Denationalization also presents problems of implementation. Determining the value of the state-owned enterprise is one problem. Another is deciding whether to sell to a private company or to the public via sale of stock. Should employees receive preferential treatment? If sale to the public is contemplated, should widespread ownership be the goal? This can be accomplished by setting a low limit on the number of shares sold to any one individual.

One of the major barriers to denationalization is the availability of capital; this is a serious problem in developing countries, but it also affected the rate of denationalization in England.[6] An even more serious obstacle is the labor issue. In many instances, state-owned enterprises are little more than thinly disguised unemployment programs, where little work is expected from the employees. As a general rule, state employees will oppose denationalization, as will politicians who court their vote.

Contracting out is perhaps the most common form of privatization, and therefore much has been learned about this practice. When the activity requires a large capital expenditure by the contractor, a long-term contract is necessary, to allow amortization of the capital equipment. But this offers an opportunity for strategic behavior by the contractor: inferior quality of work at the start of the contract period, and improved quality toward the end of the period, as renewal time approaches.[7] (Note that this is perfectly analogous to political behavior in government: Unpopular actions are taken right after elections, and popular ones just before elections.) Government must be able to intervene if the contractor's work is unsatisfactory and thereby to prevent such behavior; fair contract terms allowing such intervention must be clearly spelled out.

Vigorous opposition with no holds barred is to be expected from public employees and their unions, and therefore from elected legislators who represent many such constituents. Borrowing from successful efforts in Great Britain to build support for privatization among the affected public employees by giving them a sizable economic stake in the outcome, the U.S. Office of Personnel Management recently developed an imaginative plan to gain employee backing for contracting out. Briefly, the plan would work as follows: An activity that is a candidate for contracting out would be studied and its total cost determined. The government would then seek bids for the work and would share its savings equally with the winning bidder for three years. The latter would put its share of the savings into an employee stock-ownership plan (with the acronym, ESOP) in a newly created subsidiary that would be the contractor for the work. This novel structure would give employees—even those who are laid off—a vested interest in the economic success of the contract work. The government would realize only half the savings for the first three years, but afterward the contract would be awarded by open competitive bidding to the lowest bidder. In effect, the government "buys out" the employee opposition by sharing its savings for the first three years.[8] This ingenious plan is surely worth testing.

Implementation problems have been noted in contracting out for human services.[9] As DeHoog puts it:

Contracting authorities are not interested in promoting the goals of contracting advocates — at least not in practice in their own bastions of power. Nor are they concerned with designing and implementing competitive procedures or thorough review methods. They *are* interested in maintaining existing relationships of mutual advantage and promoting new ones. These narrow interests are facilitated by more money, more programs, and resistance to any changes in funding levels, service priorities, and contracting methods.[10]

This reasoning suggests that bureaucratic imperialists who behave in their own interests will continue to do so even when purchasing services; unless contracting procedures promote competition and have incentives to maximize efficiency, little improvement may be forthcoming.

Many of the problems in contracting for human services derive from the initial conditions. Contracting in this field was not undertaken to reduce costs or provide more services for the same expenditure[11] but to obtain federal funds that became available and to make sure they were spent. It is not surprising, therefore, that the conditions for successful contracting were ignored. There were few suppliers, specifications were vague, there was little experience with the new programs, contracting skills were undeveloped, and contract management was weak. Moreover, comfortable and amicable old relationships between the public and private sectors — a bilateral monopoly — dominated the buyer-seller relationship. (This is strikingly similar to the relationship between defense contractors and military procurement officials.) Heavy-handed political interference was commonplace in both awarding and terminating contracts. Federal, state, and local government units had contradictory requirements and imposed excessive layers of supervision. Legislative obstacles further confused the issue. In view of these frustrating experiences, it is not surprising that the contracting of human services was questioned.[12]

A careful review of the disappointment reported for human service contracting raises the following question: Would the outcomes have been very different if the work had been done in-house instead of by contractors? The reported studies can be read as an indictment of hastily created social programs implemented (i.e., funds were appropriated and spent) through contractors because in-house efforts could not be launched as rapidly. The problems posed by excessive layers of bureaucracy, conflicting intergovernmental requirements, political interference, and legislative impediments presumably would have been just as onerous had government agencies attempted to perform the work in-house. The studies do not purport to compare contract and government performance of human services; they merely point to the problems experienced with contract arrangements. One must not lose sight of the fact that the above-cited conditions for successful contracting were not satisfied. Moreover, if the objective of a program is unclear, neither a contractor nor a government agency can be monitored in a meaningful way with respect to its performance, and neither is likely to be found satisfactory.

One suggestion to overcome the problems of human services contracting is to promote competition by new, small, nonprofit agencies, although this may raise government's administrative costs. Another suggested approach, the polar opposite of the first, is to create an oligopolistic system in which the work is divided among a small number of large providers, each one providing all human services in its catchment area. A third suggestion is a system of multiple, hybrid, and partial arrangements (as these terms are used in chapter 4), involving both the public and private sectors in a variety of relationships.[13]

This last system raises concerns about "cream skimming"; that is, under a mixed system the private sector will select only the most profitable patients or services, leaving government agencies to provide residual care, care for the most expensive and least desirable clients.[14] This argument requires critical examination. It is possible to have both cream skimming *and* the lowest possible total cost to the public. This will occur whenever the per-client price charged by the private firm is less than the per-client cost of the public agency. Table 9.2 illustrates how so-called cream skimming by the private sector can nevertheless reduce the total cost to the public. The public sector can contract with a profit-making private firm to serve the easy clients, and take advantage of the savings, even while it retains the difficult-to-serve clients. In this hypothetical case, the public saves $75 (12.5 percent), even though the private firm earns a profit of $25 (25 percent).

There is a political issue here, however. If the public agency contracts with a private firm and has the latter serve the easy clients (alternative 2 in table 9.2), a superficial comparison would reveal that the per-client cost to the public is $400 for the agency and only $125 for contract service. One can imagine quite a fuss being made about this striking difference, but the invidious comparison would be utterly inappropriate, and the agency would be maligned unfairly. Rather than try to explain this outcome, a cautious bureaucrat might choose to avoid this possible problem altogether by doing all the work in-house, despite its greater cost.

This simple illustration also reinforces the point made in chapter 6 about the importance of careful and valid comparisons between public and private providers.

What about cream skimming when there is a user charge? In this circumstance, if a private firm takes over the profitable part, government is left with the unprofitable part and is deprived of the opportunity to cross-subsidize the latter with the profit from the former. Can this possibly be beneficial to the

TABLE 9.2

HYPOTHETICAL ILLUSTRATION:

"CREAM SKIMMING" CAN REDUCE PUBLIC COSTS

A. Costs and prices per client	Easy to serve	Hard to serve
Number of clients	1	1
Cost of public service	$200	$400
Contractor's cost	$100	$400
Contractor's price	$125	$500

B. Alternatives	Cost
Alternative 1. All clients served by public agency	$600
Alternative 2. Cream skimming: contractor serves only easy clients	$525
Alternative 3. All clients served by contractor	$625

public? Yes, indeed. The savings to the public at large may outweigh the loss to the government. This is an interesting situation where a policy that is good for the public is bad for the public agency, and vice versa.

Table 9.3 offers a hypothetical case of a public bus system that charges a uniform fare and serves both a profitable, high-density area and an unprofitable, low-density area. It is assumed that the number of passengers is the same in both areas. So-called cream skimming occurs, wherein a private bus line takes over the profitable area under a free-market or franchise arrangement and charges a lower fare. In this circumstance, alternative 2, the agency budget must be increased from 70 cents to 75 cents per rider, with this extra cost presumably paid by a tax subsidy. But the total cost to the public, fare plus tax subsidy, declines from $1.70 to $1.65 per rider because of the lower fare charged by the private firm. The public agency is worse off because it must seek a bigger budget, but the public as a whole is better off.

One can conclude from these simple analyses that cream skimming is not necessarily bad public policy, despite the pejorative connotation. Every circumstance must be examined carefully to determine what is best for the public, not the public agency, as their interests often diverge.

Summary

The problems with privatization arise partly from the basic concept itself, partly from the failure to satisfy the necessary conditions, and partly from the difficulties of implementation.

The ideological motivations of some advocates and some opponents of privatization sow confusion and create obstacles to its adoption. The term *priva-*

TABLE 9.3

HYPOTHETICAL ILLUSTRATION: "CREAM SKIMMING"

WHEN THERE IS A USER CHARGE

A. Per-rider costs and fares	Low-cost area	High-cost area
Cost for public agency	$.90	$2.50
Fare charged by public agency	1.00	1.00
Cost for private firm	.50	N.A.
Fare charged by private firm	.80	N.A.

B. Cost of alternatives	For two riders[a]	Average per rider
Alternative 1. All riders served		
by public agency		
Fares paid by riders	$2.00	$1.00
Subsidy paid by taxes (agency budget)	1.40	.70
Total cost to the public	3.40	1.70
Alternative 2. Cream skimming:		
private firm serves low-cost area		
Fares paid by riders	$1.80	$.90
Subsidy paid by taxes (agency budget)	1.50	.75
Total cost to the public	3.30	1.65

a. One from each of the two areas.

tization itself sometimes triggers muddled thinking and reflexive resistance. In particular, privatization can be better for the needy than traditional government programs, hence more compassionate.

Each privatized arrangement requires certain conditions in order to be successful and fully effective. Many of the problems reported for human service contracts result from the difficulty of specifying the desired results of the service and from faulty execution.

Any change encounters opposition, and privatization is no exception, however it is implemented. Political, bureaucratic, and employee resistance is the norm and must be overcome. In addition, there are policy questions about the sale, pricing, and distribution of shares when denationalizing state-owned enterprises. There may be legal impediments to novel arrangements such as vanpools, and problems with long-term contracts. On the other hand, cream skimming, where the private sector handles only the easy, low-cost work, is often derided but may be a cost-effective public policy.

Notes

1. For example, see E.S. Savas, ed., *Alternatives for Delivering Public Services: Toward Improved Performance* (Boulder, Colo.: Westview, 1977). For a generally thoughtful discussion of the limits of privatization, even though it errs in some of the ways identified in this chapter, see Paul Starr, "The Limits of Privatization," in *Prospects for Privatization,* Proceedings of the Academy of Political Science 36, no. 3 (1987): 124-37.

2. Ruth H. DeHoog, *Contracting Out for Human Services* (Albany: State University of New York Press, 1984); and Mark Schlesinger, Robert A. Dorwart, and Richard T. Pulice, "Competitive Bidding and States' Purchase of Services," *Journal of Policy Analysis and Management* 5, no. 2 (Winter 1986): 245-63.

3. Charles Blankart, "Market and Non-Market Alternatives in the Supply of Public Goods: General Issues," in *Public Expenditures and Government Growth,* ed. F. Forte and A.T. Peacock (Oxford, England: Blackwell, 1985); see also Schlesinger et al., "Competitive Bidding," 254.

4. Blankart, "Market and Non-Market Alternatives," 194.

5. F.W. Davis, Jr., et al., "Developing Ridesharing Law: A First Step to Privatizing Transportation," *Transportation Research Record,* no. 876 (1982): 9-17.

6. Paul Hemp, "Britain Forced to Slow Sale of State Assets," *Wall Street Journal,* 26 June 1986, 34.

7. Blankart, "Market and Non-Market Alternatives," 197-98.

8. U.S. Office of Personnel Management, "FED CO-OP" (Washington, D.C., 29 January 1987).

9. DeHoog, *Contracting Out;* Schlesinger et al., "Competitive Bidding."

10. DeHoog, *Contracting Out,* 28.

11. Ibid., 130.

12. Ibid., 129-34; see also Schlesinger et al., "Competitive Bidding."

13. Schlesinger et al., "Competitive Bidding."

14. Ibid.

10. Conclusion

This book arrives at the position that privatization is the key to both limited and better government: limited in its size, scope, and power relative to society's other institutions; and better in that society's needs are satisfied more efficiently, effectively, and equitably.

Privatization is both a means and an end. For pragmatists who want better government and for populists who seek a better society, privatization is a means toward those ends. The government that results from the practice of privatization is leaner and more adroit, and society is sturdier and more adaptable. For those who, on ideological grounds, seek to limit government, and for those who seek commercial opportunities in government work, privatization is an end in itself.

Some of the basic needs of a society require collective action, but most do not. Large-scale collective action requires the institution of government, with coercive powers granted by the people, but collective action on a small scale may be taken by voluntary associations.

Even when government exercises its authority to *provide* collective goods, it does not have to *produce* them. Production is not government's strong suit. Fortunately, there are alternatives. Privatization relieves government of the burden of performing many functions that it simply is not very good at doing. Privatization by prudent contracting permits government to continue providing a service but to limit itself to the roles that best suit it: articulating the demand, acting as purchasing agent, monitoring the contractor's performance, and paying the bill. By doing only these things while relegating actual operations to private firms, government takes advantage of the latter's uncontested ability to produce and deliver the goods.

Privatization by vouchers also relieves government of the production responsibility, for it enables recipients to utilize the powerful, private-sector institution, the marketplace, to obtain selected worthy goods and services on a subsidized basis. This means more for the needy, as well as greater dignity.

Privatization by government sale of, or withdrawal from, a business—load shedding—leaves it up to private organizations and institutions, acting freely in the public market of ideas and actions, to satisfy the unmet needs of society.

The theoretical reasons why privatized arrangements should be better than governmental ones are in accord with common sense; moreover, they are supported by practical experiences and confirmed by authoritative studies. Traditional tactics to improve government performance—efficiency drives, attempts to eliminate waste and to impose budget limits—generally have modest and short-lived effects. Privatization can produce large and long-lasting improvements because it involves institutional change rather than spasmodic exhortation. Indeed, privatization is a strategic approach that *causes* goverment agencies to adopt the well-known, good-management techniques because it poses a competitive threat.

It is an understatement to say that privatizing a current government function is not a simple matter. Attitudes have to be changed, and new skills have to be acquired. Coalitions of supporters have to be pieced together, and converts have to be won over. The legitimate concerns of beneficiaries and providers have to be addressed, and their unfounded fears have to be dispelled. Even beyond these issues of implementation, privatization is not without its problems. There are, of course, circumstances where privatization will not work and should not be attempted. The setting for successful contracting or franchising may be inopportune. The conditions for effective voucher systems may not exist and perhaps cannot be created. The motivation for voluntary action may be missing. The marketplace may not be ready for load shedding, and it may lack capital for denationalization. All these factors inhibit privatization, despite the ardor of its proponents.

Privatization can be looked on as the act of redesigning the life-support systems of a national or local community. The policy-making government body should separate the planning and procurement of services from their production and delivery; it can then divest itself of much of its operating responsibility. A wide variety of producers should be available through contracting and franchising by the policy maker, and through market and voucher arrangements for the citizen-consumer. Choice should be maximized, and ideally no public or private buyer should be dependent on a sole source of supply. This requires deregulation, to permit more suppliers to come forth and to develop more effective and innovative ways to provide services. The behavior of the service producer would then be driven by incentives rather than commands.[1]

Privatization of public services should lead to an outpouring of research efforts and would be an incentive for private firms to explore fundamentally new ways of providing services; monopolies, public or private, have a tendency to resist change and retard innovation. Moreover, if there were greater political tolerance of profit in the delivery of human services, there would probably be completely different kinds of schools, health-care systems, and prisons, for example, and entirely different systems for running cities.[2] Profit-making firms, spurred by competition, can be expected to develop new approaches for satisfying these needs, just as they developed free-standing kidney-dialysis clinics, "urgent medical care" centers, computer-based education, and numerous devices, fixtures, and services to facilitate mobility and independent living for the elderly. Also, it was visionary, profit-seeking developers who contributed to the revitalization of older cities by creating attractions such as the Faneuil Hall marketplace in Boston, South Street Seaport in New York, Baltimore's Inner Harbor, and San Francisco's Ghirardelli Square.

This view of government is in keeping with the very origins of the word *government*. Its Greek root means "helmsman." The role of government is to steer, not to man the oars. Privatization helps restore government to its fundamental purpose.

Government intervention has grown rapidly in both developed and developing countries. The pervasive presumption has been that the state could and should cure almost all economic and social ills and that problems would disappear once their solutions were entrusted to the state. In many developing countries, governments are almost assumed to be able to solve any problem simply by enacting a law, passing a regulation, or announcing a policy. (Sometimes the results are tragic: famine in countries where the government imposed price controls on food, with prices set so low that farmers could not afford to grow crops for sale and were reduced to subsistence farming.)

Experience has shown that some problems cannot be solved, certainly not in the short run and perhaps never, while others simply continue to exist and do not disappear as a result of having responsibility for them transferred from the private to the public sector. In fact, this transfer often aggravates the situation and creates even more problems, and it does not ensure that the allocation of resources will be either socially optimal or more efficient or even more equitable.[3]

Society is more than the state. Government is only one institution of society. As recognition of this simple fact grows, the federal government may be gradually eclipsed as the primary agent of social policy in America. It won't wither away, and some of its programs may even grow dramatically, but it may no longer play the role it did in the 1960s and 1970s. The reason is that with respect to social issues, America is not so much a single, national community as it is a nation of small, diverse communities, each of which can be empowered to define and solve for itself the problems it considers most important. The concept of national community, while of vital significance in wartime, has failed to gain popular acceptance. Consequently, Americans are turning more to society's other traditional institutions to satisfy local and individual needs, through the family, neighborhood, and church, and through ethnic and voluntary associations.[4]

Privatization is not a transient political phenomenon that will fade away when prominent proponents leave the scene. Its successes are too evident and too widespread. In the United States, it is embraced by Republicans and Democrats, liberals and conservatives. Elsewhere it has been adopted by both developed and developing countries, by communist, socialist, and capitalist regimes, and by both democratic and autocratic states.

Privatization is as old as government, by definition, but apparently the concept was first proposed as a deliberate public policy to improve government performance as recently as 1969.[5] The challenge today is to achieve a better division of responsibilities and functions between government and the private sector in order to take advantage of the strengths of each and overcome the limitations of the other. The resulting partnership can best satisfy the wants and needs of the people in a manner consistent with the fundamental beliefs and values of a democratic society.

Notes

1. Ted Kolderie, *An Equitable and Competitive Public Sector* (Minneapolis: Hubert H. Humphrey Institute of Public Affairs, University of Minnesota, 1984), 77.

2. John Diebold, Testimony, U.S. House of Representatives, *Hearing on the Impact of the Information Age on Science, Committee on Science and Technology* (Washington, D.C.: Government Printing Office, 10 September 1985).

3. Armeane M. Choksi, *State Intervention in the Industrialization of Developing Countries: Selected Issues,* Staff Working Paper no. 341 (Washington, D.C.: World Bank, July 1979), 147.

4. William J. Baroody, Jr., "America: A Nation of Communities," *Memorandum* (Washington, D.C.: American Enterprise Institute, Spring/Summer 1985).

5. Peter F. Drucker, *The Age of Discontinuity* (New York: Harper & Row, 1969). One of the earliest government reports advocating privatization was prepared confidentially for the mayor of New York: E.S. Savas, John F. McMahon, and Herbert R. Gamache, *Refuse Collection: Department of Sanitation versus Private Carting* (New York: Office of the Mayor, 1970). For a news account of that report, see Richard Phalon, "City May Use Private Refuse Haulers," *New York Times,* 6 April 1971, 1. For an amusing account of the origins of that report, see E.S. Savas, "Privatization from the Top Down and from the Outside In," in *Privatization,* ed. John C. Goodman (Dallas: National Center for Policy Analysis, 1985), vii-ix, 69-77.

Name Index

Ahlbrandt, Roger S., Jr., 224n
Albon, Robert P., 175n
Alchian, A.A., 46, 57n
Allison, Graham P., 111, 116n
Anderson, Terry L., 176n, 219, 229n
Aoki, S., 173n
Aristotle, 219
Armington, R.Q., 117n, 175n, 224n, 273n

Babitsky, Timlynn T., 175n
Baden, John, 179n
Bailis, Lawrence N., 111, 117n
Baim, Dean, 229n
Barnbrock, Jörn, 226n
Baroody, William J., Jr., 291n
Baumol, William J., 57n
Bayer, Lynn, 178n
Bellante, Don, 32n
Bendick, Mark, Jr., 226n
Bennathan, Esra, 166, 179n
Bennett, James T., 31n, 111, 117n, 122, 124n, 170, 172n, 175n, 180n, 189
Berenyi, Eileen B., 275n
Berger, Peter L., 227n
Berman, Phyllis, 178n
Bethell, Tom, 31n
Biber, J., 227n
Bish, Robert L., 32n, 92n
Blankart, Charles B., 139, 158, 174n, 178n, 179n, 287n
Block, Walter, 227n
Boaz, David, 228n, 229n
Bolick, Clint, 229n
Borcherding, Thomas E., 18, 31n, 111, 122, 173n
Boston, John, 228n
Bradbury, Katherine L., 226n
Brand, Mark J., 225n

Brans, J.P., 92n
Brecher, Charles, 31n
Bridge, Gary, 92n, 117n, 229n
Bromberg, Michael D., 225n
Buchanan, James M., 23, 31n
Burger, Warren E., 187
Burns, Scott, 174n
Burt, William D., 174n, 274n
Bush, Winston C., 32n
Butler, Evelyn, 224n
Butler, Stuart M., 31n, 57n, 147, 154, 177n-79n, 201, 224n, 226n-29n, 273n, 275n

Califano, Joseph A., Jr., 190, 225n
Camp, Camille G., 224n
Camp, George M., 224n
Carpenter, Polly, 229n
Carroll, Maurice, 226n
Carter, Jimmy, 8
Chaiken Jan, 92n, 223n, 273n
Chaiken, Marcia, 92n, 223n, 273n
Chapple, Stephen, 276n
Chipello, Christopher J., 178n
Chira, Susan, 175n
Choksi, Armeane M., 291n
Ciszewski, Robert L., 226n
Citrin, Jacob, 32n
Clarkson, K.W., 226n
Clendinen, Dudley, 99, 116n
Clymer, Adam, 12n
Coleman, James, 215, 217, 229n
Collins, Glenn, 273n
Conte, Christopher, 174n-75n
Contney, John, 178n
Coons, John E., 229n
Cox, Brian E., 275n
Crain, W.M., 176n
Crane, Edward H., 228n-29n

Crompton, John L., 229n
Cunningham, William C., 223n

Darling-Hammond, Linda, 228n
Davies, David G., 171, 175n, 180
Davies, John, 226n
Davis, F.W., Jr., 287n
Deacon, Robert T., 179n
DeAlessi, L., 46, 57n, 151, 177n
DeHoog, Ruth H., 283, 287n
Derzon, Robert A., 225n
Diebold, John, 291n
DiLorenzo, Thomas J., 31n, 170, 175n, 180n, 189, 224n
Dionne, E.J., Jr., 99, 116n
Dlugos, Lawrence, 276n
Dobbs, James C., 276n
Dorwant, Robert A., 227n, 275n, 287n
Dougherty, Philip H., 177n
Downs, Anthony, 111, 117n, 226n
Downs, George W., 175n
Doyle, Denis P., 217, 229n
Drucker, Peter F., 12n, 111, 117n, 175n, 227n, 291n
Durant, Robert F., 116n
Durman, Eugene, 92n, 227n

Edwards, Franklin R., 275n
Ellis, William D., 117n, 175n, 224n, 273n
Ellwood, David T., 117n
England, Catherine, 180n
Etzioni, Amitai, 228n

Feibel, Charles, 174n
Feigenbaum, Susan, 176n
Ferrara, Peter J., 210, 228n
Ferris, James M., 92n, 274n
Fiorina, Morris, 31n
Fisk, Donald, 92n, 122, 172n
Fiske, Edward B., 274n
Fitch, Lyle C., 111, 117n
Fitzgerald, Michael R., 116n
Fixler, Philip E., Jr., 175n, 178n
Ford, Daniel, 223n
Forte, F., 287n

Fossedal, Gregory A., 273n
Fowler, Glenn, 225n
Frazier, Mark, 122, 172n, 174n, 224n
French, H.E., III, 226n
Friedman, Dana, 228n
Friedman, Milton, 171, 204, 227n

Gage, Theodore, 224n
Gamache, Herbert R., 291n
Gardner, Delworth B., 179n
Gibelman, Margaret, 227n
Girouard, Richard J., 176n
Goldin, Harrison J., 100, 116n
Goldman, Harvey, 176n, 179n, 276n
Gonzalez, Rodolfo A., 223n
Goodman, John, 196, 226n, 228n, 238, 273n, 291n
Grava, Sigurd, 174n
Graziano, Peter, 174n

Haldi, John, 177n
Hall, George, 229n
Hall, Peter, 205
Hamada, K., 173n
Hanke, Steve H., 57n, 148, 164-65, 174n-77n, 179n, 189, 225n
Hanrahan, John D., 172n
Hardin, Garrett, 57n, 219, 229n
Harral, Clell, 174n
Harriss, C. Lowell, 174n, 225n
Hatry, Harry P., 92n, 122, 172n, 227n, 271, 276n
Hawkins, Robert B., Jr., 236, 273n
Hawley, Willis D., 117n, 172n, 274n
Hayek, F.A., 171, 180n, 204, 227n
Hayes, Frederick O'R., 178n
Hellman, Richard, 150, 176n-77n
Hemp, Paul, 287n
Henriod, Ernesto, 174n
Hermann, Robert, 228n
Hoffer, Thomas, 229n
Hollie, Pamela G., 225n
Holsendolph, Ernest, 177n
Holwill, Richard N., 179n
Hsiao, William, 225n
Hunt, Raymond G., 276n

Idi Amin, 213

Jabs, Cynthia, 177n
Jacquillat, Bertrand, 243, 274n
Jaffee, Bennett C., 276n
James, Estelle, 228n
Jaynes, Gregory, 180n
Johnson, Bruce M., 179n
Johnson, M.T., 180n
Johnson, Manuel H., 111, 117n, 122,
    172n, 224n
Johnson, Thomas A., 229n
Junk, P.E., 176n

Kaiser, J.A., 92n, 179n
Kaletsky, Anatole, 179n
Katz, Hallie M., 225n
Kessel, R.A., 57n
Kessler, Ronald, 116n, 177n
Kiesling, Herbert, 92n, 172n
Kilborn, Peter T., 116n
Kilgore, Sally, 229n
Kirby, Michael J., 175n
Kirlin, John J., 92n
Knight, Michael, 116n
Knudsen, Reinhart, 229n
Koch, Edward I., 237
Koester, Edwin H., 276n
Kolderie, Ted, 12n, 92n, 215, 228n-29n,
    291n
Krashinsky, Michael, 228n
Kristensen, Ole P., 224n
Kuhn, Bowie K., 228n
Kul, Joseph, 229n

Lane, Frederick, 116n
Larkey, Patrick D., 175n
Larsky, Michael S., 177n
Lave, Charles A., 141, 175n, 266,
    275n
Lavis, Terrence D.J., 226n
Lentz, Bernhard F., 31n
Lesson, Edward C., 225n
Levine, Arthur L., 147, 177n
Levine, Marsha, 217, 229n
Lewin, Lawrence S., 225n
Lindsay, Cotton M., 225n

Lindsey, Robert, 176n
Lipset, S.M., 12n
Logan, Charles H., 187, 224n
Long, James, 32n
Loury, Glenn C., 273n
Lowry, Ira S., 226n

McClaughry, John, 273n
McDavid, James C., 173n, 224n
McFadden, Robert D., 224n
MacGillivray, Lois A., 224n
McGuire, Robert A., 174n
Machalaba, Daniel, 175n
McMahon, John F., 291n
Maeroff, Gene I., 274n
Manchester, Lydia D., 92n, 173n
Mann, P.C., 176n
Margulies, Rhea, 225n
Marlin, John T., 268, 274n, 276n
Martin, D.L., 226n
Marx, Karl, 241
Mayo, Stephen K., 226n
Mead, Lawrence, 238, 273n
Mehay, Stephen L., 223n
Meltzer, Allan H., 31n
Mercer, James L., 276n
Meyer, Jack A., 227n, 229n
Meyer, Marshall W., 111, 117n
Meyer, R.A., 176n
Mieszkowski, Peter, 32n
Mikesell, J.L., 176n
Mokuvos, Sandra, 176n, 179n, 276n
Morlok, Edward K., 174n-75n
Moseley, Frederick A., 174n
Moynihan, Daniel Patrick, 215, 229n
Mullen, Joan, 224n
Muller, Thomas, 92n, 172n
Murray, Charles, 238, 273n
Myrdal, Gunnar, 204

Nash, Ogden, 22, 31n
Nelson, Barbara J., 92n
Nelson, Robert H., 227n
Neuberg, Leland G., 176n
Neuhaus, Richard John, 227n
Niskanen, William A., Jr., 23, 31n,
    111, 116n

Ohashi, T.M., 274n
Olsen, Edgar, 227n
Olson, Walter, 122, 172n, 174n
Ostrom, Elinor, 57n, 92n, 273n
Ostrom, Vincent, 57n

Panagiotakopoulos, Demetrios, 175n
Panzar, J.C., 57n
Parks, Rogert B., 92n
Pattison, Robert V., 225n
Peacock, A.T., 287n
Peirce, Neal R., 224n
Peltzman, Sam, 177n
Perry, James L., 140, 175n
Peterson, George E., 32n
Peyton, Tom L., Jr., 224n
Phalon, Richard, 291n
Phillips, David L., 176n
Phillips, Larry, 175n
Pierce, James M., 275n
Pirie, Madsen, 22, 31n, 201, 226n,
    274n
Pommerehne, W.W., 158, 178n-79n
Poole, Robert W., Jr., 12n, 122, 145,
    172n, 174n-76n, 178n, 220, 229n,
    265, 273n-75n
Popper, Frank J., 179n
Prichard, J.R.S., 173n
Primeaux, Walter J., Jr., 57n, 151, 177n
Pulice, Robert T., 227n, 275n, 287n
Punch, Linda, 225n
Purnick, Joyce, 116n

Rachal, Patricia, 116n
Rahn, Richard, 196, 226n
Raines, Howell, 224n
Rainey, Hal, 111, 117n
Rausch, Sharla P., 224n
Reagan, Ronald, 8, 22, 30, 31n, 141,
    147, 153, 199, 205, 208, 214-15,
    227n, 237
Regan, Edward V., 32n
Rehnquist, William, 215
Richard, Scott F., 31n
Ries, John C., 92n
Rigaudiat, Jacques, 273n
Robertson, Nan, 31n, 274n

Rogers, David, 117n, 172n, 274n
Rosenbaum, David E., 224n
Roskamp, K.W., 174n
Roth, Gabriel, 141, 151-52, 175n-78n,
    213, 228n
Roth, T.P., 274n
Rothbard, Murray N., 122, 134, 174n,
    228n

Salins, Peter D., 227n
Savas, E.S., 31n-32n, 57n, 92n, 103,
    116n-17n, 122, 124, 172n-73n,
    180n, 225n, 229n, 274n-76n,
    287n, 291n
Schenker, Alan, 31n
Schlesinger, Mark, 227n, 275n, 287n
Schneider, Friedrick, 178n-79n
Schneider, W., 12n
Schorr, Burt, 228n
Schrender, Breton R., 176n
Sclar, Elliot, 174n
Scott-Stokes, Henry, 177n
Segalman, Ralph, 273n
Shabecoff, Philip, 179n
Shafer, Jack, 177n
Sharkansky, Ira, 179n
Shaw, Jane S., 219, 229n
Singer, Fred S., 57n
Single, Eric, 228n
Sloan, Frank A., 225n
Smith, Sharon, 32n
Smothers, Ronald, 227n
Sonenblum, Sidney, 92n
Spann, Robert M., 32n, 122, 150, 173n,
    177n, 225n
Staaf, Robert J., 31n
Starr, Paul, 287n
Stevens, Barbara J., 124, 158, 160,
    173n-74n, 178n, 275n
Stewart, James K., 224n
Stine, G. Harry, 147, 176n
Stockman, David, 105, 208
Stroup, Richard L., 179n
Struyck, Raymond, 226n
Stuart, Reginald, 175n
Stuettgen, Reinhard, 175n
Summers, Lawrence H., 117n, 228n

Taylor, Charles, 274n
Taylor, Todd, 223n
Teeples, Ronald, 176n
Teltsch, Kathleen, 224n, 273n
Thatcher, Margaret, 169
Thiers, Louis A., 239
Thomas, Larry W., 116n
Tolchin, Martin, 174n, 179n-80n, 224n-25n, 228n, 275n
Tompor, Susan, 179n
Tullock, Gordon, 31n

Vaden, Ted, 177n
Valente, Carl F., 92n, 173n
Van Cott, T. Norman, 174n
Vickrey, William, 51, 57n
Viton, Philip A., 174n-75n
Vraciu, Robert A., 225n

Wagner, Richard E., 274n
Wallace, James E., 226n
Wallace, R.L., 176n
Walters, A.A., 174n-75n
Warren, Robert, 32n, 92n

Washnis, George, 92n
Webb, Kenneth, 276n
Weicher, John C., 226n
Wesemann, H. Edward, 274n-76n
Whitaker, Gordon P., 92n
Whitmore, Howard, 276n
Wildavsky, Aaron, 31n
Williams, Walter E., 103, 116n
Willig, R.D., 57n
Wilson, James Q., 29, 31n, 116n
Winslow, Ron, 116n
Wise, Arthur E., 228n
Wishart, Jennifer, 166, 179n
Witzeman, Lou, 224n
Wolf, Charles, Jr., 31n, 111, 116n
Wollman, Jane, 228n
Woodson, Robert L., 207, 210, 226n-28n, 273n
Wynne, G.G., 141, 173n, 175n

Young, Peter, 179n-80n, 274n
Yunker, James A., 176n

Zardkoohi, A., 176n

Subject Index

Academy for State and Local Government, 173
Affirmative action, 102
AFSCME (American Federation of State, County, and Municipal Employees), 123, 257
Air as common-pool good, 42
Airlines, 144
Air pollution control as collective good, 42
Air traffic control, 145
Alternative service delivery, 277
Ambulance service, contracting of, 194
Amtrak, 143-44
Anticompetitive behavior in waste collection, 129-30
Antigovernment attitude, 8
Argentina, denationalization in, 169
Arizona
  fire protection in, 184-85
  wastewater treatment in, 149
Arrangements, 11, 62-82
  characteristics of, 107-8
  choice of, 93-94
  comparison of, 107-8, 123-24
  competition among, 96-97
  costs and benefits of, 98
  for education, 213
  for electric power, 149-50
  equity of, 101, 122
  evaluation of, 95-108, 122
  examples of, 84-85
  flexibility of, 98
  hybrid, 83
  limited-government, 247
  multiple, 82-83, 264
  partial, 83-86
  ranking of, 247-48
  see also Service arrangements

Arson, 199
AT&T, 192
Audubon Society, 164
Australia
  airlines in, 144
  recreation vouchers in, 220-21

Bangladesh, family planning in, 196
Bank deposit insurance, 170-71
Banking, comparative study of, 171
Bedford-Stuyvesant Restoration Corporation, 103
Bidders' conference, 269
Bidding
  collusive, 71-72
  competitive, 262-66
  process, 69-70
Big Apple Pothole and Sidewalk Corporation, 133
Birth control, 239
Bonds, bid and performance, 268-69
Bookkeeping, creative, 4
Boston, private policing in, 182
Boston City Council, 99
Boston Housing Authority, 105
Boston University, 216
"Bracket creep," 22
Brazil, denationalization in, 169
Bribery, 99
  opportunity for, 24
  of voters, 23
Britain
  competitive bidding in, 265
  denationalization in, 169-246
  road maintenance in, 265
  sale of public housing in, 200-201
  telephone service in, 155
British Columbia Resources Investment Corporation, 243

Broadcast TV as collective good, 48
Budget maximization, 24
Budgetary imperialism, 23-24
Building codes
    as impediment to housing, 202
    in U.S. and France, 240-41
Bureaucratized systems, 10
Bus transportation, 137-41
    government monopoly of, 142
    partial arrangements for, 83
    private, 140
    school, 139
    by state-owned enterprise, 241

Calcutta, buses in, 139
California
    bus costs in, 137-38
    contracting in, 72, 205
    fire departments in, 185
    school desegregation in, 217
    traffic signal maintenance in, 136
    tuition charges in, 255
California Contract Cities Association, 68
Canada, 169, 243
    fire protection in, 184
    railroads in, 144
Capital projects, 9
Capital spending, bias toward, in government, 29
Central Intelligence Agency, 252
Central Park, 219
    restoration and maintenance of, 237
Charities
    behavioral changes due to, 238
    load shedding to, 23
    private and state, 239
Child care. See Day care
China
    forced abortions in, 239
    privatization in, 169-70
Choice in public services, 10
Citizen surveys, 271
City services. See Municipal services
Civil service, problems of, 159
Clinch River Breeder Reactor, 147

Coast Guard services, 145-46
Collective
    action, 58-59
    size of, 50
Collective goods
    arranger for, 60-61
    delivery of, 59
    examples of, 42
    growth of, 51
    measuring and choosing, 48
    payment for, by beneficiaries, 50
    production of, 228
    provision of, 93
    supply of, 47
        by voluntary associations, 58
Collusion, 100, 130, 271
Command-and-control of economy, 25
Commercial
    activities, 9
    pressures for privatization, 4-5, 9
Common-pool goods
    examples of, 42
    government-created, 94
    growth of, 51
    problems of, 46
    provision of, 94
    supply of, 45
Communication, 152-55
Community, sense of, 10
    see also Neighborhood associations
Comparative studies, conduct of, 172
Competition, 11, 272
    among arrangements, 96-97
    in bus service, 139
    continuous and periodic, 266
    in contracting, 262-66
    between contractor and government agency, 125, 128
    in education, 215
    in electric power, 150-51
    vs. monopoly, 250-55
    in police services, 182
    between public and private sectors, 264
    strategy for, 251
Competitive bidding, 262-66
Complaint monitoring, 271

Comptroller, New York State, 192
Congressional Budget Office, 156
  estimate of contract expenditures,
    265
Conrail, 143
Construction, contracting, 268
Consumers, responsiveness to, 98
Consumption property, 36-39
Contract
  award of, 263-64
  manipulation of, 273
  monitoring, 270-71, 273
  negative price of, 75
  specifications, 266-69, 273
  types of, 269
Contracting, 255-73
  arguments pro and con, 109-11
  in California, 72
  as common form of privatization,
    282
  conditions for, 255-56, 272
  cost comparisons of, 122-28, 258-62,
    272
  for custodial services, 158
  by Defense Department, 69
  definition of, 68
  for education, 216
  efficiency of, 109
  extent of, 69-75
  by federal government, 69
  flexibility of, 98
  fostering competition in, 262-66
  government role in, 68
  for human services, 283-85
  job loss due to, 258
  labor agreements concerning, 257
  by local governments, 70-71
  for military equipment, 68
  payment method for, 269
  for private police patrol, 72
  sabotage of, 267
  as service arrangement, 68-75
  for street cleaning, 131
  survey of opinions about, 112
  as threat to unions, 257
"Contracting in," 157, 264
Convention centers, 222-23

Coproduction, 82
Coprovision, 82
Corrections Corporation of America,
    186
Cost comparisons, 260, 272
  errors in, 258-60
Cost of government services, under-
    estimation of, 259-61
Cost reduction by "cream skimming,"
    284-86
Cost of retirement benefits, 260
Costs and benefits of arrangements, 98
County services, contracting of, 73-74
"Cratogenic" problems, 238
"Cream skimming"
  analysis of, 284-86
  in education, 217
  in mass transit, 142
Cultural institutions, 77
  grants for, 77
  vouchers for, 29
Custodial services, 158

Davis-Bacon Act, 149
Day care, 207-10
  load shedding of, 234
  vouchers for, 113, 208
Debt collection, 160-61
Delivery of goods, arrangements for, 94
Demand for services, 17-22
  demographic change and, 17-18
  effect of affluence on, 18
  effect of redistribution on, 18-19
  inflation and, 18
  urbanization and, 18
Denationalization, 167-69, 233, 241-47,
    272
  advantages of, 9
  in Britain, 169
  capital needed for, 282
  definition of, 241
  employee opposition to, 282
  implementation problems of, 281
  of SOEs, 167, 245
  strategy for, 243-44
Denmark
  Coast guard services in, 146

Denmark *(continued)*
  contracting in, 74
  fire protection in, 183-84
Deregulation
  of airlines, 145
  economic, 240, 281
  of taxis, 281
  of transportation, 241
Detroit, 158, 162
Developing countries
  denationalization in, 167
  education in, 213
  government enterprises in, 25
  government jobs in, 27
  road maintenance in, 13
  telephone services in, 154
  transportation in, 141
  water supply in, 148
Dispute resolution, 211-12
Distant Early Warning System, 69
Divestment, 241, 243, 245, 272
  factors to consider in, 245
  as form of load shedding, 233
  partial, 243, 246-47

Economic equity, 101
Economies
  of contiguity, 128
  of scale, 97-98
Education, 212-18, 252-55
  arrangements for, 213
  in Athens and Sparta, 253
  choices in, 214-16
  by corporations, 253-54
  cream-skimming in, 217
  expenditures for, 24
  in India, 213
  as joint-consumption good, 43
  load shedding of, 236
  in Malta, 213
  monopoly, 252-55
  in Netherlands, 215
  private, 213, 215-16, 254
  as private good, 43
  producers of, 95
  self-service in, 213
  tuition tax credit, 215

  vocational, 254
  vouchers for, 214
  as worthy good, 53
  see also Schools
Effectiveness
  comparative, 128-29
  of services, 96
Efficiency
  of arrangements, 96-97
  as societal goal, 7
  in solid-waste management, 124-28
Election campaigns, 23, 26-27
  contributions to, 29
Electric power, 149-52
  comparative costs of, 150-51
  government role in, 152
Elite, problem-finding, 24-25
Employee Stock Ownership Plan, 282
Employment
  effect of privatization on, 102-3
  for minorities, 102-4
England. *See* Britain
Enterprise zones, 205
Entrepreneurs, 103
  minorities as, 103
  teachers as, 216
Equity
  as component of justice, 7
  economic, 101
  of markets, 101
  for minorities, 101-6
  in service delivery, 104-5
  in waste collection, 129
Equity and Choice Act, 214
Exclusion property, 35, 94
  examples of, 38-39
Expenditure "caps," 30
Export-Import Bank, 166
Extortion, 99
  by government officials, 93, 100

Falck Company, 183-84
Family
  as self-service unit, 81
  as societal institution, 239
  supplanted by government, 10
Farmers Home Administration, 203

Federal Crop Insurance Corporation, 166
Federal Express, 153
Federal Housing Administration, 203
Federal Trade Commission, 106
Fire department, volunteer, 81
Fire protection, 183-85
  as collective good, 42
Fiscal
  extraction devices, 21
  illusion, 20-21
Food stamps, 96, 106
  as vouchers, 78-79, 113
Forces behind privatization, 4-10
Forest management, 162-63
France
  contracting in, 74
  telecommunication in, 155
  television in, 252
  water supply in, 148
Franchises, 75-76
  definition, 75
  flexibility of, 98
  for recreation, 218-19
  for water supply, 148-49
Fraud, susceptibility to, 99-100
Freedom, government as threat to, 7
Free-lunch programs, 94
Free-rider problem, 47
Fringe benefits, public compared to
  private, 28-29

General Accounting Office, 160, 189
  study of laundry services, 161
General Services Administration, 182
Golf courses, franchises for, 219
Goods and services, 35-39
  arrangements for delivery of, 94
  characteristics of, 35, 36
  nature of, 93-94
  transformation of, 52-55
  types of, 38
Government
  activities, commercial and adminis-
    trative, 155-62
  contracting, example of, 68-69
  effect on economy, 8

effect on efficiency, 7
effect on justice, 7
growth of, 7, 30
inefficiency of, 125
as institution of society, 290
jobs, 16, 27-28
loss of confidence in, 8
monopolies, 25-26, 97
with no employees, 16-17
reduction in revenues of, 22
role in collective action, 288
role and definition of, 290
salary levels, 28-29
sale of assets of, 30
sentiment against, 8
size of, 97-98, 106-7
as threat to freedom, 7
U.S., growth and size of, 13-17
as used by lobbies, 10
vending, definition of, 64
violations of law by, 105-6
Government programs
  beneficiaries of, 29-30
  preservation of, 21-22
Government service, 62-64
  as arrangement, 62-64
  definition of, 62
  underestimated cost of, 259-61
Government spending, 14-15
  political reasons for, 22-24
  reductions in, 22, 107, 248
Grace Commission study
  Coast Guard, 145-46
  electric power, 151
  postal service, 153
  VA hospitals, 193
Gramm-Rudman-Hollings Act, 30
Grants, 77
  for hospitals, 192
  in hybrid arrangements, 83
Great Britain. *See* Britain
Greece, railroads in, 144
Grounds maintenance, 160
Guard services, 183

Hatch Act, 27
Health care, 44, 189-96

Health care *(continued)*
  as common-pool good, 94
  cost of
    in the Soviet Union, 21
    in the U.S., 54
  grants for, 77
  for the poor, 192-93
  unsatisfactory voucher system for,
    279
Health Insurance Administration, 195
Health maintenance organizations, 190
Homeless, 115, 197, 237
Homeownership, 202-3
Hospital Corporation of America, 193
Hospitals
  comparative costs of, 191
  competition among, 190
  contracting of, 191
  for-profit, 189, 191, 192
  general, 190-93
  military, 194
  Veterans Administration, 193
  voluntary, 191
House and Senate delivery service, 153
House of Umoja, 208
Housing
  adequacy of, 198
  construction grants for, 199
  cost of grants for, 106
  low-income, 197-202
  manufactured, 202
  private supply of, 202
  problem, 197-98
  public, 105, 200-202
    in Britain, 201
  regulations, 203-5
  for senior citizens, 81
  vouchers, 78, 114, 199, 208
  as worthy good, 54
Human services
  competition in contracting for, 284
  problems in contracting for, 280,
    283-85

IBM, 192
Ideology, as basis for privatization, 4-9
Implementation obstacles, 280-85

Income
  distribution, 19
  redistribution, 7, 18-19
  in Washington, D.C., 24
Indianapolis, multiple arrangements in,
    82-83
Infrastructure, 164-66
Institutions, traditional, 10
Insurance, privatization of, 167
Intergovernmental agreements, 65-68
International Association of Assessing
    Officers, 161
International City Management Associ-
    ation, 122

Japan
  children's education in, 213
  denationalization in, 169
  telephone service in, 155
Japanese National Railways, 144
Jobs, effect of privatization on, 102-3
Joint Center for Political Studies, 102
Justice, effect of government on, 7

Kansas City, 264
Ku Klux Klan, 213

Labor
  costs for bus services, 139
  as obstacle to denationalization, 282
Lakewood Plan, 67
LANDSAT, 147
Latin America, electric power in, 152-53
Laundry services, 161
Law-breaking by government agencies,
    105-6
Legal aid, 212
Legal services, vouchers for, 114
Lighthouse, 48
Load shedding, 11, 272, 288
  by accommodation, 236
  of day care, 234
  by default, 235-36
  definition of, 233
  by denationalization, 241-47
  in public education, 236
  of recreation services, 235

Load shedding *(continued)*
of state-owned enterprises, 241
by withdrawal, 235
Local government
contracting by, 70-71
franchising by, 76
Los Angeles
contracting in, 157
grounds maintenance in, 160
guard services in, 183
intergovernmental agreements in, 67
Low-ball bids, 262, 272

Maintenance, bias against, in government, 29
Malta, education in, 213
Management flexibility in bus service, 140
Market system
conditions for successful use of, 279
decisions by, 8
equity of, 101
as service arrangement, 79
Mass transit. *See* Transportation
Mediating structures, 207-8, 239
Medicaid, 192-93
mills, 54
as unsatisfactory voucher system, 279
vouchers for, 79, 113
Medical care. *See* Health care
Medicare
discrimination in, 196
privatization of, 196
processing, 196
as voucher system, 113
Mexico, denationalization in, 169
Microcollectives, 236
load shedding to, 237
Military base support, 189
Military procurement, 68, 188
Minister for privatization, 169
Minnesota, 215, 264
interdistrict school enrollment, 216
nursing homes in, 195
Minorities
entrepreneurship of, 103

equity for, 101-6
jobs for, 102, 104
services for, 104
Model Cities program, 205
Money supply, free market for, 171
Monitoring, of contractors, 270-71
Monopoly
vs. competition, 250-55
consequences of, 250-52
contestable, 47
in education, 252-55
by government, 97, 251-52
postal, 153-54
privatization of, 244
by SOEs, 167
temporary and permanent, 265-66
Montreal, municipal contracting in, 265
Multiple, hybrid, and partial arrangements in human services, 284
Municipalities, number of, 14
Municipal services
contracting for, 72-74
intergovernmental agreements for, 66-67
for minorities, 104
privatization of, 72
see also Public services

NASA, 147
National Academy of Sciences, 191
National Center for Health Statistics, 194
National Commission on Neighborhoods, 240
National defense, 188-89
as collective good, 42
contracting of, 188
as joint-consumption good, 37
Nationalized industries, inefficiency of, 9
Neighborhood associations, 107
in load shedding, 236-37
patrols, 183
Netherlands, education in, 215
Newark, 264
contract monitoring in, 271

New Mexico, 145
New Orleans, contracting in, 264, 267
New York City
  bus operations in, 138
  citizen patrols in, 237
  contracting in, 75
  contract monitoring in, 270
  corruption in, 100
  culture vouchers in, 220
  custodial services in, 158
  education in, 216
  employee voting in, 26
  housing in, 199
  potholes in, 133
  private policing in, 182
  private streets in, 134
  recreation and leisure in, 219
  schools in, growth of, 28
  street lighting in, 135
  subways in, 140
  taxi industry in, 281
  tennis courts in, 235
  towing of autos in, 161
  zoning in, 204
New York Department of Parks, 219
New York Metropolitan Transportation Authority, 28
New York Public Library, 219
New York State
  bus costs in, 137
  school buses in, 139
New York State Commission on the Quality of Care for the Mentally Disabled, 206
Nuclear Regulatory Commission, 106
Nursing homes, 194-95
  comparative costs of, 195

Ocean fishing
  privatization of, 46
  user charges for, 250
Office of Federal Procurement Policy, 69, 155-56
Ohio, property assessment in, 161
Oklahoma City, 264
OPEC, 48

Oregon, 213
Overbuilding by government, 29
Overseas Private Investment Corporation (OPIC), 166-67

Police services
  components of, 74
  private, 72, 181-83
Populism, 10
Port facilities, 166
Positive externalities, 44
Postal service, 106
Pothole repair
  contracting for, 267-68
  patrol for, 133
  payment for, 47-48
Power Marketing Administration, 151
Pragmatic pressure for privatization, 4-6
President's Commission on Housing, 203
President's National Urban Policy Report, 205
Prisons, 185-88
  contract services in, 186
  privatization of, 186-87
Private goods, 44-45
  compared with collective goods, 50
  examples of, 43
  government spending for, 55
  load shedding of, 234
  as substitutes for collective goods, 51
  supply of, 44
  in U.S., 93
Privatization
  advocates of, 277-78
  alternatives, 109-14
  building support for, 257-58, 289
  by changing to vouchers, 281
  conceptual problems of, 277
  definition of, 3, 88
  by deregulation, 241
  examples of, 277
  interest in, 122
  as means and ends, 288
  of monopolies, 243-44
  necessary conditions for, 278-80

Privatization *(continued)*
opposition to, 61, 101, 257
paradox of, 279
by philanthropy, 114
precipitating event in, 256
pressures for, 4-10
in socialist states, 169-70, 278
strategies for, 233
as strategy for better government, 6, 289
transitions for, 89
by voluntary action, 114
Privatized arrangements, ranking of, 88
Producers, availability of, 96
Production vs. provision of goods, 288-89
Productivity
decline in, 28-29
enhancement, 277
increase in, 5-6
Property, state-owned, 162-66
Property assessment, 161
Property rights
in forest ownership, 163
in parks, 219-20
Proposition 13, 30, 122, 240, 249, 255
Pruitt-Igoe houses, 200
Public
baths, 22
housing, 105, 200-202
land, 162
safety, 181-88
works, 164-65
"Public," meaning of, 4
Public and private, 3-4
debate on, 122-24
differences between, 3-4, 111-12
Public service, elements of, 86
Public services
choices in, 10
demand for, 17-22
innovation in, 289-90
institutional arrangements for, 90
misjudging cost of, 21
overproduction of, 27
see also Municipal services

Railroads, 143-44
RAND Corporation, 189

Rangeland, 164
Ravenna Park, Seattle, 219-20
Reagan administration policy
housing vouchers, 199, 208, 281
privatization, 122, 166-67, 277
of Amtrak, 144
of mortgage insurance, 203
of oil fields, 164
of OPIC, 167
of transportation, 141
user charges, 250
water resources, 149
Reason Foundation, 122, 173
Recreation
and leisure, 218-21
as worthy good, 53
Recreation facilities
collective action for, 58
load shedding of, 235
Refuse collection. *See* Solid-waste collection
Regulation
of day care, 210
effect on demand for services, 18
of housing, 202-5
see also Deregulation
Renault, 62
Rent-a-judge. *See* Dispute resolution
Rent control, 204
Resource recovery, 131
Responsiveness to government direction, 105-6
Revenue cuts, 30
Risk aversion, 20
Riskless society, 20
Road construction and maintenance, 132-36
competitive bidding for, in Britain, 265
Rural/metro fire department, 184-85

Sale-leaseback, 165
San Francisco, 162

Scale economies, 97-98
  in bus operations, 140-41
School buses, 139
Schools
  Catholic, 217
  contracting for, 158, 216
  custodial services in, 158
  intergovernmental agreement for, 65
  in New York, 28
  private, 213, 215, 218, 253-54
  scale of, 97
  segregation, 217
  see also Education
Seattle, 219
Securities and Exchange Commission, 106
Segregation in schools, 217
Self-service, 81-82, 97
Service
  arrangements, 62-82
  arranger, 60, 95
  consumer, 60
  delivery, 60-62
  quality of, 8
Services
  division between public and private sectors, 6
  efficiency of, 97-98
  functional division of, 87
  "hard" and "soft," 267, 279
  scale of, 97-98
  specification of, 95
Ship maintenance, 189
Sierra Club, 164
Sinofication, 102
Social security, 210-11
Social Security Administration, 195
Social services, 206-8
  vouchers for, 208
Societal ills, 19-20, 25
Society
  excessive dependence on government by, 10
  as more than government, 290
SOE (State-owned Enterprise), 166-72, 241-47
  buyers of, 246

crime by, 106
definition of, 166
denationalization of, 115, 241-47
in developing countries, 169
inefficiency of, 9
sale to employees of, 246
Solid-waste collection, 124-31
  comparative performance of, 124-28
  competitive bidding for, 264
  discrimination in, 104
  ethnic dominance in, 130
  extent of contracting for, 131
  service levels of, 27
  transformed into street cleaning, 51
Solid-waste disposal, 131
Somalia, 241
South Africa, 103
Soviet Union, 106
  education in, 213
  fiscal illusion in, 21
  government services in, 62
  private goods in, 93
  privatization in, 170
Space, 46
  transportation, 146-47
Spain, 169
Special districts, 14
Spending
  coalitions, 29-30, 207, 258
  opposition to, 4-5
Sports arenas and stadiums, 221-22
Sri Lanka, family planning in, 196
St. Louis
  private streets in, 134
  Pruitt-Igoe houses in, 200
St. Paul, Minnesota, user charges in, 249
Stadiums, 221-22
Standards, public, for the arts, 20
State-owned enterprise. See SOE
Strategic Petroleum Reserve, 164
Strategies for privatization, 233
Street(s)
  cleaning, 51, 131, 280
  infrastructure, 165
  lighting, 134-36
  paving, 95, 132

Streets(s) *(continued)*
  payment for, 50-51
  private, 58-59, 133
  services, 131-36
Subsidies
  for buses, 141
  for SOEs, 166
Sweden, contracting in, 74
Switzerland, private policing in, 183
Synthetic Fuels Corporation, 147

Taxes
  collection of, 48
  effect of, on cost comparisons, 261
  international levels of, 16
  resistance to, 4
Taxi industry in New York City, 281
TEACH, 214
Telecommunication, 154-55
  in developing countries, 154
Television as collective good, 48
Tenant management, 201
Tennessee, prisons in, 186
Tennessee Valley Authority, 105
"Tie-in sales," by government monopolies, 25-26
Timber industry, 163
Toll goods, 39-44, 47
  convention centers as, 222
  definition of, 47
  examples of, 42
  provision of, 93
Traffic-signal maintenance, 136
Tragedy of the commons, 46
Transportation, 137-44
  comparative studies of, 137, 140
  in developing countries, 141, 241
  by elevator, 141
  in New York, 28
  as private, toll, and collective good, 43
  privatization strategy for, 141-42
  vouchers for, 113
  as worthy good, 53
Tree maintenance, 158-59
Trucking industry, 103
Tuition charges in California, 255

Tuition tax credit, 215-17
Turf maintenance, 159-60

Uganda, education in, 213
Underclass, 238
Union role in collusive bidding, 271
United Kingdom. *See* Britain
United Parcel Service, 152-53
U.S. Department of Defense
  contracting by, 69
  commercial activities of, 156
  as service producer, 60
U.S. Department of Energy, 156
U.S. Department of Housing and Urban Development, 66, 122, 201
U.S. Department of Interior, 220
U.S. Department of Labor, 105
U.S. Forest Service, 162
U.S. Mint, 69
U.S. Office of Management and Budget, 105, 143, 155
  estimate of savings by, 265
U.S. Office of Personnel Management, 282
U.S. Postal Service, 152-54
Urbanization, 13
Urban Mass Transportation Authority, 137
Urban services, institutional arrangements for, 84-85
User charges, 11, 248-50, 272
  costs of, 250
  purpose of, 248

Vanpools, 281
Venezuela, electric power in, 151
Veterans Administration (VA)
  commercial activities of, 156
  hospitals, 193
  role in housing, 203
Voluntary action, collective contributions for, 47
Voluntary arrangements, 80-81, 107
  legal problems of, 281
  as supplier of goods, 94
Voluntary associations
  for collective action, 58-59

Voluntary associations *(continued)*
  for fire protection, 81
  in New York City, 237
  in parks and recreation, 220
  replaced by lobbies, 10
  for social services, 206-8
Voting, 19
  by government employees, 26-27, 30
Vouchers, 78-79, 113-14, 272
  cash as substitute for, 114
  for child care, 113, 209
  conditions for successful use of,
    279
  definition and examples of, 78-79
  for education, 214-15, 217, 254
  for health care, 192
  for housing, 114, 196, 199-202
  for legal services, 114
  minority use of, 104
  privatization by, 288
  for recreation and culture, 220-21
  as service arrangement, 78-79
  for social services, 208
  for transportation, 113

Washington, D.C.
  child care in, 207

voting by residents of, 27
Waste. *See* Solid-waste
Wastewater treatment, 149
Water supply, 148-49
  as common-pool good, 43
  pollution of, 45
  as tie-in sale, 26
Wealth spreading by privatization, 246
Weather forecasting, 43, 170
Welfare, 238
Welfare state, 238-39
West Germany
  bus services in, 139-40
  cost comparisons in, 158
  custodial services in, 158
  forest management in, 162
World Bank, 132, 137
Worthy goods, 52, 54-55, 58

Yugoslavia
  contracting in, 74
  intergovernmental competition in,
    252

Zero-employee government, 16-17
Zoning, 202-4
  of day-care centers, 210, 234